ORTHO'S
BASIC HOME BUILDING

AN ILLUSTRATED GUIDE

ORTHO'S

BASIC HOME BUILDING

AN ILLUSTRATED GUIDE

Created and Designed by the Editorial Staff of Ortho Books

Project Editor
Jill Fox

Writer
Ron Hildebrand

Consultant
Daniel Fuller

Principal Illustrators
Ron Hildebrand
Mitzi McCarthy

Photographer
Saïd Nuseibeh

Ortho Books

Publisher
Edward A. Evans
Editorial Director
Christine Jordan
Production Director
Ernie S. Tasaki
Managing Editors
Robert J. Beckstrom
Michael D. Smith
Sally W. Smith
System Manager
Linda M. Bouchard
Product Manager
Richard E. Pile, Jr.
Marketing Administrative Assistant
Daniel Stage
Distribution Specialist
Barbara F. Steadham
Operations Assistant
Georgiann Wright
Technical Consultant
J. A. Crozier, Jr., Ph.D.

Acknowledgments
Cover Designer
Gary Hespenheide
Copy Chief
Melinda E. Levine
Editorial Coordinator
Cass Dempsey
Copyeditor
Toni Murray
Proofreader
Deborah Bruner
Indexer
Trisha Feuerstein
Editorial Assistants
John Parr
Nancy Patton Wilson-McCune
Composition by
Laurie A. Steele
Production by
Studio 165
Separations by
Color Tech Corp.
Lithographed in the USA by
Webcrafters, Inc.

Cover Illustrator
Mark Pechenik
Additional Illustrators
Edith Allgood
Ellen Blonder
Ron Cook
Robyn Drace
Angela Hildebrand
David Hildebrand
Frank Hildebrand
Ronda Hildebrand
Marilyn Hill
Errol McCarthy
Shandis McKray
Rik Olson
Sally Selmeier
Carla Simmons
Additional Photographer
Deborah Porter, pages 5 and 10
Photographed Homes
We wish to thank the following individuals and businesses for allowing us to photograph their projects in progress.

Bear Forest Properties, page 2
Schaal Contracting, page 10
Robert S. Huntley, Builder, page 48
The Lusk Company, builder, Carriage Oaks, page 92
Paul Coates Construction, Inc., page 144
The William Lyon Company, page 184
Kwok Chan, page 228
Richard F. and Beth Wiseman, page 246
The California Redwood Association, page 268
Morrison Homes, page 310

Special Thanks to
Edward and Dilys Fox
International Conference of Building Officials
The Owner-Builder Center, Berkeley, Calif.
Syndi J. Seid
Doug Weaver
T. Jeff Williams

Pages 2-3
Various architectural elements were combined to create this traditional house. The curved window casings and garage door framing soften the angular lines of the gable roof. The horizontal siding is paint-grade lumber that awaits finishing.

Address all inquiries to:
Ortho Books
Chevron Chemical Company
Consumer Products Division
Box 5047
San Ramon, CA 94583

1 2 3 4 5 6 7 8 9
91 92 93 94 95 96

ISBN 0-89721-235-5
Library of Congress Catalog Card Number 90-86167

Chevron Chemical Company
6001 Bollinger Canyon Road, San Ramon, CA 94583

Table of Contents

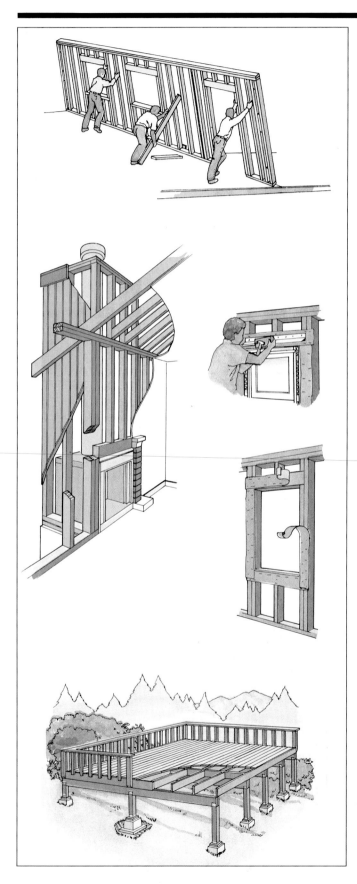

Building a house is an experience like no other. House construction takes a large commitment of time and financial resources. It has, however, instinctual and emotional overtones that make it a unique and very fulfilling enterprise. The urge to find shelter and make it distinctive is prehistoric.

A House of Your Own

Early Cro-Magnon nomads decorated their caves with paintings of the animals they hunted and tribe members so their dwellings would reflect themselves, their needs, and their interests. Doing your own building allows you to put your unique mark on a new house in the same way. *Basic Home Building* presents information for planning and building a wood-frame house. Wood-frame construction is the most common form of residential construction used in the United States. Many architectural styles can be adapted to wood-frame construction, from traditional New England saltbox to contemporary California Ranch-style designs.

This book covers the basic aspects of the residential building process. Requirements reflect the Uniform Building Code. However, you must adhere to local building codes when building your house. *Basic Home Building* takes you to the point where you can get a final inspection, have the utilities turned on, and move in.

The final finishing steps—painting, installing floor coverings, installing appliances, and otherwise customizing the house—are presented for planning purposes but step-by-step procedures are not provided. Check the Reading List on page 345 for books about house finishing.

Using This Book

The nine chapters in this book guide you through a complete house-building project, from plan drawing to choosing interior finishes. The order of the chapters matches the phases of the construction sequence. However, building a house is not a linear project. Many decisions, such as choosing the type of finish roofing you want or whether to install carpet or ceramic tile in the family room, impact construction decisions long before the carpet is laid or the roof put on.

Basic Home Building is meant to be read twice, once as a planning guide and then again as a construction guide. Read the entire book as you make your planning choices. Then use the book again as you actually build the house.

There are many alternatives in house building. You have choices of foundation types, framing methods, roof styles, exterior sidings, window and door installations, and ceiling and wall finishes. Whenever possible, several alternative methods for each aspect are given. Therefore, you won't be using every step-by-step method presented in the book.

The first chapter takes you through the planning process. It shows you alternative styles of houses, how to read and prepare plans, how to select a lot and determine costs, and how to prepare a schedule. The second chapter shows you how to lay out the site, build the foundation, erect framing, and install the subfloor.

The third chapter concerns the roof. Several roof styles and various finishes are described. Instructions are given for laying out and building a roof conventionally and with trusses. Framing, sheathing, and flashing are also described. Procedures for installing composition shingles, shakes, panel roofing, and tiles are presented.

Adding the utilities is the subject of the fourth chapter. Both planning and roughing-in the plumbing and wiring are outlined. Ideas for special systems—for building modern, smart homes—are provided as well.

The fifth chapter discusses finishing the exterior of the house, which includes installing doors, windows, siding, and trim.

Methods to make the house more comfortable are the topic of the sixth chapter. A new house should have properly planned and installed energy conservation, heating, and cooling systems to save money on utilities and help conserve precious natural resources.

Movement into and around the house is covered in the seventh chapter. Interior and exterior steps and stairway design

and building procedures—including helpful rise-and-run charts—are given. Basic construction methods for building porches and decks are also included.

The eighth chapter provides information for choosing interior finishes and instructions for soundproofing, installing wallboard on ceilings and walls, hanging interior doors, putting on moldings, and finishing the electrical systems.

The last chapter describes the final steps required by most local building departments before an occupancy permit is issued. It covers the installation of cabinets, countertops, plumbing fixtures, and bathroom accessories.

Keeping this large a project on track takes management skills. Charts throughout the book help you estimate materials, stick to your schedule, guide various construction practices, and indicate times for building inspections. A checklist at the end of each chapter outlines the procedures you should have done to that point of building your house.

This book will help you create a house that shows off your abilities and interests. Whether you are considering a large custom house in a new development or a small vacation cabin in the woods, you want a building that reflects your needs, your likes, and your lifestyle. Just like the Cro-Magnon cave paintings, your new house will leave your mark on the world for folks to see for generations.

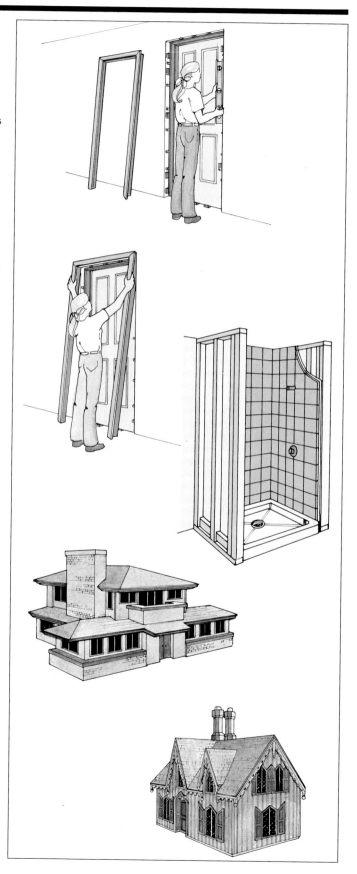

Typical House

Note: Your house may not look anything like the one pictured here, but it will probably contain most of the same features.

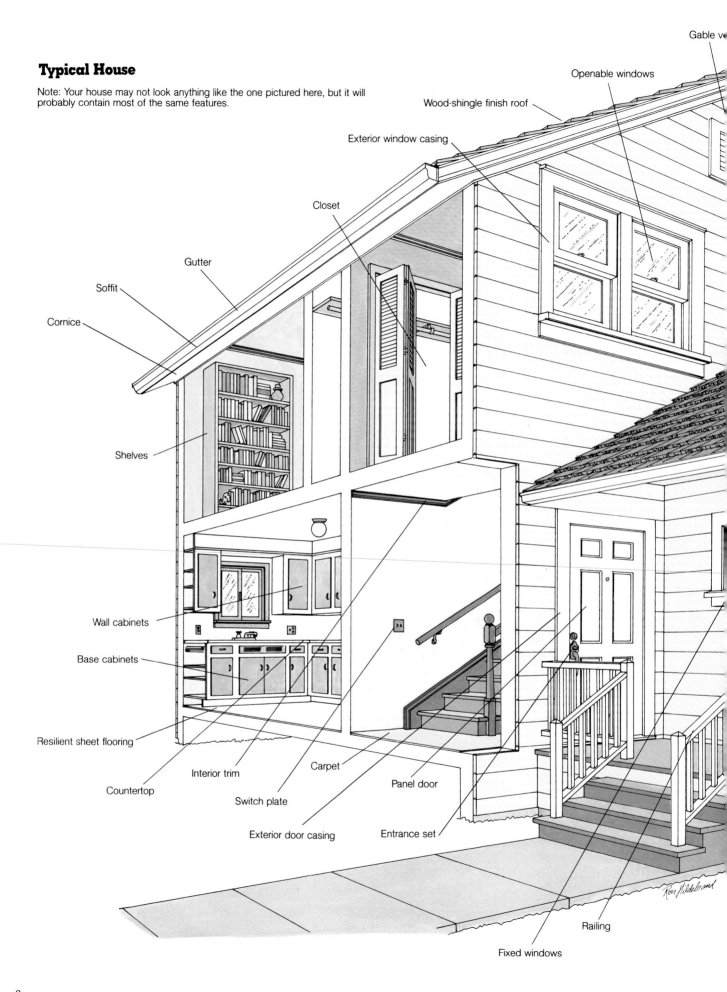

Gable v●

Openable windows

Wood-shingle finish roof

Exterior window casing

Closet

Gutter

Soffit

Cornice

Shelves

Wall cabinets

Base cabinets

Resilient sheet flooring

Interior trim

Carpet

Panel door

Countertop

Switch plate

Entrance set

Exterior door casing

Railing

Fixed windows

Ron Hildebrand

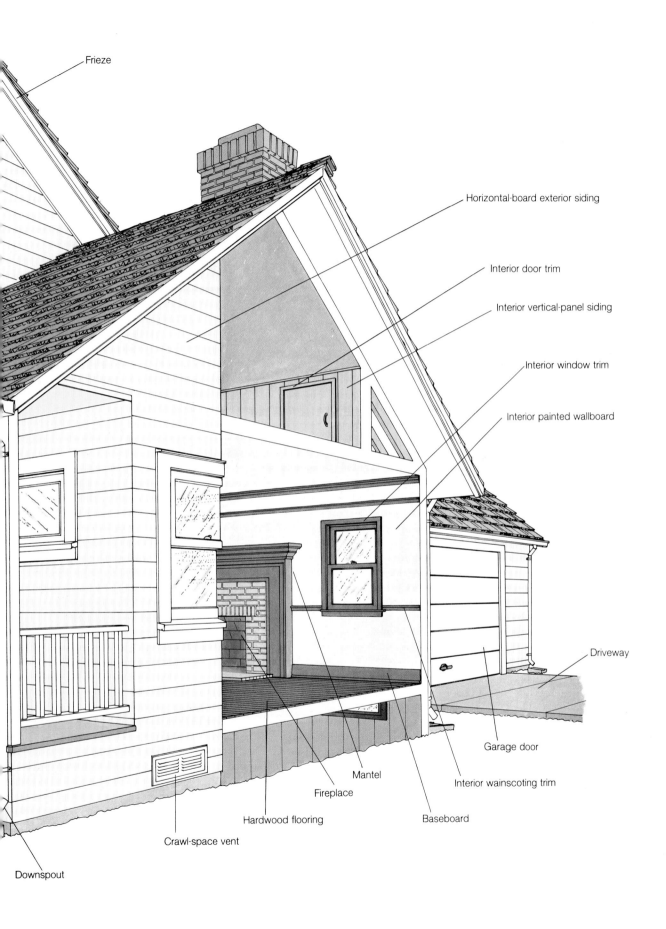

Frieze

Horizontal-board exterior siding

Interior door trim

Interior vertical-panel siding

Interior window trim

Interior painted wallboard

Driveway

Garage door

Mantel

Fireplace

Interior wainscoting trim

Hardwood flooring

Baseboard

Crawl-space vent

Downspout

PLANNING TO BUILD

Building a house takes a major commitment of time and money. However, the more time you spend planning the project, the more money you will save. This chapter will take you through the steps of determining the type and style of house you want to build, choosing a lot to put the house on, figuring the cost of materials, and coordinating schedules and talent.

The structure of this book puts these various tasks into a specific order, although the order in which you perform each step may vary. Consider each task before you start. What you'll end up with is a house plan that suits your life-style, an understanding of how a lot and a house should complement each other, an idea of the finances involved, and a concept of how to manage your upcoming project.

Planning a building project is not a simple endeavor, but it can be an enjoyable one. It will also be a creative challenge. You will be combining the business of building and the art of design to create the house of your dreams.

A new house should suit the owner and the neighborhood. Consider family needs in determining the house design and the history of the area when choosing the architectural style. On this just-completed home that combines Victorian styling with a traditional farmhouse design, the simple line of uniform, openable windows nicely balances the gingerbread trim. Notice the return of the trim at the end of eaves; such details help to define specific architectural styles.

DETERMINING YOUR HOUSING NEEDS

Two of the things you need before you can start any house are a lot on which to build and the plans to guide the building. Which you have first doesn't really matter. If you have the lot first, you can design the house to fit on the lot. If you've got the plans, you can then find a lot that will be appropriate to the house.

Gathering Ideas

Before you obtain plans, you need to determine your housing needs. The more specific you are about the type and style of house you want, the happier you'll be with the final result. If you are buying plans or having a professional draw them for you, you'll save money in architectural and design fees if you have an idea of what you want prior to drawing plans.

One priority to keep in mind at all times is the overall square footage you plan for your new house. General building costs are often figured in terms of square footage, and your budget and ability to get financing may be based on it. The size of your lot may determine the size of your house, or restrictions in your new neighborhood may determine how large—and how small—your house can be. When deciding the overall square footage, consider these factors as well as your housing needs, the number of people living in the house, and your life-style.

Other factors that determine cost are the complexity of the building, including how easy the lot is to build on and how complicated the design is, and the quantity and quality of the finish features.

Determining your housing needs takes several steps. To begin, you must gather ideas—a process that may go on for years. Then, you must survey exactly what you need from a house, room by room. Later, you must prioritize your desires, but first, be creative.

As you study architectural styles and room arrangements, you are likely to find finish materials—paints, carpets, cabinets, fixtures, and the like—that appeal to you. By all means, make a note of each find and take brochures to remind yourself of the products and where they are sold. Don't make the mistake of getting bogged down with details, however. At this stage your primary goal is to determine your housing needs. You will choose finish materials later, when you can be sure they fit your needs.

You will quickly accumulate a pile of materials that you should organize to maintain a sense of order during the planning. An accordion file (or two) works well. Not only does it organize your notes, brochures, and clippings, but it will hold bulky items such as magazines, samples, and color chips. Use categories suggested by the page headings of this chapter, or devise your own system of classification.

If you find yourself overwhelmed by information, winnow it out. Discard ideas and products you don't like. Clip photographs from brochures rather than keeping the entire thing. Be sure to save product specifications and the contact's name, address, and telephone number, however—you'll need them later on.

In designing a new house, there are many sources to which you can turn for inspiration.

House Tours

Going into houses—whether new, old, or somewhere in between—allows you to "feel" the home in a way that no photograph can convey. If there are historic or heritage homes in the area you plan to build, take tours. Notice the style of the houses and try to determine why they were built the way they were. In the past, when transporting materials was more difficult than it is today, builders chose local materials to minimize shipping costs. This gave the house the look of belonging to a place, and the materials, of course, adapted well to the climate. In days before central cooling and heating systems, homes were built to use the sun for heating and the prevailing winds for cooling. Today, using these ideas from an earlier time can lower shipping costs during building and lessen utility costs over time. In addition, your new home will adapt well to the climate, fit into the natural landscape, and harmonize with the style of the area.

Model homes present a wide variety of ideas for new houses. Models incorporate the latest styles in realistic settings. Look at models above and below your price range to get a spectrum of house styles and building procedures. Don't forget condominiums and town houses in your search for new concepts in house design. These homes are often smaller-than-average living spaces and, when well designed, use space very effectively.

Many organizations raise money by sponsoring showcase-style home tours. Check the calendar section of a local newspaper for these events; they are an excellent way to get ideas. Often, the homeowner or designer is available to answer questions.

Don't overlook the homes of your friends and family. When you visit, observe how the space is arranged, what features you like, how activity centers are laid out, and how rooms work together. You may find a gold mine of information by asking, "What do you like about your house?" To see how things are put together, ask to look in the basement, in the attic, and elsewhere.

Most important, look at your own house, where you live now and—in your memory—the houses you've lived in in the past. List what you like and don't like about the living space, what you want and don't want in a new place, how space could be used more effectively, and the needs that have prompted you to think about building a new house.

Showrooms

An efficient way to learn about the latest in home products is to visit the showrooms of manufacturers or sales outlets of building materials. Along with the specific products on display—doors, windows, heating and cooling systems, and kitchen and bathroom fixtures, for example—there are often mock-ups of full rooms, full exteriors, and house plans showing how these products can be used in a new house.

Home Shows

Public home shows also provide a variety of home product ideas. These displays present many different manufacturers' wares in booths staffed by knowledgeable employees. Home shows usually present booths sponsored by installer organizations as well, and company representatives can offer lots of advice to the owner-builder.

Brochures

If you are unable to pick up brochures at showrooms or home shows, contact manufacturers to obtain information on their products. Their brochures, many of which are in color, include specification sheets that give actual dimensions that you can incorporate into your home design. Manufacturers' brochures may also list dealers in your area.

See whether the local library carries *Sweet's Catalog*. This catalog is a compilation of brochures from many different manufacturers, and it is a valuable tool for architects, designers, and builders. Arranged by topic and manufacturer, *Sweet's Catalog* contains hundreds of photographs and illustrations, and it can give you still more ideas about products and how to select and install them.

Books and Magazines

If you have not already loaded up your shopping cart with home-oriented books and magazines, do so now. Every one of them is full of innovative plans and new ways to use space, materials, and products.

If you have access to a large public library or to the office of an architect or a contractor, look over some of the magazines that are distributed only to the trade. You may see ideas that are slightly more futuristic than in the consumer magazines and certainly ahead of already built homes.

Plan Books

Books of house plans offer perhaps the best chance to see many different ideas. The plans are usually copyrighted; you must send away for—and pay for—complete plans.

If you are using these books just for ideas, pay attention to how the rooms connect, how doors and windows are situated, where closets and other storage areas are located, and how many activity areas fit into different-sized homes.

A Wish List

One of the most useful aids in determining your housing needs is a list of absolutely everything you want from your new house. As you discover an element you want to incorporate, jot it down. Although you think you'll remember everything you've seen, it is a good idea to make a formal, written list of these ideas to use in developing or obtaining your house plans.

Those who study the human creative process have adopted four rules to guide brainstorming. Use these rules as you develop your wish list.
• There are no bad ideas at this point; list everything you've ever wanted.
• The wilder the idea, the better; it is easier to tame down an idea than to dream up one.
• Go for a quantity of ideas; the more ideas, the greater the likelihood of useful ones.
• Remember that combination and improvement will be necessary.

Involve everyone who will live in the house. If you have children, have them contribute their ideas about what they want from the house, too. Have meetings to share ideas. Participants should also suggest how the ideas of others can be turned into better ideas or how two or more ideas can be joined to form a third one.

Remember, this is your list, made especially for you and your family. There is no magic formula for you to follow.

Use your wish list as you select your house style (see page 16). Be sure that the way the rooms fit together, the number of floors, the size and type of kitchen, and the general feel of the house all carry out your wishes.

Use your wish list as you develop the floor plan for your house. Keep the wish list handy as you make your bubble plan (see page 24). The time when you are creatively putting together your floor plan is the best time to start implementing your wishes.

Your wish list will remain helpful even after the house is well on its way to completion. After the roof is on, but before the exterior and interior are finished, you still have a chance to make last-minute changes (see page 137). Drag out the wish list again, and see if you are following your original intentions.

You'll also need the wish list later as you choose fixtures, appliances, and interior finish materials, and when you create your landscaping.

Keep in mind that many items on the wish list won't make it into the final house. Many will, however, and these will be the features that will make your house unique as well as a joy to live in.

Making a Survey

Refine your list by surveying each room in the house. Think about how you use these rooms in your current home; consider what you like and what you don't like about each.

As you go about your survey, think about your everyday activities, such as making a meal, doing laundry, or cleaning. Note any wasted motions and awkward steps. If you're doing more walking than working, think how the basic layout could be changed to make the activity more efficient.

Determine the traffic patterns in your existing home to see if you can make your new home more comfortable. Check the access from outdoors and between rooms to see what works and what doesn't.

Pay attention to what happens when friends come over. Note where people gather. Think about how you like to entertain—in a formal dining room or outside on the patio—and how you can design a home to best fulfill your style.

Consider the changing needs of your family. If you are about to have children, your needs will be different from those of a family about to send their youngest child off to college. Anticipate future needs as best you can.

Living and Family Rooms

Defining a living room and a family room is as difficult as defining the family itself. The character of living rooms and family rooms should be determined by the size, taste, and

Planning Room Sizes

Building codes specify the minimum size of rooms intended for various uses. This chart shows the minimum floor areas required by the Department of Housing and Urban Development, but local codes may vary. Since the minimum sizes are quite small, the table also shows a preferred size, which would be more comfortable. Where figures are omitted, there is no minimum size.

Room	Minimum Floor Area* (Square ft)	Sample Size (Ft)	Preferred Size (Ft)
Bedroom	80	8 × 10	11 × 14
Master bedroom	—	—	12 × 16
Family room	110	10½ × 10½	12 × 16
Living room	176	11 × 16	12 × 18
Other habitable room	70	7 × 10	—
Bathroom	35	5 × 7	5 × 9
Toilet compartment	—	2½ × 4	3 × 4½

*Means net floor area within enclosing walls, excluding built-in fixtures, closets, or cabinets.

activities of the people who use them. But there are parameters that any family can consider to design these living spaces. Determine how much overall square footage you want to devote to these general-use rooms. Think about whether you want a formal living room and a separate family room or one large space for all types of gatherings. Think now about fireplaces and wood-burning stoves and in what rooms you'd like to place them.

This is a good time to catalog items that you want to be sure will fit into your new house. Measure any large pieces of furniture and art, and keep track of where you'd like to place them. If you'd like to see your grandfather clock as you enter your home, for example, make sure you design plenty of space for it in the entrance hall.

Kitchen and Dining Rooms

The heart of the home, the kitchen and eating areas, may be the hardest rooms to design. It is not within the scope of this book to teach kitchen design, and there are already many helpful books on the subject (see page 345). At this point you need to consider generalities of the kitchen. Think about the size and shape of kitchen that would best meet your needs. List the appliances that you must have and those that you'd like to have in the new space. If you plan to use your current appliances in the new house, measure them and allow appropriate space. List everything you do in your kitchen now, and figure out the best way to support these activities.

Decide if you want an eat-in kitchen or a working kitchen with a separate eating room. Think about whether you want

to devote space to a formal dining room or if one general-purpose eating area will do.

The spaces that go along with the kitchen also require planning. If you want a large pantry, you must devote space to it. If you want a separate laundry room, baking center, or plant-potting room, allow space for them.

Consider the location of your kitchen as it relates to other rooms and as it relates to the outdoors. If you want a kitchen that is sunny in the morning, make sure you place it on the east side of your new house. If you really don't want the afternoon sun blasting in while you're trying to cook, make sure you don't place the kitchen on the west side. Or, you may prefer a kitchen that looks out on the backyard or toward an interesting view.

Bedrooms

Bedroom planning consists of determining how many bedrooms you want in your new house, how large you want them to be, and how you want to place them. Consider your current and future bedding needs. Decide whether you want to separate the master bedroom from the other bedrooms. If you are building a vacation home, you may want simple dorm-style rooms, which can accommodate many cots and sleeping bags, rather than individual bedrooms.

Also consider your need for rooms similar to bedrooms. If you'd like a home office, for example, make sure to include it on your wish list. If a library or den seems like something your family needs, be sure you plan for it.

Bathrooms

Every house needs at least one bathroom. Beyond that the options are innumerable. Although it is tempting to give everyone in the family a private bathroom, these rooms are—on a square-foot basis—the most expensive rooms to build. You need to figure out how many full bathrooms and how many partial bathrooms you must have for your needs. One way to solve the morning bathroom crunch is to compartmentalize the different aspects of the bath, placing the toilet in its own room, the washbasin in another, and the shower or tub in another.

Also consider the features you want in a bathroom. You must have at least one toilet, one washbasin, and one shower or bathtub. Then consider the options: spas and luxury tubs, bidets, multiheaded showers, double sinks, and installed towel warmers. Remember that each bathroom feature is an added expense. For a list of publications that can help you with bathroom design, see page 345.

Garage and Storage

A garage is not usually counted in the overall square footage of a house, but it is a major design and construction element. You must determine if you want a garage and how many cars you want it to store. Also think about other vehicles you need to store, such as RVs and boats. These vehicles need higher ceilings than cars do, and you'll have to make design accommodations for them.

Also think about spaces connected to the garage—workshops, tool and equipment rooms, and other storage areas.

When considering garages and storage areas, remember: Always ask if these areas are being counted in the square-foot measurements of the house. By no means are these areas free to build, but they are sometimes left out of square-foot figures.

Internal Systems

As you determine your housing needs, most of your decisions will be affected by aesthetic preferences. In comparison, choosing internal systems—plumbing, electrical configuration, heating and cooling capability, installed vacuums, and wiring for sound and security—can seem glamourless. Consider, however, that to a large degree these systems determine the comfort, convenience, and safety of your home. Time you spend planning internal systems will be time well spent.

Prioritizing Goals

Before you begin the actual design work, be aware of factors that will affect the project. It is easy to see these factors as limitations, as restrictions on your creativity, but they are really more like boundaries that define your arena of possibilities. These factors include the local building codes, the size of your lot, the slope of the lot, the stability of the soil, and your budget. All are important and are addressed in this book.

Take as much time as you can at this stage of developing your ideas. Planning costs little, and you and your family will reap the benefits.

Zoning and Restrictions

Every area is divided into zones that specify what kind of buildings or activities may be conducted there. The usual zone designations are for single-family, multiple-family, apartment (including condominiums and cooperatives), light commercial, heavy commercial, light industrial, and heavy industrial use. Check with the local government to see how the area you like is zoned. Most people who want to own a single-family house prefer that it be in an area zoned for single-family dwellings.

All areas have building codes. These specify the minimum standards for the quality of construction and materials. Many code requirements are much the same throughout the country, but some local codes are more demanding than others. Some codes, for example, demand cast iron for drain and waste pipe instead of the newer plastic pipe. (Building codes are discussed in detail later; see page 43.)

Be aware, when selecting a lot, that some areas have deed restrictions in addition to the zoning requirements. Some are municipal restrictions; others are spelled out in the Codes, Covenents, and Restrictions (CCRs) of a particular development or community. Either type may specify minimum square footage of a house, minimum setback requirements, or minimum or maximum height limit or number of stories. CCRs often dictate answers to aesthetic questions regarding architectural style, finish material, color, and the like. Some areas also impose environmental restrictions that prohibit cutting trees or installing overhead wires or dish antennas. Before you buy a lot or design a house to go on one, be sure you are aware of all the factors that can limit your options.

CHOOSING A HOUSE STYLE

You already have some knowledge about the kinds of houses built in this country. You see them every day and you know what you like. You may have dreamed of the kind of house you'd build, if you ever built one.

Architectural Styles

When you get really serious, the decision about the type of house to build will probably be easier if you have better knowledge about the kind of houses you see around you and how they came to be the way they are. If you are going to enlist an architect or designer to help plan your house, you need this knowledge to discuss the styles and accoutrements you like.

When considering the house that is best for you, keep several factors in mind. Some architectural styles suit certain regions better than others. Some features suit certain styles better than others—especially if you want a one-story home. If you have already purchased your lot, look around the neighborhood. Some homeowners' associations dictate the architectural styles. In most cases you'll want to build a home in keeping with, at least, the general style and size of the houses that will surround it.

This section will present background on popular architectural styles. The dates given indicate when a particular style was most popular. Don't let the dates limit you. All these styles continue to be built today. Building a house of a style that

represents a particular era—especially the era in which your area was settled—can be challenging. The reward is a house that looks as if it has been part of the landscape for years.

Most homes don't fall neatly into style categories. Instead they are variations of the definitive styles that have been modified by climate, life-style, building materials, and builders' skills.

This adaptation leads to what is called vernacular architecture. Your present house and those of your neighbors probably reflect the vernacular tradition. Most of these styles, as they have developed, can be made from the basic wood-frame construction this book will describe.

The following portfolio of styles will probably identify the architectural roots of the house you want to build. It will also guide you in deciding which features you like and want to include. Be aware of how roof slope; dormers; number of stories; and number, type, and placement of windows and porches contribute to the style. Please do not try to take features from different styles and incorporate willy-nilly all the things you like into one house. The features of each style have been designed and modified over the years to create a functional and eye-pleasing whole.

Saltbox

The saltbox, or lean-to, house derives its name from the long slanted lid of the saltbox found in Colonial general stores. In the South a saltbox is called a catslide house. Wherever it's found it has a distinctive gabled roof with a long lean-to slope in the rear. On two-story houses the roof extends to the first floor; on one-story houses the roof extends nearly to the ground. The settler usually placed this longer roof so it faced the harsh wind and weather from the north.

Some historians attribute the longer roof to early colonists who attached a lean-to shed to the original house when they needed more room. The style exactly mimics English stone, stucco, and wooden houses of the sixteenth and seventeenth centuries, however. These English houses almost always had the asymmetrical roof as an integral part of the original construction. In most cases then, the lean-to is probably not just an afterthought, but a feature the builder planned from the beginning. That's not to say additions weren't added to the original house; many were, but they usually did not include the long saltbox roof.

Windows on the front and sides are multipaned and openable. Those on the back are small and few in number. Roofs often feature dormers. A massive central chimney is common in this style.

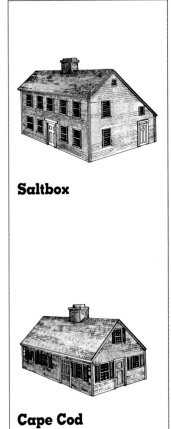

Saltbox

Cape Cod

In New England, most saltboxes are shingled and left to weather naturally. In some areas they are finished with horizontal boards.

Early American And Cape Cod

Both styles are designed around a large central stone chimney. They are usually symmetrical when viewed from the front. The kitchen is traditionally placed in the center of the house, with living and dining rooms up front and bedrooms in the back.

An Early American can have 1½ or 2 stories, with bedrooms in the attic area and dormer windows in the roof as

Greek Revival

Georgian Revival

well as windows in the gables. Sometimes the roof starts a couple of feet above the floor of the attic area, and "eyebrow," or "lie-on-your-stomach," windows are under the eaves.

A Cape Cod can have 1 or 1½ stories. If it has bedrooms upstairs, the only windows are in the gable ends. It never has dormers. The Cape Cod is known all across the country as the typical small American house. It is a descendent of the little English cottage, and it has lost very little of its charm in its

travels. The Cape Cod can be found in coastal towns in the West and East and in the suburbs of the Midwest, usually complete with picket fence and rambling roses. Because the Cape Cod is easy to build and maintain, it was the most popular style of home built from the 1920s through the 1950s. Even now, in the new construction of small homes, it is rivaled only by the California ranch style.

Both Early American and Cape Cod houses have a moderately sloped gable roof, multipaned or single-paned openable windows, and a simple front entrance. The exterior is shingled or finished with horizontal boards. Shutters often adorn windows.

In Colonial America all styles of houses had attachments of one sort or another. The most common was a wing, usually off to one side. Its rear wall was usually in line with the back wall of the main section; its front wall was set back from the front of the house.

The attachment often contained the kitchen and usually had a substantial chimney and kitchen fireplace. (Kitchens were originally placed in wings as a fire-prevention technique.) This chimney could be either at the gable end of the attachment or in a more central location, where it would provide a flue for the kitchen as well as for a fireplace in another room.

Georgian Revival

Over the course of the eighteenth and nineteenth centuries, Colonial styles were influenced in varying degrees by classical European styles. New World architects adapted these styles to their own vernacular and made order, symmetry, and proportion their watchwords.

The Georgian house was the first of the revivals. Builders began constructing such homes about 1750, and the style continued to be popular until well after the Revolution. Bricks had become more plentiful and less expensive so these houses are sided with brick and have multiple brick chimneys.

The Georgian Revival house has a flatter roof than the Early American home; some Georgian Revival homes have hip roofs. Other features include ornamented front doors and windows. Inside, too, the plain pine walls and beamed ceilings of earlier styles give way to paint in a variety of colors, wallpapers, and ornamental cupboards and paneling.

The Georgian is a well-proportioned, compact box, usually two stories high, with its rooms formally and symmetrically arranged off a central hall. The Georgian kitchen was often in a wing off to one side in the back.

Greek Revival

Interest in classic styling continued after the Revolution. By the early 1820s another new style was being built, the Greek Revival, which is sometimes thought of as the first truly American architectural style. The grandest houses of the

Greek Revival copied Greek temples and were built from scratch. Many owners, however, just added a colonnade along the front of an existing house. Sometimes they built from traditional plans and added trim that resembled a pediment and attached pilasters or vertical boards to corners to suggest columns. The Greek Revival became the most popular style of house in the American Midwest during the 1830s and 1840s.

These houses have a low-gabled, pedimental roof and dormers or a flat roof with a triangular false front to give the appearance of a temple. A rectangular transom over the front door, usually accompanied by rectangular sidelights, is common. Wide, bold but simple trim is at the roofline and frames the doors. A portico, or porch with columns, is common, although square posts or pillars may be used in a colonnade arrangement instead. Windows on the first floor tend to be taller than those on the second. Greek Revival houses, whether large or small, are usually painted white to suggest marble, and they frequently display shutters of dark green or black.

Two floor plans were developed for Greek Revival houses. In one, the gable end became the front of the house. This was the most obvious way to crown the front with a classic pediment. This floor plan consisted of two rooms with a wide hall beside them, running the full length of the house. The stairs were on the outside wall of the hall, and the hall behind the stairs became the kitchen.

Gothic Revival

Romanesque

Victorian

In the second plan, the pedimented gable again dominated the front of the building, but the main entrance was on the side of the house. The front door was within a recessed porch a short way up the side, and a colonnade supported the second floor above the porch. A parlor and den or bedrooms were at the front of the house. An entrance hall with stairway and the dining room were in the middle, and the kitchen and utility rooms in the back.

Gothic Revival

From the 1830s to the Civil War, the Gothic Revival style emerged all around the country. These houses were romantic in that they appealed to fantasy or suggested the remote or mysterious. Stone mansions resembled little medieval castles; modest dwellings suggested storybook cottages. The Carpenter Gothic, or gingerbread house, was the most popular version of this style during the 1850s.

Key characteristics of this style are its distinctive roof, with steep gables and pinnacled peaks, tall chimneys, and an occasional tower or spire. Another feature, especially on Carpenter Gothic houses, is the wealth of trim. There is wooden fretwork, usually deep and intricately patterned, along the eaves and gable edges; decorative balustrades atop porches; and fancy molding around the window and door casings.

The windows vary. On the same house you might find multipaned openable windows; stained-glass fixed windows;

and lancet windows, or windows with pointed arches.

The Gothic style is asymmetrical, with projections everywhere—wall dormers, bay windows, balconies, and porches or verandas, as well as the towers and spires mentioned before. The usual exterior covering is brick, stone, stucco, or vertical board and batten. The customary roof material is slate.

Since the houses are so asymmetrical, the floor plans vary greatly. The whim of the owner and creativity of the builder determine the sizes, shapes, and placement of each of the rooms.

Romanesque

This style was loosely patterned after the villas of northern Italy. This style enjoyed immense popularity in the East, mostly because its boxy two- or three-story form worked well as a city row house. Also, it could be dressed up or down, depending on the taste and pocketbook of the builder. Romanesque architecture flourished in the plan books of the 1810s.

Features of the Romanesque style include a hip roof with a very low slope and wide eaves. The eave is usually supported by heavy brackets or deep moldings. An ornamental cupola is often built on top of the flat-looking roof to add height and grandeur. The front is formally balanced, with windows and doors symmetrically placed. A central portico or small porch, embellished with Italian-style architectural detailing, adds importance to the entrance. The windows are grouped in twos and threes and

dressed up with rounded tops or are square with rounded panes of glass. The exterior covering is usually stone or brick, although stucco is sometimes used and worked to look like stone. There are octagonal designs of this style that are wood-framed and have an exterior siding of horizontal boards.

Victorian

The Victorian building era flourished from about 1860 to 1910. Elements from many past styles were woven into a rich tapestry. The result was a picturesque vogue that appeared in urban row houses, modest small-town dwellings, and the luxurious mansions of the robber barons from coast to coast.

During the 50 years of the Victorian period, many substyles appeared. Industrialized construction techniques and mass-produced components made a dizzying array of materials available to the architect and builder. In addition, with a rail system that stretched from coast to coast, materials could be transported to all parts of the country.

Italianate, Victorian Gothic, Queen Anne, Chateauesque, Richardsonian, as well as Classical and Colonial Revivals were all products of this age of innovation. Within this period and to this very day, architects as well as builders have mixed and matched these styles and incorporated local forms and materials to create their own vernacular Victorian styles.

The Victorian is distinctly asymmetrical with steep gables, sometimes in combination with a hip roof. It has second- and even third-story projections that may be gabled, hipped, or rounded. Corner turrets or bays are common, as are rounded corners that suggest a turret.

Different and often contrasting materials are used to cover each story; often the materials are mixed within the stories as well. Stone, brick, decorative boards both vertical and horizontal, patterned shingles, turned and carved ornaments, and fretwork are all used freely. Sheltering porches and wraparound verandas visually enlarge the first floor and open the house to the outdoors. Porches and balconies often appear on upper floors as well.

Decorative round and octagonal windows and transoms abound, glazed with stained or beveled glass. Regular windows are double-hung and openable. Windows in the turrets and bays often contain curved panes. Fixed windows of stained or beveled glass adorn walls at the top of stairs and above porches.

Shingle

This style first appeared in small seaside resort hotels and large summer cottages in New England around 1880. The simplicity and emphasis on natural wood was a welcome departure from the classic styles in vogue at the time. Exposure in plan books in the late 1880s helped foster the popularity of the Shingle-style home in the Midwest and West. This laid the foundation for the early Bungalow designs that were to follow.

The Shingle style was derived from the Queen Anne Victorian and earlier Colonial styles. The Shingle-style home features a moderately sloped gable roof and a wide base and ample porches and verandas. These are large open extensions of the living area that provide shade and allow access to cooling breezes. The horizontal nature of the design is emphasized by the lines of the naturally weathered shingles, the unobtrusive foundation of rough stone, and the wide groupings of several small multipaned windows that are definitely a throwback to Colonial times.

Inside, the design emphasizes function and flow. This is a trend that continues in almost every residential style that has developed since the Shingle style.

Bungalow

This style was born in California, but it spread quickly across the country, thanks to its exposure in movies and its availability through mail-order catalogs as a precut kit house. The simplicity and adaptability of the Bungalow style encouraged regional variations, and it became the favorite small house design of the early twentieth century.

The Bungalow-style house has a compact appearance with a gently sloped gable roof. It always has 1 or 1½ stories and a prominent front porch sheltered by a continuation of the roof. The roof is supported by tapered posts or flared extensions of the solid railing.

Natural materials are featured in this design. Cobblestones or rough-finished brick cover the foundation. Chimneys and naturally weathered or lightly stained shingles finish exterior walls and roof, giving the Bungalow-style house its characteristic rustic look. Occasional stucco-finished examples usually have a tile roof.

The interior floor plan is as simple and functional as the style itself. The front door leads directly from the porch into the living room. The remaining rooms connect from the center room, without a hallway wasting space.

Prairie

The name of this style derives from its low horizontal form, which was designed by Frank Lloyd Wright in the early 1900s to harmonize with the flat midwestern landscape. The Prairie House embodied a new philosophy of design that required a house to reflect the needs and living patterns of those who lived there. It stressed continuity of space and living areas open to natural light, air, and views through and across the interior to the outdoors. By the 1920s Prairie-style homes were widely built from coast to coast.

A key feature of this style is a flat roof with wide overhangs that project like sunshades and form a distinctive low profile. Chimneys anchor the structure vertically, and multilevel rooms and half-walled terraces and balconies extend from it horizontally, like shelves. Large bands of openable windows let in the light and air. Often these windows continue around corners to produce a ribbon effect.

Common materials include light-colored brick and stucco trimmed with horizontal bands of dark wood. The plan is open, with living areas flowing around the central core.

Shingle

Bungalow

Prairie

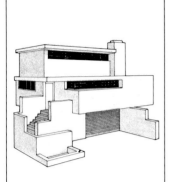

International

Mediterranean

Ranch

International

In the early 1930s the International Style arrived from Europe and went on to become a significant influence on modern architecture. It was the forerunner of the clean-lined classic contemporary style seen everywhere today. It is noted for its stark simplicity and flexible, functional interior arrangements.

This style consists of a series of unadorned cube shapes with a flat roof, smooth, continuous surfaces, and an absence of cornices or projecting eaves. Most windows are arranged in horizontal bands separated by sections of plain wall. Clerestories often line the upper portions of the facade.

Man-made materials, especially those used in industry, are the primary materials. Concrete, glass, steel, and plastics have precedence over natural materials. The concrete is sometimes textured by placing vertical or horizontal elements in the forms, or it may have a stucco or plaster finish. Although there is a balance and geometry of form, the parts are never symmetrical. Balconies and parts of the upper floors often cantilever over the ground or lower terraces. International-style houses display little or no ornamentation inside or out, and they are rarely any color but white. The homeowner uses paintings, sculpture, and other art forms to interrupt the austerity.

Mediterranean

Spain introduced several varieties of architecture to the New World. These varieties left lasting impressions on American vernacular styles. The Spaniards first settled along the Florida coast and later in the southwest territories that became Arizona, California, and New Mexico. The Mediterranean style was quickly adapted to the hot climate of these locations.

Materials were chosen to withstand the climatic extremes of hot days and cold nights. Thick walls of adobe brick and a flat roof of dried mud or packed earth were laid on rough-hewn poles set into the walls. The windows were small, deeply set, and unglazed; heavy wood shutters kept out the cold and intruders.

The low-profile, single-story design was arranged around a courtyard or patio, which provided a cooling effect. The building was often in a squared U shape with a covered loggia along the inner walls to provide a shady walkway.

In the milder, seasonally rainy climate of southern California, a slightly different style emerged. The walls were thinner. The roof was slightly pitched for drainage and covered with tile. The handmade tile was curved over the thighs of its makers before it was baked in the sun. The windows were larger for better ventilation and light.

Modern Mediterranean-style homes incorporate the center patio, often including a fountain; the abundant use of ceramic tile on floors, walls, and also as a decorative element; a tile roof. In most cases, stucco has replaced adobe as an exterior finish.

Ranch

The California or western Ranch style as we recognize it today appeared in California around the turn of the century. The Ranch-style house was initially a descendent of the southwestern ranch house of the 1830s, but it has close ties to the gabled, wood-frame houses brought west by the pioneers and the Bungalow style, which evolved about the same time. The Ranch-style home picked up its L or U shape and patio from the Mediterranean style. Ranch style adopted a Frank Lloyd Wright–designed feature, the picture window, and incorporated the sliding glass doors of the International style. These elements add a sense of spaciousness.

Materials vary widely and may be mixed and matched. Commonly, walls are finished with stucco, wood boards (either vertical or horizontal), shingles, brick, or stone. Roofs can be finished with tile, wood shingles or shakes, or composition shingles.

The Ranch-style house is single storied or split-level. Generally without a basement, it has only a crawl space below grade; this allows the floor to be at ground level. It has a low-slope gable roof that frequently projects to shelter a walkway or create a covered patio. The typical floor plan offers informal living and dining rooms, a large kitchen with nearby family room, two or three bedrooms, and two or more bathrooms. Living and family rooms usually open onto one or more patios or decks.

SELECTING A LOT

If you already own a lot or know where you want to build your new house, choosing the lot will not be a problem. You will now have to design your house to fit the size, slope, and other attributes of the lot. If you don't have a lot and you've decided on a particular size and style of house, you now have to find a lot on which your dream house can be built.

Investigating The History

There are many factors you need to consider in choosing a site on which to build a house. Some involve you and your family, not the house itself. For example, you'll need a location within a suitable distance of your employment. You should consider the distance to your family's recreational needs. If you have children, the suitability of the local school district is an important factor. Shopping convenience; the availability of medical services; the convenience of entertainment, cultural, and religious activities; and public safety are all things to think about when choosing a building site.

An investigation of the future plans for the neighborhood and the legal history of your lot can reveal important factors that will affect the long-term value of your house and the well-being of your family. For example, it would not be to your benefit if an airport or tannery was planned on the tract of land adjacent to your lot. If you're not familiar with the area around a lot you're

considering, be sure to ask around. Talk to a realtor, banker, or some prospective neighbors—see how they feel about the area and its prospects.

An investigation of the legal history of your lot includes a title search. Most lenders require this to be sure there are no outstanding liens against the property and that all previous transfers have been done correctly. If you are buying the lot without a loan or if your lender doesn't require a title search, order one yourself; it's well worth the expense.

Title insurance has become the norm in real estate transactions today. Title insurance protects you against costs and property loss due to an improper transaction—if a previous owner's spouse did not sign the sales contract, for example.

Make sure the physical characteristics of the property are as described to you. In particular, confirm the boundaries

of your property. If you cannot find survey monuments at the apparent corners of the lot, you may want to have the land surveyed by a registered, licensed surveyor—just to be sure you are buying what you think you are buying. Some jurisdictions require an official survey before the sale of property can be recorded or before building permits can be issued.

Soil and Geology

The soil and geological conditions of the land can have a profound effect on your plans for construction. Information about these conditions is especially important if you need to drill a well or install a septic system. It can also affect the kind of foundation you'll need for your house and—if you are in earthquake country—how the framing must be tied to the foundation. Check with realtors or other owners in the area to see if there have been any problems with the soil or geology. The United States Department of Agriculture Soil Conservation Service is a dependable, disinterested source of data on the soil and the geology of an area. Departments of agriculture and geology at a local university may be of help as well. In some places you need a soil report by a licensed geotechnical engineer in order to obtain building permits.

Be sure to determine if the ground is stable. United States Geological Survey maps indicate earthquake faults. Even if the area is earthquake free, ask

locals about the stability of other houses in the neighborhood—especially in hilly areas. You may need to hire a geologist to determine if the site is suitable for the house you want to build.

The lot itself must be able to accommodate the house you have in mind. After you have allowed for the setbacks required by local zoning, is the remaining lot wide and deep enough for your house and landscaping? Is the contour flat and relatively level? If it is sloped, you'll need to design the house to fit the contour.

If the slope or soil requires a special foundation, what are the costs of designing and building it? Make sure the costs fit within your budget. In addition, find out whether the difficulty of the work eliminates the possibility of doing it yourself.

Utility Services

Determine the availability of electricity, natural gas, sanitary sewerage, and telephone services—especially if you are buying land in a rural area. Contact the organizations that provide these services to get up-to-date information.

Even in built-up areas, find out where the utility hookups are; their locations can affect construction costs. Also find out about hookup fees. These fees can be quite high.

OBTAINING PLANS

The ability to read house plans will help you decide on the kind of house you want. An experienced person can look at house plans and visualize the house as if he/she had been in it and were simply remembering how it looked and felt. Developing this ability will help you immeasurably in getting the kind of house you want.

Buying Plans

There are many ways to come up with plans for a house. The least expensive way is to buy a ready-made house plan, which includes specifications and materials lists. Such plans may have to be adapted to local codes. They are available from several sources. Some building materials outlets and lumber-yards have catalogs of plans. Also check the books, magazines, and other publications devoted to producing and distributing plans. You just look through all the plans and elevation drawings, find the house you like best, and pay the purchase price of the plans.

Some sources for plans not only provide the plans and specifications, but all the materials as well. These providers are the companies that manufacture precut, prefabricated, or ready-built modular homes. They will ship all the precut pieces or modules to your site for you to assemble. All you have to do from scratch is the foundation, plumbing, and electrical work. If you wish, the manufacturer will even provide the contractor to build the foundation and assemble the house. You can find listings of these manufacturers in the telephone directory under "Buildings,

precut, prefabricated, or modular." These companies usually have local agents or distributors in metropolitan areas.

House plans can also be secured on a no-cost basis from some building-supply companies if you agree to buy all your building materials from them. Some of these firms even have a design or architectural service that will help you make limited modifications to a ready-made plan.

Making Custom Plans

If you have specific and unusual ideas for your house and you want to incorporate these ideas without compromise, you want to build a custom house. To build a custom house, you must have custom plans.

Professional Plans

The most expensive way to design a custom house is to hire an architect or house designer. An architect is a state-licensed professional with the education, experience, and ethical standards required to use the label *architect*. A house designer may also be very competent, have a suitable education, much

experience, and high ethical standards, but not an architect's license. Some states, however, do regulate house designers. The architect, having the prestige of the license, is usually more expensive. Either an architect or a designer can design your house totally and individually and provide plans and specifications for a fee—usually 5 to 10 percent of the total construction cost. For a larger fee, your architect or designer can also supervise the construction.

If you are going to hire a professional to draw your plans, there are at least two ways to go. You can tell your expert, in general terms, what you want, back off, and leave all the creativity up to the professional. Or, you can decide very specifically what you want and become deeply involved in the creative process—to the point of making your own rough drawings. Then you can hire a professional to finalize the plans. Keep in mind that, in some areas, building departments will not issue permits and lenders will not loan money unless a professional has, at the very least, consulted with you in creating the plans.

If the second way is for you, taking a few preliminary steps will help you reach many conclusions before you start paying hourly rates to have someone help you. These steps include gathering your ideas, making a bubble plan, and drawing rough plans.

Self-Drawn Plans

Before you begin plan drawing, gather together your wish list (see page 13) and the drawings

and photographs you have been collecting. You should have chosen the house style. If you have chosen your lot, be sure to get a site plan, which will list the exact dimensions and contours of the lot; include streets, utility lines, and easements, and cite the setbacks you must maintain.

The tools you need to develop your preliminary plans aren't elaborate or expensive. Purchase the items that follow at a local stationery, art-, or office-supply store.
• A pad of ⅛- or ¼-inch graph paper, 8½ by 11 inches for sketching and 18 by 24 inches for working plans
• A pad of tracing paper, 18 by 24 inches
• A straight-edged ruler
• Several soft- to medium-soft lead pencils
• A soft rubber or gum eraser
• Plastic templates for drawing symbols for fixtures, appliances, and furniture

The optional items that follow will make the plan drawing easier.
• A drawing board or portable drafting table
• A T square
• A 45-degree triangle and a 30/60-degree triangle

Measurement and Scale

Obviously the drawings on the plans cannot be the actual size of the house. Even the construction details of small parts of the house are usually larger than the paper house on which the plans are printed. However, the views of the house and all its parts must be shown in some way that allows the builders to see everything in the proper relationship.

To accomplish this, all the plans are drawn to scale—that is, 1 foot on the actual house is shown as a smaller dimension on a drawing. The most commonly used scale on house plans is ¼" = 1'0" (read "One-quarter inch equals one foot, zero inches"). Site plans are ⅛" = 1'0". Elevations—which are used mostly to visualize the house, not for construction detail—are drawn to ⅛" = 1'0". And detail drawings—which include very important construction detail that must be shown clearly—are usually ⅜" = 1'0", ½" = 1'0", or ¾" = 1'0". In the legend on each page of plans, you will find the scale of the major drawings on that page. If other drawings on the page use a different scale, it is noted under or near the title of each drawing.

Be sure that a scale is referenced on all your drawings and that you are sure of the scale you are working with before buying materials.

A few years ago, as part of an attempt to promote the use of metric measurement in the United States, some books on building and building materials included metric equivalents in parentheses after measurements of feet and inches. The metric system is not yet in general use, however; all tools, hardware, lumber, and other building materials—even those manufactured in countries that use metric measurements—are still discussed in terms of feet and inches. That is how materials are measured and sold in America. Therefore, except for on the metric conversion chart (see page 352), this book will not mention metric measurements or metric equivalents.

Typical Site Plan

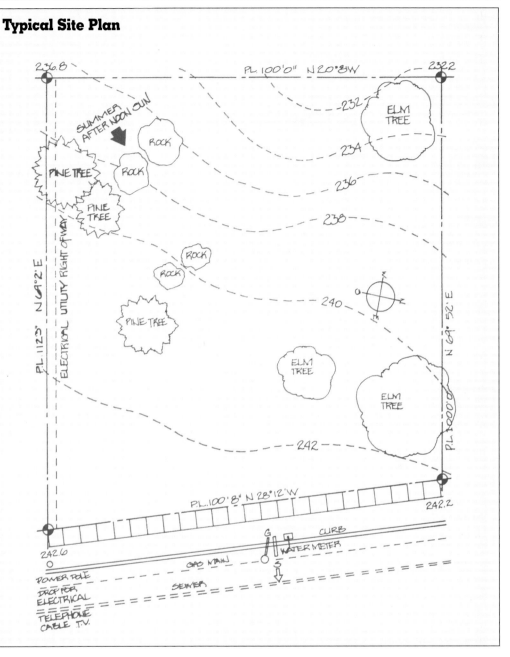

The Site Plan

The first thing you need to begin your house plans is an accurate site plan. A site plan will show your correct property line; easements; existing contours; and stubouts and underground lines for natural gas, electricity, water, telephone, cable television, and other utilities. Contour lines connect points of similar elevation, indicating the formation and slope of the land. All plans should include a directional indicator (showing north, south, east, and west).

The community building department or assessor's office, and perhaps the real estate company you purchased the lot from, should be able to provide you with a site plan from their files. Check to be sure that whatever is indicated on the plan is still correct and completely up-to-date. If possible, take the plan out to the site and verify the property line measurements before you complete the deal on the lot.

If a copy of your site plan is not available, you may need to

Typical Bubble Plans

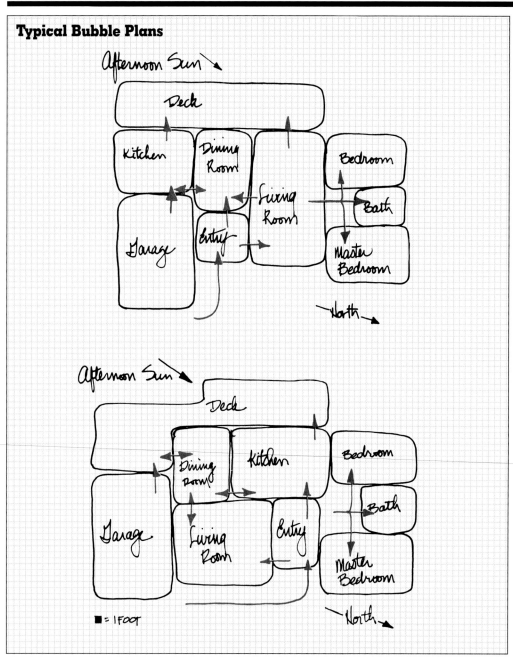

Bubble Plans

Your first plans should be rough sketches or doodles. These should merely show spaces and zones in relation to each other and in an arrangement based on your wish list (see page 13). You can include arrows to show traffic patterns and circles, or "bubbles," for the rooms and areas. Link the bubbles together to show halls or passageways. You do not have to be too careful about size, shape, or scale, although it is good to make sure the plan relates to the lot.

You can use some floor plan you like as a pattern or just make one up as you go along. At this stage you are seeing how various parts will relate to each other in the space of your prospective home. For instance, the kitchen and dining areas should be near each other, if not connected. But you might also like your breakfast area to be near the backyard and your formal dining room between the living room and entry hall. You might like your kid's bedrooms near your own or clear across the house. You might want your work area next to your bedroom or near the kitchen, where you can make coffee. Experiment with many arrangements. Go crazy. Have fun. Paper is cheap, but concrete and lumber are not. Spend as much time as you can making bubble plans.

Rough Plans

The next step is to refine the best of the bubble plans into more representational plans. Now the size, shape, location, and relationships become more important. You still don't have

have your property professionally surveyed. A topographic survey will show the property boundaries and contour lines. This is particularly important on a lot with a steep slope. A relatively level lot will not need to have a plan that shows contours. If utility information is not on the site plan or survey, contact all local

utility suppliers for information concerning easements, stubouts, and underground lines; add these to the drawing.

Use the site plan during a visit to the lot to help determine where the house should be positioned. Take some time to verify that all stubouts and property-marking indicators are correctly placed—on the plan and on the lot.

Then look around the lot. Before you decide where on the lot you want to place the house, complete the site plan by drawing in existing elements such as major trees and shrubs that you want to save, as well as any structures on the lot that will need to be demolished.

to be exact with the measurements, but your rough plans should show the proportion of one room to another. For example, the living room and bedrooms should be larger than the bathrooms. At this stage it is wise to include closets, stairways, the thickness of walls, and porches, just so you are aware that they must be included somehow.

Now is also the time to start thinking about environmental factors. Determine where you'd like the sun to hit the house in the morning or where you'd like shade in the afternoon. Decide where the driveway and garage won't interfere with living areas. If there is a view, determine from which windows you want to see it.

Use the graph paper to speed the measuring process. Choose a convenient scale; usually ¼″ = 1′. Use the tracing paper over your graph-paper drawing to duplicate certain rooms, and then move or turn the paper to refine your ideas. Turn the tracing paper over to flop parts of your plan to see how it works the other way. Change the labels around, too. Just because a room is designated a laundry or bedroom doesn't mean it can't serve another function as well. Walls are not permanent at this stage, either. Try everything you can think of to make your plan better.

Try not to be too compulsive about plan drawing. Relax—play and have some fun while you're planning. The design process should take some time. Don't expect to finalize everything in one session. Make photocopies and play around with various options.

Soon you will have refined all your ideas to the point that

you have incorporated most of the best possibilities. Now is the time to begin planning dimensions. Many building materials come in 4- by 8-foot panels; construction lumber is sold in 2-foot increments. Plan to use these standard sizes wherever you can in your design. Incorporating standard

dimensions can save you a lot of money over the course of construction. Now is also the time to be sure bathrooms, bedrooms, and kitchens are large enough to accommodate furniture, fixtures, and appliances.

When you have come this far, you are ready to take your rough plans to the professional. Figure on a couple of sessions to review your plans, and work

with the architect or designer to arrive at adjustments based on his or her expertise.

The professional will provide you with structural plans that you use to obtain building permits, determine the amount of materials you need, and eventually build your house.

Typical Rough Plan

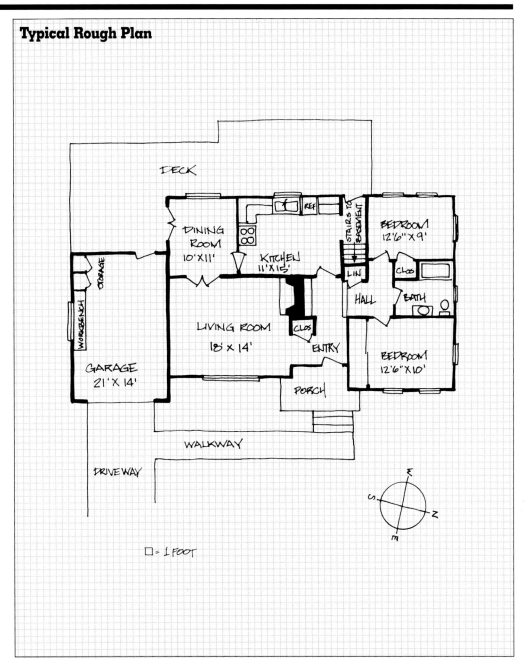

Alphabet of Lines

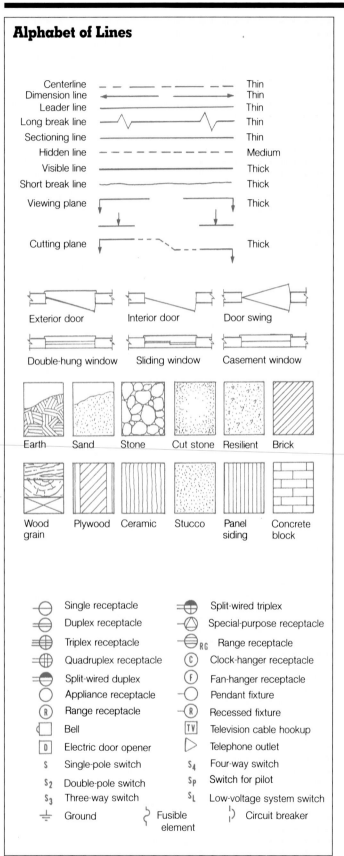

Centerline	Thin
Dimension line	Thin
Leader line	Thin
Long break line	Thin
Sectioning line	Thin
Hidden line	Medium
Visible line	Thick
Short break line	Thick
Viewing plane	Thick
Cutting plane	Thick

Exterior door Interior door Door swing

Double-hung window Sliding window Casement window

Earth Sand Stone Cut stone Resilient Brick

Wood grain Plywood Ceramic Stucco Panel siding Concrete block

Single receptacle		Split-wired triplex	
Duplex receptacle		Special-purpose receptacle	
Triplex receptacle		Range receptacle	RG
Quadruplex receptacle		Clock-hanger receptacle	C
Split-wired duplex		Fan-hanger receptacle	F
Appliance receptacle		Pendant fixture	
Range receptacle	R	Recessed fixture	R
Bell		Television cable hookup	TV
Electric door opener	D	Telephone outlet	
Single-pole switch	S	Four-way switch	S4
Double-pole switch	S2	Switch for pilot	Sp
Three-way switch	S3	Low-voltage system switch	SL
Ground		Fusible element	
		Circuit breaker	

Reading Plans And Specifications

Your ability to read and understand the plans and specifications for the house you want to build is crucial. Unless you can tell from the plans how something should be, you will not be able to build it yourself or, if it's being built for you, know if it's being built correctly. The plans do not detail each method used in the construction of each and every part of the house; there are some standard methods of construction, such as building forms for the foundation or putting together a stud wall, that a carpenter must know. But the size, materials, and other specifications for every part of the building appear in the plans and every part must be built accordingly.

Each drawing consists of lines that delineate the object, symbols for materials or parts that are too small or complex to show, dimensions to give the size, and notes to explain elements not apparent in the drawing. Understanding what some of the symbols mean will make plans easy for you to comprehend.

Visible Lines

Medium to heavy solid lines—called visible lines—delineate the outline of an object and the visible edges on the side facing the viewer.

Hidden Lines

Medium dashed lines—called hidden lines—delineate the outline or edges that are hidden behind the surfaces facing the viewer. These lines can also show an edge nearer to the viewer than the main object but out of the plane of the main object. For example, hidden lines might show hanging cabinets above the counters in a view of a kitchen.

Centerlines

Usually light or thin lines—called centerlines—are made up of alternating and evenly spaced short and long dashes, with a long dash at each end. They are used to show where a component should be placed if it is to be in the center of an area. Centerlines also show that an object is symmetrical. Circular or elliptical objects have a centerline at each axis. Sometimes a centerline is formed by two short dashes that cross. This symbol indicates the center of a circular object or each axis of an ellipse.

Dimension Lines

Light or thin lines—called dimension lines—end with slashes at the edges of the object they describe. If it is not practical for the end of the line to touch the edge of the object, extension lines are used to move the dimension line to a better location on the drawing, usually just outside the outline of the object. Dimension lines are also used to describe angles, in which case they appear as arcs between the object outlines or extension lines.

Extension Lines

These lines are the same weight as the dimension lines they assist. Extension lines are always straight lines perpendicular to the dimension lines at the point of contact.

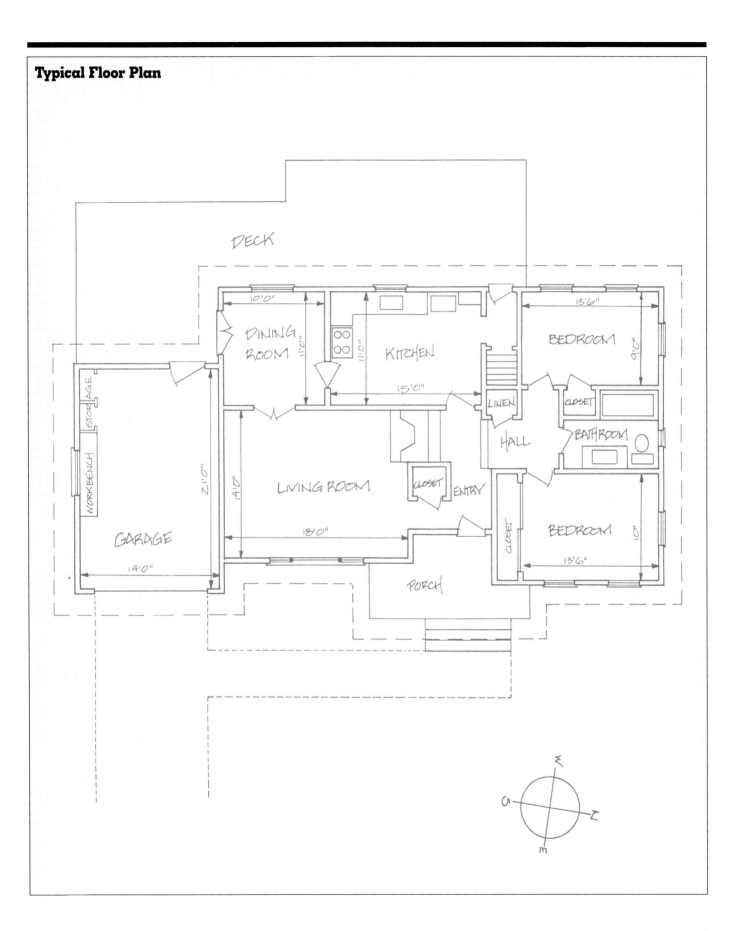

Cutting Plane Lines

Slightly lighter than visible lines, cutting plane lines are heavier than dimension lines. Cutting plane lines appear in the side view through which the section is "cut." An arrow at each end of such a line shows from which direction the object is viewed in the section drawing. Each end is labeled with letters (A-A, B-B, or the like) to indicate the section drawing to which it relates.

Break Lines

The same weight as visible lines, break lines indicate the boundaries of a missing portion of an object. The break appears because the object is too large to fit in the space provided on the sheet or because the object contains repeating segments that need to be shown only once.

Leader Lines

Very light or thin lines that connect a note or other reference to a part of an object are called leader lines. They often end in an arrowhead or dot. The arrowhead indicates the surface, line, or point that is referenced; the dot indicates the area within the object to which the note refers.

Symbols

Technical drawings include standard symbols for construction units such as doors and windows, electrical devices, plumbing fixtures, building materials, types of finished surfaces, types of woods, and types of masonry. There should be an index of symbols in your plans.

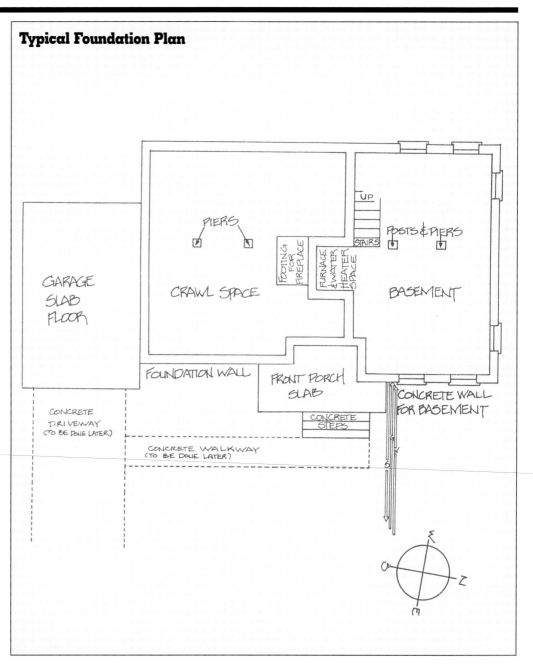

Typical Foundation Plan

GARAGE SLAB FLOOR

PIERS

CRAWL SPACE

FOOTING FOR FIREPLACE

FURNACE & WATER HEATER SPACE

UP

STAIRS

POSTS & PIERS

BASEMENT

FOUNDATION WALL

FRONT PORCH SLAB

CONCRETE WALL FOR BASEMENT

CONCRETE DRIVEWAY (TO BE DONE LATER)

CONCRETE STEPS

CONCRETE WALKWAY (TO BE DONE LATER)

Organizing The Plans

House plans are nothing more than a ritualized method of drawing what an object looks like so you can understand it or build it. Usually, presentation drawings and working drawings are required for any construction job.

Presentation drawings are used to impress or sell the project to the client. These are called architectural renderings, and they are usually idealized drawings of the completed project. The drawing is usually done in pencil or ink and colored with colored pencils or watercolors. They are always of the finished project, complete with landscaping, automobiles and people, and beautiful billowing clouds. Often these drawings are distorted to look wider, longer, higher, or any other way that will impress the client; they might not be accurate. Architectural renderings are used in presentations, on the walls of sales offices, and in advertisements—never on the job where the actual work is to be done.

Typical Roof Plan

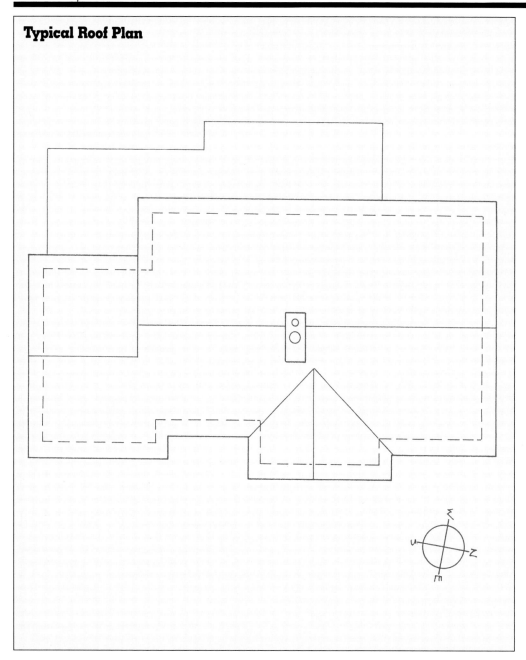

Floor Plans

These plans show where the major parts of a house are and how they relate to each other. They include walls, rooms, closets, cabinets, stairs, porches, doors, windows, electric wiring, switches, lights, outlets, gas and electric appliances, and plumbing fixtures. Everything that constitutes a house should appear somewhere on the floor plans, although the floor plans alone might not show enough detail to be used as a guide for building.

Foundation Plans

The perimeter foundation; piers; slabs; footings for fireplaces, porches, cellar, or basement; and anything else that is built on or in the ground are indicated on the foundation plans. The foundation plans usually contain several section drawings and details of the foundation. These show the placement of reinforcing steel, thicknesses of footings and foundation walls and the like, and copious notes.

Roof Plans

The location of the peaks, valleys, hips, dormers, and the overhang are indicated on the roof plan. A roof plan often includes several details, especially if the roof has unusual angles or other features not found in a standard roof. This plan also includes the triangular symbol for the slope of each part of the roof, and it shows the rise and run—that is, how many inches the slope rises (vertically) for each foot of run (horizontal distance). Roof slope is discussed in detail in the third chapter.

The working drawings are accurate representations of the project, used to show the building department, construction supervisors, and workers how it will be contructed. Shown separately or superimposed on the structural plans are drawings of the foundation, each floor of the house, the mechanics, and the roof. There may also be elevation and section drawings and some detail drawings. They are usually drawn in pencil on vellum sheets. The completed drawings—and any subsequent revisions—are made into sets of blueprints for the use of all the parties concerned with the project. These sets are called blueprints because, until the 1950s, the reproduction method made all the black pencil lines white and the white background dark blue. Since that time better methods of reproduction have been developed. Now blueprints are usually black or dark blue lines on a white background. Compared to old-style blueprints, modern plans are easier to read and much easier to make notes on with a pencil or pen.

Typical Mechanical Plan

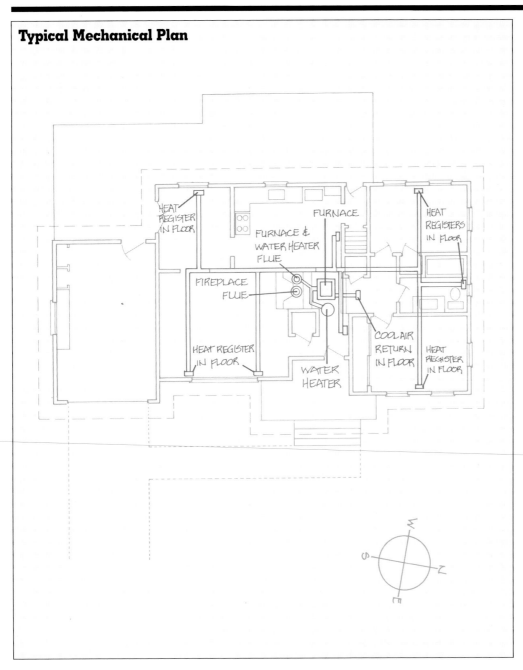

Mechanical Plans

Not all sets of plans include a mechanical plan. Sometimes—in relatively straightforward installations—the furnace, registers, and cold-air returns are shown on the floor plan, but the location of the ducts is left up to the builder. For any complex or out-of-the-ordinary system, however, a mechanical plan shows the placement of all the duct work, other heating fixtures, and appliances. It includes details of special framing that may be needed.

The mechanical plan may show plumbing lines and electrical wires, or these may be drawn on separate sheets. If complicated, kitchen and bathroom mechanics may be drawn separately.

Elevations

Side views of any exterior or interior walls are called elevations. Usually all the exterior views of a house are included in the plans. The views are fairly representational pictures of the house and show placement of construction features.

Also included is the grade, or ground line, as it relates to the house and all necessary dimensions.

Interior elevations are drawn only when a wall has some built-in features. These can be cabinets, shelves, windows, arches, stairways, or any other feature for which the builder needs a side view.

Details

Drawings used to show construction particulars not apparent in the plan or elevation drawings are called details. Details are used as needed to clarify complicated construction features or show something too small to be shown on the full floor plan. Details are usually in a scale larger than that of the floor plan, and they include more dimensions and notes.

Sections

Usually drawings of vertical "slices" of the building or parts of the building are called sections. Each section drawing is labeled "Typical Section" or with two letters (for example, "Section A-A"). A typical section—of a foundation, for instance—is the view you'd get if you cut through the foundation and looked at the cut end. If the section drawing is a view at a particular point along the length of the foundation, it will be labeled with the letters to indicate where this view is on another drawing of the foundation. On the other drawing, usually a plan or elevation, there is a corresponding pair of letters at the ends of a section line, which shows where the section was "cut." Arrows indicate the direction of the view in the section drawing.

Notes and Specifications

All the written materials on or accompanying a set of plans are concise statements concerning the methods or materials to be used in the construction. Specific notes appear on the drawings themselves to clarify or add information not apparent in the drawing. These notes may explain a procedure or material to be used or a standard that must be maintained.

General notes refer to many of the drawings, materials, methods, or procedures used in several phases of the construction. These notes are usually grouped together and marked with reference letters or numbers that also appear on the drawings where the note applies.

In addition to the notes on the plans, there may be a separate booklet of written material called the specifications. This booklet contains everything that can be written about the construction of the house. All the materials, finishes, fixtures, appliances, methods, and procedures to be used on the job must be delineated in the specifications. Separate energy calculations may also be required.

The specifications, often referred to as specs, also lay out the responsibilities of all those involved in the project. If you are getting bids on all or any parts of the job, the specifications constitute the legal document on which the bid is based. A copy of the specifications should be attached to the signed contract. If, after a bid is accepted, you want to include something in the house that isn't in the specs, you will have to pay extra for it.

Typical Elevations

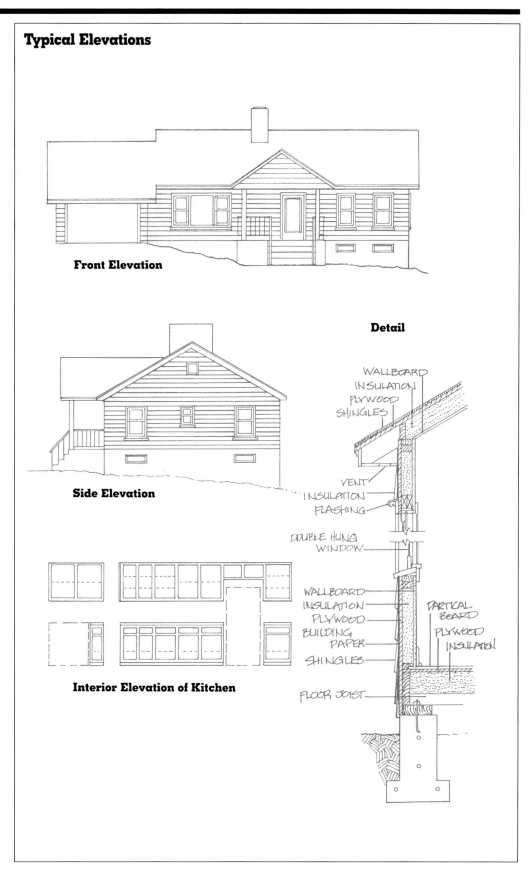

Front Elevation

Side Elevation

Interior Elevation of Kitchen

Detail

WALLBOARD
INSULATION
PLYWOOD
SHINGLES

VENT
INSULATION
FLASHING

DOUBLE HUNG
WINDOW

WALLBOARD
INSULATION
PLYWOOD
BUILDING
PAPER
SHINGLES

PARTICAL
BOARD
PLYWOOD
INSULATION

FLOOR JOIST

FINANCING AND COSTS

The amount of money you spend to build your new house depends on your financial situation and the requirements of the new house. If, like most people, you need to borrow money to buy or build a house, you'll find that the banks and savings and loans have very strict requirements for lending.

Getting a Loan

A general rule of thumb used to be that the cost of a family's housing should not exceed three times its average annual income. In recent years, however, homes sometimes cost as much as four or five times the family's annual income. Lenders may insist that the amount spent on all the housing expenses—mortgage, insurance, and maintenance—not exceed 35 percent of the family's take-home monthly income.

It is much harder to get a loan to build a house than to buy a ready-made house. There is less value in a vacant lot than in a house that is already built, where the house is there to see and appraise. A house can have its market value established by a realtor or appraiser without too much difficulty; to a lender, however, a set of plans and good intentions aren't worth as much as tangible real estate. If you own the lot outright—especially in places where lots are valuable—you will have an easier time borrowing money.

Lenders look at your ability to repay and how well the loan is secured—that is, the loan-to-value ratio. A loan is secured by how much of your own

money you are putting into the project and the value of the completed project.

It is even more difficult to get a construction loan for a house you are going to build yourself than for a house built by a professional. An owner-builder, like you may become, has no track record. And the bank has no idea of your work habits or expertise. It doesn't know if you'll ever finish the job and, if you do, whether it will be built well enough to sell for the amount of the loan. If a conventional lender will lend you the money to build, it may be at a high interest rate.

Institutions that may be able to either make the loan themselves or give you leads to others who will include banks, savings and loans, credit unions, mortgage brokers, finance companies, and real estate brokers.

Look in the local telephone directory under "Building Construction Consultants" for companies that specialize in providing advice, services, and materials to those interested in

building their own houses. Sometimes a consultant can lead you to loan sources. If you can't find such a firm, call any construction consultant and inquire whether the the firm provides services to owner-builders or ask for a referral to a company that does.

Special government financing programs offer assistance for some kinds of construction. Try the Department of Housing and Urban Development (HUD); the Federal Housing Administration (FHA); the Veterans Administration (VA); and state, county, or city housing programs.

You may find that the best way to finance your self-built home is to borrow the money from relatives or friends. They will certainly have more confidence in you than a bank would. You can secure their loan just as you would with a bank, with a deed of trust on the property and the improvements, and make monthly payments to them just as you would to any lender. When the house is finished, you can get a regular mortgage on it and can pay them back.

Estimating Rough Cost

Until you have a set of plans and specifications, you cannot accurately estimate the cost of building your house, so you can't know how much money you'll need for construction. On the other hand, you can't draw up a set of plans until you know how your house must be to fit within your price range.

You have a catch-22 problem here. The solution is a little homework.

You can get an idea of what various kinds of construction will cost by discussing the matter with contractors, builders, and real estate professionals in your area. They will be able to give you a fair idea of the cost-per-square-foot of various kinds of construction. Be aware that every house has certain fixed costs and that cost-per-square-foot begins after these basic costs have been figured. Because of these fixed costs, small houses usually cost more per square foot than comparable-quality large houses.

If you plan on doing some of or all the work yourself, get a breakdown on how much of the cost per square foot is labor; how much is materials; and how much is other costs, including insurance and taxes for laborers, permits, utilities, and general overhead. Within each of these categories you can determine a cost range. Then, you can tailor your plans to stay within your budget.

Estimating The Materials

Once you have your plans, you can make a very accurate estimate of the materials it should take to do each part of the job. Estimating materials, called materials takeoff, is one of the

Dressing for Safety

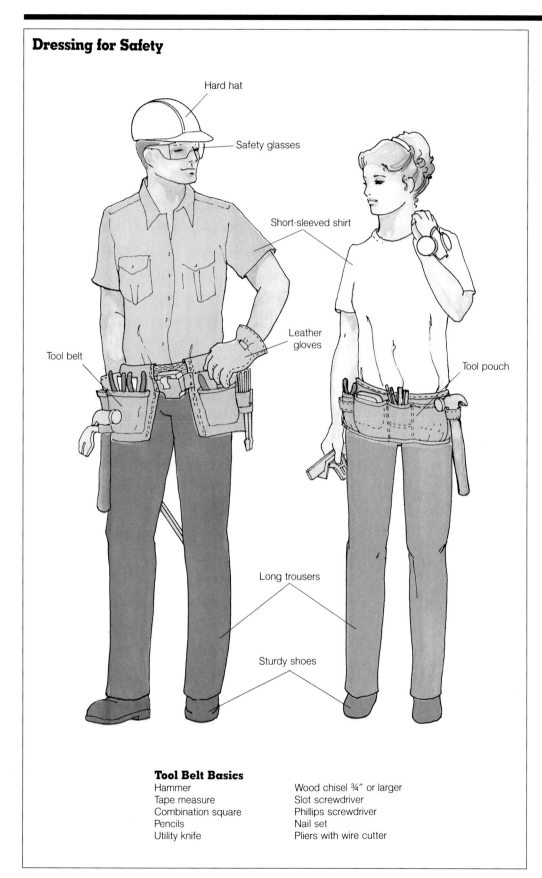

Hard hat

Safety glasses

Short-sleeved shirt

Leather gloves

Tool belt

Tool pouch

Long trousers

Sturdy shoes

☐ Site survey completed
☐ Life-style list completed
☐ Plans drawn
☐ Specifications listed
☐ Costs estimated
☐ Contractor bids secured
☐ Contractors selected, if used
☐ Construction loans in hand
☐ Construction insurance secured
☐ Building permits obtained
☐ Materials-ordering schedule completed

Tool Belt Basics

Hammer	Wood chisel ¾" or larger
Tape measure	Slot screwdriver
Combination square	Phillips screwdriver
Pencils	Nail set
Utility knife	Pliers with wire cutter

FOUNDATIONS & FRAMING

"What have I gotten myself into?" might be the first thing you mumble as you walk onto your lot to start the construction of your very own house. Feeling this way is understandable. The plans, specifications, and list of materials look overwhelming. When you think of all the different jobs and procedures necessary to construct a house, it's even more mind-boggling. But, take heart. Neither Rome nor any house was built in a day. You aren't going to build it all at once. You have to do only one step at a time. This chapter will describe the steps for marking the site, building the foundation, and doing the framing. When you've read it, you will see just how simple most of the steps really are.

The symmetry of this saltbox is broken by the addition of a double-car garage. Although the house style is old, the composition shingles on the gable roof are just an example of the modern materials used throughout the construction. Skylights—planned in the roof at the framing stage—provide additional light in the front rooms of the house.

LAYING OUT THE SITE

The first step in actual construction is laying out the site. This means accurately marking, with a stake, where the corners of the building will be in relation to the boundaries of the lot. Then these corners are marked with batter boards. The boards will establish and maintain the position of the foundation as the footings and foundation walls are completed.

☐ Tool belt
☐ Steel tape measure
☐ Wood stakes
☐ Mason's twine
☐ Framing hammer
☐ Sledge hammer
☐ Builder's level or hose level
☐ Line level

For Excavation

☐ Spray paint or powder
☐ Round-tipped shovel
☐ Square-tipped shovel
☐ Pickax
☐ Backhoe
☐ Wheelbarrow

Determining Reference Lines

There are two common ways of accurately determining the location of the building on the site. One is to measure from one or more established reference lines, such as a street, sidewalk, or property line marked with a fence or surveyor's stakes. For this you'd use a 100-foot steel tape measure. The second way is to use a transit and work from a surveyor's benchmark. This method requires expensive equipment and more instruction than this book can accommodate.

If the lot is fairly level, the reference-lines method works well. If the lot slopes very much, it's better to let a survey professional lay out the site with a transit.

To determine reference lines, you will need a 100-foot steel tape measure, a bundle of stakes, a ball of mason's twine, and a hammer. A plumb bob will also be useful; see if you can borrow or rent one. Buy ready-made stakes or make them yourself from 1 by 2 or 2 by 2 lumber. Cut the lumber into stakes about 1 foot long, and sharpen one end of each with a hatchet or saw. Mason's twine is a special, heavy-duty string made with just enough stretch and strength to mark the position of courses of bricks. It is also perfect for marking foundations, and it is available at most any place that sells building materials.

Take the site plan from your set of plans and orient it with the site. That is, lay it on the ground or hood of your car so that north on the plan coincides with north at the site.

Locate objects on the site—the street, trees, and fences—and find the corresponding symbols on the plan so you see how the plan relates to the site. A surveyor should have marked the property lines with stakes. Verify that these are in the correct positions. Measure carefully from the stakes to find the position of the first corner of the house.

When you find the position of the corner of the house on the site, drive in a stake to mark it. On the plan, measure the distance from that corner of the house to the next corner. Multiply by whatever scale your plans are drawn to, measure that distance on the site, and mark the next corner with a stake.

Find the remaining corners of the house the same way. If your house is made up of right angles and you have established at least two corners, you can use the 6-8-10 method (see illustration opposite page) to find additional corners.

If your house has more than four corners—that is, if it is made up of a series of rectangles—lay out one large rectangle that encompasses all or most of the building. Then use the corners of this large area to lay out the remaining corners.

Once all corners are staked, check all distances from the property lines. Then check all the right angles of your building by using the 6-8-10 method or measuring diagonally across each rectangle. The length of the diagonals of a rectangle are exactly the same if the corners are square.

Drive a nail into the top of each stake and stretch mason's twine tightly from stake to stake. This string shows a rough outline of the house you are about to build.

Placing the Grade-Line Stake

The grade line is another important reference point used to make measurements. Find this line on the site plan. The site plan shows the level of the ground where it meets the foundation. From the grade line you will locate the top of the foundation and the depth of the excavation for the footings.

A surveyor's benchmark is often used to establish a grade line. You can also use an existing street, curb, or sidewalk. To establish the grade line near the site of the building, drive a stake near one of the corner stakes, but outside the perimeter of the foundation. By using a line level or water level, mark on the stake the level of the benchmark, curb, or whatever.

A line level works well over short distances—12 feet or less. Over longer spans the string will sag, so a more accurate device must be used.

A water level is nothing more than a long length of transparent tubing or a hose with short transparent tubes at each end. Just fill the hose with water and have a partner hold one tube against the first stake and measure the distance between the water level and the established reference mark. While your helper holds the tube against the stake, take the other end of the tube to the rest of the stakes and put a mark on each at the waterline. Then measure up or down from this mark

Laying Out the Site

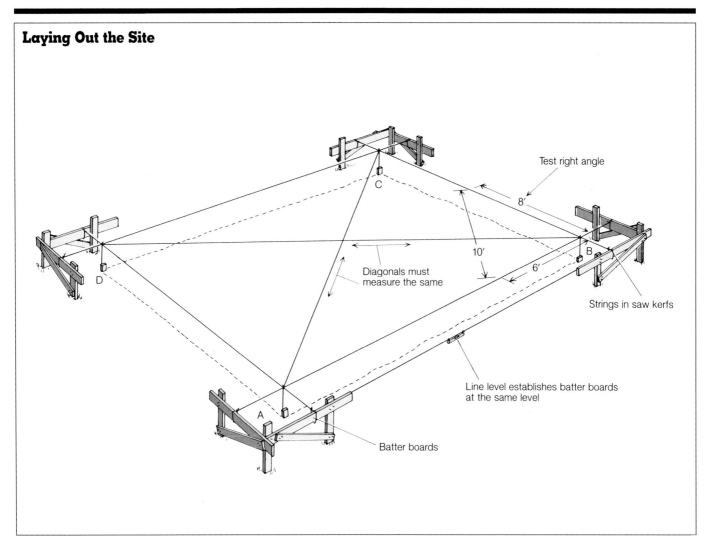

Test right angle

Diagonals must measure the same

8'

10'

6'

Strings in saw kerfs

Line level establishes batter boards at the same level

Batter boards

the same distance that your partner measured at the first stake and make a new mark. This is the grade-line mark.

Batter Boards

Batter boards must be put at all major corners of a building. They are L-shaped arrangements of boards, usually 1 by 4s, that you should set up well back from the actual construction. The batter boards are secured to stakes driven into the ground and braced with diagonals. On a roughly level site, the tops of the batter boards and saw kerfs or nails mark the

exact height and outside edge of the foundation wall. String stretched tightly between the saw kerfs or nails will help you put the foundation in the correct location.

How far you place the batter boards from the edge of the building is determined by how the foundation footings will be dug. If you will be digging the foundation footing trenches by hand, place the boards about 4 feet outside the stakes. If the trenches are to be dug with a backhoe, either set the boards 2 feet back so the backhoe operator can reach over them or set them 10 feet back so the backhoe can maneuver inside them.

Start constructing the batter boards by driving 2 by 4 stakes into the ground vertically at each corner. Be sure the stakes are higher than the finished top of the foundation wall. You can figure this height by measuring the planned foundation height from the grade-line stake as it relates to the grade line on the plans.

Using a line level, water level, or builder's level, mark the height of the foundation wall on the batter-board stake closest to the grade-line stake.

A builder's level, usually available at rental agencies, works well for this job because

it is simple and, for this purpose, takes no training to use. Just find a place from which you can see all the batter boards clearly. Sight through the builder's level and make it level at the exact height of the mark you established on the first stake. Then just rotate it from stake to stake and tell your helper where to mark.

Now nail the 1 by 4 batter boards across the stakes so the top of each is on the marks. You have now established the precise elevation of the top of the foundation wall. Now you need to mark the outside edges and widths of the foundation wall and footings.

Renting Equipment

The list of tools and equipment needed to build a house is a long one. However, you don't have to buy all of them; almost any tool can be rented.

In particular, consider renting power tools. Many are large and take up a lot of storage space, or are for specific tasks only and will be used rarely, and others are expensive. Most communities have good equipment-rental agencies, some of which specialize in construction equipment. Check the local telephone directory for agencies in your area.

Excavation equipment is specialized. Except for very simple jobs, a backhoe is used for foundation excavation. A backhoe is a tractor-style vehicle with a bucket attached to a rigid bar. The bar is hinged to a boom that is drawn to the machine when in operation. Backhoes can be purchased, of course, but for the construction of one house, renting makes more sense. Backhoes are large pieces of equipment that take experience to handle proficiently. Many backhoe owners—often contractors or farmers who use the machine regularly—will rent out the equipment, as well as operate it for you. If possible, find backhoe owners/operators to do your excavation work; their experience should prevent costly mishaps.

Stringing the Foundation

Decide the wall of the house that must be placed most accurately. It probably is the wall facing the street or the one closest to the legal setback limit. Stretch mason's or nylon twine above the twine you put between the stakes on the ground. Tap nails temporarily into the top of the batter boards, and tie the twine onto the nails. Now use the 100-foot tape measure to check the position of the twine in relation to the original reference points. Relocate the twine, if necessary, by tying it to other nails driven into the tops of the batter boards.

Continue around the perimeter of the house, stretching lines of twine so they cross just above the stakes in the ground. Make sure that the lines are the right length. Use the 6-8-10 method or measure the diagonals of the rectangles to be sure each angle is 90 degrees.

When you have squared the building, mark the batter boards at each line and cut a ¼-inch-deep saw kerf at each mark. The saw kerfs are more reliable than nails for this purpose—they cannot bend or work themselves loose. Just tie a large knot in the end of each line and the kerf will hold it securely. When the lines must be removed for digging the footing trench or moving materials, they can be quickly replaced in the kerfs.

If your house plan calls for additional foundation walls or piers within the perimeter, now is the time to mark their location. If your house has a slab foundation for a garage or other room, its limits must also be located accurately. For walls, rows of piers, or a slab, set up supplementary batter boards as far outside the perimeter as the batter boards at the corners. If you must set up batter boards within the perimeter, be sure they will be well clear of any trench digging. For 1 or 2 piers, measure very carefully from the perimeter twine and mark the center of each pier with a meticulously placed stake.

Next check your foundation plan to find the width of the foundation footing and wall. For a one-story house the Uniform Building Code (UBC) requires a footing 12 inches wide and 6 inches thick; 15 inches wide and 7 inches thick for a two-story house. The foundation wall must be 6 inches wide for a one-story house, 8 inches wide for two stories. Local codes may differ, especially in areas of unstable ground or earthquake danger.

Using the first saw kerf on the outside edge of the foundation wall for reference, mark the width of the wall and footing on each batter board. Make another saw kerf at each mark. Now, as needed during construction, you can stretch mason's twine to mark either the footing or the foundation wall.

Excavating for The Foundation

All foundations must be excavated to some degree. The depth of the excavation depends on the weather in your area and the type of utilities you will be running under the house. Check the plans for the correct excavation depth for your house.

You can do all the digging by hand if yours is a simple foundation with shallow footings, say 12 to 15 inches deep, and only a foot or so wide. If it needs deep footings, a sunken crawl space, or a basement, you will need to hire a backhoe and operator.

The width of the footing trench or the outline of a slab or basement is delineated with batter boards and mason's twine. Now, mark the width or outline on the ground so you will know where to dig. To do this, stretch mason's twine between each pair of footing saw kerfs in the batter boards. In one hand hold a plumb bob on a string; in the other hold an aerosol can of spray paint or a coffee can of lime or flour. As you walk, let the plumb bob string slide along the marking string and spray a line or dribble the white powder behind the plumb bob.

If the trenches are to be dug by hand, mark both edges. If a backhoe will be digging the trenches, mark only the outside edge. To get the desired width of trench, specify the width of the bucket on the backhoe.

After marking the trench, go back over all your lines and double-check to be sure they are accurate. Then remove all the twine lines so they are not in the way of the digging. You can replace those lines or the foundation-wall lines exactly where they were because of the care you took in placing the saw kerfs.

BUILDING THE FOUNDATION

You'll need the assistance of one or two people for five days to completely build the foundation of your house. Though building a foundation is not difficult work, it is physically demanding. On a difficulty scale of 10 points, consider building a foundation a 5. One member of the team should have rough carpentry skills.

☐ Tool belt
☐ Steel tape measure
☐ Wood stakes
☐ Mason's twine
☐ Framing hammer
☐ Sledge hammer
☐ Builder's level or hose level
☐ Wire cutter
☐ Rebar cutter and bender
☐ Strike-off board
☐ Kneeling boards
☐ Bull float
☐ Wood floats
☐ Steel finishing trowel
☐ Edging trowel
☐ Power finisher

For a Concrete-Block Foundation
☐ Mason's trowel
☐ Mason's chisel
☐ Mason's hammer
☐ Chalk line
☐ Steel tape measure
☐ Combination square
☐ Framing square
☐ 24-inch level
☐ Carpenter's pencil

☐ Line blocks
☐ Mason's twine
☐ Mortarboard
☐ Jointers
☐ Gloves
☐ Wheelbarrow

For a Stem-Wall Foundation
☐ Tool belt
☐ Framing hammer
☐ Sledge hammer
☐ Handsaw
☐ Power circular saw
☐ Wire cutter
☐ Rebar cutter and bender
☐ Tamping poles
☐ Mason's trowel

For a Post-and-Pier Foundation
☐ Round-tipped shovel
☐ Square-tipped shovel
☐ Pickax
☐ Tool belt
☐ Framing hammer
☐ Power circular saw
☐ 24-inch level
☐ Combination square
☐ Builder's level or hose level
☐ Plumb bob
☐ Carpenter's pencil

Choosing the Foundation

Houses have concrete-slab, perimeter-wall, post-and-pier, full-basement, pier-and-grade beam, or all-weather wood foundations.

The correct foundation for your house depends on the design of the building, the configuration of the lot, and the local building codes. Intricate designs, hillside locations, and homes with full basements generally require professional engineering and construction. If this is your situation, you can have professionals install the foundation and then pick up the construction work from that point.

Typical homes built on flat lots by the owner-builder use a combination of three foundations: concrete slab for garages, perimeter for exterior walls, and post-and-pier for interior walls.

Concrete Slab

This is an economical means of supporting a house because it is foundation and subfloor all in one. A concrete-slab foundation keeps the floor as close to the ground as you can get, an advantage where a high floor would cause a problem. A concrete slab is the floor of choice for garages and basements.

In areas where the ground freezes deeply, the walls of the house must be supported by a foundation that extends below the frost line. In such cases you should form and pour the slab and foundation separately.

In warmer regions, where soil conditions are favorable, a thick-edged slab may be desirable. This is a slab with a reinforced footing around the edge. In most cases you can pour slab and footing at once. Instructions for installing a concrete-slab foundation begin on page 56.

Perimeter Wall

The perimeter-wall foundation is the most common foundation built today. It can be used on either level or somewhat sloping ground. It raises the house away from the dampness of the ground and the destructive insects that abound there. It provides a crawl space under the house for access to utilities. This type of foundation is good for supporting a wood-floor system. The footings are poured concrete and the foundation walls are either poured concrete or concrete block.

For house construction, footings and concrete walls are usually poured in one operation. For a concrete-block wall, the footings are poured first. When they have hardened, the block wall is built on top of them. Instructions for installing a perimeter-wall foundation begin on page 62.

Post-and-Pier

Typically used for small buildings—such as outbuildings, toolsheds, and playhouses— post-and-pier foundations are not usually allowed as the only foundation for a residence. However, they are often used in conjunction with perimeter foundations for supporting interior walls and girders. Post-and-pier footings must be placed on undisturbed soil and can be used in any climate. Instructions for installing a post-and-pier foundation begin on page 71.

Full Basement

In areas where freezing conditions require a deep foundation, it may be desirable to excavate a full or partial basement. The floor slab and footings are always poured concrete. The basement walls are usually concrete block because it's almost as easy to lay the blocks as it is to engineer and construct the forms for the concrete. If your plans call for a full basement, get professional help to build the tall forms and make the pour.

Pier-and-Grade

This kind of foundation is made of reinforced concrete piers set deeply into the ground. The piers are tied together with reinforced concrete beams at ground level. It is designed to support structures on steep slopes or on unstable ground. This foundation must be professionally engineered and constructed. Forms for the beams are built on grade and usually follow the contour of the ground.

All-Weather Wood

Techniques were developed a few years ago for building basement and crawl-space foundation walls with pressure-treated lumber. These foundations require proper materials and special assembly and back-filling procedures. If this type of foundation sounds interesting to you, seek advice from an engineer or contractor who specializes in this kind of construction.

Building The Footings

Building codes require a footing beneath the edges of a slab, under all perimeter-wall foundations, and under the piers of a post-and-pier foundation. The footing trench must be planned and dug with great care. How deep should it be? How wide? What if the ground isn't quite level? The answers to these questions are in the Uniform Building Code, but local codes may vary. Be sure someone has checked local codes before you complete your plans. Then check the plans carefully before digging.

Footing Trenches

If your soil can hold sharply cut trenches, it can support the sides as well as the bottom of the form. If soil conditions prevent sharply cut corners and sturdy vertical sides, use form boards for the sides. In this case you'll need to dig the trenches wide enough and slope the sides so you can work safely in the trench while you build the forms.

A footing trench must be dug in undisturbed soil, not fill. If you dig too deep and must backfill the excavation, most codes require that the fill be engineered fill or concrete. Engineered fill is designed specifically to enhance the structural integrity of the soil. Requirements will vary; check local codes.

All footings must be deep enough to lie below the frost line. If you are building in an area where the ground does not freeze, the required depth for the base of the footing is usually 12 inches for a one-story

house, 18 inches for two stories. The footing trench around the edge of a slab must be at least 12 inches deep or below the frost line.

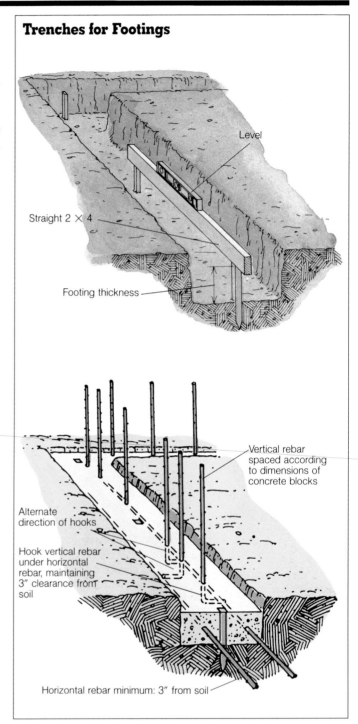

Trenches for Footings

Level

Straight 2 × 4

Footing thickness

Vertical rebar spaced according to dimensions of concrete blocks

Alternate direction of hooks

Hook vertical rebar under horizontal rebar, maintaining 3" clearance from soil

Horizontal rebar minimum: 3" from soil

Rebar for Footing Reinforcement

The UBC and the more stringent local codes require that most slab and wall-foundation footings be reinforced with steel rebar. Note the details on

Forms for Footings

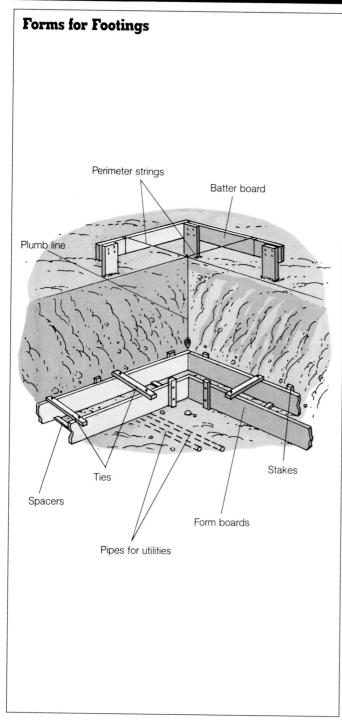

Perimeter strings

Batter board

Plumb line

Ties

Spacers

Pipes for utilities

Form boards

Stakes

your foundation plan and the specifications for the size, number, and location of the bars. See page 59 for lapping requirements.

Horizontal rebar within the footing must be held above the ground on dobies (concrete cubes or pieces of brick or stone in the bottom of the footing trench). The rebar can be secured further by wiring it to the dobies if necessary.

Vertical bars, if required in a poured concrete or concrete-block wall, must have their bottom ends wired to the horizontal rebar. If there is no horizontal rebar, they must be bent to a right angle and suspended or set on dobies so the vertical bars do not contact the ground or get too near the edge of the footing.

Rebar in concrete-block foundations must be placed accurately so it fits exactly in the holes in the blocks. To do this, lay a row of accurately positioned blocks beside the footing trench. Then mark the center of the holes every 4 feet or at whatever spacing the specifications require. Check local codes for the exact requirements, but usually these bars need be only as high as the top of the third course of blocks. If the foundation requires more courses, wire additional lengths of rebar to the first length as you set the blocks.

Wall Footing

A common type of form for a wall footing has side boards of 2-inch lumber as wide as the thickness of the footing. Hold the boards in place by nailing wood or metal stakes to them and attaching braces that go diagonally from the top of these stakes to the bottom of stakes a foot or so away. Keep the tops of the form boards in alignment by nailing spreaders (2 by 2 or 1 by 2 sticks) across from the top of one to the top of the other.

Footings for basement walls should contain a key slot for better resistance to water where the wall joins the footing. A key slot is a groove that

runs down the middle of the footing. This groove is usually formed by nailing a 2 by 4, beveled on both sides, to the bottom of the spreaders. When the wall is poured or built with blocks, concrete or mortar takes the shape of its mold, creating a formidable water barrier.

Post-and-Pier and Column Footings

These footings should be square, with the same thickness and width as corresponding wall footings. They must also be below the frost line in areas where the ground freezes. To anchor a wood post, set a ready-made concrete pier with a wood block attached to the top of the footing. To anchor wood or steel posts directly to the footing, set manufactured metal post anchors or bolts into the footing when you pour it.

Other Footings

Install special footings to support fireplaces and chimneys, furnaces, porch stairs, and other heavy areas. Form these so you can pour them at the same time as the foundation footings. Build the forms the same way you build the forms for the foundation footings, but refer to the plans and detail drawings for depths, widths, and thicknesses. Also, check to see if any bolts or anchors must be placed into the concrete of the footing when you pour it.

Concrete Slab

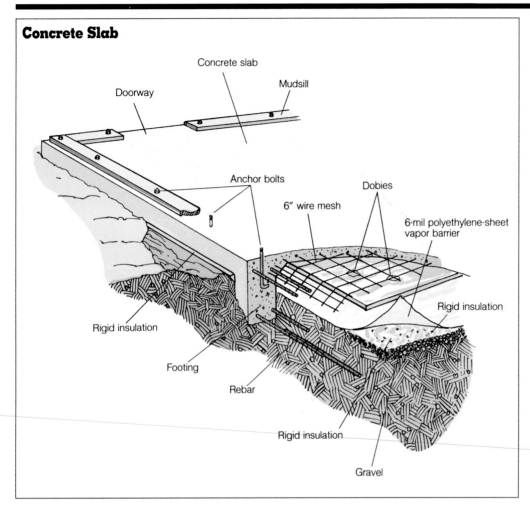

Concrete slab

Doorway

Mudsill

Anchor bolts

6" wire mesh

Dobies

6-mil polyethylene-sheet vapor barrier

Rigid insulation

Rigid insulation

Footing

Rebar

Rigid insulation

Gravel

Installing a Concrete-Slab Foundation

The slab is the foundation of choice for a garage, shop, or laundry room. In some areas it can even be the choice for the whole building if you are building a small vacation house or a studio or shop behind your main house. A big advantage in using a slab is that, once you pour the foundation, you are ready to put up the walls. You avoid using the time and materials necessary to construct a separate floor.

In areas where the ground freezes in the winter, the perimeter and bearing walls within a structure must be supported by foundation footings or piers that extend below the frost line to solid unfilled soil. In such a case pour the footings and piers separately, before pouring the slab.

Proportions for 1 Yard of Concrete

The chart that follows gives the proportions for mixing 1 cubic yard of concrete. You can tell by the weights that, if you need more than a yard or so or need air entrainment, you should have it delivered by a transit-mix truck. If you need only a small quantity, you can mix it yourself in a rented cement mixer or a construction wheelbarrow.

To make a 1-cubic-foot batch, divide each of the proportions by 27 (there are 27 cubic feet in a cubic yard). The first row of proportions divided by 27 would yield 21 pounds of cement (about one quarter of a sack); 60 pounds of sand; 44 pounds of gravel; and 10½ pounds of water (1⅓ gallons).

Project	Aggregate Size	Lb of Cement	Sacks of Cement	Lb of Sand	Lb of Gravel	Total Lb of Aggregate	Lb of Water	Gallons of Water	Air Entrainment
Foundations and	⅜"	565	6.0	1,630	1,190	2,820	285	36	—
footings	¾"	520	5.5	1,310	1,730	3,040	260	33	—
	1"	490	5.2	1,260	1,870	3,130	245	31	—
Slabs, patios, and	⅜"	580	6.2	1,570	1,190	2,760	290	36	7%
foundations in	¾"	580	6.2	1,250	1,730	2,980	290	36	6%
cold climates	1"	535	5.7	1,170	1,870	3,040	270	34	6%

Note: 1 sack of cement weighs 94 lb; water weighs 8 lb/gal.

Pipes Under the Slab

Supply and waste plumbing lines, heating ducts, and electric utility lines can all be placed beneath the slab. Check your plans, dig trenches, and install them as needed. To prevent damage from freezing if the building is not occupied during cold weather, water supply lines should be placed in trenches of the same depth as those outside the building. Dig the trenches for the supply lines so they are just wide enough for the piping, then backfill the pipes with well-tamped gravel or compacted fill that cannot settle later.

Forms

Mark the outline of a slab foundation with batter boards and strings, as described earlier. In this case, however, the batter boards don't have to be as far above grade. Simply mark the ground with spray paint, lime powder, or flour. If the trench is to be dug by hand, mark it after the perimeter forms are in place. If the trench is to be dug with a backhoe, mark only the outside edge and wait until the digging is completed before you construct the forms.

The ground for a slab is rarely level. However, if the lowest and highest measurements are within a foot of each other, there's no problem. The low spots can be filled in with gravel and additional concrete. If the discrepancy is greater than a foot, however, level the area before you continue.

Start placing the form boards at the highest corner and work toward the lowest corner. The top of the form should be at least 8 inches above grade at the highest point. Build the forms around the outside edge with 2-by lumber held by stakes. Use the twine lines to align the forms. The inside face of each form should be just beneath the perimeter string. Drive a stake along the outside edge of the board and nail it to the board. Place a level on the board and make sure the board is true. Then stake the board at the other end. Continue around the perimeter.

As you finish each side—or when you've gone all the way around—you must straighten and brace the form boards. Sight down the boards to see if they bow in or out. Pull them into line under the twine, and add additional stakes every 18 to 36 inches to keep them from bowing out under the weight of the concrete.

At the low areas of the site, under the form board, there may be gaps of a few inches to almost a foot. Fill the gaps with additional boards nailed to the stakes, then pile dirt against the outside of the form to strengthen it.

You must now add diagonal braces every 4 to 6 feet, especially where you have added extra boards. To do this, drive a stake 2 feet or so away from the form, and nail a brace from the top of the form to the bottom of this stake.

Building Forms

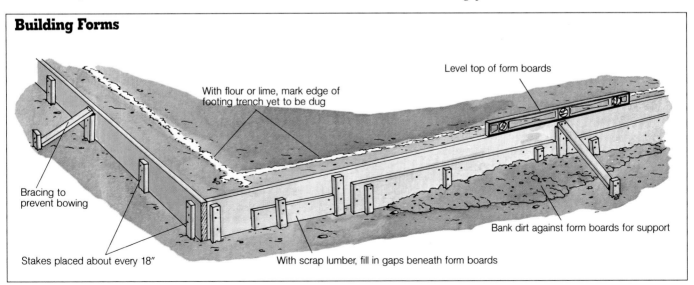

With flour or lime, mark edge of footing trench yet to be dug

Level top of form boards

Bracing to prevent bowing

Stakes placed about every 18"

With scrap lumber, fill in gaps beneath form boards

Bank dirt against form boards for support

Screed Guides

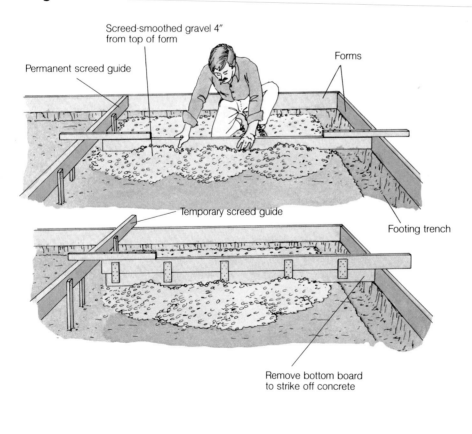

Temporary screed guide

Permanent screed guide

Footing trench

Forms

Screeding

Screed-smoothed gravel 4"
from top of form

Permanent screed guide

Forms

Temporary screed guide

Footing trench

Remove bottom board
to strike off concrete

After the forms are in place, dig the footing trench according to local code requirements. Be careful to cut the sides vertical and make all corners as sharp as possible. Again, if you dig too deep, do not fill the depression with dirt. Either leave it and let it fill with concrete or fill it with gravel that will not settle later.

Screeds and Screed Guides

Slabs of concrete must be struck off—that is, cut off even with the top of the forms with a long board called a screed. Garages or other rooms of 20 feet or more are too wide for a board to reach across. There are two ways to solve this problem. One is to install in the slab permanent dividers made of treated or naturally rot-resistant wood. The other is to install temporary screed guides that can be used both to level the gravel base and to strike off the slab itself.

Screed guides are usually 2 by 4s supported on stakes. Permanent guides must be even with the top of the forms, and if you use more than one, they must be equidistant from each other and the forms that are parallel to them. Screed guides are usually 8 to 10 feet apart.

Temporary guides, too, are usually 2 by 4s. They are nailed on top of the form boards instead of even with them. Nail the ends of one or more 2 by 4s on top of the forms, level them, and stake them in place at several points. These guides will be removed after you pour and strike off the concrete. A screed for use on permanent dividers is just a 2 by 4 long enough to reach across two dividers with a foot or two to spare. A screed for use with the temporary guide next to a form must also be a foot or so longer than the space between the guides and the form. This screed must have one ear—usually a 1 by 2 stick nailed to the top of one end. The screed for use between two temporary guides has to be about a foot shorter than the space between the guides; it should have two ears.

Gravel Fill

Gravel fill must be placed on the ground under the slab; see your specifications and building code for the requirements. Use a gravel rake or a screed made as described, but use cleats to attach an additional 2 by 4 to the bottom of the guide. The extra 2 by 4 ensures that the surface of the gravel is 4 inches below the top of the forms, the standard thickness of a floor slab. For thicker slabs, adjust the screed boards accordingly. If using a rake, measure down from the twine.

Vapor Barriers

A vapor or water barrier prevents significant amounts of water from working its way through the concrete slab. Also, it helps the concrete cure by keeping it wetter longer.

The barrier is usually formed of 6-mil polyethylene sheets that you spread over the leveled gravel. Overlap the sheets at least 12 inches, and do your best not to puncture or tear the plastic. Spread a layer of sand over the sheets.

Establishing a Vapor Barrier

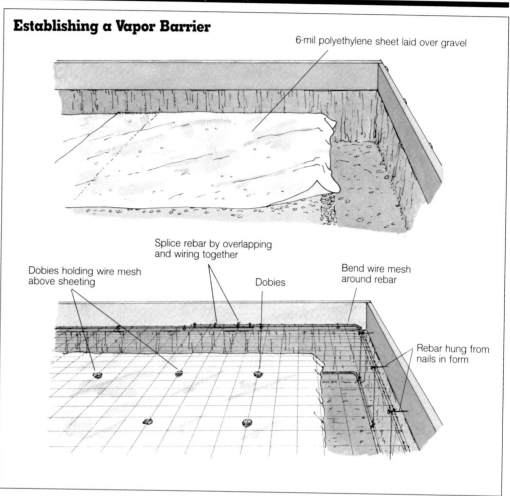

6-mil polyethylene sheet laid over gravel

Dobies holding wire mesh above sheeting

Splice rebar by overlapping and wiring together

Dobies

Bend wire mesh around rebar

Rebar hung from nails in form

Rebar

Steel reinforcing rods, called rebar, must be placed in the footing trench in at least 2 layers. Place the first about 3 inches from the bottom and the other about 2 inches below the surface of the finished slab. Intermediate layers, if required, will be shown in the details on your foundation plan.

Where two rebars meet they must overlap at least 24 inches for ½-inch bar and 30 inches for ⅝-inch bar. Normally, ½-inch bar is all that you need in slab foundations. Use tie wire, available at most building-supply stores, to wire rebar together. To bend rebar for corners and to cut it quickly,

rent a special tool. For small jobs cut rebar with a hacksaw or a circular saw that has a metal cutoff blade. You can bend rebar by putting one foot where you want the bend and pulling up on the remaining length.

To hang rebar, drive nails into the inside surface of the form boards and wire the top bar to them. Place the bottom bars on dobies set on the bottom of the trench. Using tie wire, tie vertical rebar to the horizontal bars and tie the second top bar to the verticals and the first top bar. Be sure to keep all rebar at least 2 inches from the form boards and 3 inches from the sides of the trenches.

Reinforcing Mesh

Steel reinforcing wire mesh should be installed 2 inches above the vapor barrier and 2 inches beneath the surface of a 4-inch slab. Use 2-inch dobies to support the mesh in the middle. Tie the mesh to the rebar in the trench. If you need more than one width of mesh, be sure they overlap at least 6 inches and that you wire them together.

In climates requiring deeper footings, where slab and footings are to be poured separately, you must plan the connection between the slab

Pouring Concrete

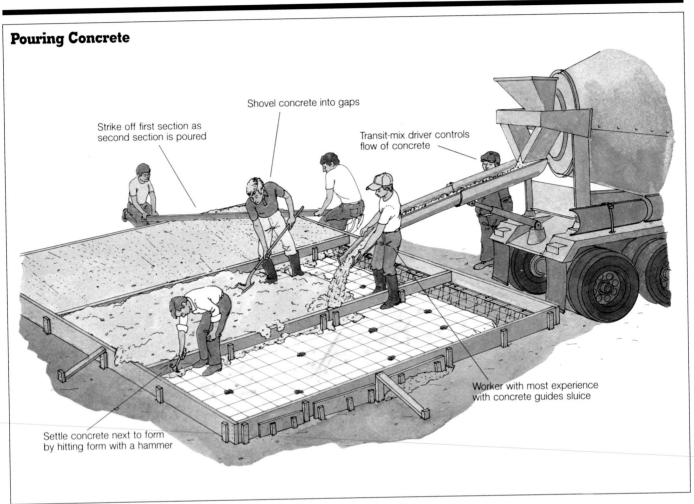

Strike off first section as second section is poured

Shovel concrete into gaps

Transit-mix driver controls flow of concrete

Worker with most experience with concrete guides sluice

Settle concrete next to form by hitting form with a hammer

and the footing. If the slab is to rest on the footings, place hooked lengths of rebar in fresh concrete after you pour it. Then wire the mesh to these before you pour the slab. If the footing walls are to extend above grade and the slab is to be poured within them, they don't have to be tied together with steel. In this case, form and pour the footing walls the same way you would form and pour a perimeter foundation. Then place special filler material or rigid insulation between the footing wall and slab to form an isolation joint.

New technology allows fiberglass strands to be mixed into concrete, thus eliminating the need for steel reinforcing mesh. Consult with the local building department, contractor, or concrete company to see if this method is available or desirable in your area and for your project.

Pouring and Finishing

When you are ready to pour the concrete, contact the building inspector to have the form work approved. The inspector will check that the footing trench is deep and wide enough, that there is adequate steel in place and that you tied it together in an approved manner, that the gravel or sand fill is in place and adequate,

that the reinforcing wire mesh is properly installed, and that there is the required space (usually 4 inches) between the surface of the fill and the top of the forms.

Be prepared for the arrival of the transit-mix truck. It is advisable to have a wheelbarrow or two and at least two helpers at the time of the pour.

Start pouring in the area farthest from the truck. As you fill the footing trench, watch that the concrete does not push the reinforcing rods out of alignment. Pour concrete into only one section of the slab at a time. When you finish pouring that section, move to the next section while your helpers strike off the first section with a

screed. If you've poured too much concrete to move readily with the screed, use a shovel to throw the extra concrete into low spots or into the next section.

When using temporary screed guides, where the strike-off board must fit between the guides, you cannot saw the screed back and forth very much to settle the large aggregates. In this case use a shovel or tamper to settle the concrete. But don't overdo it, or you will cause too much separation of the aggregates and water. As the work progresses, have a helper rap the sides of the forms with a hammer to settle the concrete smoothly against

Finishing Concrete

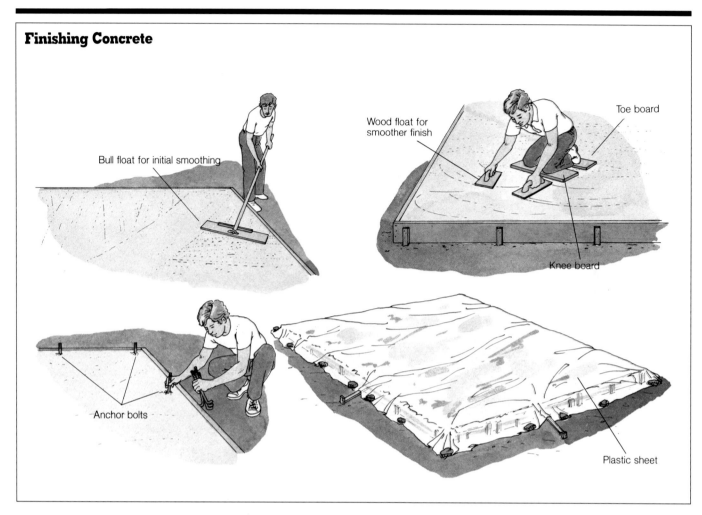

Bull float for initial smoothing

Wood float for smoother finish

Toe board

Knee board

Anchor bolts

Plastic sheet

the boards; you don't want air pockets to be visible when you remove the forms.

After you pour the concrete and strike it off, it must set for a while before you begin to smooth it. Keep a close watch on the setting concrete in hot weather, because the first part may begin hardening while you are still pouring the remainder. If you notice hardening, have a helper begin smoothing the concrete with a bull float before you finish pouring the other sections.

Place anchor bolts for the mudsill when you finish striking off and bull floating. Using a tape measure as a guide, place the bolts 1½ inches away from

the edge of the slab and about 4 to 6 feet apart, depending on the area. Be sure there is a bolt about 6 inches from the end of each sill. Do not place any bolts in door openings. If you are in a high-wind or earthquake area, where studs must be bolted to the foundation, measure carefully to place an anchor bolt adjacent to a stud at whatever intervals the specifications stipulate.

Once you've smoothed the concrete roughly and it has set enough to support kneeling boards without leaving much of an impression, begin the finish floating. Kneeling boards

are approximately 3-foot-square pieces of ½-inch plywood with 2 by 2s nailed along two edges for handles. Use kneeling boards in pairs, with one board under your knees and the other under your toes.

Go over the surface once with a wooden float for a coarse finish; then repeat the procedure with a steel float for a smooth, slick finish. For large slabs you can rent a power finisher, sometimes called a helicopter or whirlybird because it has 4 to 6 blades that spin around and smooth the concrete. Begin using the steel float or helicopter when the sheen has disappeared from the surface and the concrete is hard

enough to walk on without leaving a deep impression. Before the concrete hardens completely, cut between the forms and the concrete with a trowel to make form removal easier. Wait until the concrete hardens completely before removing the forms.

Cure the slab for a day or two by covering it with a sheet of plastic with all the edges and seams weighted down to trap moisture. An alternative is to cover the slab with straw or burlap and keep it damp by spraying water on it whenever the covering begins to show signs of drying.

Installing a Perimeter Foundation

The old-fashioned way to build a perimeter foundation is to pour the footing, then build the forms, and later pour the wall. This method is still used when walls are to be built of concrete blocks or if the poured concrete walls are formidable, as when they are the walls of a basement. If your house has a basement, it is wise to have professionals form and pour the foundation.

If you are building a house on ground that is nearly level and your house won't have a basement, the following descriptions of concrete-block and stem-wall foundations should make it possible for you to build the foundation yourself.

You may have to add a few special features when you build the foundation: openings for access to the crawl space, holes beneath or through the foundation for utility access, and pockets or pilasters to support girders that end at the foundation wall. See the illustration on page 69 for ways to handle these necessities.

Concrete-Block Foundations

A concrete-block foundation wall requires footings (see page 54). When you've poured the footings and they have cured for a couple of days, you are ready to construct the foundation wall.

There is a great deal of regional difference in how concrete blocks are made. Spend some time checking the blocks at a supplier. Although the blocks may be different, the

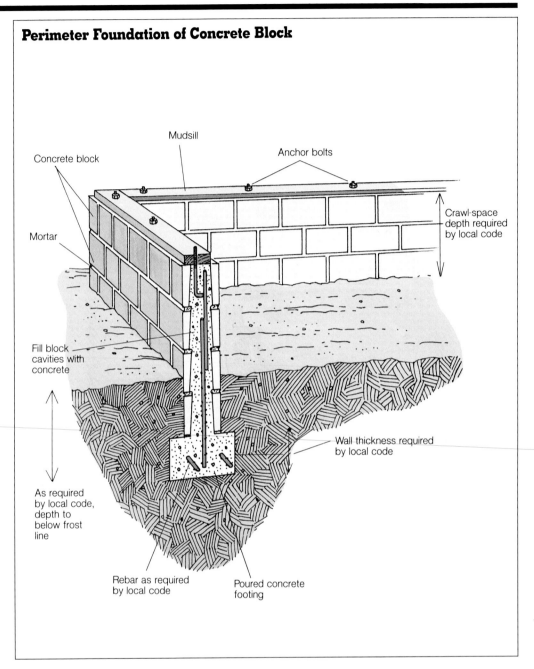

Perimeter Foundation of Concrete Block

Mudsill

Anchor bolts

Concrete block

Mortar

Crawl-space depth required by local code

Fill block cavities with concrete

As required by local code, depth to below frost line

Wall thickness required by local code

Rebar as required by local code

Poured concrete footing

basic construction practices used to build a concrete-block foundation wall are the same.

Concrete blocks are nominally 6, 8, or 10 inches wide; 8 inches high; and 16 inches long. Half blocks are also available. The actual measurements are about ⅜ inch less than the

nominal measurements, to allow for mortar at the joints. The 8-inch-wide block is standard for the foundation walls of a one- or two-story house.

The mortar to hold these blocks together is concrete without gravel. The recipe for mortar is 1 part masonry cement, which includes lime; 3 parts fine sand; and just

enough water to make it workable. You'll soon get the hang of how much water to use as you work with it. You can buy ready-mixed bags of mortar, but unless you are doing a very small job, a mix is expensive relative to buying cement and sand in bulk.

Beginning a Concrete-Block Wall

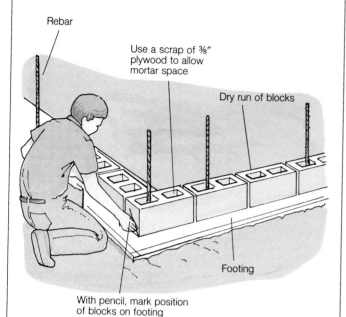

Rebar

Use a scrap of ⅜″ plywood to allow mortar space

Dry run of blocks

Footing

With pencil, mark position of blocks on footing

Rebar

Level

Mortar bed

Estimating Material for a Concrete-Block Wall

To find the square footage of a concrete-block wall, multiply the height of the wall by the length of the concrete-block perimeter foundation. Then divide the total square footage by 100 and multiply that number by the appropriate numbers in the table to determine the total number of blocks and the cubic feet of mortar you'll need.

Concrete-Block Size (In.)	Wall Thickness (In.)	Number of Blocks	Cubic Ft of Mortar, ⅜″ Joints	Cubic Ft of Mortar, ½″ Joints
8 × 4 × 12	4	146	4	5
8 × 4 × 16	4	110	3¼	4
12 × 4 × 12	4	100	3¼	4
8 × 6 × 16	6	110	3¼	4
8 × 8 × 16	8	110	3¼	4
8 × 10 × 16	10	110	3¼	4
8 × 12 × 16	12	110	3¼	4

If you are building the wall by yourself, mix your mortar in a wheelbarrow. Mix the cement and sand thoroughly with a shovel or hoe, then add water and pull the mixture back and forth with a hoe until the texture is smooth. Since the mortar will dry out and start to set up quickly, mix only a half wheelbarrowful at a time—about the amount you can use in an hour or so.

If you have several helpers, you will want to rent an electric mixer. Just as the pros do, one worker can mix mortar and carry it and blocks to the others, who are doing the laying.

Blocks

The first step in laying blocks is to restring the perimeter twine on the batter boards so you know exactly where the outside edge of the blocks must be. Lay a row of blocks in position on the footing, directly beneath the line. A plumb bob will ensure accuracy. Put a ⅜-inch spacer (plywood scraps work well) between each pair to separate the blocks the same distance as the mortar will.

If you've planned the house so the length of each outside wall is divisible by 8 inches, the blocks should fit perfectly. You'll have to use half blocks at the corners of the next course anyway, even if whole blocks fit. If they don't, you must use a cut block in each course to make the length come out right. This partial-block insert should be near the middle of the wall; start with a whole or half block on each end and work toward the middle. Make sure the blocks line up with the vertical rebar.

Mark the exact location of the corner blocks and remove all the blocks from the footing. Spread a layer of mortar the length of the corner block at the end of the first wall, and

Laying Blocks

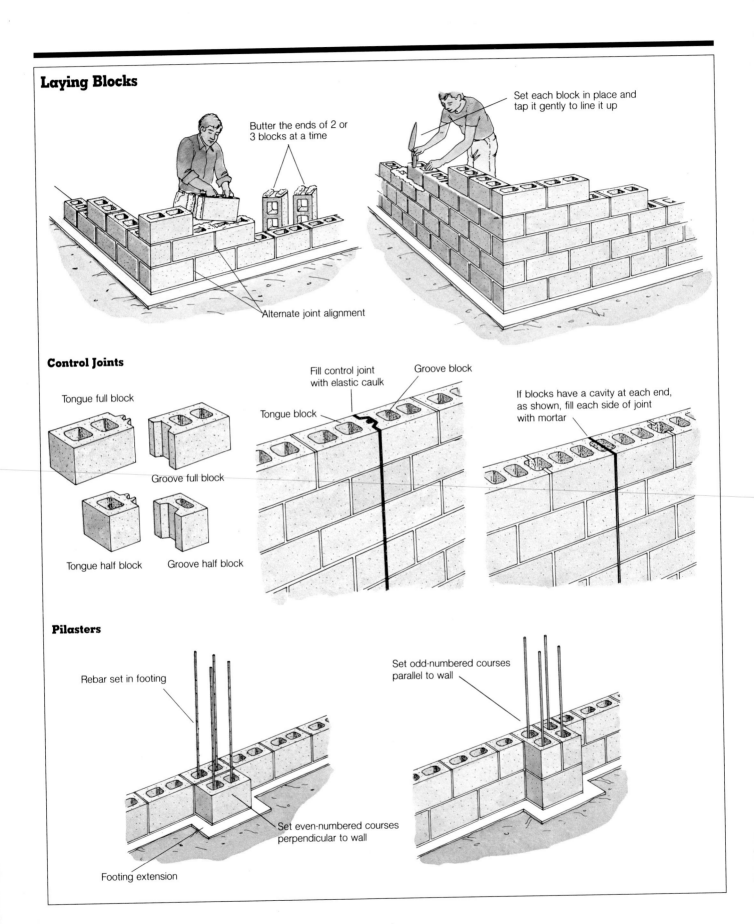

Butter the ends of 2 or 3 blocks at a time

Set each block in place and tap it gently to line it up

Alternate joint alignment

Control Joints

Tongue full block

Groove full block

Tongue half block

Groove half block

Fill control joint with elastic caulk

Groove block

Tongue block

If blocks have a cavity at each end, as shown, fill each side of joint with mortar

Pilasters

Rebar set in footing

Set even-numbered courses perpendicular to wall

Footing extension

Set odd-numbered courses parallel to wall

place the corner block firmly in it. Set the block by tapping it with your trowel handle until the block is square and level and the required ⅜-inch of mortar lies under it.

Note that the hollow-core spaces and web of a concrete block is different on each side. On one side the holes are smaller and the surface is wider. Be sure this wider side is up when you lay the blocks so the mortar holds in place properly. You'll determine quickly which is the wider side because the blocks are easier to pick up with the correct side up.

When you've set the two corner blocks, stretch a length of mason's twine between their upper outside edges, using line blocks to secure the twine. This is the guide to keep each course of blocks straight and level. Spread a solid layer of mortar about 1 inch thick and a little wider than a block for the distance of 2 or 3 blocks. Butter each block on one end only, then press it into place against the preceding block. Lay each block on the mortar and tap it into place. Don't let the blocks nudge the twine enough to push it out of line.

Once you've completed the first course, build the leads—that is, the corners or ends of a wall placed and built up to its final height. When you've done this, it's a piece of cake to fill in the rest of the wall accurately. Note that in a standard block wall, every other course ends with a half block.

The last block you set in each course will be a middle block. When you come to it, cut it to fit if necessary. Then butter both ends and slide it carefully into place on its bed of

mortar. You can cut concrete blocks easily with either a radial arm saw or a portable power saw equipped with a Carborundum abrasive masonry blade. Be sure to wear eye protection and a dust mask when doing the cutting.

Anchor Bolts

Most codes call for the hollow spaces in load-bearing walls to be filled with concrete, especially the spaces that contain rebar and those where anchor

bolts will be set. The anchor bolts will hold down the mudsill and some studs in areas calling for tie-downs.

Fill the cavity with concrete and place an anchor bolt 6 inches from the end of each mudsill and at 4- to 6-foot intervals along the sill. Set the bolts so 2½ inches of the threaded end protrudes above the wall.

Finishing the Joints

When the mortar in the joints has hardened so that it will just

barely take a thumbprint, you must start finishing the joints. Use a convex or V-shaped jointing tool to compress all the joints. This will force some more mortar out beyond the edge of the block, which should be trimmed off with the edge of the trowel. Let the mortar dry partially, then restrike the joints to form a neat, distinct joint. Finally, brush the wall after the mortar has dried to remove any dirt or small fragments of mortar.

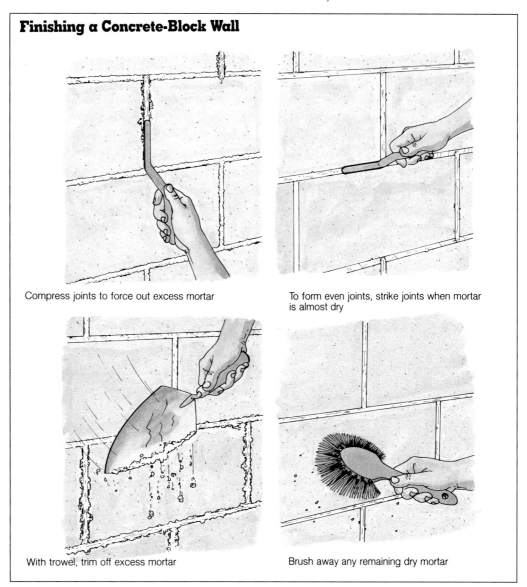

Finishing a Concrete-Block Wall

Compress joints to force out excess mortar

To form even joints, strike joints when mortar is almost dry

With trowel, trim off excess mortar

Brush away any remaining dry mortar

Stem-Wall Foundations

With the stem-wall foundation method, widely used by professionals, you build the footing and wall forms and then pour both together. The transit-mix truck has to make only one pour, which makes concrete delivery economical and fast. To make it even more economical, the 2 by 6, 2 by 8, 2 by 10, or 2 by 12 material you use for the forms can be used later for the floor joists and rafters. Your floor joists and rafters may be stained with concrete, but who cares; they don't show and you don't have to buy special lumber to build the forms.

To build a perimeter stem wall, lay out the foundation in the usual way, using batter boards. Suspend the form boards over the footing trench on steel stakes. (You can use 2 by 4s instead of steel stakes, but the steel is easier to drive accurately into hard ground and much easier to remove when the concrete has hardened.) When you pour the concrete, it will fill the trench and then come up inside the forms.

Start by marking and digging the footing trench. With the perimeter lines in place, build the wall forms, starting with the outside boards at the highest corner of the house.

Drive stakes into the trench about every 4 feet. Since the form boards are 1½ inches thick and the stakes will be nailed to the outside of the boards, use a tape measure to position the stakes 1½ inches outside the perimeter string.

Poured-Concrete Perimeter Foundation

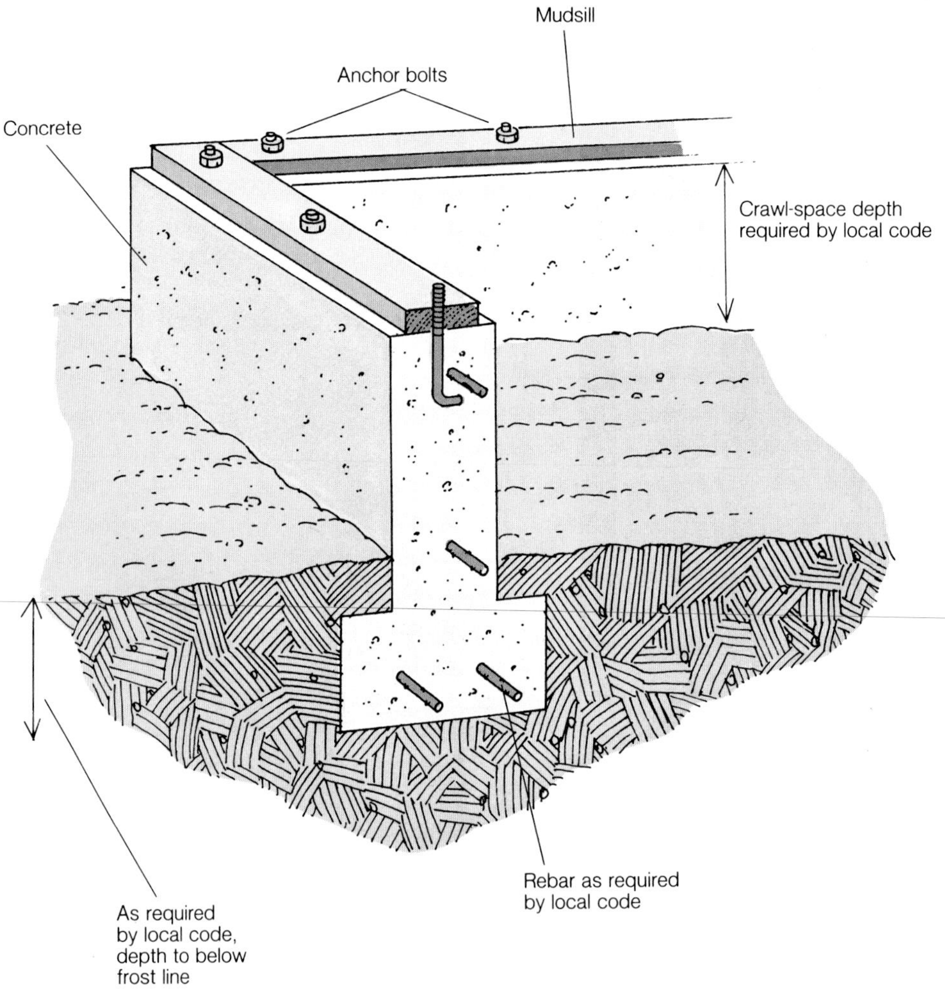

Mudsill

Anchor bolts

Concrete

Crawl-space depth required by local code

Rebar as required by local code

As required by local code, depth to below frost line

Nail the boards to the stakes with the inner edge directly under the string.

To set the stakes so they are close to vertical, hold them at the top between your thumb and forefinger as you set them in place. Then hold them in that position as you hammer them into the ground. They needn't be positioned perfectly because you will true up and brace the entire wall after you have assembled it.

Outside Form Boards

With the stakes in place, nail the boards in place. For this you will need at least one helper to hold one end of the board as you set and nail the other. Again, start at the highest corner, with the top of the first board even with the twine and extending about a foot beyond the corner where the lines cross. The end of the adjoining wall will butt against this first wall. Hold the board just a hair away from the

Beginning a Poured-Concrete Foundation

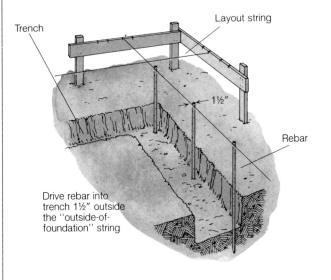

Trench

Layout string

1½"

Rebar

Drive rebar into trench 1½" outside the "outside-of-foundation" string

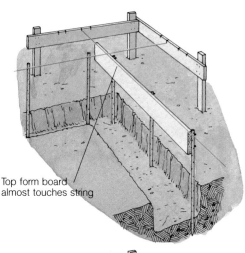

Top form board almost touches string

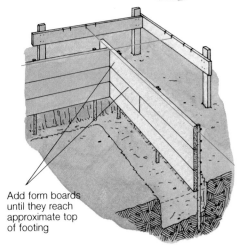

Add form boards until they reach approximate top of footing

Estimating Material for a Poured Foundation Wall

To find the square footage of a poured foundation wall, multiply the height of the wall by the length of the concrete perimeter foundation. Divide the total square footage by 100, then multiply that number by the wall thickness to find the cubic feet or cubic yards of concrete required.

Concrete Perimeter Foundation Wall Thickness In.	Concrete Required per 100 Square Ft of Wall	
	Cubic Ft	Cubic Yd
4	33.3	1.23
6	50.0	1.85
8	66.7	2.47
10	83.3	3.09
12	100.0	3.70

twine, but not touching it. Nail through the holes in the stake with 8d duplex nails. Have your helper keep the top board perfectly in line with the twine as you hammer 2 nails through each stake and into the board. When necessary, drive additional stakes to support the end of each board or the one that abuts it.

After you place the top boards for the first wall, put on the second and remaining courses. The number of courses will depend on the height of the wall and the width of the boards. The last course should extend a little into the trench, to within as many inches from the bottom as you want the thickness of the footing. You may have to rip the bottom board so it doesn't hang too far into the trench. By not cutting any of the others, you save most of the wood for later use.

The first wall must be braced to plumb (perfectly vertical) before butting and nailing the wall next to it. Otherwise, the corners will never hold.

When you come to the first corner, allow the ends of the form boards to extend beyond the twine. Butt the ends of the next wall against the first and nail them together. Continue placing stakes and boards in this manner until you've completed the outside form wall.

Bracing

At this point the wall may be up, but it's not going to be straight or strong enough. Bracing the wall securely cannot be overemphasized. You will never feel more sick to your stomach than if the wall suddenly gives way and you see tons of concrete running onto the ground.

Make your braces from 2 by 4s. You'll need a brace about every 4 feet, at all the corners, and wherever you butt form boards together without a steel support stake to hold them in line. Count how many braces you'll need, and set up an assembly line with your helpers to make them all at once. The bottoms should be 2 or more feet long, and the upright legs about the same height as the wall. Cut the ends of the diagonal pieces at 45 degrees. Cut all the pieces, then nail all the braces together with duplex nails so you can use the lumber later in construction.

To use these angle braces to hold the wall perfectly plumb, nail a brace to the wall and then pull the wall into line directly under the twine. While you hold it there, have a helper drive a wood stake into the ground at the back end of the brace and nail the brace to the stake. This will keep the brace from slipping off the stake under the weight of the concrete.

Reinforcing Steel

After you've straightened and braced the exterior wall, the next task is to hang the reinforcing steel. Reinforcing steel is made from courses of rebar. Hanging it is easier to do before you build the interior form wall. Rebar must be suspended in the footing and in the foundation wall. Place at least 1 rebar in the center of the footing and another 2 to 3 inches from the top of the wall—check your specifications or with the building inspector to learn about requirements in your area. If the foundation wall is more than 18 inches high, hang a third course of rebar between the top and bottom courses. The rebar must be bent to go around the corners of the foundation. Wherever one length of bar meets another, they must overlap by at

Building the Forms

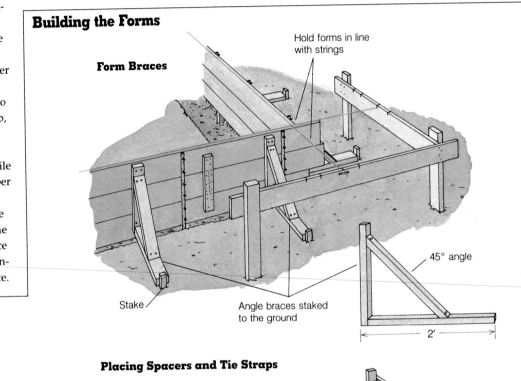

Form Braces

Hold forms in line with strings

45° angle

Stake

Angle braces staked to the ground

2'

Hanging Steel

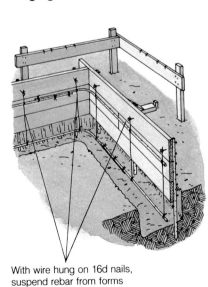

With wire hung on 16d nails, suspend rebar from forms

Placing Spacers and Tie Straps

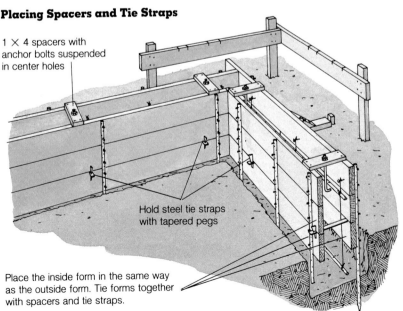

1 × 4 spacers with anchor bolts suspended in center holes

Hold steel tie straps with tapered pegs

Place the inside form in the same way as the outside form. Tie forms together with spacers and tie straps.

least 24 inches, and you must secure them with tie wire.

To hang the rebar in the forms, every 3 feet or so drive a 16-penny (16d) or 20d nail into the form boards at the height of the top bar. A 20d nail is 3¾ inches long. In a 6-inch thick wall, you can drive the nail into the wood ¾ inch and the end will be right in the middle. Wire the top rebar to the end of the nail. Leave enough wire to hang the next rebar or two below the first. Be sure to keep all the steel and wire well away from the forms so there will be plenty of concrete around them to make them effective.

Form Boards

The first step in forming the interior wall is to place the twine that will mark the inside edge of the foundation wall. Stretch the twine between the kerfs in the batter boards. Just as you did for the outside wall, place the support stakes 1½ inches beyond the twine. Assemble the inside wall just as you assembled the outside wall. You must cut more boards for the inside, however, because the corners must fit inside the outside wall.

It is easier to straighten the interior wall than the outside wall. Just tie the inside wall to the outside wall with spacers. For a 6-inch wall the spacers should be 9 inches long and cut from 1 by 4 lumber. The extra 3 inches let you nail the ends of each spacer flush with the outside edge of the form boards and leave the wall exactly 6 inches thick.

Drill a ¾-inch hole in the center of each spacer. Then place the anchor bolts in these holes so they will be suspended by their nuts during the pour. Cut enough of these spacers to place one 6 inches from the end of each mudsill and no more than 6 feet apart between the ends of the sills.

At each course of boards use steel form ties and wedges to keep the form boards from spreading apart from the weight of the concrete.

You will be pouring concrete into these forms. Be sure that you have allowed for all openings, including those for access and utilities, and hold-down anchors.

Later, when the concrete has set, remove all of the wedges to strip the forms away and snap off the protruding pieces of the form ties.

Utility Access

Since you will need access to the crawl space under the house, you must form an opening in what will be the wall. Using redwood or pressure-treated lumber, you will make a form—a three-sided box that you will drop into the wall where you want the opening. The bottom of the box will be positioned just above ground level. The open top of the box will be covered by the mudsill. Hold the form in the wall and nail it into place. Drive a few nails into the uprights to hold the boards in place when the concrete is poured. When pouring, be sure to work the concrete with a shovel so it flows under the bottom of the opening. If girders will be used to support floor joists, the inside of the concrete wall can be "keyed" to accept the ends of the girders. This is done by cutting a 2-inch length from the end of one girder, or using a similar piece of scrap, and nailing it to the inside form precisely where the girder will fit. Use batter boards set for the interior posts and piers as your guide. The top of the key must be flush with the top of the mudsill, not the top of the wall,

Allowing for Access

Crawl-Space Access

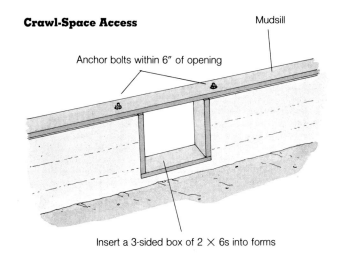

Mudsill

Anchor bolts within 6" of opening

Insert a 3-sided box of 2 × 6s into forms

Utility Access

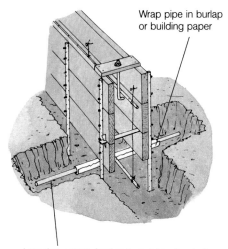

Wrap pipe in burlap or building paper

Lay pipe across footing trench to allow holes through footing

Keying for Beams

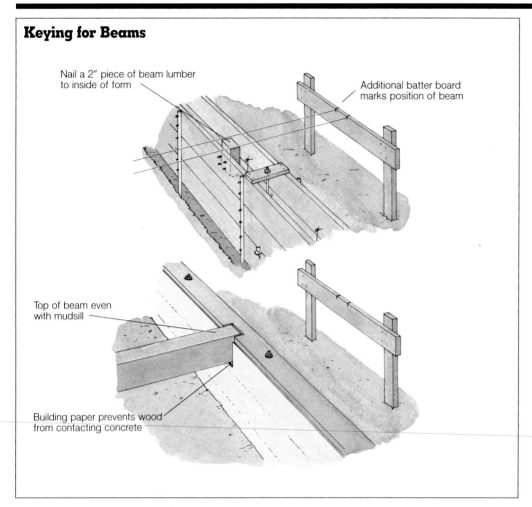

Nail a 2" piece of beam lumber to inside of form

Additional batter board marks position of beam

Top of beam even with mudsill

Building paper prevents wood from contacting concrete

---

so be sure to raise the block 1½ inches above the wall surface. When the forms are stripped, the block will have a 2-inch-deep indentation in the wall where the girder end will fit.

If you are planning on placing water pipes, conduits for electricity, or heating ducts underground and running them into the house, you will have to form holes in the footing or foundation wall, as needed. This is easily done by placing a length of electrical conduit or plastic drainpipe across the footing ditch or between the

forms before pouring the concrete. If in the footing, dig a trench so the pipe extends about 12 inches beyond the footing on each side—this will enable you to find the pipe easily after the pour is complete. In addition, remember to wrap any conduit or drainpipe in insulation or building paper before the pour. This provides a cushion around the conduit and prevents the concrete from eventually cutting through the conduit or pipe as the footing expands and contracts.

Also place a wrapped pipe across the footing ditch to create a hole for the plumbing waste line.

Additional pipes can be dropped into the footing if you feel it may be necessary to drain water from under the house during the wet season.

Delivery of Concrete

Order the concrete as discussed on page 56. Before the big, expensive load arrives, go over the forms one last time to see that everything is square and plumb and that you hung the steel properly. Be sure that you brace everything well. Lean over the forms and push out on

the walls as hard as you can in several places. If the forms move, you haven't braced them well enough.

Have at least two helpers on hand—the more help you have with concrete the better. Supply plenty of work gloves and shovels. One person, standing at the back of the truck, will work with the driver to control the chute and go around the forms placing the concrete. Another will follow behind the chute with broom handles or a long stick, prodding and poking at the concrete to make sure it settles into the bottom and all corners of the forms. This person should watch that the concrete does not force the rebar out of line and against or too near the form boards. A third person should rap on the forms with a hammer to chase out air pockets. Duplicating workers at each position will keep the project moving along quickly. Concrete work happens very quickly. Consider renting a concrete vibrator to help settle the concrete and eliminate any voids.

On the first pass with the concrete, fill the footing trench and a couple of inches up into the forms; don't fill the trench too high at first or the concrete will force its way out of the trench. On the second pass, fill the forms to the top, if they are 18 inches high or less. If they are higher, make a third pass to fill them. Making more than a single pass allows the concrete from the previous pass to set up a little, thus reducing the pressure on the forms that would result if you filled them to the top all at once. Don't permit delays in passes, however. If the concrete hardens too much, the next pass will not adhere properly to the prior pass, resulting in a weakness known as a cold joint.

Once you fill the forms, smooth the top with a piece of wood or a float. A smooth, flat top allows the mudsill to lie flat and bolt tighter to the foundation.

The best schedule for pouring concrete is to pour in the morning and pull the stakes at the end of that day. When you strip off the forms, remove all nails and scrape any concrete from the boards so you don't dull or ruin a blade when you cut the wood later to form joists and rafters.

A transit-mix truck holds about 8 yards of concrete. If you will use more than that, arrange to receive a second truck rather than having the first truck go back for a second load. Ideally, the second truck should arrive just as you have finished spreading the first load, but it is hard to time this exactly. If the second truck has to wait on you for very long, it will cost you money.

When you must wait for the second truck to arrive, keep the area where you stopped the pour continuously wet. When you start pouring there again, work over the old and new concrete with a jitterbug tamper to prevent a visible joint.

During an interruption in the pour, wash all your tools and wheelbarrows. If you don't the concrete will harden on the equipment.

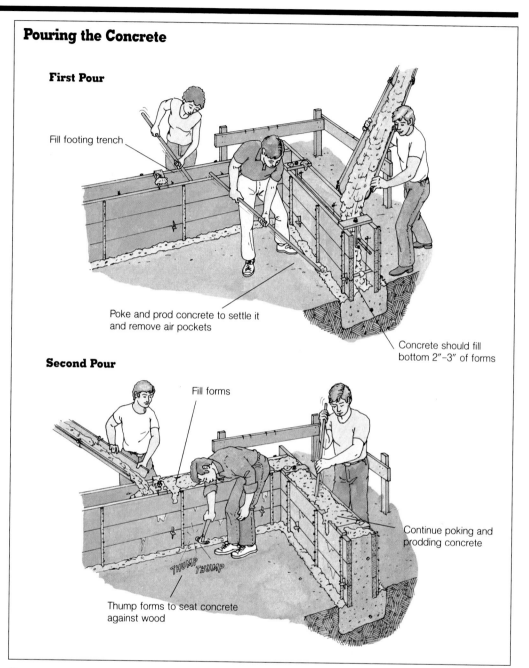

Pouring the Concrete

First Pour

Fill footing trench

Poke and prod concrete to settle it and remove air pockets

Concrete should fill bottom 2"–3" of forms

Second Pour

Fill forms

THUMP THUMP

Thump forms to seat concrete against wood

Continue poking and prodding concrete

Installing a Post-and-Pier Foundation

Pier blocks are precast tapered blocks of concrete. They are 12 inches square at the bottom and about 8 inches square at the top. Each has a 6-inch square of redwood or other rot-resistant wood secured to the

top. Because pier blocks form such a wide base, a footing is not always required; check local codes.

Whether you use a perimeter-wall foundation or all posts and pier blocks, you may need one or more rows of pier blocks

inside the perimeter wall to support the middle of the house. The number of pier blocks you need and the distance between them is established by the size of the girders. The number will probably be clear to you by studying the foundation plan of your house. If not, check the discussion of

Post-and-Pier Foundation

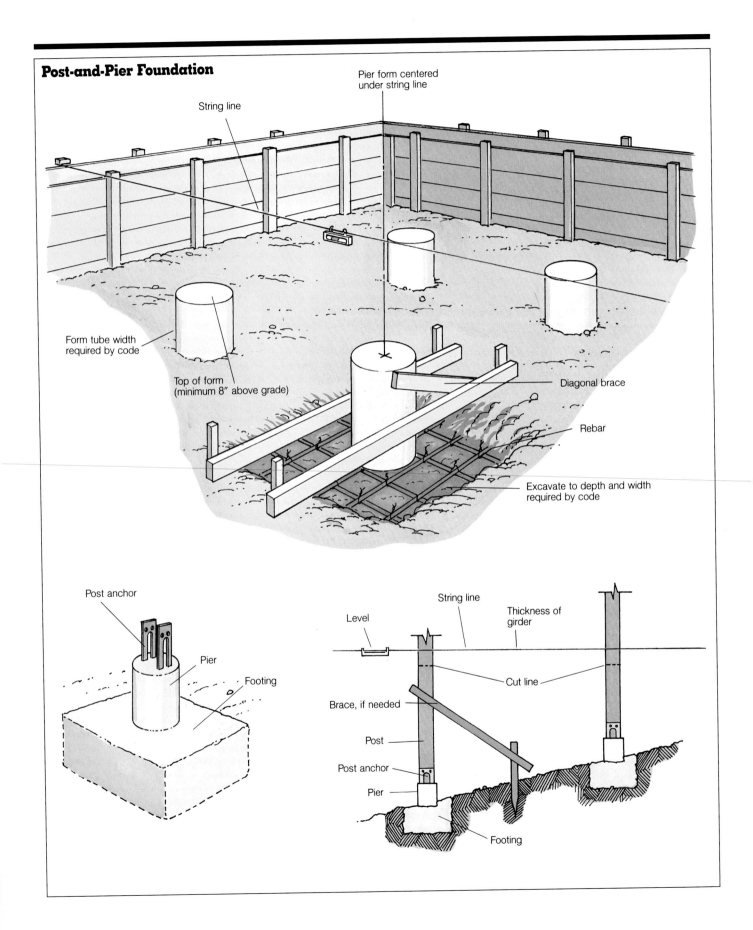

Pier form centered under string line

String line

Form tube width required by code

Top of form (minimum 8″ above grade)

Diagonal brace

Rebar

Excavate to depth and width required by code

Post anchor

Pier

Footing

Level

String line

Thickness of girder

Cut line

Brace, if needed

Post

Post anchor

Pier

Footing

beams and girders in the framing section (see page 76) and the span charts (see page 88).

Pier blocks, on the ground or on footings, provide a stable support for the posts. The posts provide a level support for girders or beams that function like foundation walls. In fact, in certain circumstances, buildings can be entirely supported by post-and-pier foundations. Most municipal building codes, however, insist on a perimeter-wall foundation combined with posts and pier blocks.

To install pier blocks, dig footing holes 6 to 12 inches deep and as wide as required by the code, usually 15 to 18 inches. Fill the footing holes with concrete. Before the concrete sets up, string the auxiliary batter boards you set up for the girders. Use a plumb bob to center the pier blocks on the twine and set them on the footings while the concrete is still wet. Level them in both directions.

Note that the pier blocks do not have to be placed at the same level. You can correct any differences in height by cutting all the posts at the same level after you have placed them on the pier blocks.

A superior alternative to precast pier blocks is cast-in-place footings and piers. Dig footing holes the same as for pier blocks. Then suspend a short length of forming tube, at least 8 inches in diameter, above the hole to the level of the girder. Cut two 2-by-4s long enough to straddle the hole to support the tubing. Then pour concrete into the footing hole and forming tube at the same time. Set a metal post anchor into the concrete before it hardens.

Pier-and-Grade Beam Foundation

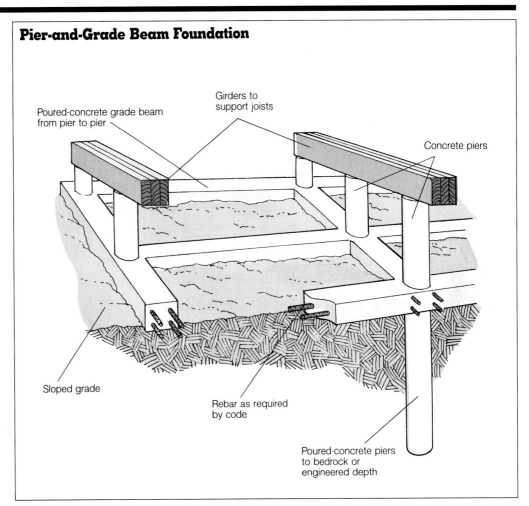

Girders to support joists

Poured-concrete grade beam from pier to pier

Concrete piers

Sloped grade

Rebar as required by code

Poured-concrete piers to bedrock or engineered depth

Estimating Material for a Poured Concrete Footing

To find how much concrete you'll need, measure the total length of the footing in feet. Divide the length by 100, then multiply the dividend by the appropriate number from the table.

Footing Thickness (In.)	Cubic Yd of Concrete per 100 Linear Ft of Footing Footing Width					
	6"	8"	10"	12"	18"	24"
2	0.31	0.41	0.51	0.62	0.93	1.24
3	0.46	0.62	0.77	0.93	1.39	1.86
4	0.62	0.82	1.03	1.23	1.85	2.46
6	0.93	1.23	1.54	1.85	2.78	3.70
8	1.23	1.64	2.06	2.47	3.71	4.94
10	1.54	2.06	2.57	3.09	4.64	6.18
12	1.85	2.47	3.09	3.70	5.56	7.40
18	2.78	3.70	4.63	5.56	8.34	11.12
24	3.70	4.92	6.17	7.41	11.12	14.08
36	5.56	7.40	9.26	11.12	16.68	22.24
48	7.41	9.88	12.35	14.81	22.22	29.62

$\mathbf{B}$UILDING THE FRAMING

Above the foundation of a house is the structural framework. This skeleton of the house provides strength and stability. It is the unseen structure to which all visible parts are attached. It is important to build it right so your house will stand straight and strong for many years.

☐ Tool belt
☐ Framing hammer
☐ Sledge hammer
☐ Handsaw
☐ Power circular saw
☐ Table saw or radial arm saw
☐ Steel tape measure
☐ 24-inch level
☐ Combination square
☐ Framing square
☐ Carpenter's pencil
☐ Chalk line
☐ Tin snips
☐ 12-inch crescent wrench
☐ Caulk gun
☐ 8- or 10-foot stepladder

Choosing a Style

The time and number of people you'll need to frame your house depends on the size of the building. Obviously, the smaller the house and the larger the work crew, the faster the job will go. You do need at least one helper during most of the framing operation. You can try and organize an old-fashioned "barn raising" to get the job done as quickly as possible. Keep in mind, however, that on a difficulty scale of 10 points, consider building the

framing a 7, and at least one person should be a skilled carpenter.

Most houses in this country are of wood-frame construction. Even if the exterior is brick or stone veneer or stucco, the main structure is usually the same as that in homes with sidings of wood, composition materials, or shingles.

In general, wood-frame construction costs less than other methods. It allows you to build a bigger house for the money. In addition, this type of construction is very durable. It holds up well in all kinds of weather, and it is generally the best in earthquake areas.

The wood frame is multifunctional. It is structural and the skeleton in which all the internal systems—plumbing, electrical, heating and cooling—of the house fit. The wood frame is also the backing on which you attach the interior wallboard, the exterior siding, and the trim.

There are two classes of wood framing: post-and-beam and conventional. Conventional framing, in turn, includes two common types: balloon and platform. Each type has its advantages and disadvantages.

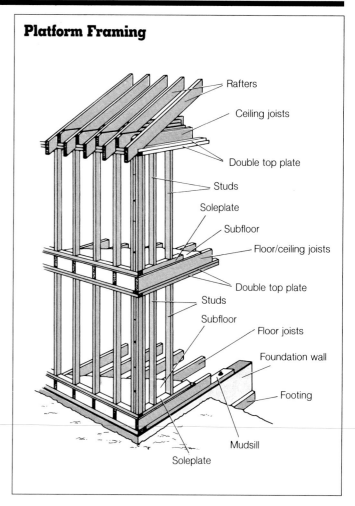

Platform Framing

- Rafters
- Ceiling joists
- Double top plate
- Studs
- Soleplate
- Subfloor
- Floor/ceiling joists
- Double top plate
- Studs
- Subfloor
- Floor joists
- Foundation wall
- Footing
- Mudsill
- Soleplate

Post-and-beam framing was the main type of framing until the late nineteenth century. It is still popular in some areas—New England, for instance—where some people want their homes to have a historical flavor. Post-and-beam construction has a framework of vertical supports (posts) connected by horizontal spanning members (beams). The timbers are large, perhaps 4 by 12 inches or even 8 by 12 inches. Most often the builder leaves the framework exposed in the interior and sometimes on the exterior, making this type of construction easy to identify. Walls between the posts and under the beams divide the space within the house, but the

walls are not bearing the load of the structure. Because it is not commonly used by the owner-builder, this book will not describe building post-and-beam framing. If you are interested in this style of framing, check local codes to see if it is allowed in your area.

Conventional Framing

Both kinds of conventional framing—balloon and platform—consist of many small pieces of wood, mostly 2 by 8s and 2 by 10s used as joists and studs and 2 by 6s to 2 by 12s used as rafters. These are assembled so the stresses of supporting the structure are evenly

Estimating Board Feet of Joist Lumber and Nails per 100 Square Feet of Floor or Ceiling Area

To estimate your lumber needs, multiply the length by the width of any floor or ceiling area. Divide the product by 100, then multiply the dividend by the appropriate number on the chart.

To estimate the quantity of nails you'll need, divide the total by 1,000 and multiply by the number opposite the appropriate joist size.

Size of Joists (In.)	Board Ft per 100 Square Ft of Area				Lb of Nails per 1,000 Board Ft
	12" OC	16" OC	20" OC	24" OC	
2 × 6	130	105	90	80	12
2 × 8	175	140	120	105	10
2 × 10	215	175	150	135	7
2 × 12	260	210	180	160	6

Subfloor

A subfloor is a wood floor laid over the joists and beneath the finish floor. The subfloor material and when you install it depend on the finish floor material.

The strongest and best subfloor material is plywood. Commonly, this is CDX plywood, at least ⅝ inch thick, with tongue-and-groove edges. Oriented strand board (OSB) is an economical substitute.

Rough plywood is a fine subfloor under a wood finish floor or most carpeting. If the finish floor will be resilient sheet flooring, vinyl tile, or other thin material, you need to install a smooth underlayment over the plywood. Otherwise, knotholes or other deep irregularities in the plywood will cause breaks in the finish materials. Use smooth hardboard, smooth particleboard, or—for ceramic tile—special tile-backing units for the underlayment. Be sure to check the finish floor specifications before installing the subfloor.

Install a plywood subfloor after all the rough wiring, plumbing, and mechanical work is complete and has passed a building inspection. Wait to install hardwood, particleboard, or tile-backing units until the roof and siding are completed. Though plywood can weather rainstorms, these others cannot.

Install the subfloor sheets perpendicular to the joists. Start by snapping a chalk line on the platform 4 feet away from the outside edge of the rim joist or ends of the field joists. To prevent the floor from squeaking, apply construction adhesive to the tops of the joists with a caulking gun before laying each sheet. Install a full sheet first; continue with staggered rows so the joints don't meet over the same joist. Install the underlayment sheets in the same manner, making sure to offset the seams.

Secure the sheets with 8d ring-shank, or spiral-shank, nails every 6 inches along the edges and every 10 inches within the panel.

Framing the Walls

Before reading further, study the diagram of typical wall framing (see page 80). It shows a typical stud wall and identifies all the parts you are likely to need in building such a wall for your house. Note especially that the spacing of the studs is always 16 inches on center except for the last stud on the end. The 16-inch measurements start at one end and continue evenly, despite windows, doors, or the corner posts of intersecting walls.

These 16-inch increments should start at the left front corner of your house (the corner on your left if you are facing the front of the house) and go left to right and front to back across the entire house in all walls. Keeping this stud-spacing pattern consistent makes putting up exterior siding and interior wallboard or paneling much easier. It allows you to use full panels more often and eliminates much cutting. Also, it makes finding studs easier when you are trying to hang a picture or install a shelf after you've lived in the house awhile.

The stud walls must be square on the floor platform. If, in spite of best efforts, you did not make the platform perfectly square, there is a way to make the final corrections and begin laying out the walls at

the same time. This is done while making top plates and soleplates.

Plates

For the top plates and soleplates of a wall, use straight 2 by 4s at least 12 feet long. One person can raise a 12-foot wall section without help. However, if you'll have help raising the wall when it's built, use 16-foot 2 by 4s because longer wall sections are easier to keep straight once raised.

If your house is longer than 16 feet, you must use more than one piece for each plate; you will butt them together at one of the 16-inch marks. A stud will bridge that joint and support both pieces. You cannot have a joint in a soleplate or top plate that is unsupported by a stud.

Start by placing 2 by 4s flat on the subfloor against the longest sides of the house. Place the outer edges of the 2 by 4s flush with the edges of the subfloor, and cut the ends of the boards flush with the side edges of the subfloor. These 2 by 4s will be the soleplates.

If all but the last length of 2 by 4 is in multiples of 4 feet, the joints will always be over studs. The last length should be at least 4 feet long. If necessary, cut the next-to-last length shorter, but still at a 16-inch mark, so the last length will be at least 4 feet.

When you've laid down the soleplates on the longest sides of the platform, place the ones for the shorter sides between the ends of the long ones. Again, make sure the end pieces are at least 4 feet long and that all joints fall on 16-inch marks.

Stud Wall

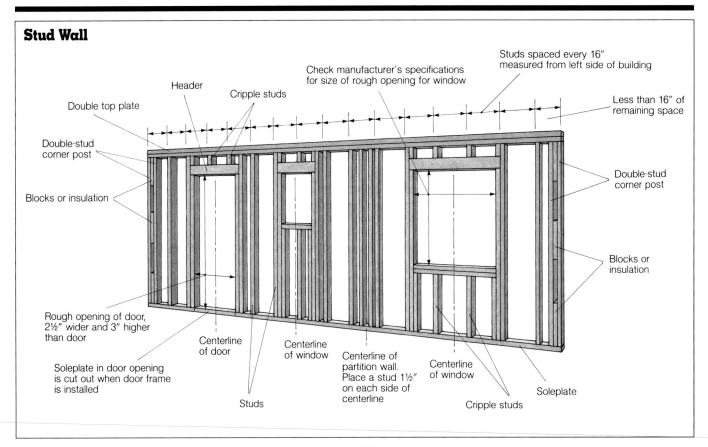

Double top plate

Header

Cripple studs

Check manufacturer's specifications for size of rough opening for window

Studs spaced every 16" measured from left side of building

Less than 16" of remaining space

Double-stud corner post

Double-stud corner post

Blocks or insulation

Blocks or insulation

Rough opening of door, 2½" wider and 3" higher than door

Soleplate in door opening is cut out when door frame is installed

Centerline of door

Centerline of window

Centerline of partition wall. Place a stud 1½" on each side of centerline

Centerline of window

Soleplate

Studs

Cripple studs

Measure the diagonals of all the rectangles formed by your soleplates. Both diagonals in one rectangle should be equal. If this is true for all rectangles, your platform is square and there is no problem. A variance of ¼ inch or so from square is acceptable. If the platform is not perfectly square, let the soleplates hang over the edge or set them inside the edge of the platform to make the plates square. When the house is finished, the siding will extend below the joint of the wall and platform and hide the imperfection.

Measure and snap chalk lines to indicate the interior edges of the walls.

Place the soleplates and top plates side by side, and mark the door and window openings on them. Laying out these openings at this time will let you know where full-length studs can be eliminated. Also lay out all the soleplates and top plates for the interior walls and mark their positions on the subfloor in the same manner. When you've laid out all the plates, label them clearly, and set all aside except those of the longest wall.

Stack the pieces carefully and in the proper order so you can reassemble the plates as they were laid out. You will construct the walls in the following order: longest sides, ends, short jogs or remaining exterior walls, interior walls that intersect the exterior walls, and the remainder.

Plate Marking

Clear the platform except for the plates with which you are working. Align the plates along the edge. Starting at the left front corner, lightly mark on the top plate the 16-inch interval to the first stud. Because it's difficult to center a stud on a mark, come back ¾ inch from the first light mark and draw a dark mark. From there continue making dark marks at 16-inch intervals on the top plate. Put your combination square on the first dark mark and draw a line simultaneously across both plates. Then, on both plates, put an X on the side of the mark where the stud goes. In the same fashion, continue marking both plates and drawing Xs.

When you reach the end of the plates, go back and mark the positions of the double-stud corners and partition posts. Also mark the positions of the king and trimmer studs for windows and door openings. For the sizes of rough openings, check the illustrations in this book, the details and specifications in the plans, and any instructions that come with doors and windows.

Wall Construction

After you build each wall on the subfloor platform, you will raise and brace to its proper position. The process is essentially the same whether the section of wall is plain or if it has doors or windows.

Marking Plates for Studs

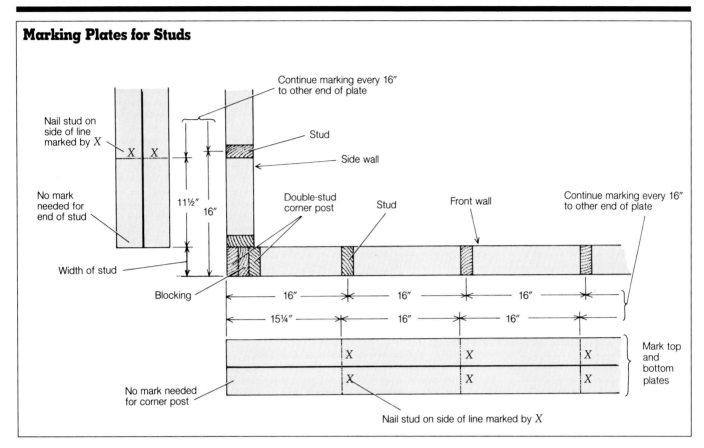

Nail stud on side of line marked by X

No mark needed for end of stud

Width of stud

11½"

16"

Blocking

No mark needed for corner post

Continue marking every 16" to other end of plate

Stud

Side wall

Double-stud corner post

Stud

Front wall

Continue marking every 16" to other end of plate

16" 16" 16"

15¼" 16" 16"

Mark top and bottom plates

Nail stud on side of line marked by X

The first step is to lay the soleplate on the line where it will be raised and the top plate a little more than the length of the studs away. Set both on edge so the marks face each other. For an 8-foot ceiling, standard studs are 92¼ inches long. To save time you can buy studs already cut to this length or, if you have 8-foot 2 by 4s, count how many you'll need and cut them all at once.

The studs are 92¼ inches long so that when you add the thickness of the soleplate, the top plate, and cap plate (often called the double top plate), the total height of the stud wall is 96¾ inches. This creates a wall that will accommodate the ceiling board and flooring.

Next, build the corner posts for the ends and any interior-wall intersections. The end walls and those that meet the

posts do not have posts. You will nail the single stud at the end of these walls to the corner post when you raise the walls into place. Make the corner posts by sandwiching 3 pieces of 2 by 4 scrap, about 12 inches long, between 2 studs.

Lay all the corner posts and studs for the wall on edge in position between the plates. Butt each of them against the marks on the soleplate. Stand with one foot on the stud to keep it from moving, and hammer two 16d common or box nails through the plate into the ends of the studs. Do the same with the top plate, and you have finished a basic stud wall. At this point the wall is obviously not square, but don't worry. Square it after you stand it up in position.

Estimating the Board Feet of Lumber For Stud Walls

Find the square footage of the stud walls by multiplying the height by the length in feet; multiply this figure by the appropriate number in the table. The result is the approximate board feet of material you'll need, including the corner posts, doors, windows, and top and bottom plates. Any special framing must be added to this figure.

To estimate the quantity of nails you'll need, divide the total square footage by 1,000 and multiply by the appropriate number in the table.

Size of Studs (In.)	Spacing OC (In.)	Board Ft per Square Ft of Area	Lb of Nails per 1,000 Board Ft
2 × 4	16	1.20	22
	24	1.10	19
2 × 6	16	1.54	17
	24	1.45	15

Framing Openings

Windows

Doors

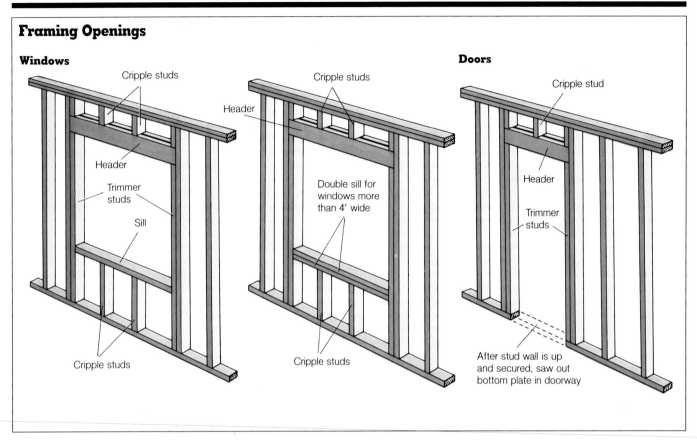

Cripple studs

Header

Trimmer studs

Sill

Cripple studs

Cripple studs

Header

Double sill for windows more than 4' wide

Cripple studs

Cripple stud

Header

Trimmer studs

After stud wall is up and secured, saw out bottom plate in doorway

Windows

Except for an occasional bit of architectural creativity, the tops of windows and doors should all be the same height. Standard house construction calls for this height to be 82½ inches from the top of the soleplate to the bottom of the header. To account for the 1½-inch bottom plate, cut all trimmer studs, which support the headers, 81 inches long. The width of the door and the width and height of the windows are determined by you or your designer and are shown on the plans.

The rough window openings should be ½ inch larger on all sides than the outside dimension of the window. This allows you room to maneuver the window somewhat before

nailing it. By maneuvering the window, you can ensure that it is square and that it will not bind when opened. Trim will cover the spaces between the rough opening and the window.

For structural support, place a header above all openings. Headers can be fabricated from pieces of 2-by lumber or can be precut to length at the lumberyard from 4 by 12 stock. Study the plans and the illustrations in this book to find the length of the headers. Note that the header should overlap the trimmer studs on each side, so it needs to be cut 3 inches longer than the width of the rough opening.

If you make all the headers from 4 by 12s, you eliminate this figuring. If you make your headers from scraps, read the note that follows to figure out how deep a header must be.

Note: For maximum spans of 3½, 5, 6½, and 8 feet, the header must be 6, 8, 10, and 12 inches deep, respectively. Also, headers fabricated from 2-by lumber must have a piece of ½-inch plywood sandwiched between the 2-bys to make them the same thickness as the 2 by 4 studs.

The bottom of each window opening is a 2 by 4 sill that fits between the trimmers and rests on the cripple studs. Some local codes call for double sills.

When you lay out the window and door openings on your soleplates and top plates, check the illustrations to note the locations of the king studs and trimmers. Put the king studs in place. Place the headers between the king studs, then cut the trimmers to fit

under the headers. Set the sills between the trimmers, then install the cripple studs to support the sills. Finally, double up the sills, if required.

Doors

Framing the door openings is similar to framing the windows, except you have to consider the thickness of the door jamb based on how it's going to be constructed. Whether you buy prehung doors or make the jamb and hang the doors yourself, the framing process is much the same.

Standard doors are 80 inches high. When framing, you must adjust the door opening to accommodate the finish floor, threshold, and top jamb.

Many plans give measurements from the end of the house to the centerline of the doorways. Mark this centerline

Framing Windows

Corner Posts

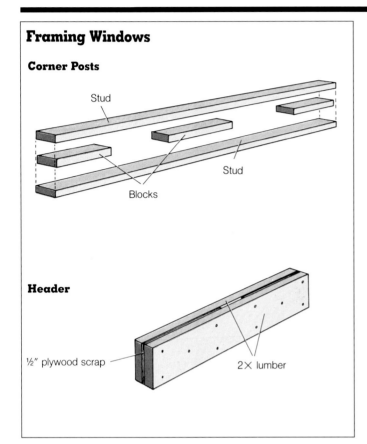

Stud

Stud

Blocks

Header

½" plywood scrap

2× lumber

Header Sizes

Most codes do not have tables to guide you in sizing headers over doors and windows; they just contain formulas for calculating beam sizes. However, the following sizes are generally accepted sizes for headers in various situations.

Location	Size of Header (4 by or Built-up 2 by)	Maximum Span (Ft)
Single story or top story	4 × 4	4
	4 × 6	6
	4 × 8	8
	4 × 10	10
	4 × 12	12
Lower floor, with floor above	4 × 4	3
	4 × 6	4
	4 × 8	7
	4 × 10	8
	4 × 12	9

Note: Increase sizes where accumulated loads concentrate on a header.

---

with a big C on the soleplate. You can usually adjust the opening a few inches one way or the other so you can use an existing stud as one of the king studs. However, be careful of design requirements that may have doors positioned for specific reasons. Divide the width of the doorway in half, and measure and lightly mark that distance each way from the center mark. To accommodate the thickness of the door jamb, add 1¼ inches to each side and mark these points with a dark mark. Later, you will fill the 1¼-inch gap with shims to true the door.

Install the king studs on the marks next to the trimmer stud

Number of Studs per Linear Foot of Wall

To find the total number of studs you'll need for each wall, measure the wall length in feet and find that number on the chart. Add 2 studs for each corner or intersection; add 2 more for each door and window.

Number of Studs Needed		Length of Wall in Ft																	
	2	3	4	5	6	7	8	9	10	11	12	13	14	15	16	17	18	19	20
16" OC	3	3	4	5	6	6	7	8	9	9	10	11	12	12	13	14	15	15	16
24" OC	2	3	3	4	4	5	5	6	6	7	7	8	8	9	9	10	10	11	11

marks. Cut the trimmers to fit the opening, which should equal the height of the door plus finish floor, threshold, and top jamb. Install the trimmers next to the king studs. Set the header on top of the trimmers and nail it in place. Cut and nail the cripple studs on the 16-inch marks above the header.

Special Supports

At some point you'll need to install extra support members to support pipes, chimneys, plumbing fixtures, light fixtures, recessed fixtures, towel and grab bars, or other items. Consider adding supports between studs at points you

plan to hang large mirrors and pieces of art. These special supports are rarely identified in plans, but they should be installed while framing.

Most supports, also called blocking, are 2 by 4s nailed between the studs. For details, see the illustrations in this book that show specific fixtures.

Bracing Walls

Let-in Bracing

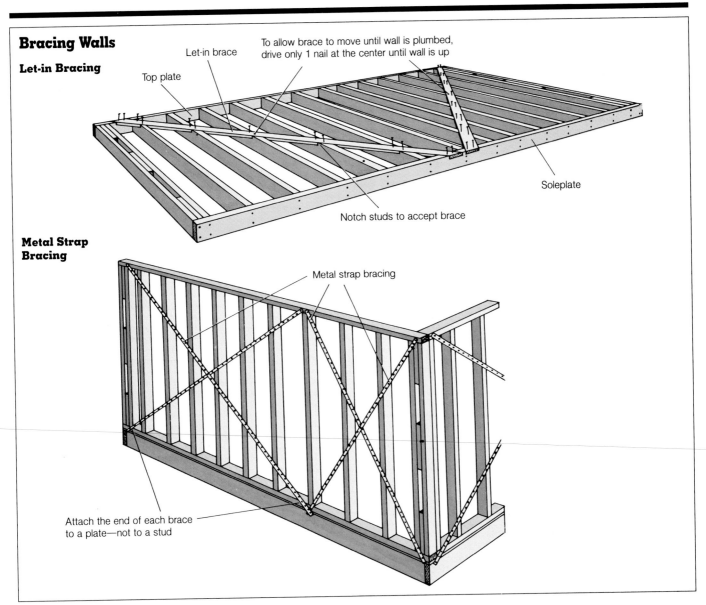

To allow brace to move until wall is plumbed, drive only 1 nail at the center until wall is up

Let-in brace

Top plate

Soleplate

Notch studs to accept brace

Metal Strap Bracing

Metal strap bracing

Attach the end of each brace to a plate—not to a stud

Wall Bracing

If your house will have plywood siding as a finish material, you probably won't need additional diagonal bracing on the stud walls. However, all other kinds of siding do require an underlayment of plywood sheathing for support (see above illustration) or metal straps for bracing. Sheathing is usually required in earthquake zones and areas of high winds. Check local building codes.

Metal Strap Bracing

Special metal straps for bracing are commonly available in 10- and 12-foot lengths. The straps are installed in crossed pairs or in T shapes, which are installed into a saw kerf in the plates. You will nail the bracing to the outside of the exterior stud walls after the walls are up and trued. The braces are thin enough not to interfere with the exterior sheathing.

Metal strap bracing comes with holes for 8d nails every 2 inches. To secure the bracing after you true the walls, nail one end of the brace to the top plate, then nail it to each stud in turn, and finally nail the other end to the soleplate.

Wall Raising And Truing

You will raise and brace each exterior wall as you build it. Two people can easily raise a 16- to 20-foot wall. The walls will not usually slip off the platform, but if you want to be safe, tack a couple of sticks to the side of the joist to catch the edge of the soleplate as you lift. Raise each wall smoothly and evenly, being particularly careful not to let it bend at the butt joints of the plates. When you have it vertical, have one person steady the wall while the other braces it.

Make your braces from 1 by 4s or 2 by 4s. The first braces go on each end, from high on the wall to the side of the end

Truing Walls

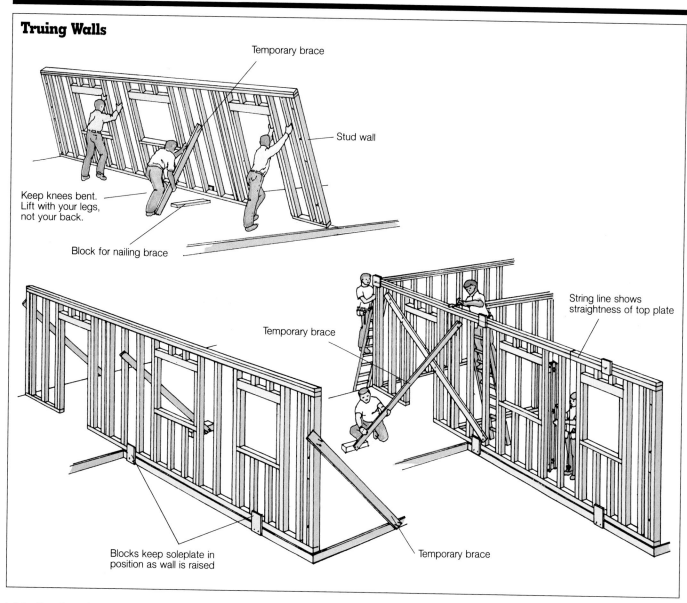

Temporary brace

Stud wall

Keep knees bent. Lift with your legs, not your back.

Block for nailing brace

Temporary brace

String line shows straightness of top plate

Blocks keep soleplate in position as wall is raised

Temporary brace

joists. Tap the soleplate into position at the outline mark you drew earlier, and put a few nails through the soleplate to hold it in place. Don't drive the nails completely until you've trued the walls. Additional braces should be at 6- to 8-foot intervals.

Have one person use a level to see if the wall is plumb while another person secures the braces. Nail pieces of scrap wood to the subfloor, and nail

the intervening braces from near the top of the studs to these scraps.

When all the walls are completed and up, do a final truing. To make sure all the walls are square with each other and with the platform, make yourself a plumb board as shown in the illustration (see above).

You need to straighten and brace walls in two directions—along the wall and in and out and perpendicular to the wall. Have one person on a ladder at the end of a wall push or pull

the wall into plumb while another person nails the braces to hold the wall in place. Don't drive the nails completely in until you've trued all the walls. Long walls have a tendency to bow in or out in the middle; before you nail on the cap plate, sight down each wall and make sure they are straight. Mason's twine pulled from end to end, with a little block of wood to hold it slightly out

from the top plate, may help you set an accurate sighting. Straighten the wall by adjusting the center bracing.

To set final proof that your walls are true, measure the diagonals from the top corners of the walls as you did earlier with the soleplates. If both diagonals in all rectangles are equal, the walls are true and you can nail all the corners together and nail all the braces down. Secure the soleplate permanently with 2 nails between each stud.

85

Building Ceiling Joists

Joists With Rafters

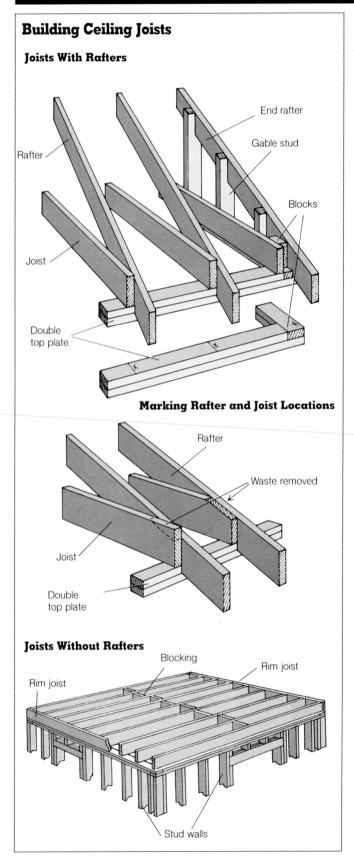

Rafter

End rafter

Gable stud

Blocks

Joist

Double top plate

Marking Rafter and Joist Locations

Rafter

Waste removed

Joist

Double top plate

Joists Without Rafters

Blocking

Rim joist

Rim joist

Stud walls

Interior Walls

Lay out and construct interior walls in the same manner as exterior walls. They are designed both to divide the house into rooms and to support the ceiling joists if the house is too wide for a single span.

If an open area where ceiling joists need to be supported has been designed into the house, you must span that open area with a beam of proper size. Check the framing plans, a span chart, and with the building inspector to be sure the beam is constructed according to code.

The installation of the cap plates is the final step in the construction of the stud walls. Select the straightest possible 2 by 4s for the cap plates. The cap plates on end walls and those on interior walls that meet exterior walls should overlap the cap plates of the walls they meet—just the converse of the top plates. When you put the cap plate on, don't let any cap plate butt joints fall within 4 feet of the butt joints in the top plate. The joints in the cap plate do not have to fall directly over the ends of studs as joints in the top plate do.

Installing Ceiling Joists

When you have completed and secured all the walls, you are ready to install the ceiling joists. The ceiling joists tie the house together horizontally and provide a place to attach the ceiling. If there is a second story, the first-floor ceiling joists are the floor joists for the next floor and another platform on which to build more walls.

The joists of the top floor, especially, are there to resist the outward pressure of the rafters on the walls.

If your house has a second story, mark the joist positions on the cap plates just as you did on the mudsills. Proceed with the second-story platform just as you did with the first one. Frame the second story in the same manner as the first. Remember that, before you install the upstairs subfloors, you must first put in the backer material for the ceiling wallboard below.

Ceiling joists on the top floor are different from ceiling joists that are also floor joists. Joists on the top floor do not have to carry the same kind of weight that floor joists do, and this affects spacing. Top-floor joists are spaced according to the rafters.

Because ceiling joists fit alongside the rafters, you need to mark the rafter locations first. Before you proceed with the ceiling joists, read "Laying Out the Roof Framing" (see page 98), so you can learn how to mark rafter locations accurately.

Rafters are usually spaced 24 inches on center, but in areas where heavy snow loads are possible and in areas of extremely high winds, you may be required to space them 16 inches on center.

You will mark the rafter locations on the cap plate just as you marked the stud locations on the soleplate. Starting from the same end of each side wall, measure off either 16 inches or 24 inches as required. Then back up ¾ inch and use your square to make a line across the plate. Again put an X beside the line to show on which side

Chart 4.* Low- or High-Slope Rafters. Allowable spans for 30 lb per square ft live load (supporting drywall ceiling)

Rafter Size	Rafter Spacing	Allowable Extreme Fiber Stress in Bending F_b (psi)														
		500	600	700	800	900	1,000	1,100	1,200	1,300	1,400	1,500	1,600	1,700	1,800	1,900
2 x 6	16.0″	6–6	7–1	7–8	8–2	8–8	9–2	9–7	10–0	10–5	10–10	11–3	11–7	11–11	12–4	12–8
		0.24	0.31	0.39	0.48	0.57	0.67	0.77	0.88	0.99	1.10	1.22	1.35	1.48	1.61	1.75
	24.0″	5–4	5–10	6–3	6–8	7–1	7–6	7–10	8–2	8–6	8–10	9–2	9–6	9–9	10–0	10–4
		0.19	0.25	0.32	0.39	0.46	0.54	0.63	0.72	0.81	0.90	1.00	1.10	1.21	1.31	1.43
2 x 8	16.0″	8–7	9–4	10–1	10–10	11–6	12–1	12–8	13–3	13–9	14–4	14–10	15–3	15–9	16–3	16–8
		0.24	0.31	0.39	0.48	0.57	0.67	0.77	0.88	0.99	1.10	1.22	1.35	1.48	1.61	1.75
	24.0″	7–0	7–8	8–3	8–10	9–4	9–10	10–4	10–10	11–3	11–8	12–1	12–6	12–10	13–3	13–7
		0.19	0.25	0.32	0.39	0.46	0.54	0.63	0.72	0.81	0.90	1.00	1.10	1.21	1.31	1.43
2 x 10	16.0″	10–11	11–11	12–11	13–9	14–8	15–5	16–2	16–11	17–7	18–3	18–11	19–6	20–1	20–8	21–3
		0.24	0.31	0.39	0.48	0.57	0.67	0.77	0.88	0.99	1.10	1.22	1.35	1.48	1.61	1.75
	24.0″	8–11	9–9	10–6	11–3	11–11	12–7	13–2	13–9	14–4	14–11	15–5	15–11	16–5	16–11	17–4
		0.19	0.25	0.32	0.39	0.46	0.54	0.63	0.72	0.81	0.90	1.00	1.10	1.21	1.31	1.43
2 x 12	16.0″	13–3	14–6	15–8	16–9	17–9	18–9	19–8	20–6	21–5	22–2	23–0	23–9	24–5	25–2	25–10
		0.24	0.31	0.39	0.48	0.57	0.67	0.77	0.88	0.99	1.10	1.22	1.35	1.48	1.61	1.75
	24.0″	10–10	11–10	12–10	13–8	14–6	15–4	16–1	16–9	17–5	18–1	18–9	19–4	20–0	20–6	21–1
		0.19	0.25	0.32	0.39	0.46	0.54	0.63	0.72	0.81	0.90	1.00	1.10	1.21	1.31	1.43

Chart 5.* High-Slope Rafters. Allowable spans for slope over 3 in 12; 30 lb per square ft live load (heavy roof covering)

Rafter Size	Rafter Spacing	500	600	700	800	900	1,000	1,100	1,200	1,300	1,400	1,500	1,600	1,700	1,800	1,900
2 x 4	16.0″	4–1	4–6	4–11	5–3	5–6	5–10	6–1	6–5	6–8	6–11	7–2	7–5	7–7	7–10	8–0
		0.18	0.23	0.29	0.36	0.43	0.50	0.58	0.66	0.74	0.83	0.92	1.01	1.11	1.21	1.31
	24.0″	3–4	3–8	4–0	4–3	4–6	4–9	5–0	5–3	5–5	5–8	5–10	6–0	6–3	6–5	6–7
		0.14	0.19	0.24	0.29	0.35	0.41	0.47	0.54	0.61	0.68	0.75	0.83	0.90	0.99	1.07
2 x 6	16.0″	6–6	7–1	7–8	8–2	8–8	9–2	9–7	10–0	10–5	10–10	11–3	11–7	11–11	12–4	12–8
		0.18	0.23	0.29	0.36	0.43	0.50	0.58	0.66	0.74	0.83	0.92	1.01	1.11	1.21	1.31
	24.0″	5–4	5–10	6–3	6–8	7–1	7–6	7–10	8–2	8–6	8–10	9–2	9–6	9–9	10–0	10–4
		0.14	0.19	0.24	0.29	0.35	0.41	0.47	0.54	0.61	0.68	0.75	0.83	0.90	0.99	1.07
2 x 8	16.0″	8–7	9–4	10–1	10–10	11–6	12–1	12–8	13–3	13–9	14–4	14–10	15–3	15–9	16–3	16–8
		0.18	0.23	0.29	0.36	0.43	0.50	0.58	0.66	0.74	0.83	0.92	1.01	1.11	1.21	1.31
	24.0″	7–0	7–8	8–3	8–10	9–4	9–10	10–4	10–10	11–3	11–8	12–1	12–6	12–10	13–3	13–7
		0.14	0.19	0.24	0.29	0.35	0.41	0.47	0.54	0.61	0.68	0.75	0.83	0.90	0.99	1.07
2 x 10	16.0″	10–11	11–11	12–11	13–9	14–8	15–5	16–2	16–11	17–7	18–3	18–11	19–6	20–1	20–8	21–3
		0.18	0.23	0.29	0.36	0.43	0.50	0.58	0.66	0.74	0.83	0.92	1.01	1.11	1.21	1.31
	24.0″	8–11	9–9	10–6	11–3	11–11	12–7	13–2	13–9	14–4	14–11	15–5	15–11	16–5	16–11	17–4
		0.14	0.19	0.24	0.29	0.35	0.41	0.47	0.54	0.61	0.68	0.75	0.83	0.90	0.99	1.07

* Charts 2, 3, 4, and 5 are reproduced from the 1991 edition of the *Uniform Building Code*, copyright 1991, with permission of the publisher, the International Conference of Building Officials.

THE ROOF

The purpose of a roof is to protect the house and its occupants. To do that, a roof must be strong, durable, and weatherproof. Along with this function goes form. The roof is a prime design element. The roofline defines the exterior style of the house; the finish material—both the material and its color—determines the way you can trim the house, the color you can paint it, and how long it will be until you'll have to put on a new roof.

This chapter begins with a gallery of roof styles. Many roofs are actually a combination of several styles. The finish material is a major budget item and should be chosen with care. Common choices are shown beginning on page 94. Once you've determined the style and finish, just follow the step-by-step building instructions for layout, framing, and finishing, taking every safety precaution possible.

A combination of roof types adds architectural interest to this compact Ranch-style house. The garage roof is a gable; the roof just above it and the one above the front door are hip roofs; to the left of the door is a shed. Other appealing integrated details include the built-in front window box and the quoins, or corner blocks, that flank the garage.

SELECTING A ROOF STYLE AND FINISH

Your roof should add beauty and style to your house. When you select the roof style and the finish material, be sure they are compatible with the style of house you've chosen.

Roof Styles

There are seven roof styles: flat, shed, gable, gambrel, hip, mansard, and butterfly. Any other style is a variation or combination of these basic styles.

The most common roofs built by the owner-builder—and the only roof styles described in this book—are gable roofs, hip roofs, and combinations of these two styles.

A shed roof, for instance, is just half a gable roof. A gambrel roof plan is the same as a gable roof plan except the gambrel has two rafters on each side instead of one and another board—like a ridge board—between them. The mansard roof is a combination of a hip roof and two hip roofs, one with a shallow slope inside another with a very steep slope.

The correct roof style and finish for your house depends mainly on the architectural style of the house. If you are building in an established neighborhood, look at the surrounding rooflines and use of finish materials.

No roof style is intrinsically better than any other. Some, however, suit certain weather conditions better than others. Flat roofs are fine in areas where there is little rain or snow; steeper roofs are needed where heavy snow loads must be endured. When choosing the correct roof style and slope for your house, consider that it should withstand the strongest rain, snow, and wind loads that your area has ever had.

The Slope

All roofs—even "flat" roofs—have a slope to allow drainage. This slope may be referred to as the pitch. Roofs have a 3 in 12 or 9 in 12 slope. This is often written "3:12" or "9:12" and means that for every 12 inches of run, a horizontal measurement, a roof has 3 or 9 inches of rise, a vertical measurement.

The slope of your roof is determined partly by the style of the house and partly by the weather in the area where you will build. The slope will be given on the roofing plan.

The style of roof and its slope dictate to some degree the roofing material used. Flat roofs, for example, are almost always built-up—that is, composed of alternate layers of roofing felt and hot-mop tar, with the final layer of tar embedded generously with fine gravel. Roofs with a slope of 3 in 12 or flatter can be built-up. Hot tar would run off steeper roofs so, for them, other materials are desirable.

Roofing additions—such as wings, ells, dormers, or cupolas—should have the same style roof and the same slope as the main structure unless a particular design reason dictates a different style.

Finish Materials

For your purposes, finish materials fall into two categories: those that can be installed by the owner-builder and those that should be installed by a qualified professional firm. Tar-and-gravel, cold-mop, composition-roll, slate-tile, and aluminum-shingle roofs are beautiful choices for homes. However, they should all be installed by experienced workers. If you are interested in one of these finish materials, seek professional help.

This section will describe common roofing materials that can be installed by the owner-builder. Roofing materials are sold by the square; one square equals 100 square feet of roof.

Composition Shingles

Also called asphalt shingles, these are the easiest roofing finish to install and the most widely sold. About 70 percent of houses in the United States are roofed with them.

Composition shingles come in many colors and with shading to give them a three-dimensional look. The most widely available configuration is the 3-tab cut. Interlocking, 1-tab, and 2-tab styles have become less available over the last few years because of the popularity and easy application of the 3-tab style. Composition shingles can be used on almost all styles of houses because their colors help them mimic the roofings used on buildings of the classic styles.

Composition shingles are commonly made with sealing strips across the middle, where the bottom of the next tier will fall. After the shingles are applied to a roof, the heat of the sun melts the strips and binds the shingles together. This prevents them from blowing up in strong winds and helps them resist curling.

Composition shingles have a core of cellulose fibers or fiberglass. This is coated with asphalt on both sides and topped with a protective layer of fine mineral aggregate. The aggregate can be in any of several colors or combinations of colors, including black, grays, browns, reds, blues, and greens. Each manufacturer has catalogs with color samples and photos of how the various styles appear when covering different roof styles.

The 3-tab shingles come in different qualities. The quality of a shingle is judged primarily by the weight. The heavier a shingle, the longer it's guaranteed to last. Standard shingles run between 205 and 300 pounds per square and are usually guaranteed to last 15 to 30 years.

Composition shingles should not be used unless the roof has at least a 3 in 12 slope; a 4 in 12 slope is preferred.

Wood Shingles And Shakes

Wood shingles are smaller and lighter than shakes. They are usually sawn on one side or both sides to give them their typical profile. Shakes are usually split by hand, which accounts for their higher cost. Most shingles and shakes are cut from western red cedar.

Shakes and shingles are graded by the numbers 1, 2, and 3. Grade 1 shingles are cut vertically from heartwood. They are highly resistant to rot and free of knots. For roofs you should use only grade 1.

Grades 2 and 3 have progressively more sapwood and knots. Grade 1 or 2 can be used for siding. Grade 3 is used mostly for starter rows on roofs and siding and for shimming as needed around the construction site.

Shingles come in lengths of 16, 18, and 24 inches. They are sold in bundles, with 4 bundles equaling 1 square. A square of shingles covers 1 square of roof if installed with a 5-inch exposure. More exposure, of course, allows more coverage.

Shakes are sold in bundles of 18- or 24-inch lengths. They come in two weights: medium or heavy. A 5-bundle square of 24-inch shakes covers 100 square feet with a 10-inch exposure.

Both shakes and shingles are usually applied over spaced 1 by 4s or 1 by 6s, rather than over solid sheathing, to allow more air circulation. This is especially necessary with shingles because they are smoothly sawn and fit tightly together. For this reason, never put roofing felt under shingles. Do put it under shakes, however,

because their irregular surface does allow air to circulate.

Do not use either shakes or shingles on roofs with a slope less than 4 in 12. On a shallower slope they will not shed water quickly enough, and the wind will tend to blow water under them.

Clay and Concrete Tile

Tiles are strong, beautiful, and heavy. When you put them on a roof, you can almost count on them being there for the life of the structure.

Clay tiles, which have been used for centuries on both sides of the Atlantic Ocean, have been challenged recently by concrete tiles, which offer many advantages. Concrete tiles are lighter, cheaper, easier to install, and come in a wide variety of colors and shapes. They can be curved like mission tiles, as well as ribbed, S-shaped, or virtually flat. Some varieties of concrete tile are light enough to be put on a standard roof frame.

Clay tiles, on the other hand, weigh about 1,000 pounds per square. If you want a clay tile roof, you have to have it especially engineered and build it to carry the weight.

Any kind of tile is more expensive than composition shingles. But, you rarely have to replace tiles—they never wear out.

Metal Panels

Panel roofs are long lasting and fairly easy to install. Metal roof sections are corrugated or ribbed to fit together. Steel roofs have been available for over one hundred years. They are quite inexpensive, but they

are heavy and will eventually rust out, no matter how carefully they're maintained. Galvanized steel panels, which are often painted, last longer. Aluminum panels are quite popular because they are lightweight, will not rust, and are easy to handle and cut. Aluminum, however, expands and contracts considerably in heat and cold and tends to loosen and pull out nails. Be sure to follow the manufacturer's instructions when installing an aluminum roof.

Metal roofs are rarely used on urban homes. They are found on barns and other utility buildings on farms, on vacation cabins in mountain areas, and in tropical and subtropical climates. Unless properly insulated, metal roofs are noisy in a heavy rain and downright ear-shattering in a hailstorm.

Roofing Felt

Roofing felt—though not a finish material—is an important component of a properly installed roof.

Roofing felt is asphalt-impregnated underlayment paper. It is used under almost all kinds of roofing materials and under most siding materials as well. It is waterproof, but it is not a vapor barrier—that is, it will allow some air and water vapor to pass through, so areas within the building can breath and dry out if they are damp.

Rolls of roofing felt are designated by their weight per square. A roll usually weighs 60 pounds. If it is 15-pound felt, it will cover 4 squares; a roll of 30-pound felt will cover 2 squares.

Considering Special Needs

Before you make the final decision on the finish material for the roof of your house, there are a few things to consider.

Fire Resistance

Composition shingles are rated A, B, or C by Underwriters Laboratories (UL), based on the base material and the quality of the shingle manufacturing. Look for a Class A rating when buying shingles for your house. Class A shingles are capable of withstanding "severe exposure to fire" and well worth their cost.

Wood shingles and shakes, unless treated with fire retardant, are very susceptible to burning. They are especially vulnerable to catching fire when embers from nearby forest fires or brushfires fall on them. Shakes and shingles that have been pressure-treated with UL-approved fire retardant are more expensive, but much safer in fire-risk areas. Some local building codes require this fire retardant.

All tile and metal roofs are fireproof. Metal roofs, however, have a low fire rating because they conduct heat so readily that the framing under them can ignite.

Wind Resistance

Composition shingles are also tested by Underwriters Laboratories for wind resistance. The test involves installing the shingles according to the manufacturer's instructions and submitting them to 60 miles-per-hour winds for two hours. The label of approved shingles carries the UL insignia. Look for it if you are going to build your house in an area prone to high winds.

Wood shingles and shakes are naturally resistant to wind damage because of their rigid form. Over time, however, the nails holding them will tend to work loose, and the resistance of the roofing will diminish. How long this takes depends on how well they are nailed in the first place.

Tiles are very wind resistant. Their weight makes them almost immovable except in a cyclonic wind.

Metal panels are reasonably wind resistant as long as they are nailed down securely. If a corner manages to work loose, however, the whole panel will rip off in even a moderate wind. It is important, then, to install the panels securely with the recommended nails and nail spacing. In areas of high winds, it would be wise to use even longer nails than recommended.

Code Restrictions

Be sure that the finish roofing you want is allowed in your area; roofing finishes are often restricted by local codes and covenants. Some codes restrict the type of finish material allowed, banning certain colors of composition shingles, for example. Others dictate the type of roof you must install; an area trying to imitate a Spanish-style village might allow tile only. Such rules are occasionally based on aesthetics only, but usually safety issues come into play. For instance, wood roofs are often outlawed in areas where forest fires or brushfires

are likely. There are alternatives that are just as stylish—and less dangerous to you, your family, and your investment.

Estimating Roofing Materials

To obtain roofing materials, you must know the square footage of the roof. Square footage is found, of course, by multiplying the length times the width, just as you learned in grammar school. The easiest way to calculate the roof area is to take the measurements from the plans.

Roof Area

To get the square footage of your roof from the plans, use a scale to measure all the appropriate edges; mark them as shown in the illustration. Since the plan is flat and the roof is sloped, the area the plan can represent is considerably less than the actual area of the roof. Likewise, the measurements along the hips and valleys are longer than they appear on the plan. To compensate for this, you'll need slope, hip, and valley conversion charts.

To get the actual area, multiply the length and width of the plan area to get square feet. Measure the width and length of chimneys, skylights, and any other areas that are not covered with roofing; subtract their footage from the total. Then look for the slope of your roof in the Slope Conversion Chart (see page 97), find the slope factor opposite the slope, and multiply

the total by this number. The result is the actual square footage.

If all the roof is the same slope, you can find the grand total of the plan area and multiply it by the slope factor. If your roof has areas of different slopes, you must calculate each different area separately and add them to get the total.

If the roof has overhangs on dormers or intersecting wings or ells, the areas of the overlapping overhangs must be counted twice. The edges of the lower surface should show as hidden (dashed) lines on the plans. Be sure to measure to this line when calculating the area of the lower surface.

Once you have calculated the square footage of the roof, add 10 percent for breakage and damage, then divide by 100 to determine the number of squares.

Linear Materials

Ordering materials for the roof also means ordering starter strips; drip edges; flashing for valleys, hips, chimneys, skylights, and other edges; ridge shingles or tiles; and gutters and downspouts. Level edges, such as ridges and eaves, are shown to scale on the plans, so you can measure the plans to calculate the areas needing coverage.

Rake edges—edges perpendicular to the ridges, such as gables and sides of chimneys and skylights—are on the same slope as the roof. You must multiply the length of rake edges by the slope factor to get the actual measurement.

The hips and valleys are not at right angles to the ridges;

therefore, they have a shallower angle than the slope. To get the actual measurement of these, multiply their length by the hip/valley factor in the Slope Conversion Chart (see page 97). Again, the factor is opposite the slope number.

Additional Materials

You will also need flashing units for vent pipes, as well as roofing cement and nails. The exact number and sizes of vent pipes do not usually appear on the plan or in the specifications. The specifications usually say, "Soil and waste vents shall be cast-iron pipe, in required sizes." Wait until the rough plumbing is completed before you order the vent flashing. Then measure all the pipes that protrude through the roof and buy the flashing units that fit over them.

Roofing cement comes in tubes and cans of 1 or 5 gallons. It's fine to buy more than you need. If you don't use it all, seal it tightly and put it away. It will last practically forever, and it's handy to have around for emergency repairs.

As for nails, allow 2½ pounds per square of 1¼-inch roofing nails for composition shingles. For wood shingles, buy 2 pounds per square of 3-penny (3d) galvanized box nails; for shakes, 2½ pounds per square of 4d galvanized box nails; for slate, 2 pounds of 4d or 5d galvanized or copper common nails. For tile, ask the supplier or check the manufacturer's instructions to learn the recommended nails.

Calculating Roof Area

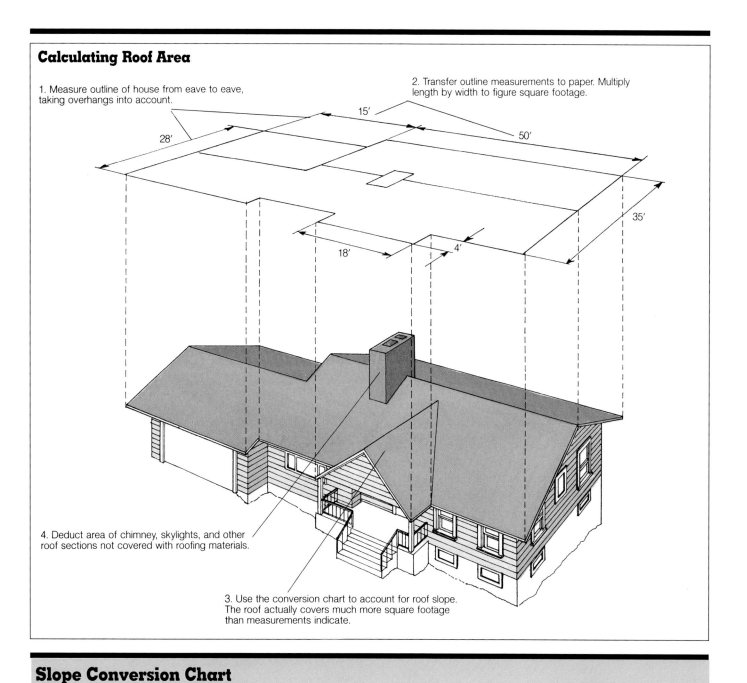

1. Measure outline of house from eave to eave, taking overhangs into account.

2. Transfer outline measurements to paper. Multiply length by width to figure square footage.

4. Deduct area of chimney, skylights, and other roof sections not covered with roofing materials.

3. Use the conversion chart to account for roof slope. The roof actually covers much more square footage than measurements indicate.

15'
28'
50'
35'
18'
4'

Slope Conversion Chart

Since a roof is sloped it actually covers much more area than it would appear to on your outline.

Slope (In. per Ft)	Rake/Area Factor	Hip/Valley Factor
4	1.054	1.452
5	1.083	1.474
6	1.118	1.500
7	1.157	1.524
8	1.202	1.564
9	1.250	1.600
10	1.302	1.642
11	1.356	1.684
12	1.414	1.732

LAYING OUT THE ROOF FRAMING

The layout procedure is the same for both gable and hip roofs. One person can do it all, although it is easier to have a helper. It takes about a half day to lay out a simple roof. No special skills are needed beyond the ability to read a tape measure and do basic arithmetic; on a difficulty scale of 10 points, consider roof layout a 5.

- ☐ Tracing paper
- ☐ Straightedge ruler
- ☐ Architect's scale
- ☐ T square
- ☐ Triangles (45 degree and 30/60 degree or adjustable)
- ☐ Pencils
- ☐ Eraser
- ☐ Drawing board or drafting table

Framing Styles

There are two ways to frame a roof: with joists and rafters or with trusses. Conventional framing is built of joists and rafters, individually cut and installed. In open-beam ceilings, the rafters are larger and farther apart than those in other conventionally framed roofs, and open-beam ceilings include heavy collar beams in addition to ceiling joists. Even so, the construction of all conventionally framed roofs is virtually the same. The alternative way to frame a roof is to have trusses made and just put them

in place. Some roofs call for combining both framing styles. This chapter will describe both; check your plans to see which is used for your roof.

Drawing a Framing Plan

Before ordering trusses, or cutting the rafters, or even laying out the positions of the rafters or trusses on the top plates, you must have a framing diagram. A roof framing diagram may be included in the working drawings. If not, you'll have to make one for yourself. Always make a very detailed plan to determine the kinds of members and the number and position of each. Draw the plan to scale, and include each member in it. Do not order roofing

materials or begin roof construction without a framing diagram in hand.

If you are framing conventionally, do not try to determine the actual length of each rafter from the diagram. Instead, take the dimensions directly from measurements of the wall framing after it has been straightened and trued.

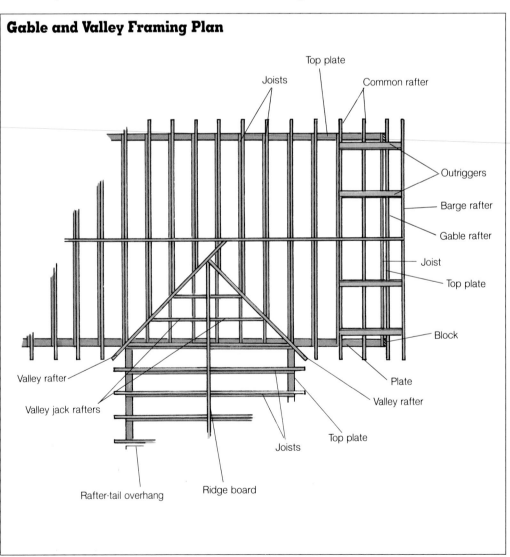

Gable and Valley Framing Plan

Joists · Top plate · Common rafter · Outriggers · Barge rafter · Gable rafter · Joist · Top plate · Block · Plate · Valley rafter · Valley rafter · Valley jack rafters · Joists · Top plate · Rafter-tail overhang · Ridge board

Laying Out and Cutting the Ridge Board

The ridge board is the top of the triangle in a conventionally framed roof. If the roof has more than one ridge, you will make the main, or longest, ridge board first. Ridge boards should be made from 1- or 2-inch stock one size wider than the rafters. If you are going to make the rafters from 2 by 6s, for example, then make the ridge board from an 8-inch board. If the ridge will be longer than a single board, splice 2 boards so they butt together at a point where a rafter attaches.

For a gable roof, the theoretical length of the ridge board is the length of the building between the outside edges of the top plates. The actual length of the board includes the width of any overhangs.

For a hip roof, the theoretical length of the main ridge board is the length of the building less twice the run of a main roof common rafter. The theoretical ends are where the centerline of the ridge board and the centerlines of the hip rafters intersect.

For hip roofs, the actual length is the theoretical length plus either the thickness of a common rafter or the 45-degree thickness of a hip rafter,

depending on how you make the attachment (see illustration on page 107). Place half the width of the addition at each end.

To mark the positions of the rafters on the ridge board, lay the ridge board along a top plate and transfer the rafter-position marks.

Laying Out and Cutting Common Rafters

You will need a carpenter's framing square to lay out and cut rafters. On it is a table that you will use to find the unit length of common rafters. You will also need the lengths of the run and span; to find these

lengths, measure the top plates after the walls have been straightened and trued. And, you will need to know the slope of the roof. With the framing square and this information, you are ready to lay out the first rafter.

Laying out a rafter is not as difficult as it may first appear. Just keep in mind that the roof design is based on two right triangles. The span is the base; the rise is the right angle of both triangles; and the rafter is the hypotenuse, which will be angled at the slope you have selected for your house. The following example uses the 6 in 12 slope shown on all the accompanying illustrations.

Laying Out the Ridge Board

Gable Roof

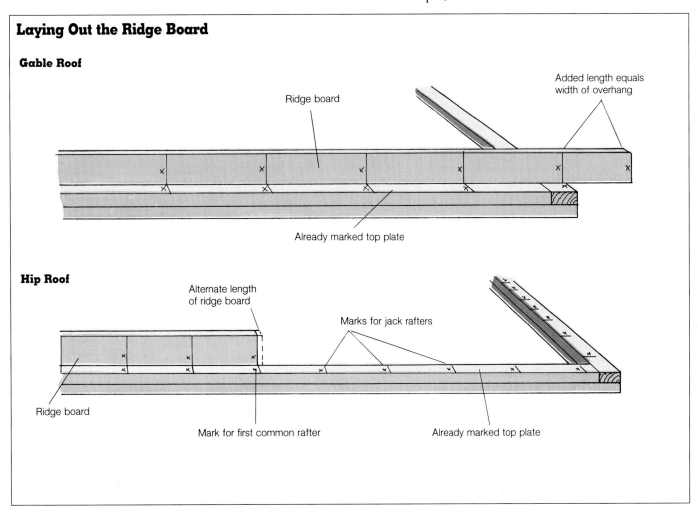

Added length equals width of overhang

Ridge board

Already marked top plate

Hip Roof

Alternate length of ridge board

Marks for jack rafters

Ridge board

Mark for first common rafter

Already marked top plate

Framing the Roof

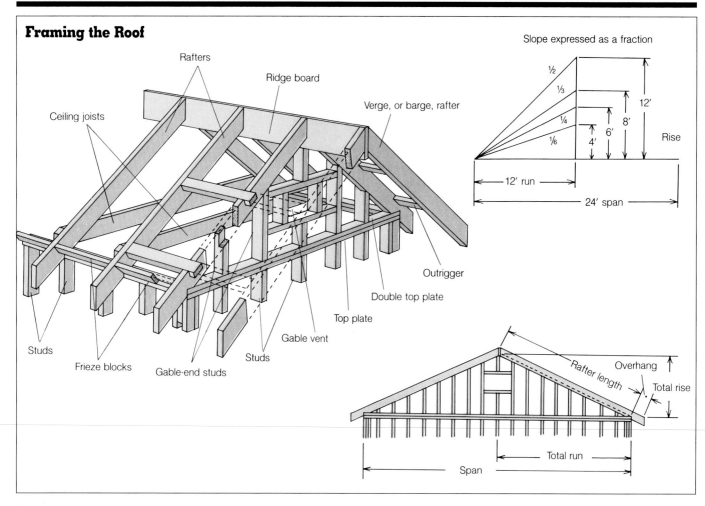

Rafters
Ridge board
Verge, or barge, rafter
Ceiling joists
Outrigger
Double top plate
Top plate
Gable vent
Studs
Frieze blocks
Gable-end studs
Studs

Slope expressed as a fraction

½
⅓
¼
⅙

12'
8'
6'
4'

Rise

12' run

24' span

Rafter length
Overhang
Total rise
Total run
Span

Common Rafter Length

The theoretical length of a common rafter is the distance between the outer edge of the top plate and the ridge, measured along a line at the slope angle. The length along the measuring line can be calculated in three ways: (1) by using the Pythagorean theorem you learned in high school math, (2) by using the rafter table on the framing square, and (3) by stepping off the length with the framing square.

The Pythagorean theorem states that the square of the hypotenuse of a right triangle is equal to the sum of the squares of the other two sides

$(A^2 = B^2 + C^2)$. Therefore, the length of the rafter can be figured if you measure the rise and the run and do some multiplication and addition. If this is too much mathematics, use one of the other methods.

To use the rafter table on the framing square, you just need to know the slope and the length of the run (half the length of the span or width across the house between the outer edges of the top plates). In the example, the slope is 6 in 12 and the run is 12 feet. To determine the rafter length, look under the 6-inch mark on the outer edge of the framing square blade. The top row is

labeled "Length Common Rafter Per Foot Run." In the top row are the figures "13 42," which mean that for every foot of run the rafter is $13\frac{42}{100}$ inches long. Multiply 12×13.42 on your calculator, and you get 161.04 inches. The .04 is just a little over $\frac{1}{32}$ inch, so you can disregard it—framing houses is not that exact a science.

To step off the length with the framing square, place the tongue and blade on the rafter board with the 6-inch and 12-inch marks just as for making the plumb cut (see the section that follows). Then, keeping the square in this position, step it down the rafter as many times as there are feet in the run—in this example, 12 times.

The Plumb Cut

The first step in making the first rafter is to mark the plumb cut, which forms the top end of the rafter that fits against the ridge board. Have a 2 by 6 on the subfloor in front of you. Lay the framing square on the right end, with the 6-inch mark on the outside edge of the tongue on the edge of the board nearest you. Then rotate the square so the 12-inch mark on the outside of the blade is on the same edge of the board. Draw a pencil line across the board, along the outside edge of the tongue. That is the required angle for a 6 in 12 plumb cut. You will make the cut later.

The Bird's-mouth

Measure the length of the rafter along the bottom edge of the rafter board—in this case, 161 inches. Mark the length on the rafter board. On this mark place the 6-inch mark on the tongue of the square. Place the 12-inch mark on the edge as you placed it in making the plumb cut. Draw another pencil line across the board, along the outside of the tongue. Now, still holding the 6- and 12-inch marks on the edge of the board, slide the square toward the plumb cut. Position it so the distance from the bottom edge of the board to the line you have just drawn is 4 inches. Draw a pencil line along the bottom edge of the blade. The triangular section

formed by the two lines is called the bird's-mouth, and it will fit precisely on the top plate of the stud wall.

The Tail Cut

Measure from the rafter-length line, away from the plumb cut, along the blade of the square, the distance of the overhang. Again draw a line along the tongue of the square while it is positioned on the 6- and 12-inch marks—the line should be parallel to the plumb cut. You have marked the tail cut, which forms the end of the rafter that will form the eaves of the house. It may be left as is or have a fascia board or rain gutter attached to it.

The Level Cut

If your roof is to have a cornice with a level soffit, cut the bottom of the rafter level before the rafters are installed. See the soffit details on the plans or read the section on cornices (see page 112) to decide where to make this cut.

The Shortening Cut

This is a simple step, but it must not be overlooked. Rafter lengths are measured as if they butted together at the ridge. Measuring perpendicular to the plumb cut, subtract half the thickness of the ridge board from the length at the plumb cut. Measure ⅜ inch if you are using a 1-by ridge board; measure ¾ inch for a 2-by. Draw the cut line with your square

exactly parallel to the original line for the plumb cut.

Barge Rafters

If your roof has an overhang, you will need two rafters for each gable end. These are the rafters that will be at the ends of the gable overhangs. They are put up last and supported by outriggers. These gable-end, or barge, rafters are exactly like common rafters except that they have no bird's-mouth and do not have shortening cuts unless the ridge board extends beyond them. Barge rafters double as trim boards. Choose the material with the siding and roofing finish in mind.

Cutting Rafters

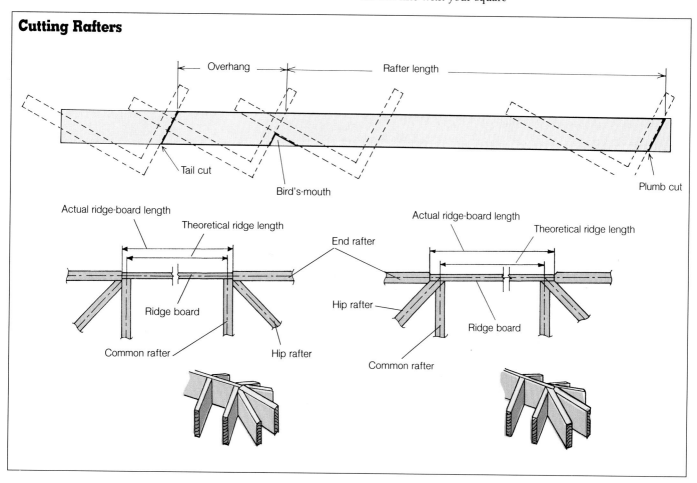

107

Mark and cut barge rafters at the same time you mark and cut common rafters.

Cutting Common And Barge Rafters

Cut out the first common rafter, the one you did all the layout on, very carefully. Use it as a pattern to cut out 2 more. Put this first pair in place at one end of the house to be sure you have an accurate fit. If everything fits correctly, use the pattern rafter to cut all the remaining rafters. Don't forget to cut the barge rafters, and don't forget that they have no bird's-mouths. The barge rafters will be installed along with the outriggers (see page 111).

Cutting Hip and Valley Rafters

Hip and valley rafters will be installed at 45 degrees to the common rafters, but they will have the same rise. They may be the same thickness as the common rafters, but they should be one lumber size wider to be large enough to allow full bearing by the beveled end of the jack rafters. That is, if the common rafters are 2 by 6, the hip and valley rafters should be 2 by 8. Local codes often require valley rafters to be doubled to carry snow or wind loads. Make each hip and valley rafter cut as it is measured and marked.

Rafter Length

The length of a hip or valley rafter can be calculated in all the same ways as that of a common rafter. The run, though, instead of being half the span, should be the hypotenuse of the equilateral triangle formed by the run of the last common rafter and the length of the top plate between the corner of the building and the first common rafter. In other words, the run should equal $\sqrt{2} \times$ the common rafter length. The easiest way to figure the length of the hip or valley rafter is by using the table on the framing square.

Using the example of the 6 in 12 roof that was used in determining the length of the common rafters, look under the 6-inch mark on the blade of the square. The first row showed the length of the common rafter as $13^{42}/_{100}$ inches per foot of run. In the second row, labeled "Length Hip or Valley Per Foot Run," you'll see *18*. This means the length of the hip or valley rafter is 18 inches per foot of common rafter run. The theoretical length of the hip or valley rafter is 18×12 inches, or 216 inches. At this point the length is still theoretical because you have not yet figured the shortening cut or the tail cut of the rafter.

Marks for The Plumb Cut

When you marked the plumb cut on a common rafter for a slope of 6 in 12, you set the triangle on the board so the 6-inch mark on the tongue and the 12-inch mark on the blade

were at the edge of the board. Since the run of the hip or valley rafters is the hypotenuse of the equilateral triangle for which the run of the common rafter is one side, then the inch number on the blade used to figure the angle of the plumb cut is the hypotenuse of a 12-inch equilateral triangle.

The hypotenuse of a 12-inch equilateral triangle is always 16.97 inches ($\sqrt{12^2 + 12^2} = 16.97$). Therefore, to get the angle of the plumb cut, on the edge of the board set the 6-inch mark on the tongue and the 17-inch mark (that is, 16.97 rounded up—close enough for rafters) on the blade. Draw the plumb cut along the edge of the tongue just as you did for the common rafter.

Marks for The Other Cuts

With one exception you will measure the bird's-mouths, tail cuts, and level cuts on the hip and valley rafters the same way as on the common rafters. The exception is that rather than using the 12-inch mark on the blade, use the 17-inch mark. As a result, the hip and valley rafters—and their amount of overhang—will be longer than the common rafters. Make each cut as you measure and mark it.

Side Cuts

The hip and valley rafters should be at a 45-degree angle to all the other roof members. Therefore, where the ends meet other members, they must be cut at 45-degree angles. At the top end, the hip or valley rafters butt into the corner

against both the last common rafters on the sides and the center common rafter on the end. Therefore, they must have a double, or corner, cut. Hip and valley rafters must be shortened at the point where they intersect the ridge board, in the same manner as common rafters.

The tail cut at the bottom end of the rafter, if there is to be a fascia board, must have a double side cut to which the fascia board is nailed.

If you have a doubled valley rafter, each one should be at a 45-degree angle in opposite directions at both the plumb and tail cuts.

Dropping and Backing

Since the hip and valley rafters are made of wider stock than the jack rafters, if the bird's-mouth is the same depth on each, the top of these rafters will extend above the surfaces of the jack rafters and get in the way of the sheathing. You can fix this by dropping the valley rafter and either dropping or backing the hip rafter. *To drop* means to cut the bird's-mouth deeper by the amount of the difference in depth; this brings the edges even. *To back* means to bevel the edges of the hip rafter because it contacts the wall at an angle. The center will connect but the edge will be high. Beveling the edge gives a better surface for nailing on the sheathing.

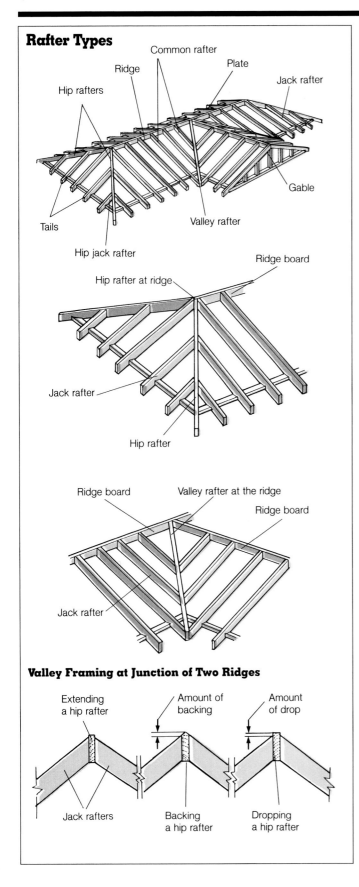

Rafter Types

Common rafter

Ridge

Plate

Jack rafter

Hip rafters

Tails

Hip jack rafter

Valley rafter

Gable

Ridge board

Hip rafter at ridge

Jack rafter

Hip rafter

Ridge board

Valley rafter at the ridge

Ridge board

Jack rafter

Valley Framing at Junction of Two Ridges

Extending a hip rafter

Amount of backing

Amount of drop

Jack rafters

Backing a hip rafter

Dropping a hip rafter

Adding Jack Rafters

Jack rafters are the shortened common rafters that connect to hip or valley rafters or both. For all figuring of length and angles, the unit rise of a jack rafter is always the same as the unit rise of the common rafters. The spacing of the jack rafters is always the same as the spacing of the common rafters.

Hip jack rafters have a bird's-mouth and tail cut, extend from the plate to the hip rafter, and have a 45-degree plumb cut at the top end. Valley jack rafters have a 90-degree plumb cut at the top, extend from the ridge to the valley rafter, and have a 45-degree tail cut.

Cripple jack rafters go from a hip rafter to a valley rafter without contacting either a plate or a ridge board.

Hip Jack-Rafter Length

To figure the length of hip jack rafters, study the framing diagram. Note that the center or longest rafter in the hip, the one that is an extension of the ridge board, should be the same actual length as the common rafters on the side of the roof. Each of the jack rafters should be progressively shorter than this center rafter. Calculate how much shorter by using the factor number from the framing square table for common rafter length and using the rafter spacing as the run.

For example, using the sample roof with a 6 in 12 slope and a rafter spacing of 16 inches, the length of the progressive shortening is 17.89 (17⅞) inches. You get this by

multiplying the spacing in feet (16 inches = 1.33 feet) by the number on the framing square blade (13.42).

Valley Jack-Rafter Length

The length of valley jacks is figured in exactly the same way as that of hip jacks except that there is no center rafter. You have to start with the last common rafter before the jacks and make the longest and subsequent jack rafters progressively shorter by the same factor.

Cuts for Jack Rafters

Lay out and cut the longest jack rafter first, complete with all the allowances and angles. Once the common and hip rafters are up, put the longest jack rafter in place to check the fit; trim it if needed; and when it's perfect, use it as a pattern for all the rest. Draw a center-line down the top and mark the shortening-factor measurements. On hip rafters, measure from the top. On valley rafters, measure from the bottom.

To find the length of cripple rafters—those between a hip and a valley rafter—measure the actual distance between the hip and valley rafters at the position of one cripple. Mark the angle of the cripple rafter to fit, then cut the rafter. Make any necessary adjustments, then use the first cripple rafter as a pattern for the rest.

Erecting The Rafters

Putting up the first 2 pairs of rafters, 1 pair on each end of the ridge board, is a difficult stage of conventional framing. One method is to hold the ridge board in place on a couple of notched 2 by 4s while you nail the rafters into place. If you have 2 helpers, have 1 hold the ridge board and 1 pair of end rafters in place and have the other hold the other end of the ridge board so it's level; you toenail the rafters to the cap plate and then to the ridge board. The weight of the 2 rafters against the ridge board and top plate will hold everything in place until you get them nailed.

When the first 2 pairs of rafters are up, check a few things before you proceed. First check that the ridge board is centered over the house. Then make sure that the ridge board is level. Finally, if it's a gable roof, check that the end rafters are plumb and even with the ends of the house.

When everything checks out, use two 1 by 4s to brace the ridge board from near its center to the end-wall studs. Nail one end of the rafters to the ridge board; nail the other end to the ceiling joists where they meet on the side walls.

Continue the framing by adding all the end common rafters, the hip and valley rafters, and the jack and cripple rafters. Refer to the illustrations to see exactly how all the pieces fit together. When nailing rafters to the ridge board, face-nail the first rafter of each pair and toenail the second rafter. Alternate the direction of face-nailing and toenailing with each pair of rafters as you proceed along the ridge.

Collar Beams

Local codes, especially in areas with heavy snow, often require double-pitch rafters to be reinforced with collar beams. Sometimes the collar beams are required only on every second or third set of rafters. A collar beam is a horizontal member that ties opposing rafters together above the side-wall top plates. If you want an attic, the collar beams can function as the ceiling joists.

Specifications don't usually give the length of the collar beam. Instead they give you the height of its bottom edge above the side-wall top plates. To find its length, measure up from the bottom of a ceiling joist to the points on the upper edge of 2 opposing rafters that are the required height. Measure the distance between these points to find the length of the collar beam.

Lay out the angle to cut the beam by laying the framing square on the edge of the beam just as you did to draw the plumb-cut angle on the rafters. However, instead of drawing the line along the tongue of the square, this time draw the line along the blade. When in place, the angle on the collar beam should exactly match the top edge of the rafter to which it is nailed.

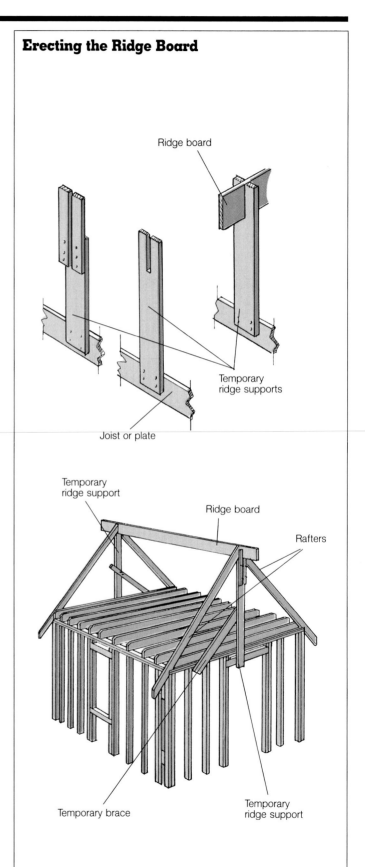

Erecting the Ridge Board

Ridge board

Temporary ridge supports

Joist or plate

Temporary ridge support

Ridge board

Rafters

Temporary brace

Temporary ridge support

Rafter Details

Collar Beams

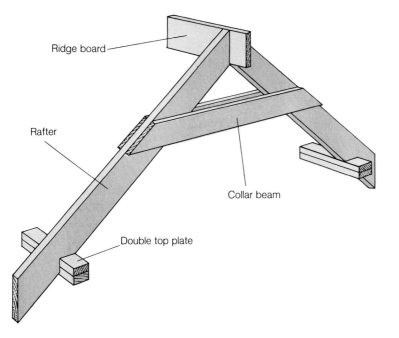

Ridge board

Rafter

Collar beam

Double top plate

Gable-End Studs

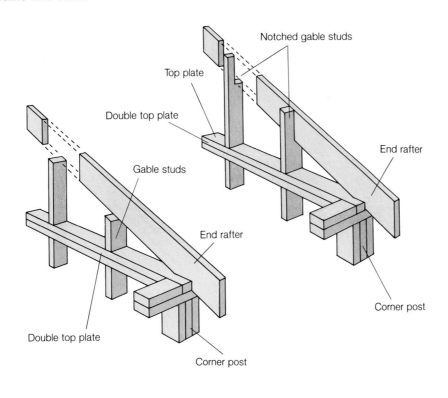

Notched gable studs

Top plate

Double top plate

Gable studs

End rafter

End rafter

Corner post

Double top plate

Corner post

Gable-End Studs

When all the roof members are up, you need to use studs to fill the triangular end walls formed by the rafters. These studs are the members to which you will nail the exterior siding. Gable-end studs fit between the cap plate and the end rafter directly above the end-wall studs.

To mark the length of each stud, hold a length of 2 by 4 in place above the cap plate behind the end rafter. Make sure the 2 by 4 is plumb, then draw a line where the rafter crosses it. Cut it at that angle and toenail it into place.

To make a stronger end wall, mark both the bottom and top of the rafter on the 2 by 4. Then cut a 1½-inch notch in the end of the stud so the rafter rests on half of it and the other half is nailed to the back of the rafter.

Outriggers and Barge Rafters

If you are building a gable roof with an overhang, you will need to install outriggers to support the barge rafter. Make the outriggers from lengths of 2 by 4. You will space them every 4 feet, starting at the bottom so they will line up with the sheathing boards when the boards are installed.

Cut a notch for each outrigger in the last rafter on each end of the roof. Nail the outriggers into these notches so they butt against the second rafter. Then nail the barge rafter to the ends of the outriggers and to the ridge board.

Framing a Skylight

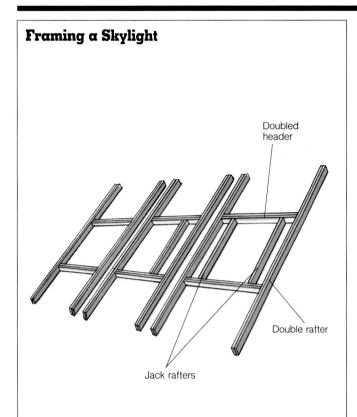

Doubled header

Double rafter

Jack rafters

Framing Frieze Blocks

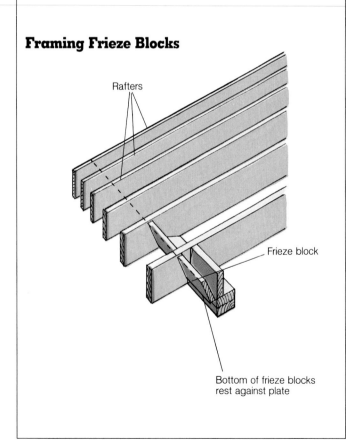

Rafters

Frieze block

Bottom of frieze blocks rest against plate

Framing Roof Openings

Any openings in the roof that are larger than the space between two rafters have to be specially framed. Such openings may be needed for chimneys, skylights, dormers, or large ventilators. These openings are framed in the same manner whether you are framing with trusses or framing conventionally.

If an opening interrupts rafters or joists, the roof must be framed with double headers and, in most cases, double rafters or joists as well. The extra rafter or joist in these situations is called a trimmer. The headers are normally installed so they are plumb. Skylight headers are installed perpendicular to the rafters.

Adding a Chimney Saddle or Cricket

A cricket is a small pitched roof, similar to a dormer, that is placed on the upper side of a chimney. Its purpose is to shed snow and ice, preventing them from building up and damaging either the roof or the chimney. A cricket for a small chimney, say up to 3 feet wide, can be made from 2 triangular pieces of ¾-inch exterior plywood. Like a gable dormer roof, a cricket requires a saddle that will be sheathed with the same material as the rest of the roof. See the illustrations on pages 117 and 141 for the construction details of chimney saddles.

Build the cricket in place as part of the framing procedure or build it on the ground and nail it to the sheathing before the roofing is applied.

Installing Frieze Blocks

The overhang on the gable end of a house is called the rake. The edges of the roof where rafters end are called the eaves. Under the eaves is either a cornice or frieze blocks. Frieze blocks support the space between the rafters under the eaves and usually are made from the same stock as rafters. Cut the blocks to fit precisely between the rafters. To align them, toenail the 2 end blocks into place first, positioning them so they are perpendicular to the sheathing, with their top edges flush with the top edge of the rafters and their inside bottom edges against the cap plate. Snap a chalk line across the tops of the rafters between them. Line up the rest on the chalk line and toenail them into place.

Building Cornices

There are three basic kinds of cornices: open, closed, and box. Each of the three has many more variations than can be described here. The sections that follow will present only the essentials. If you are interested, you can find many derivatives, complete with construction details, in books and magazines or by asking your architect or designer.

To make a strong, good-looking, and long-lasting closed or box cornice, make a groove in the fascia board to support the outside edge of the soffit panel. The inside edge of the soffit rests on a frieze board nailed to the wall of the house.

You can use any of several materials for the soffit. Plywood, wallboard, and hardboard make fine choices because they come in large sheets and can be stained or painted to fit in with any style of house.

Special aluminum soffit material is available in rolls. It comes with fascia and frieze runners that you nail to the house and soffit material that you slide into place. The aluminum rolls are available in various sizes from less than 1 foot to 4 feet wide. The rolls are available with perforations so individual vents are not necessary.

Open Cornices

The simplest open cornice has frieze blocks nailed between the rafters, as described earlier. To make it slightly more decorative, extend the siding material up between the rafters and attach short strips of decorative molding where the siding meets the roof sheathing.

With an open cornice you can leave the ends of the rafters exposed, either plain or cut in some decorative way, or you can nail a fascia or band board to the ends. The fascia board can be the full width of the rafters. For a more delicate appearance, make a level cut below the tail cut on the rafter and apply a narrow fascia, either plain or with trim boards.

The roof sheathing is always clearly visible with an open cornice. Be sure the sheathing over the tail piece of the rafters is attractive. It can be plywood that you paint to match the house, or it can be tongue-and-groove sheathing stained or left natural.

Closed Cornices

A closed cornice has no constructed overhang at all. Instead, just an inch or so of the roofing material peeks past the edge of a frieze board or piece of trim at the top edge of the house wall.

To create a closed cornice, make the rafters with no bird's-mouth or tail piece. Just make a seat cut at the cap plate, and cut the end of the rafter vertical and flush with the outside edge of the plate. The siding goes right up to the top edge of the rafters, where it meets the sheathing. Decorate the edge of the roof, just below the tiny overhang of the shingles or tiles, with a frieze board and shingle trim.

Box Cornices

Box cornices have either a sloping soffit or a level soffit. For a sloping soffit, enclose the rafters alone with a fascia board, soffit, various kinds of frieze boards, and moldings.

For a level soffit, attach level lookouts from the ends of the rafters to the wall sheathing and enclose the rafter ends and the lookouts with a fascia board, soffit, frieze boards, and trim boards.

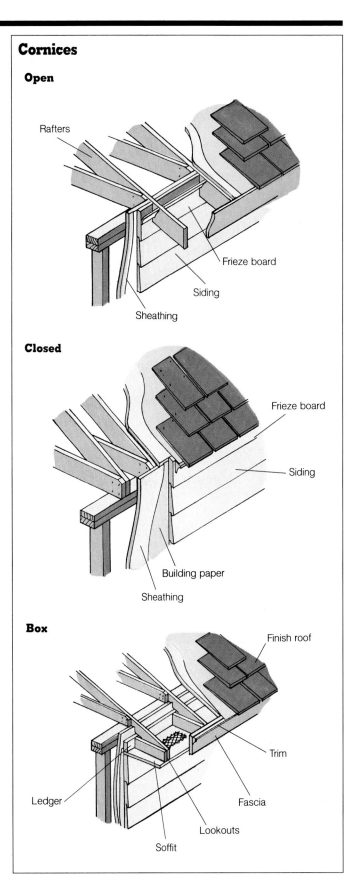

Cornices

Open

Rafters
Frieze board
Siding
Sheathing

Closed

Frieze board
Siding
Building paper
Sheathing

Box

Finish roof
Trim
Fascia
Lookouts
Ledger
Soffit

Allowing for Vents

Unless it is living area, every attic should be ventilated. In hot weather, proper ventilation prevents the attic from becoming a hot box that spills unwanted heat down through the attic floor (even if the attic is insulated) and into the living area.

In cold weather, proper ventilation helps prevent moisture from condensing in the insulation, framing, or on the outside of the roof, which may cause damage to the finish material.

If your house has a gable roof, vents in the top corners under the gable overhang will allow air to move freely through the attic area. The vents may be commercially manufactured of steel, aluminum, or wood; manufactured vents come with complete installation instructions. An alternative to buying a vent unit is to drill 3 or more 2-inch holes in the siding and cover them on the inside with screen to keep insects, birds, and bats out.

The local code will specify the amount of vent area—typically 1 square foot of free vent area for every 150 square feet of attic. A 2¼-square-foot gable vent, with louvers and screening, would have 1 square foot of free vent area.

If you have a hip roof, it will need vents in the cornice. These can be holes you drill in the frieze blocks or soffit and cover with screen on the inside, or they can be commercially available vents that you install according to manufacturer's instructions. Vents in the frieze blocks should be protected somehow so attic insulation doesn't block them.

Attic Vents

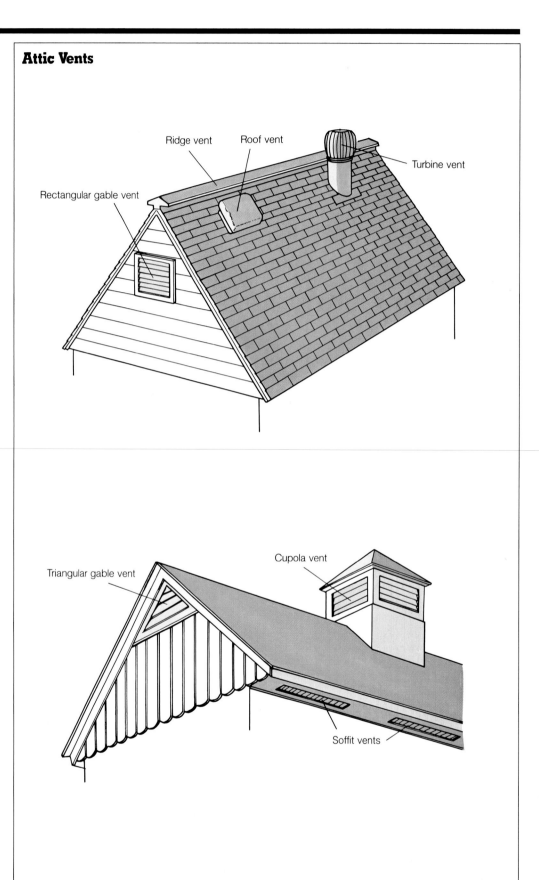

Ridge vent

Roof vent

Turbine vent

Rectangular gable vent

Triangular gable vent

Cupola vent

Soffit vents

layer at the beginning, there would be nothing for the first course to overlap. This starter layer is installed after the roofing felt, drip edge, and valley flashing are in place.

The easiest way to provide this starter layer is to apply a 7- or 8-inch-wide roll of mineral-surfaced roll roofing made especially for this purpose. Nail it along the eaves where the first course of shingles will go. It should overhang the edge by about ½ inch.

If you neglected to buy a starter roll or if it's your preference, you can use shingles as a starter course. Just cut the tabs off the starter shingles and install them top edge down so the upper edge overhangs the drip edge by about ½ inch. Be sure the joints in the starter course are not where the joints of the first course will be.

Shingling A Gable Roof

Before you start the first course, choose the shingle pattern you want. The three normally used are the 6-inch, 5-inch, and 4-inch patterns. The terms refer to the distance each shingle is offset from the one below it so the cutouts don't line up and allow water to penetrate. All these patterns will protect the roof equally well.

Whatever shingling pattern you use, the installation proceeds in the same manner. The section called Ridge Shingling (see page 126) tells how to finish the roof.

The 6-Inch Pattern

This is the easiest style to install and is the one shown in the instructions on most

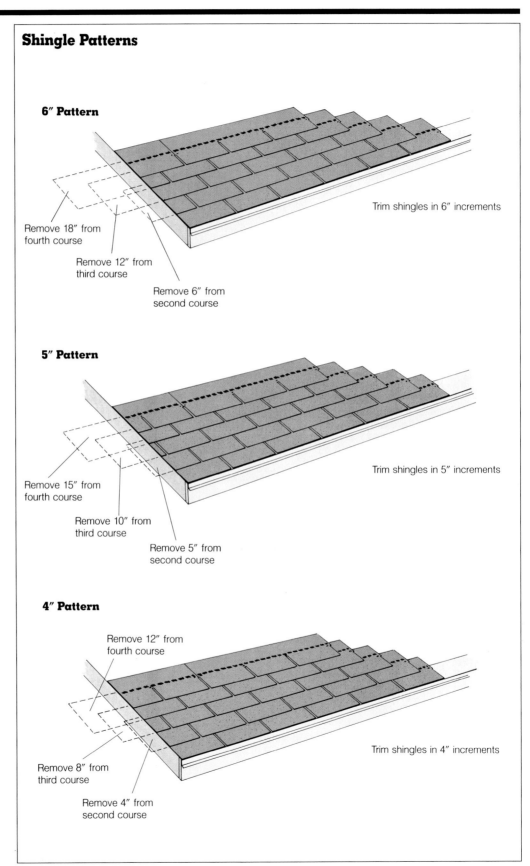

Shingle Patterns

6″ Pattern

Remove 18″ from fourth course

Remove 12″ from third course

Remove 6″ from second course

Trim shingles in 6″ increments

5″ Pattern

Remove 15″ from fourth course

Remove 10″ from third course

Remove 5″ from second course

Trim shingles in 5″ increments

4″ Pattern

Remove 12″ from fourth course

Remove 8″ from third course

Remove 4″ from second course

Trim shingles in 4″ increments

bundles of shingles. At the start of each course, you will cut off part of the first shingle, working in 6-inch increments. The remaining shingles in the course will be whole ones until you get to the end of the course. The resulting pattern aligns each cutout directly above another cutout in every other course.

The 6-inch pattern presents a problem that you must keep in mind. In roofs of 40 feet or longer, any misalignment of the shingles can be very apparent from the ground. Keep the cutout lines straight by snapping vertical chalk lines on the roofing felt to keep the shingles lined up all the way across.

Start the 6-inch pattern by nailing a full-length temporary shingle in the bottom corner. The bottom edge should overhang the eave by ¾ inch or so, and the side edge should be flush with the rake. If the rake edge has no flashing, overhang the shingle ½ inch. Put another temporary shingle at the opposite end of the roof and snap a chalk line between the top edges of the two. Remove the 2 temporary shingles. Nail the first course even with this line to make it perfectly straight.

Now cut 6 inches, or ½ tab, off the trailing edge of the first shingle in the next course. Use the hatchet gauge to set the proper 5-inch exposure at both ends of the shingle, and nail it down. For the third course, remove 12 inches, or a full tab, from the first shingle and nail it in place. Continue in this manner, removing 6 inches more each time, through the sixth course, where you will remove 30 inches, or 2½ tabs.

Carry each course partway across the roof, far enough to keep the pattern going. Start the seventh course with a full shingle again and repeat the process. When you get to the ridge, go back and fill in each course across the roof from the bottom up.

Do not attempt to start rows by alternating whole shingles and shingles with ½ tab removed—this is guaranteed to create a leaky roof. When starting each course, always remove an additional 6 inches. Save the cutoff pieces of shingle and use them as needed to fill out the ends of the courses where partial shingles are needed.

To keep the cutouts aligned vertically, snap a chalk line every 10 to 15 feet and on both sides of any interruptions, such as dormers or chimneys. The process of working around an interruption is described under the heading Making Neat Tie-ins (see page 126).

The 5-Inch Pattern

This pattern is widely used by professional roofers because the 5-inch increments are the same as the exposure. This so-called random pattern eliminates the problem of aligning vertical cutouts on long roofs.

Begin the first course, as always, with a full-length shingle. Start the second course with 5 inches removed from the trailing end of the first shingle. There is a trick to doing this work quickly. After the first shingle is down, put the second-course first shingle on top of it and use the hatchet gauge to move it 5 inches in the direction you are shingling. Grasp the overhanging portion

right at the rake edge, flip the shingle over, and cut it. Put the cut shingle back in place and use the gauge to adjust the exposure at each end and the distance from the end of the first shingle. Nail it down. Always set the shingle according to the hatchet gauge, not the cut end, which may be slightly inaccurate. When the roof is complete, you can trim the edge more precisely or cover it with a drip edge.

The third course is done the same way: Offset it from the second course by 5 inches, a total of 10 inches off that shingle. Continue in this manner through the seventh course, from which you remove 30 inches. Taking 5 inches off the eighth course would leave only 1 inch of shingle, so just start the eighth course with a full shingle and start the process over again.

Keep working up the roof, filling out each course only far enough to keep the pattern going. Cutting and laying shingles along the rake while you work up the roof is the slow part, but do it very accurately. When you reach the ridge, go back to the eaves and fill out each course, working from the bottom up.

After every 3 or 4 courses, check that your work is not drifting out of line. Do this by measuring from the bottom edge of the first course at each end of the roof up to any given course. The measurements should be the same. If one course has drifted, snap a chalk line to straighten the next course. Don't remove a crooked course unless it is radically out of line. When the roof is finished, it's not likely anyone will notice it except you.

The 4-Inch Pattern

This style is needed only on low-sloped roofs—roofs with slopes of 2 in 12 or 3 in 12. In these cases, instead of the standard 2 inches for extra protection against the wind blowing water under the roofing, overlap the roofing felt from 18 to 19 inches.

As with other patterns, start the first course with a full shingle. Then trim the first shingle in each successive course by 4-inch increments. Continue through the ninth course, from which you trim 32 inches. Then start the tenth course with a full shingle.

Shingling A Hip Roof

Begin by choosing the 6-inch, 5-inch, or 4-inch shingle pattern. A little more cutting is required to shingle a hip roof than a gable roof. Start in the low corner—left or right depending on whether you are right-handed or left-handed (see page 127)—and place a starter course and a first course as you would with a gable roof except cut the side of the shingle to follow the line of the hip. Start the second course in the same way you would start the second course of a gable roof except now you'll have to measure the 6, 5, or 4 inches from the break between 2 shingles instead of the edge of the roof.

Continue up the roof as described for the gable roof until you reach the ridge. When you have shingled all the sections of the hip roof, you now have shingles butting each other at the hips and at the ridges.

Hip Shingling

Since ridge shingles cover the top of the last hip shingle, the hip shingles must go on first. Either make your own hip shingles by cutting them from full shingles, which is tedious, or buy them ready-made. If you decide to cut your own, cut them as shown in the drawing below to get a really smooth fit.

Put the first shingle in place at the eave so the middle is at the corner of the roof and the corners of the shingle hang over the edge. Trim along the roof edge so there is a ½-inch overhang beyond the regular shingles.

Tack a temporary hip shingle into place at the top of the hip. Snap a chalk line between the edges of one side to keep the hip shingles straight. Remove the temporary shingle at the top, and apply the hip shingles from bottom to top along the snapped line. Place nails 1 inch from the edges and just below the adhesive line. Use the hatchet gauge to give each hip shingle a 5-inch exposure.

Do the same on all the other hips. Where hip shingles meet at the ridge, trim them so they meet smoothly, but do not overlap them. Now cut a ridge shingle up from the bottom about 4 inches. Lay it on the ridge so the top of the 4-inch cut is right at the beginning of the ridge and the bottom is over the hip shingles. Bend these tabs down to the hip shingles. They will overlap in the middle. Drive a nail through the overlapping pieces, and cover the nail head with a dab of roofing cement.

Cutting Hip Shingles

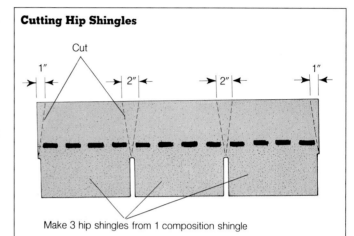

Cut

1" 2" 2" 1"

Make 3 hip shingles from 1 composition shingle

Installing Hip Shingles

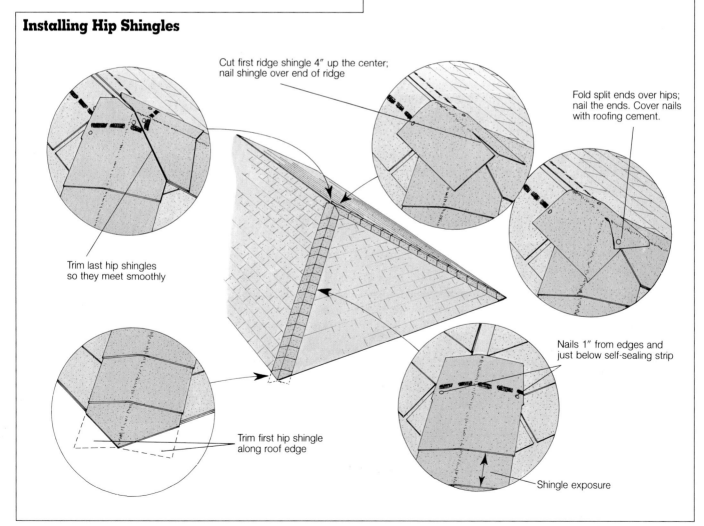

Cut first ridge shingle 4" up the center; nail shingle over end of ridge

Fold split ends over hips; nail the ends. Cover nails with roofing cement.

Trim last hip shingles so they meet smoothly

Nails 1" from edges and just below self-sealing strip

Trim first hip shingle along roof edge

Shingle exposure

Ridge Shingling

Generally, ridge shingles should be placed so the exposed ends are facing away from the prevailing weather. This means the first shingle you place should be at the lee end of the roof—the end away from the direction the weather comes. For either a hip or gable roof, put a ridge shingle at each end and snap a chalk line along one edge to keep them all straight. Use a 5-inch exposure and place the nails 1 inch from the edges and just below the adhesive.

Trim the top portion of the last shingle. Nail it securely at all 4 corners with 1½-inch roofing nails, and cover the nail heads with generous dabs of roofing cement.

Next to a vertical wall, such as a chimney or a dormer, use step flashing as described on page 140.

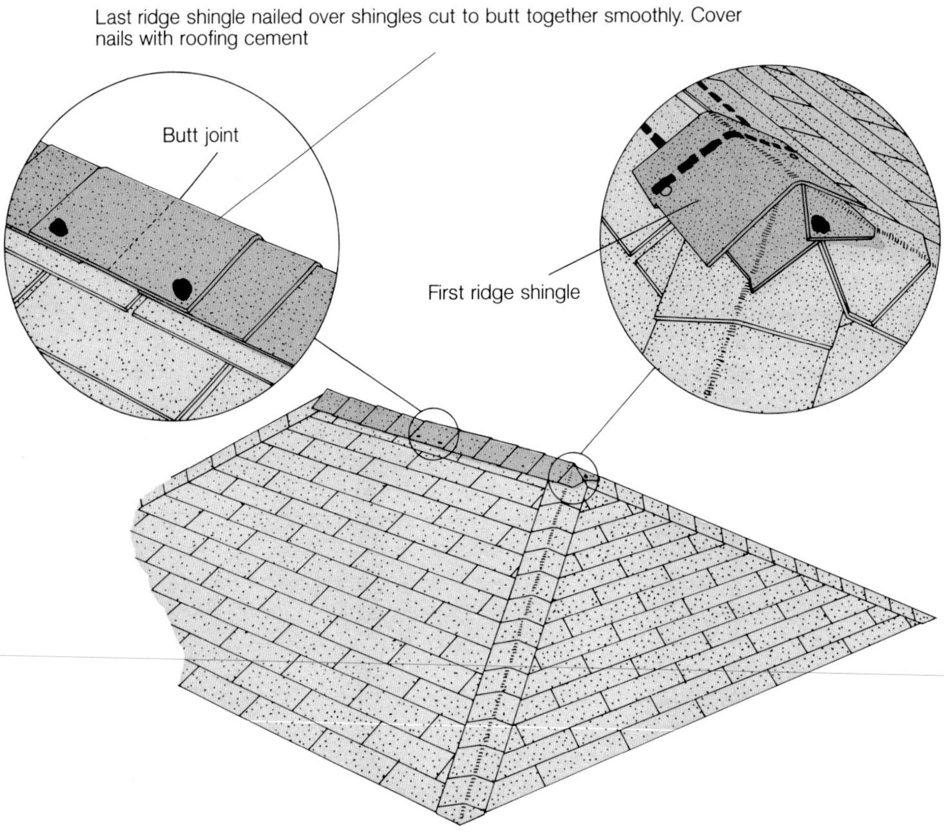

Making Neat Tie-ins

Making a tie-in means working around a dormer, chimney, or other roof interruption so that the shingles on and around the interruptions are vertically aligned with those on the rest of the roof. Tying in a dormer is the most difficult; tying in other interruptions is a similar process. Check the illustrations to see the differences.

Shingle up the roof toward the ridge. Lay the last course at the base of the interruption so that the shingles go past the dormer. Next, shingle the dormer roof. Then complete the valley on that side.

For the actual tie-in, lay the main-roof course immediately in line with the top of the

Installing Ridge Shingles

Last ridge shingle nailed over shingles cut to butt together smoothly. Cover nails with roofing cement

Butt joint

First ridge shingle

dormer roof to a point about 4 shingles beyond the far side of the dormer roof ridge. Just tack these 4 shingles at the top so the courses that will be brought up to them can be slipped underneath.

Continue roofing above this line of shingles all the way to the ridge. Now, using the cutouts of these upper shingles as guidelines, snap a chalk line from the ridge to the eave near

the far edge of the dormer. Move over 36 inches and snap another line. Use these chalk lines to line up the cutouts as you bring the courses up the far side of the dormer. Slip the tops of the last course under the tabs of the course you tacked into place earlier.

Generally, as you reach the far side of the dormer, you will have to cut each shingle an irregular amount so it fits against the side of the dormer wall and still lines up with the

chalk lines. The second chalk line 36 inches away is a means of checking your work.

It's a good idea to snap horizontal lines across the roof on the far side of the dormer to keep the bottoms of the shingles aligned, too. When measuring for these horizontal lines, measure from the first course you have already installed or be sure to add the amount of the overhang, if you are measuring from bare eaves.

Shingling Techniques

Whatever type of material you use, all shingling is hard, repetitive work. Always wear comfortable, loose-fitting clothing that won't bind when you bend and sit. Wear sneakers or other soft-soled shoes both for a firm grip on the roof and so you don't deform the composition shingles. Bending the shingles can be a real problem in hot weather.

Shingling is especially hard on the knees and the seat of your pants. For protection, cut a length of inner tube long enough to reach from waist to knee. Trim it so it slips around the leg you sit on and goes up your back. Cut slits for belt loops at the top, and attach it so your belt holds it up. Or purchase comfortable, ventilated kneepads.

Shingle Nailing

If you are right-handed, start shingling from the bottom left side of the roof. If you are left-handed, start on the right. If you are lucky enough to have a partner who is opposite-handed from you, you can both work together on the same roof with great ease and comfort. As you shingle, you will work up and in the direction of your favored hand.

By far the most widely used composition shingle is the 3-tab shingle. Each shingle is about 36 inches long with 2 cutouts that make each one look like 3 separate shingles when they are installed. Each end of the shingle has half a cutout that, when fitted against another shingle, forms a full cutout.

Fasten each shingle to the roof with 4 roofing nails. Place 1 about an inch from each end and the other 2 above each cutout. If the shingles have a self-sealing strip, place the nails just below it, not in or above the adhesive.

Wood shingles and shakes are always nailed down with only 2 nails in each shingle, regardless of their width. Place nails about ¾ inch from the side edges and 1 to 2 inches above the exposure—that is the distance from the bottom of one course of shingles to the bottom of the next.

This exposure, also called the weather, varies depending on the kind of shingles or shakes and the slope of the roof. Check the manufacturer's instructions for the ideal exposure for the roofing material you are using. Set the exposure evenly with the help of the gauge on the roofer's hatchet. Always check the exposure at both ends of a shingle or shake, especially with a wide composition shingle, to keep the courses straight. If, after you've put in 2 nails, you see that a shingle or shake is crooked, don't try to realign it or leave it as is. Remove it and nail it down correctly.

It is important that the first course be perfectly straight. To align composition shingles, let the first one overhang the drip edge by about ¾ inch. You can use the first joint of your index finger for a gauge. Place another shingle the same way at the other end of the roof. Now snap a chalk line between the 2 top edges and on it line up the top edges of all the shingles in that course. If you are not experienced at shingling, snap a chalk line every few courses to keep the shingles straight as you go.

For wood shingles and shakes, place 1 shingle at each end of the roof as described in this section. Press a tack into the butt edge of each, and stretch a string between them. Line up the bottoms of all intervening shingles or shakes on the string.

With all types of shingles or shakes, ensure straightness by measuring up from the bottom shingle on each end of the roof and snapping a new chalk line to align the shingles on. Do this every 3 or 4 courses.

Make sure that the nails you use at the exposed eaves and gable ends are short enough so that they don't poke through and show when you look under the eaves.

Tools for Shingling

The slowest part of all roofing is simply handling and driving all those nails. This process can be greatly speeded by using either a nail stripper or a pneumatic staple gun.

A nail stripper is a metal box that you strap to your chest. The box has a slanted bottom and slots so, when you put nails in the box and shake it, the nail shanks fall through the slots. You can then grasp a row of nails between your index finger and thumb, slide them out of the box, and they are in position to be driven one at a time—without further adjustment in your hand. Don't hold nails in your mouth. Just tap each nail once to start it, and again to drive it home.

The pneumatic staple gun makes shingling even faster. Just load the gun with staples. Then press it against the spot on the shingle where you want a fastener, and pull the trigger. Be sure to hold the gun perpendicular to the roof so the staple is driven in straight and not at an angle. You can rent a staple gun and air compressor at most equipment rental outlets.

Shingle Cutting

All shingles must be cut to fit properly around vents, along the rakes, in valleys, and beside flashing. Wood shingles should be cut with a circular saw for straight cuts and a saber saw, jigsaw, or coping saw for curves. Composition shingles should be cut with a utility knife or with the razor blade in the roofer's hatchet, if you have the kind that has one.

Always turn the composition shingle over and cut on the back side. Cutting on the mineral surface will quickly ruin your blade. Score the shingle deeply, then bend it until it breaks. Don't use a straight edge as a guide for each cut, or the work will go extremely slowly. Just eyeball the line you want to cut and cut it. Practice makes perfect.

![I]NSTALLING A SHAKE ROOF

Putting on a shake roof is somewhat more difficult than putting on a composition shingle roof; on a difficulty scale of 10 points, consider installing a shake roof an 8. It will take two people four days to cover a simple roof with wood shakes. Except for the ability to plan ahead, no special skills are needed.

☐ Tool belt
☐ Roofing hatchet
☐ Utility knife
☐ Compass or saber saw
☐ Hammer
☐ Steel tape measure
☐ Framing square
☐ Carpenter's pencil
☐ Chalk line
☐ Tin snips
☐ Putty knife
☐ Nail stripper
☐ Extension ladder

Preparing the Roof

As a natural product, wood shakes do not have the uniformity of composition shingles.

Before installing wood shakes, arrange the shakes according to their slightly different sizes so that you can place the sizes randomly—random placement will look better than having all the large shakes in one area and all the small shakes in another.

Shakes come in 18-, 24-, and 32-inch lengths and in medium and heavy grades.

There are three types of shakes: taper split, hand split and resawn, and straight split. The first two are thick at the bottom end and taper to a thin top. Straight-split shakes are of equal thickness throughout their length. These are not suitable for houses because the shakes are so bulky. As a general rule, shakes function the best on roofs with at least a 6 in 12 slope, particularly in wet and humid climates.

Common exposures for shakes are 7½ inches for 18-inch shakes, 10 inches for 24-inch shakes, and 13 inches for 32-inch shakes. These exposures provide the standard two-ply coverage. You will have a markedly better roof with three-ply coverage. This means giving a 24-inch shake a 7½-inch exposure and an 18-inch shake a 5½-inch exposure. The shorter exposures are more costly, but they are probably worth it in terms of the life of the roof.

Install wood shakes over sheathing (see page 115) and an underlayment of roofing felt (see page 118).

Before installing the roofing felt for a shake roof, nail a drip edge along the eaves and the rake. Then you will install 30-pound roofing felt. The first strip laid along the eaves should be 36 inches wide. All the other strips should be 18 inches wide.

If you can't buy 18-inch-wide rolls of roofing felt in your area, cut a 36-inch roll in half. Cut it while it is rolled by going around it using a portable circular saw with an old blade or a carbide blade.

Lay the first strip of 18-inch felt twice the exposure distance from the bottom of the starter course. If you are using 24-inch shakes with a 7½-inch exposure and the bottom edges overhang the eaves by 2 inches, then the bottom edge of the first strip of felt should be 13 inches from the edge of the eaves.

Wood-Shingle and Shake Nailing Pattern

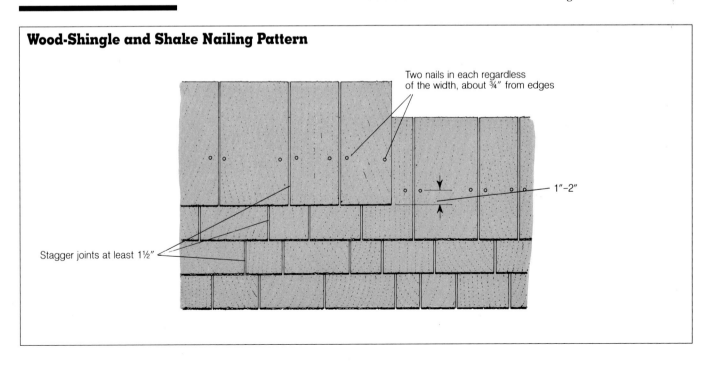

Two nails in each regardless of the width, about ¾" from edges

1"–2"

Stagger joints at least 1½"

The bottom edge of each succeeding strip should be 7½ inches up from the bottom edge of the previous one. Lay the last strip of felt at the ridge so it extends over the ridge to the other side. On a hip roof, weave the strips together in overlapped joints at the hips.

With a nail every 6 feet or so, nail the top edges of each 18-inch strip of felt to the sheathing. These will hold the felt temporarily, until the shakes are nailed down. Lay the felt for all the shakes you can install in one day.

Installing The Shakes

Position—don't nail—the starter course of wood shakes so each is ½ inch from the next and the bottom edges overhang the eaves by about 2 inches. Extend the side edges of the shakes over the rakes by ¼ to ⅜ inch. For a neat appearance, use shakes with straight, smooth edges for the rakes.

Before nailing, slide the top ends of the shakes under the 18-inch strip of roofing felt. You'll repeat this sliding-before-nailing process with each succeeding course. On a properly installed shake roof, from the top you see only shakes; from in the attic underneath you see only felt.

Be sure to maintain the ½-inch gap between shakes to allow for expansion. Place 7d galvanized or aluminum box nails 1 inch from each side and where they'll be 2 inches under the next course. The nails must be long enough to penetrate at least ¾ inch into the sheathing. If you split a shake, consider it 2 shakes. Separate the pieces

by ½ inch and nail each down with 2 nails.

Use the roofer's hatchet as an exposure guide. Mark the handle 7½ inches or 5½ inches from the head by wrapping a strip of adhesive tape around it. Joints in adjacent courses should never be closer than 1½ inches. No joint between 2 shakes should be directly above another joint less than 2 courses below.

As you near the ridge, lay 3 or 4 shakes vertically to check the exposure of the last course. If it will be appreciably different from the others, adjust the last few courses to bring it closer to the same exposure as the rest.

Check that the shakes are straight after every 3 or 4 courses. To do this, measure the distance from the eaves to the bottom of the shakes in 3 or 4 places along the course. If you find that the courses you lay are drifting, snap a chalk line

equidistant from the eaves for the next course to bring yourself back to where you ought to be.

The tops of the final 2 courses at the ridge will extend over the ridge. Just leave them that way until you are all finished with that side of the roof. Then snap a chalk line flush with the ridge, and cut off all of them at once with a portable circular saw. Adjust the cutting depth of the saw so it just cuts the shakes and doesn't penetrate the sheathing.

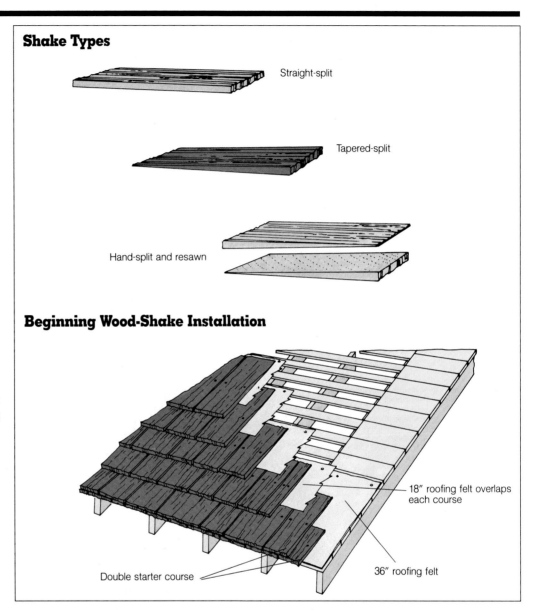

Shake Types

Straight-split

Tapered-split

Hand-split and resawn

Beginning Wood-Shake Installation

18" roofing felt overlaps each course

36" roofing felt

Double starter course

Installing Shakes

Valley Shakes

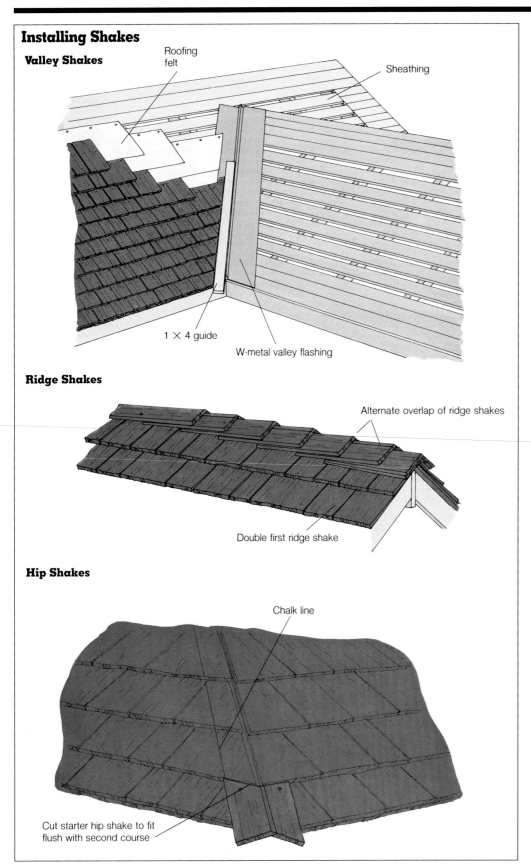

Roofing felt

Sheathing

1 × 4 guide

W-metal valley flashing

Ridge Shakes

Alternate overlap of ridge shakes

Double first ridge shake

Hip Shakes

Chalk line

Cut starter hip shake to fit flush with second course

Valley Flashing

Use 20-inch-wide W-metal to flash the valleys in the open way (see page 120). To keep the edges of courses straight, lay a 1 by 4 board in the valley, against the dividing ridge of the flashing. Trim the last shake in each course or the first shake when you start shingling the other side of the valley, so the shake fits flush against the board. This will provide an ample 7-inch runoff space between the shakes.

Because you are starting courses from the other side of the valley, you can mark the angle of the first shake and then cut all the other first shakes for each course. Try to select shakes of varying widths, mostly wide ones, so you can stagger the joints.

Shakes on Hips And Ridges

When coming up to a hip, you will trim the last shake in the course just as described for trimming the last shake next to a valley. Except, in this case, trim the top rather than the bottom. Or, if you want, let all the courses go over the hip a little and then cut them all with a circular saw as described for trimming the tops of shakes over a ridge. On the other side of the hip, mark and cut the first shakes for all the courses at once, just as you'd mark and cut for a valley.

The angled double shakes for hips and ridges are factory-made with mitered edges and glued joints. Install them so the mitered joints alternate from side to side. Hip and ridge

Installing Shakes Around Vents

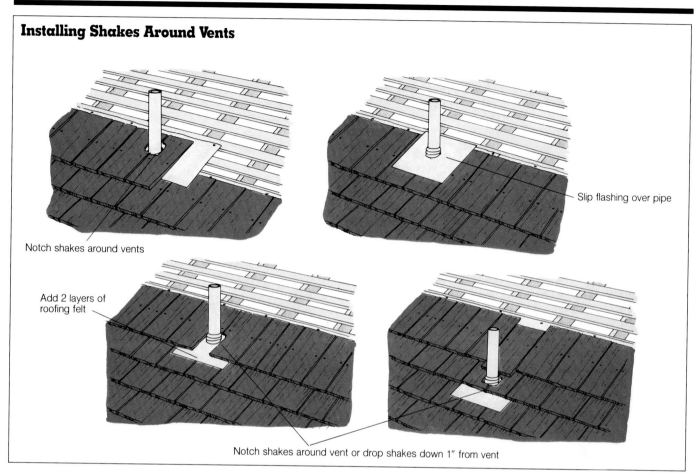

Notch shakes around vents

Slip flashing over pipe

Add 2 layers of roofing felt

Notch shakes around vent or drop shakes down 1" from vent

shakes must be attached with nails long enough to pierce the shake and penetrate the sheathing by at least ¾ inch.

When installing the mitered hip shakes, snap a chalk line from the edge of the first one to the edge of one put temporarily at the top. Use this line to align the edges. Put a double hip shake at the eave. For a smoother-looking job, trim the starter shake in a *V* so it fits against the bottom edges of the second-course shakes.

Then, put the first hip shake over the starter shake, and continue up the hip. Use 10d galvanized or aluminum box nails to secure the hip shakes.

At the top, trim the inner edges of the hip shakes where they meet each other and trim the tops flush with the ridge.

Shakes Around Vents

When putting shakes around vent pipes, lay the course to the pipe, then use a compass saw or power saber saw to cut a semicircle on each side to form a close fit. Slip the standard vent-pipe flashing over the pipe. Then cut 2 layers of 30-pound roofing felt to fit over the flashing, and extend it at least 1 foot above and on each side of the pipe. (See above illustration.) The course above the vent can be notched at the bottom as well or, if it is too far away to cover the joint at the vent, it can be dropped down to within an inch of the vent to cover the joint.

Next to a vertical wall or a dormer, use step flashing as described on page 140.

Exposures for Wood Shingles And Shakes

The exposures under 2-Ply Coverage are standard; those under 3-Ply Coverage cost more but provide a markedly superior, longer-lasting roof.

Material	Length (In.)	2-Ply Coverage (In.)	3-Ply Coverage (In.)
Shingles	16	5	3¾
	18	5½	4¼
	24	7½	5¾
Shakes	18	7½	5½
	24	10	7½

131

INSTALLING A PANEL ROOF

Aluminum and galvanized steel panels make excellent roofing finish for farm structures, small factories, and vacation cabins. Fiberglass panels, factory-treated to resist darkening by sunlight, are widely used for greenhouses and patio covers. Panels come corrugated and in various ribbed shapes. All are installed in a similar fashion.

□ Tool belt
□ Hammer
□ Handsaw
□ Power circular saw
□ Steel tape measure
□ Framing square
□ Combination square
□ Carpenter's pencil
□ Chalk line
□ Tin snips
□ Putty knife
□ Caulk gun
□ Extension ladder

Preparing the Roof

On a difficulty scale of 10 points, consider installing a panel roof a 6. Two people can put panels on a simple roof in a day. It takes no special skills, but the instructions—both here and those that come with the product—must be read carefully and understood thoroughly before you begin the project.

Lightweight and easy-to-install aluminum panels readily shed snow, but can be noisy in a heavy rain or hailstorm. Insulation reduces the problem to some extent.

The appearance of metal roofs can be improved and made less outbuilding-like by ordering factory-painted panels. Unfortunately, this nearly doubles the price and makes a metal roof almost as expensive as composition shingles. Fortunately, you have other alternatives. You can paint the roof yourself, but you must first clean the metal with muriatic acid. Or, you can let the roof weather for at least a full year and then paint it with an exterior-grade metal paint. For the most attractive metal roof, have one installed by professionals, using commercial-grade materials and standing-seam fastening techniques.

Panels for do-it-yourself roofing come in lengths ranging from 8 to 20 feet and from 24 to 48 inches wide. You can order them precut to whatever length you want. They are most easily installed on gable roofs. Cutting for hips and valleys is complex. If you must cut panels, use a Carborundum abrasive blade in a circular saw. Be sure to wear safety goggles when using a circular saw.

All types of panel roofing is nailed to 1 by 4 board sheathing installed in the open style (see page 116). Space the 1 by 4s either 2 feet or 4 feet on center, depending on the steepness of the roof. In heavy-snow country the roof should have a 8 in 12 slope at the least and sheathing boards spaced every 2 feet. Usually, no underlayment is needed under panel roofing, but check local codes to be sure. Closure strips, however, are necessary. Read the section that follows for details.

If your roof has valleys, install W-metal flashing on the sheathing (see page 120). Drip edges are not necessary.

Putting on The Panels

Because the panels come in so many different lengths—and you can order them to the exact size you want—you should be able to install a roof with no leftover pieces. For roofs that require more than one panel from eaves to ridge, order long and short pieces and then overlap them to fit. The overlap should be between 12 and 18 inches, with the longer lap used on shallower sloped roofs, say 4 in 12. For added protection from water and snow leaks through the overlap, you will place a thick bead of caulk under the bottom edge of the overlapping panel.

Place the first panel in the low corner, just as with other roofings. Allow a 2-inch overhang at the eaves and overhang the rakes by ¼ to ⅜ inch. The first panel must be placed perfectly straight and true to the roof. The others around it will interlock to it, so there is little tolerance for error.

The 26-inch-wide panels, when nailed to rafters placed 24 inches on center, allow for a 2-inch overlap on each side. Over sheathing board, put 4 nails across each panel over each board.

Aluminum panels are nailed down with aluminum screw-nails with a neoprene washer under the head. Using steel nails on aluminum roofs will cause a chemical reaction that will destroy both metals eventually. Use steel nails on a steel-panel roof. Always place nails in the ridge of a corrugated panel rather than in one of the valleys, where more water flows. Drive the nails so the washer is seated firmly against the panel but causes no indentation. Hex-head screws are also available for this job.

Steel and fiberglass panels are installed in the same way as aluminum panels but with one exception: Because the steel is too tough to nail through and because fiberglass shatters when nailed, you must predrill the nail holes.

Closure strips are pieces of wood or fiber material about 1 inch wide and up to 8 feet long or longer. These strips are flat on one side and, on the other, are cut in a wavy pattern to match the corrugation or other pattern in the panel. Place closure strips under the panels at the top and bottom to seal the weather out.

Hip and Ridge Caps

Hip and ridge caps are factory-supplied to match the roof-panel configuration. They commonly overlap each other by half a panel width and are simply nailed in place. Other factory-supplied pieces—rake and corner trim and pieces for flashing at walls and around chimneys and vents—are also available; you may want to install one or more specialty pieces on your building. Check with a building-supply dealer—and an agricultural building supplier—to learn about all the extra pieces and accessories that are available with each kind of roofing you are considering. In addition, ask for instruction booklets from the manufacturer of each type.

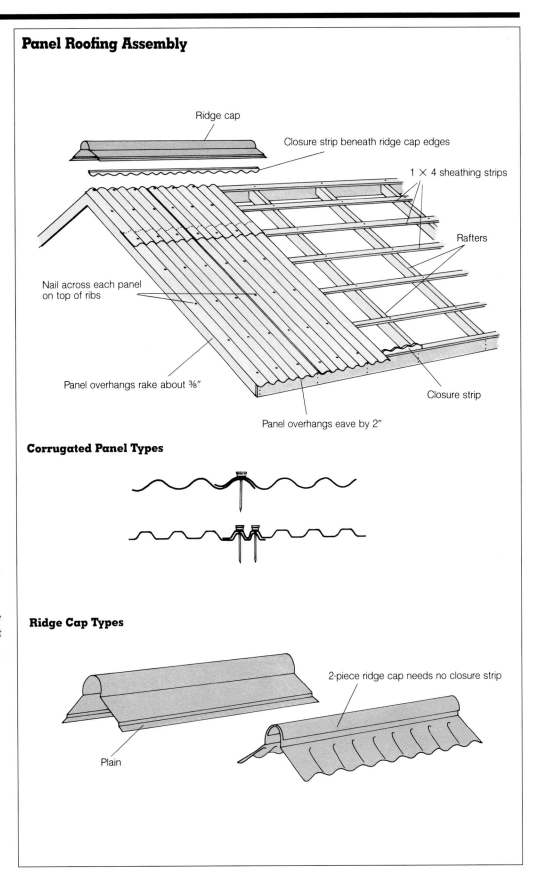

Panel Roofing Assembly

Ridge cap

Closure strip beneath ridge cap edges

1 × 4 sheathing strips

Rafters

Nail across each panel on top of ribs

Panel overhangs rake about ⅜"

Closure strip

Panel overhangs eave by 2"

Corrugated Panel Types

Ridge Cap Types

2-piece ridge cap needs no closure strip

Plain

INSTALLING A TILE ROOF

Clay tile is both expensive and heavy. Roof framing must be able to handle about 1,000 pounds for every roof square (100 square feet) covered in tile. However, recent innovations in concrete fabrication have reduced both the price and the weight of roofing tile.

- ☐ Tool belt
- ☐ Hammer
- ☐ Tin snips
- ☐ Power circular saw and a blade with Carborundum abrasive
- ☐ Coping saw and a blade with Carborundum abrasive
- ☐ Utility knife
- ☐ Steel tape measure
- ☐ Framing square
- ☐ Carpenter's pencil
- ☐ Chalk line
- ☐ Putty knife
- ☐ Extension ladder

Preparing the Roof

Tile is now widely made in lightweight concrete that weighs less than 700 pounds per square. This tile can be installed on a standard roof built to endure the weight of composition shingles.

On a difficulty scale of 10 points, consider installing a concrete tile roof an 8. It is more time-consuming than installing other roof finishes described in this book. It will take two people four days to cover a simple roof with tiles.

The instructions—both here and those that come with the product—must be clearly understood.

Concrete tiles come in a variety of colors and patterns. These make it possible to complement or match the siding of your house, and they work well with almost any architectural style. Roofing-supply outlets can give you catalogs, brochures, and lots of current advice on the kinds of tiles available. This information will include the weight per square and instructions on how you can install these roofs yourself.

This section will describe how to install one of the new flat concrete tiles that can mimic slate, shakes, or clay tile, depending on the color you choose. If in doubt about the weight your roof can support—even if you use the new lighter concrete tile—discuss the matter with the local building department before ordering.

Tiles cannot be put on a roof with less than a 3 in 12 slope without risk of rain blowing

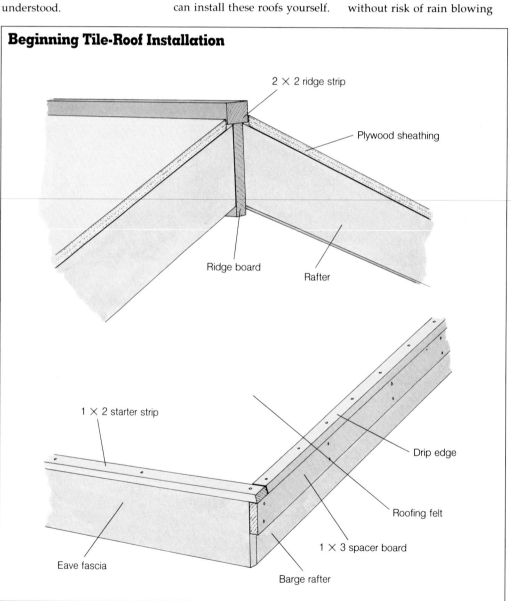

Beginning Tile-Roof Installation

2 × 2 ridge strip

Plywood sheathing

Ridge board

Rafter

1 × 2 starter strip

Drip edge

Roofing felt

1 × 3 spacer board

Eave fascia

Barge rafter

Continuous Flashing

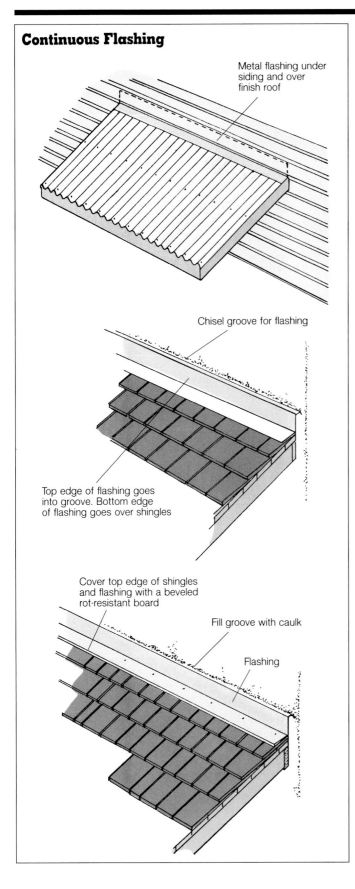

Metal flashing under siding and over finish roof

Chisel groove for flashing

Top edge of flashing goes into groove. Bottom edge of flashing goes over shingles

Cover top edge of shingles and flashing with a beveled rot-resistant board

Fill groove with caulk

Flashing

Installing Continuous Flashing

Use continuous flashing on vertical walls where a roof meets the front wall of a dormer, where a shed roof is brought up to a wall, or where a slanted edge of a panel roof meets a vertical wall.

For flashing to work, gravity must carry water from one surface to the next, always going downhill and always leading the water away from cracks or openings where it could get into the structure. In this case the siding of the wall must be over the flashing, and the flashing over the roof.

Often, on finished roofs, you aren't able to see the flashing where it meets a wall. This is because paint, a decorative piece of wood, or an extra course of shingles is on top of the flashing to hide it. But the flashing must go on top of the roofing for it to do its job.

Plan the last 2 or 3 courses of roofing before the wall so the last one, which will go under the flashing, will be as wide as possible—8 inches or so is best. The flashing referred to here is a continuous strip of aluminum or galvanized steel at least 10 inches wide. The metal must be bent in the middle to the exact angle made by the wall and the roof.

If you have several pieces of flashing like this, it is not too expensive to have the cutting and bending done by a sheet-metal shop. A shop has the tools to make the bends straight and perfect, without wrinkling the metal. A sheet-metal shop can also make other special pieces of flashing that are soldered or welded—for around skylights, for example (see illustration page 208.)

If you want to bend the metal yourself, use a couple of long straight boards. Lay one board on the sheet of metal with one edge in the middle, where you want the bend. Slip the other board under the metal and lift it so it bends the full length of the metal at once. This is sort of a trial-and-error process that might take you a while to get the hang of, but keep at it and you should get reasonable results. Be sure to wear heavy gloves when you do this; metal is sharp and unforgiving when you slip.

If the vertical wall has not yet been covered with siding, the job is quite simple. Put the roofing on the roof up to the vertical wall. Nail the flashing to the sheathing on the wall so it lies on the roofing, but do not nail the flashing to the roof. This allows the wall and roof to move or settle at different rates, without disturbing the flashing seal. Then put the wall underlayment and the wall siding over the top of the flashing.

If the wall is to be stucco, the flashing goes under the felt underlayment under the stucco. If the stucco has already been applied, bend the top ½ inch of metal flashing at a 90-degree angle. Insert this flange into a saw kerf cut into the stucco and caulk the joint thoroughly.

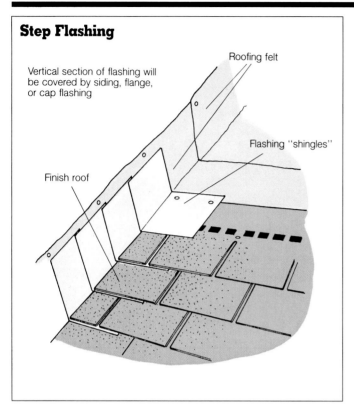

Step Flashing

Vertical section of flashing will be covered by siding, flange, or cap flashing

Roofing felt

Flashing "shingles"

Finish roof

Installing Step Flashing

Use step flashing where the slanted edge of a shingled roof meets a vertical wall, such as around the sides of a dormer, chimney, or skylight. For panel roofing, use continuous flashing where a slanted roof meets a wall.

With step flashing each course of shingles is protected by its own flashing "shingle" of metal. The metal pieces should be 10 inches wide and 2 inches longer than the exposure of the shingles. This lets the flashing extend 5 inches up the wall and 5 inches over the shingle it protects. This section will describe how to install step flashing with composition shingles, but the process is exactly the same for wood shingles or shakes.

You can make your own step flashing, have it made at

a sheet-metal shop, or buy premade flashing wherever you buy roofing materials. To make your own, cut the metal to size. Then cut 2 boards to a little larger than half the size of each metal piece. Between the 2 boards clamp half the metal in a vise, and, with a rubber mallet, hammer the metal over the board to form the angle required. It's much easier to buy step flashing premade.

As in the case of continuous flashing, roofing and step flashing must be installed before the siding is put on the wall. When you put the underlayment of roofing felt on the roof, extend it up the wall 6 to 7 inches.

To install the flashing, put the first piece on top of the starter shingle under the first course and place it so the bottom edge of the flashing is flush with the bottom edge of the starter course. Nail the flashing to the roof with 2 nails

about 1 inch from the top. Do not nail the step flashing to the vertical wall.

Next place the first shingle of the first course on top of the first piece of flashing so the bottom edge of the shingle is flush with the bottom edge of the flashing. Place the next piece of flashing on top of the first-course shingle so its bottom edge is 5 inches above the bottom edge of the first shingle; that is the amount of the exposure.

Place the second-course shingle over the flashing, flush with the bottom edge of the flashing. Continue in this manner so that each piece of flashing is just covered by the first shingle in the next course. The only places you should be able to see the metal, after the vertical tabs are covered by siding, are in the cutouts of every other course or so, depending on the shingle pattern you have chosen to use.

Flashing a Chimney

This is the most difficult and important part of flashing a roof, since many leaks originate around chimneys. Although a careful amateur can do it well, call in a contractor if you have any doubts about your abilities.

Most chimneys today are actually wood-frame boxes surrounding a metal flue pipe. Typically, these boxes are covered with siding to match the house. The boxes are flashed in the same manner as any other roof protrusion. Install a saddle at the bottom (see page 112), steps at the side (see above), and a cricket at the top (see page 112), all made from galvanized steel.

Traditional masonry chimney flashing consists of base flashing and cap flashing (also called counter flashing). The two overlap but must not be joined together, since the chimney and the house may settle at different rates. Start flashing the chimney as soon as you have installed the roof up to the chimney. If you are having a mason install the chimney, make clear to this person exactly where you want the flashing. This flashing is usually made of lead or galvanized steel.

If your chimney is wider than 2 feet or if you live in an area of heavy snow and ice, you will need to construct a cricket along the up side of the chimney. The cricket diverts snow and water that would otherwise freeze and build up behind the chimney and cause leaks. Framing a large cricket was described in the section about roof framing (see page 112). If you didn't frame the cricket when framing the roof, it must be done now. Cut the cricket from 2 pieces of ⅜- or ½-inch exterior-grade plywood. (See the illustration on page 141.) Nail the cricket pieces to the roof deck.

The next step is to coat the bricks all around the base of the chimney with asphalt sealant. Also spread roofing cement on the up side of the chimney where flashing will be placed. Press each piece of base flashing into the roofing cement. The sealant helps the cement adhere to the bricks.

Now fabricate a saddle or cut a piece of base flashing for the down side of the chimney, as shown in the illustration on page 141. Bend it as the dashed lines indicate so it fits around the chimney. Hold this piece of base flashing against the chimney and trace around it with a pencil. Cover the penciled area, including the shingles in front of the chimney, with roofing cement and embed the base flashing into it. You can hold the flanges in place by driving a couple of concrete nails through them into the mortar between the bricks. There is no need to remove the nails later.

Continue by placing step flashing alongside the chimney. Each piece of step flashing must be embedded in roofing cement, and the end of each shingle placed on the flashing must be embedded in the cement. Note how the first and last piece of step flashing is bent to fit around the chimney.

Now cut pieces to form corner-base flashing and cricket-base flashing. These pieces should fit around the back of the chimney and over the cricket, as shown in the illustrations. They must extend at least 6 inches up the side of the chimney. In addition, the cricket-base flashing should extend beyond the cricket and onto the roof behind the chimney at least 6 inches. Nail the cricket-base flashing to the roof.

If the cricket is large enough, say 2 feet or longer, and to be shingled, you don't need to make the cricket-base flashing. Just shingle the cricket as you would a dormer (see page 103).

Now comes the installation of the cap flashing. You will set it into the mortar of the chimney, 2 bricks above where the base flashing reaches, and extend it down to within 1 inch of the roof. Use a narrow cape chisel to remove mortar between the bricks to a depth of 1½ inches.

The first piece of cap flashing is put on the down side of the chimney. Cut and bend it. Then, along with some new mortar (which you've mixed according to the instructions that follow), fit the piece into the chiseled gap.

Cut enough pieces of cap flashing to cover the 2 sides of the chimney. Note how the first piece is part of the large front piece bent around the corner and how the last pieces on the sides are bent around to the back. Each piece should overlap the next by 3 inches.

Finally, cut and fit the cap flashing on the up side. Trim the bottom in an upside-down V to fit over the cricket.

Mortar

Cap flashing for a chimney must be held in place with mortar. Make the mix by combining 1 part portland mortar cement with 3 parts fine mortar sand. (You'll probably have enough with 3 cups mortar and 9 cups sand.) Put the dry ingredients in a bucket, add water slowly, and stir constantly. Continue adding water until the mix is just the consistency of thick whipped cream. The sand particles should be mixed so thoroughly that they are invisible.

Fill the joint and insert the flashing into the center of the space. Push it firmly into place. With your finger, smooth and press the mortar above the flashing.

After a couple of hours, wet the mortar with a fine spray; wet it again the following day. Keeping it wet will help it harden slowly and prevent cracking.

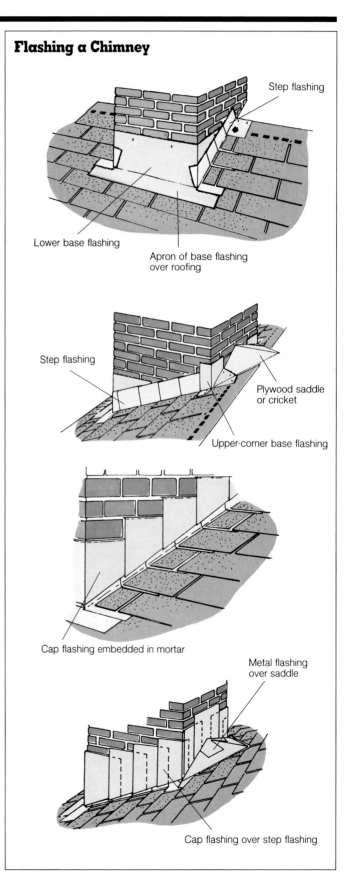

Flashing a Chimney

Step flashing

Lower base flashing

Apron of base flashing over roofing

Step flashing

Plywood saddle or cricket

Upper-corner base flashing

Cap flashing embedded in mortar

Metal flashing over saddle

Cap flashing over step flashing

INSTALLING GUTTERS AND DOWNSPOUTS

Gutters are installed on the eaves to collect runoff from the roof and channel it into downspouts that direct it away from the house. Without these, water can drip from the eaves onto people and gardens, causing bad tempers and soil erosion. Worse, water can saturate the soil and seep into the crawl space and through basement walls.

- ☐ Tool belt
- ☐ Hammer
- ☐ Screwdriver
- ☐ Handsaw
- ☐ Hacksaw
- ☐ Steel tape measure
- ☐ Chalk line
- ☐ Caulk gun
- ☐ Extension ladders
- ☐ Scaffold plank

Selecting Gutters And Downspouts

On a difficulty scale of 10 points, consider installing gutters and downspouts a 5. It will take two people (one to hold, one to install) one or two days to complete the project.

There are different styles of gutters and downspouts, but they all connect in a similar way and are mounted along the eaves in the same manner. However, some gutters and downspouts—those with a top flange or strap hangers—go over the roof sheathing but under the finish roofing and must be installed prior to the finish roofing. Some gutters and downspouts come prepainted.

You'll probably want to wait to install these until after the rest of the house is painted or mask them to protect them from paint splashes.

Gutters and downspouts are most commonly made from galvanized steel, aluminum, copper, or vinyl plastic. Copper and wooden gutters exist and can probably still be found, but they are expensive and probably used only by those who are trying to restore very old houses absolutely authentically.

Aluminum and galvanized gutters and downspouts are sold either factory-painted or bare, which allows you to paint them to match your house, if you wish. Vinyl ones come in a wide variety of colors.

Gutters and downspouts are sold in 10-foot lengths, which makes them easy to handle and transport. Longer ones can be specially ordered if you have a need. Gutter width is usually 4, 5, or 6 inches. As a general rule, for roofs of 750 square feet or less, 4-inch-wide gutters are adequate. Use 5-inch gutters for roofs up to 1,500 square feet; for roofs over 1,500 square feet, you'll need 6-inch gutters.

Gutters are sometimes half-round, but more commonly they have what is called a forged shape. Some are rectangular

shaped to resemble a simple fascia board. Downspouts are either round or square and are often corrugated, which gives them extra strength.

The gutter sections can be hung from the eaves with any of a variety of devices. Spikes, clips, and strap hangers are the three kinds of brackets most commonly available and used. Strap hangers provide the strongest support, but they must be installed before the roof is put on; it is virtually impossible to nail them to a completed roof without damaging the roofing material. Attach clips to the fascia board after it is painted (see illustration, opposite page). Drive spikes through predrilled holes in gutters and into fascia boards. Downspouts are secured to the side of the house with ¾-inch-wide straps and nails or screws.

Estimating Materials

Study the illustrations to familiarize yourself with all the parts and their names. No matter what style of gutters and downspouts you select, the parts and names are much the same.

First measure the length of all the eaves to calculate the number of gutter sections and supports. You will need 1 support for every 3 to 4 feet of gutter. Count the number of inside and outside corners and count the number of left and right end caps.

A drop outlet is needed for every 40 feet of gutter, so calculate the number needed. Usually, 3 elbows are needed for each drop outlet—2 to reach the side of the house and 1 at the end of the downspout pipe. If you have many levels

in your house, you may need more to go around them.

Count the number of downspout pipes needed and add a few extra in case some must be cut to use as connectors between the elbows at the top. Don't forget the straps for the downspout pipes—1 strap for every 6 feet of pipe.

Now count how many slip connectors you need to join the pipe. Remember: You don't need one where the gutter sections meet at corners or drop outlets.

Finally, add up the number of splash blocks or leaders you'll need under the downspouts.

Attaching Gutters And Downspouts

Gutters need to slope about 1 inch for every 20 feet of length. If you have a run of 40 feet or more, then slope the gutters from the middle of the run and put a downspout at each end. To lay out the gutter slope, tap a nail into the top of the fascia board at the high end of the slope. Measure the run and drop 1 inch every 20 feet. Tap a nail at this position at the other end. Between the 2 nails snap a chalk line to use as a guide while attaching the gutter.

Lay out all the components on the ground below the eaves. Measure the gutter runs and note the downspout locations. Then cut the gutters accordingly. If the gutters are unpainted metal or plastic, cut them with a hacksaw. Use tin snips on painted gutters to minimize shattering of the enamel paint. To steady the gutters while you saw, slip a length of 2 by 4 in the gutter about an inch back from the cut, then squeeze the gutter against the wood. Use a file to remove burrs from the cut edges.

Gutters should be installed by at least two people, if possible. One person supports the far end while the other person installs the gutter and its supports and works toward the holder. If you don't have a helper, hang the far end in a loop of light rope or cord at the proper level and work toward it.

When all the pieces are connected and secure, go back and seal each joint with caulk to minimize leaks.

Connect the downspout elbows to the drainpipe on the drop outlets by drilling holes on opposite sides and inserting sheet-metal screws. Do not use any more screws than needed—the screws catch debris and cause clogs. Connect the elbows to the downspouts in the same manner.

Bend the straps to fit the downspouts, then screw or nail them to the siding. The method is the same for all materials and styles of downspouts. Fit the elbows on the ends of the downspouts and put the splash blocks under them.

If you wish to carry the water farther from the house, attach a length of downspout to the elbow. This extension can be buried and run to a dry well, as the next section describes, to daylight, or to a storm drain if that's legal in your area.

Finally, put strainer baskets over the downspout holes and aluminum or vinyl mesh over the gutters. They'll keep out leaves and other debris that can clog the system. These items are available wherever gutters and downspouts are sold.

Dry Wells

If you think you might have trouble keeping roof runoff diverted from your foundation, you can install dry wells—one for each downspout. Dry wells are holes in the ground about 4 feet across and 4 feet deep, placed 6 to 10 feet or more from the house and filled with rock or gravel. Runoff from the house is directed into the dry wells, where it has time to seep deeply into the ground.

When you dig the holes, fill them with course gravel or stones and replace the sod on top. Bury a length of pipe from a downspout to the well, with just enough slope to ensure water movement—at least ¼ inch to the foot.

☐ Roof framing completed
☐ Exterior wall sheathing installed
☐ Chimneys and vents installed
☐ Roof sheathing installed
☐ Flashing installed
☐ Finish roofing installed

Installing Drainage Systems

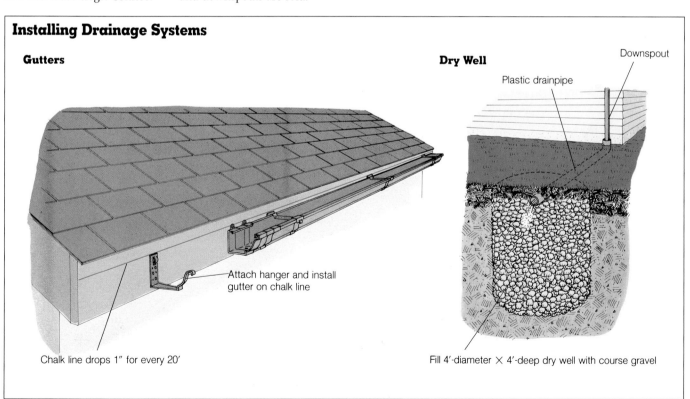

Gutters

Attach hanger and install gutter on chalk line

Chalk line drops 1" for every 20'

Dry Well

Downspout

Plastic drainpipe

Fill 4'-diameter × 4'-deep dry well with course gravel

UTILITY HOOKUPS, PLUMBING & WIRING

There are a few things you need to do regarding your utilities before you start building at all. Most important, you need to know that you have access to them. When you purchase your lot, verify the availability of electricity, natural gas, water, sewer, telephone, and cable television. If you are in an area without public systems, you'll have to make arrangements to supply your own.

This chapter explains how to install plumbing and electrical systems that will be connected to public utilities. It also details other systems you'll want to install at this point in construction: smoke alarms, intercoms, doorbells, and vacuum systems.

Although this house has the European look of solid brick, it is actually a wood-frame house with a brick veneer. The house has standard framing covered by plywood sheathing. A 1-inch space separates the sheathing and the veneer. Brick veneer should be professionally installed. The roof is an especially steep-sloped hip finished with wood shingles.

MAKING THE CONNECTIONS

There are alternatives to all public utility systems. You can use generators for electricity, you can use propane or solar power for heating water and for home heating, truck in water or drill a well, install a septic system for sewage, live without a telephone (unless you have teenagers, of course), and install a satellite dish or antenna for television reception.

☐ Your house plans
☐ Graph paper
☐ Tracing paper
☐ Straightedge ruler
☐ Architect's scale
☐ T-square
☐ Triangles (45 degree and 30/60 degree or adjustable)
☐ Pencils
☐ Eraser
☐ Templates for fixtures and appliances
☐ Drawing board or drafting table

Connecting to Public Utilities

Even if you have publicly provided systems, you still need to do some planning prior to breaking ground for your house. You must know the location of each utility to plan where it will enter the house. The hookup points should be indicated on the lot survey, if you obtained one when you bought the lot. If not, you'll need to check with each utility company to find the locations. Verify the locations on the site. The placement of hookups will affect foundation work because

you must dig the trenches for various lines. Later, you must know where these lines are to make sure you do not disrupt them with landscaping projects.

If you are in an area where the existing utility lines are a long way from your building site, you must arrange for the various utility companies to extend their services to your site. These extensions can be costly. Be sure to check all the costs of connecting utilities before you purchase the lot.

Look on the site plan and you'll find how and where all the utilities will enter your house. In most areas where you can build a house or summer cabin, the utilities are located in pipes under the street or road or on poles in front of the site. The typical site plan shows these public utilities by using specific kinds of lines and labels.

Your site plan probably includes a long dashed line labeled "Sewer Main" and, in the middle of the street, a dashed line with a "g" between the dashes labeled "Gas Main." Between the curb and the sidewalk, you may find a solid line labeled "Water Main," with a small box in it with the label

"W.M." for the water meter. Wire-fed utilities such as electricity, telephone, and cable television are most often on a utility pole (which, on the map, is labeled "P.P."), but they, too, might be in an underground conduit. If they are, a map label says so.

Also on the site plan you should find a note with an arrow on each utility line. The arrow indicates where your utility line will connect with the public utility line. The label probably says something like "E water line and N line connect here." The "E" means existing and the "N" means new. It could be even more specific, such as "Pole drop for TELE, TV, + ELEC underground. Stepped utility trench for SEWER, TELE, TV, + ELEC," with arrows pointing to parallel dashed lines. The labels "S," "T," "C," and "E" between the dashes show which line is which.

The business of utility connection is potentially difficult and confusing. Inspection must occur at several stages. You need to coordinate the utility companies; the building department; other government agencies; and, if you are hiring help, the contractor who will actually do the work.

On the site plan each utility line either ends with an arrowhead at the outside wall of the house or goes into the house or garage and ends in a box. This box or group of boxes is often referred to as the service entrance. Each metered utility—gas and electricity—ends in a box labeled "Gas Meter" or "Electric Meter." The meter or the arrowhead indicates where the utility company will bring its lines and where you start being responsible for them.

Most of the time the utility company is responsible for digging the trenches and running the pipe or cable to its meter. In the case of the sewer, you are usually responsible for actually connecting your sewer line to the public sewer system. The local public works department will probably give you specifications regarding how to do this, and it will inspect your work before you are allowed to fill in the trench.

You are responsible for digging trenches as necessary to run your water supply pipe to the water meter at the street. The water company runs the pipe to the meter and puts in the meter.

If electricity comes to you on power poles and you want the wires to run from the pole to a service head on your house, you must put up the service head. You put in your own service panel and run the supply line from it to a meter socket and then to the service head on your entrance mast. The power company then installs the meter and runs cable from the pole to the service head.

If your electric power service is underground or you want the wires to come underground from the pole to the house, you need a trench. Responsibility for digging it depends on how far away the utility hookup is. You usually have to do the digging on your property, and the utility company usually does the trenching on public property.

In the trench you will install the kind of conduit specified by the power company—the conduit is usually plastic pipe. Run it from the meter socket to the underground power source or

Air Chambers

Because water is not compressible, the force of it stopping quickly in a pipe can cause a loud bang and damage to the plumbing. To prevent these problems, some plumbing codes require air chambers, or cushions. Air trapped in a chamber compresses to cushion the shock when a nearby faucet or valve is turned off quickly. An air chamber is a vertical section of pipe on a supply line. It has a cap on top and is usually hidden within a wall.

The air in an air chamber will eventually dissolve in the water, making the chamber useless as a cushion. If your cushions must be put within walls or in other locations where they are not easily serviced, consider installing manufactured shock absorbers. These are made with inert gas and an internal bellows so they remain effective without servicing.

The Hot-Water System

A home hot-water system consists of a heater and a pipe system that sends hot water to the hot-water faucets. The heater is fueled by gas, oil, electricity, or the sun, depending on the fuel that is available in the area and your preference. Most heaters cannot heat water as fast as you can use it, so they have tanks in which to store a quantity of hot water.

A home water heater is generally available with a tank of 30 to 82 gallons. Gas and oil-fired heater tanks are usually 30 to 75 gallons. Electric heaters, because they heat water more slowly and have a longer recovery time, are made with up to 82-gallon tanks. In "rapid-recovery" electric water heaters, an upper heating element operates independently to heat the top quarter of the tank quickly. When the top part is heated, the upper element turns off and the lower element turns on to heat the rest of the water slowly.

The size of your water-heater tank should depend on how much hot water your family needs at the time of peak usage, usually the morning or evening, when everyone takes a bath or shower. Typically, the number of bedrooms in a house is used to determine the capacity of the water heater. For a one- or two-bedroom house, a 40-gallon tank is recommended; with three bedrooms, buy a 50-gallon tank; and so on. If you have several children, you may want a tank larger than recommended.

If your house will have the master bedroom on the opposite end of the house from the children's bedrooms or if your house will have a natural division between two or more areas where hot water is used, you might consider installing two or more small to medium-sized water heaters instead of one large one. This is being done more and more these days.

In large houses with long runs from the water heater, hot-water–pipe loops are becoming common. These loops contain a small pump, which runs continually, so hot water is always only a few feet away from any given faucet.

Pressure Relief Valves

According to the Uniform Plumbing Code (UPC), all water-heater storage tanks must have a temperature-pressure relief valve. This valve will relieve the pressure and thereby prevent an explosion if the thermostat on the heater malfunctions and the temperature or pressure inside the tank exceeds established limits. To properly install one of these valves, you must also attach an overflow pipe that directs any escaping water or steam outside or to a floor drain.

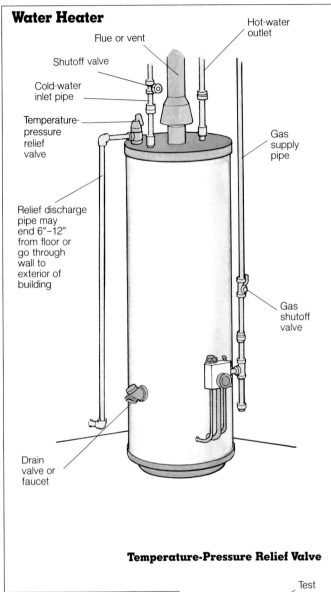

Water Heater

Flue or vent

Shutoff valve

Cold-water inlet pipe

Temperature-pressure relief valve

Hot-water outlet

Gas supply pipe

Relief discharge pipe may end 6"–12" from floor or go through wall to exterior of building

Gas shutoff valve

Drain valve or faucet

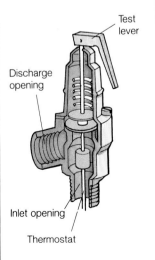

Temperature-Pressure Relief Valve

Test lever

Discharge opening

Inlet opening

Thermostat

Alternative Water Heating

If you've seen black panels on the tops of houses, you've seen one alternative to the tank-type water heater. The black panels are part of a solar system, an environmentally friendly method. There are other alternatives for heating water as well. Besides helping to save resources, these alternatives may also save you money on utility bills. You might still want a tank-type water heater, but you should be aware of what else is available.

On-Demand Water Heating

On-demand water heaters, also called tankless or instantaneous water heaters, are common in Japan and Europe. Because of the copper shortage during World War II, however, they haven't been used in the United States to any great extent. On-demand heaters have a heat exchanger similar to a radiator in a car. When the hot water is turned on, it runs through a grid heated by a large gas flame or heating coil. This type of heater heats the water only as it is used; the heat does not have to be activated periodically to keep a whole tank of water hot. Therefore, an on-demand heater uses up to 20 percent less fuel than a conventional tank heater.

The drawback is that the amount of water that can be heated is limited. If one person is taking a shower and another turns on the hot water in the kitchen to do dishes, the shower water may become cool very quickly. These heaters do come in very small sizes, though, so it is possible to have a separate one for each bathroom, the kitchen, and the laundry.

Solar Water Heating

If you are considering saving energy by using solar power in your home, water heating might be the best place to start. Even at its most complex, solar water heating is less expensive than active solar space heating. And since hot water is needed the year around, the cost is amortized more quickly, too.

Solar energy is also a great way to heat water for a swimming pool, if your new house will include this fun feature.

Combined Systems

Combining a couple of water-heating systems may make the best sense for your home. A solar water-heating system connected to a conventional tank-type water heater is a typical combination of systems. The water supply that would normally enter the water heater as cold water can be piped into the solar heating system first. When someone turns on the hot-water faucet, water is drawn from the solar storage tank into the gas or electric water heater. It's possible that more than half the heating has already been done by the sun—that much less heating needs to be done by gas or electricity.

Another way to save fuel is to use both tank-type and on-demand heaters. Have a tank heater that you set at a lower-than-normal temperature. Then use one or more on-demand heaters to bring the water temperature up as desired when the hot water is turned on. The flow of water through the on-demand heater will be greater than it would be if it had to heat cold water.

Check with solar heating stores or "alternative" building-supply dealers for information and advice on these economical methods of heating water.

Choosing Supply-Line Pipe

Supply pipes are made of copper, threaded steel, or plastic. The choice of material is a decision you'll have to make based on what is allowed in your area by the building codes, the cost of the pipe and the labor to install it, and your own preference. This book will give an overview of the advantages and disadvantages of each material and a general feeling of how to work with it. For actual step-by-step instructions on installing new pipe and fixtures, read Ortho's book *Basic Plumbing Techniques* or a similar publication (see page 345).

There are three basic ways to join pipe and fittings to each other and to fixtures and appliances. The first and probably most common is with threaded, or screw-together, joints. The second is with fused joints—that is, with soldering, welding, brazing, or cementing. The third is with compression joints. In a compression joint an unthreaded pipe and fitting are pressed together with a threaded nut.

Steel, brass, and copper pipe in standard, or schedule 40, thickness are almost always connected by threaded joints. Copper tubing and plastic pipe have some threaded fittings, but the pipe itself is almost never threaded.

Copper tubing is usually soldered or held together with compression fittings. Plastic pipe and fittings are almost always "welded" with solvent cement that melts the plastic and fuses them together. PB (polybutylene) plastic tubing is joined with compression fittings; it cannot be solvent-welded.

Thin-walled brass pipe, such as the 1¼-inch or larger chrome-plated drainpipe under your sink, is sometimes threaded but is usually held together with flexible-ring compression joints. If it is threaded, the threads are very fine and were cut at the factory—you can not thread this kind of pipe yourself.

Old-fashioned thick-walled copper and brass pipes have the same threads and fittings as modern galvanized steel pipe, but the old-fashioned pipes are rarely seen these days. Copper pipe is no longer available at all. Brass pipe is available but is so expensive that it is used only in small amounts for decorative purposes or to separate steel pipe from copper tubing to minimize the galvanic action that occurs when the two are used in the same system.

Steel Pipe

Galvanized steel pipe, often called iron pipe, has been used in more homes than any other kind of pipe. Almost all homes built prior to 1955, and many since then, have threaded steel pipe throughout.

Although the life span of galvanized steel pipe is usually considered to be 20 to 30 years, many homes built in the early 1900s have steel plumbing systems that are still being used. Most of these have had some parts repaired or replaced, but many of are still going strong.

Availability, relatively low cost, and long life span are the main reasons for using steel pipe. Its strength and ability to withstand bumps and pressure make it useful in hostile environments, too.

Steel pipe has a couple of drawbacks, also. Even though it's galvanized, steel pipe will eventually rust out. Another problem is that the relatively rough interior surface where the pipe and fittings meet provides a place for mineral deposits from hard water to build up. The buildup may eventually block the pipe altogether. The installation of a water softener can prevent this, but only in the pipes served by the softener. If you opt to run hard water to faucets used for cooking and drinking, the pipes that carry the hard water will tend to collect deposits.

If you plan on doing the plumbing installation yourself, there are other negative attributes to threaded steel pipe. You will need a number of tools and some skill to work with it. Thick-walled iron is very unforgiving because of its rigidity. You will need to be much more accurate in your measuring and cutting than with copper tubing or plastic pipe, which are more flexible than steel. If you cut a piece of steel pipe too long, you will have to recut it and rethread it. If you make it too short, you will have to replace it entirely.

Threaded pipe and fittings of all materials have standard

pipe thread whether they are threaded at the factory or hardware store or whether you do the threading yourself. In only a few places in a plumbing system will you find any deviation. Thin-walled brass tubing used for sink drains usually has a fine factory-made machine thread, compression fittings have machine threads like those on nuts and bolts, and faucets often have threaded ends. Kitchen and bathroom faucets are threaded for an aerator and outdoor faucets are threaded for a garden hose.

Pipe thread is unique in that it is tapered. It is cut at an angle, so the thread at the end of the pipe is smaller in diameter than the thread ½ inch up the pipe. The taper, which is about ¾ inch per foot, causes the joint to tighten as it is screwed together; the taper "seals" the joint.

Typical Code Requirements for Pipe Sizes

Codes specify the exact size of all drainpipes; the sizes are not minimums. The sizes of the fixture outlet, trap (outlet and trap must be the same size), and vent depend on the amount of water flowing through the fixture. Codes measure the flow in fixture units. The chart summarizes typical code requirements. Remember that codes specify pipe sizes in fixture units, not by fixture type.

Fixture	Fixture Units	Trap Size (In.)	Vent Size (In.)
Toilet	4	3	2
Washing machine	3	2	1½
Shower	2	2	1½
Bathtub	2	1½	1¼
Kitchen sink	2	1½	1¼
Washbasin	1	1¼	1¼
Kitchen or laundry	Varies	2	1½
Bathroom	Varies	3	2
Whole house	Varies	3 or 4	Total=size of main drain

Steel-Pipe Sizes

Galvanized steel pipe and fittings are manufactured in diameters from ¼ to 2½ inches. However, a hardware store or plumbing-supply outlet that caters to homeowners rather than contractors usually stocks only the sizes commonly used in houses: ½-, ¾-, and 1-inch items and sometimes a limited quantity of 1¼- and 1½-inch pipe and fittings. The 2½-inch size is not usually stocked but can be special ordered.

Pipe with threaded ends comes in standard lengths of 10 and 20 feet. Many dealers will cut lengths to order, but if you are putting in your own system, you'll have to get all the cutting and threading tools and do almost all of it yourself, on the job.

Copper Tubing

The price of copper tubing varies in its relation to the price of steel pipe because the price of copper on the world market is volatile. Even when copper costs more than steel, however,

using copper usually costs less than using steel, because copper is so easy to work with that the cost of installing it is low.

Copper is lighter than steel and is therefore easier to carry and put in place. Though the bore size of copper tubing and steel pipe may be the same, the tubing is quite a bit smaller on the outside. Copper tubing, then, needs smaller holes in studs and floors and less clearance for joints and fittings. Because flexible tubing can be bent around corners, it takes fewer fittings than steel pipe; the fittings for tubing are quicker and easier to install.

The tools needed to install a copper-tubing system cost far less than those needed to install a similar steel system. In most cases copper is more resistant to corrosion than steel, so you have much less trouble with rusting out. And, because copper tubing and joints are smooth inside, they are not as prone to mineral buildup.

Another attribute of copper tubing that can save you money is its superior water-carrying capacity. Because of the interior smoothness of both the tubing and the fitting connections, you can often use copper tubing one size smaller than the steel pipe to accommodate the same water flow.

The fittings for copper tubing are similar in most ways to those for steel pipe. The tubing, however, requires fittings called adapters to connect to the ends of threaded pipes or fittings.

Copper-Tubing Sizes

Two kinds of copper tubing are available. Soft tubing, which is easily bent, comes in 60-foot coils. Hard tubing is rigid and, just like steel pipe, must have elbow fittings to turn corners. Hard tubing comes in lengths of 10 and 20 feet.

Copper tubing comes in the same sizes as iron pipe—from ¼ to 2½ inches in diameter. The actual outside diameter (OD) of the tubing is ⅛ inch larger than the nominal size, and the inside diameter (ID) varies with the thickness of the tube wall. Copper tubing for supply lines comes in three tube wall thicknesses: K, L, and M. K denotes the thickest size; L, the medium size; and M, the thinnest size. Unless the local building or plumbing code specifies otherwise, M is usually considered adequate for residential water systems within the house.

Plastic Pipe

Not all building codes allow plastic pipe. If it is permitted in your area, plastic is a good material to choose for an owner-builder installation. Plastic pipe is lighter to move and easier to join than any of the metal pipes. To join plastic, you don't need expensive special tools or have to use a potentially hazardous flame or molten metal. Plastic pipe is joined by using solvent cement or compression fittings, and the resulting joints are just as permanent and watertight as those on any metal pipe. Plastic pipe is much less expensive than metal pipe.

Plastic can be cut with almost any saw or a tubing cutter. The flexible plastic pipe can be cut with a knife. Because plastic is chemically and electrically inert, it can be used with fixtures or appliances of any metal—without the threat of galvanic action. Plastic will not rust or corrode and, because it is smooth inside, will not collect mineral deposits as readily as iron.

Opinions vary as to the long-term quality of plastic pipe. Some say plastic would melt or burn in a fire, others say it hasn't been around long enough to be proven, and still others say labor unions oppose it on the grounds that it takes fewer hours to install and hence provides fewer jobs. In any case, if the local code prohibits plastic pipe, don't use it. The building inspector will make you remove it all and replace it with pipe that does meet the code.

Plastic pipe has other disadvantages, too. Unlike iron pipe, plastic pipe and fittings cannot be used to support the weight of a fixture. What's more, plastic expands considerably and tends to soften; if not properly supported, it can sag when exposed to hot water over an extended period. Closely spaced and loose-fitting supports solve this problem satisfactorily. Like copper, plastic must be protected from mechanical damage, such as that caused by errant nails and heavy objects.

Plastic pipe commonly used for supply lines is made from one of three kinds of plastic: PVC (polyvinyl chloride), CPVC (chlorinated polyvinyl chloride), and PB (polybutylene). PVC and CPVC are rigid, white or sometimes pastel-colored plastics. CPVC is the newer of the two and is the best when you want plastic hot-water pipes. It can also be used for cold-water pipes.

The newest member of the group is PB pipe. It is flexible, black or dark gray, and more costly than the others. It cannot be joined with solvent cement; it requires compression fittings. PB is now used mostly in irrigation systems and by gas and water companies for service mains. It is not well known or readily available for residential use, but it is rapidly gaining acceptance for this purpose because of its flexibility and strength. It has good heat resistance and is approved in many areas for hot-water lines.

Plastic-Pipe Sizes

Plastic pipe comes in all the same nominal sizes as iron and copper pipe. Adapter fittings connect plastic pipe to metal fittings and the metal fittings of fixtures and appliances. The same fittings are available for plastic as for metal pipe.

The DWV System

At the end of the water supply pipes are fixtures or appliances where the water is used. The system that carries the used water away is the waste-water drainage system or, as it is called in the trade, the drain-waste-vent (DWV) system. Because of the nature of the household and body wastes in waste water and soil water, more than just drainpipes are needed to take this water away.

Waste materials contain large amounts of bacteria and other microbes, both beneficial and harmful varieties. Anaerobic bacteria, which live in an environment without free oxygen, thrive in human digestive tracts. When these bacteria are in septic tanks and sewer lines, they produce a foul-smelling, poisonous, and flammable mixture of gases commonly called sewer gas. This gas must be kept out of homes.

To prevent sewer gas and other pests and contaminants from coming up the drainpipes and into homes, DWV systems include traps. A trap is a U-shaped curve in a pipe or fitting that remains filled with water at all times. Sewer gas and most other things cannot get past the water to come into the house through the drains.

Each time you empty a sink or flush a toilet, the water in the traps is also flushed away and new water takes its place. This means, theoretically, that the dirty water isn't in the trap long enough to grow large colonies of bacteria.

To get rid of the sewer gas and to prevent the siphoning of water out of the traps, all house drain systems have vents. Vent pipes come off drains downstream of the traps and go up through the roof. Sewer gas passes up the vents

Water Supply and Drain Systems

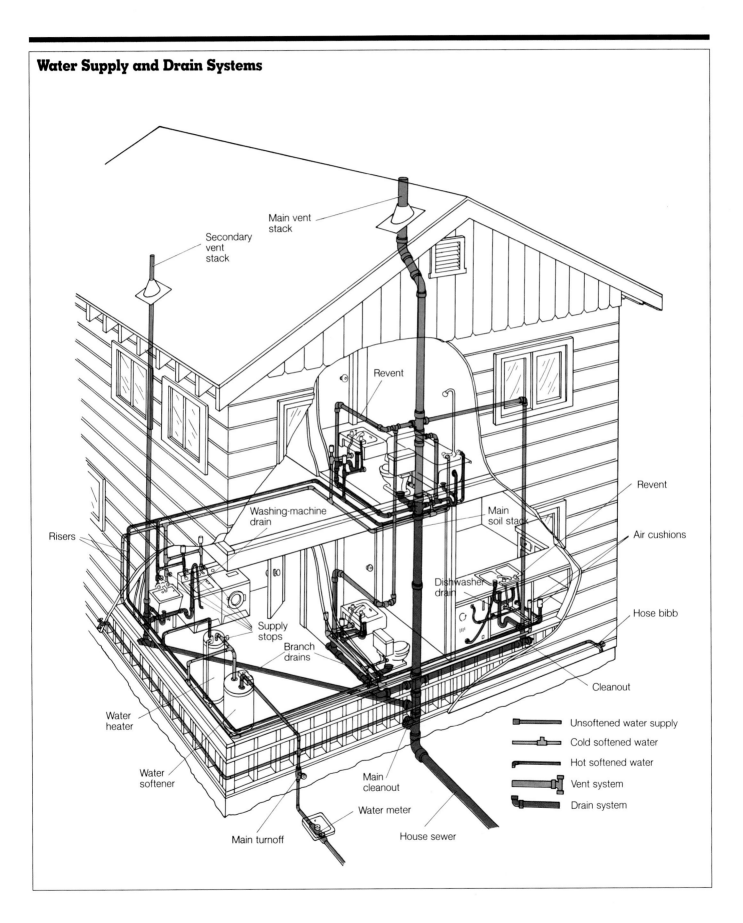

Main vent stack

Secondary vent stack

Revent

Washing-machine drain

Risers

Main soil stack

Revent

Air cushions

Dishwasher drain

Supply stops

Hose bibb

Branch drains

Cleanout

Water heater

Unsoftened water supply

Cold softened water

Hot softened water

Vent system

Drain system

Water softener

Main cleanout

Main turnoff

Water meter

House sewer

This table cites the maximum distance allowed from a fixture of a certain diameter to a vent stack. Local codes may vary.

Diameter	Distance to Vent
1½"	4½'
2"	5'
3"	6'

and disperses harmlessly into the air. When water flows down the drain, air is sucked down the vents and into the drainpipes, equalizing the air pressure on each side of the traps. This prevents the water in the trap from being siphoned out and sewer gas from entering the house.

Since all drains are subject to clogging from time to time, you must always provide them with cleanouts. These are Y or T fittings with screw-on covers that give you or a plumber a place to insert rods or augers to dislodge the clogs.

Drainpipes

Drainpipes differ from water supply pipes in at least two important ways: Drainpipes are larger and their content flows at lower pressure, usually by gravity alone. The smallest drainpipes in the house—probably the ones coming from bathroom washbasins—are never smaller than 1¼ inches in diameter; most building codes state a preference for 1½ inches. The smallest drain from a toilet is 3 inches in diameter.

Metal drainpipe 2 inches or less in diameter is usually made of galvanized wrought iron, galvanized steel, cast iron, or copper tubing. Most building codes now allow plastic pipe

for DWV systems in single-family homes, but there are usually some restrictions.

The DWV system in a house is arranged like a tree. The smallest branches are near the top. These small pipes always flow into pipes the same size or larger. The larger pipes flow into even larger pipes, until they all flow into the soil stack, building drain, and building sewer—the largest pipes in the system. The sizes of all these pipes are specified in the building code. A typical arrangement of pipes is shown in the illustration on page 155.

Drainpipe Sizes

Unlike some specifications in the building code, pipe sizes are not minimum sizes. You must use the sizes specified—not larger or smaller sizes. The mathematics used to specify pipe sizes for gravity drainage prescribes sizes that are just right for the job.

Pipe that is too small won't allow the proper amount of material through and may clog or unduly retard the flow. Not so obviously, horizontal drainpipe that is too large is also undesirable because it results in slower movement of the

waste through the pipe. This slower speed reduces scouring action and lets heavier particles settle. In addition, the greater thermal mass of the larger pipe causes greater cooling and solidifying of grease. All these things contribute to the possibility of clogging. Finally, larger pipe adds unnecessarily to cost, whether the pipe is horizontal or vertical.

The proper-sized pipe provides enough capacity to prevent backups; promotes the scouring action of swift movement; and avoids siphoning sewer gas into the house by allowing enough vent air to enter the system. For drainpipe, the proper-sized pipe is almost always the smallest permitted by the code.

Besides making the drainpipe smaller, there is another way to increase the velocity of the waste within the pipe: by increasing the slope of the horizontal parts of the system. Codes require that horizontal branches slope ¼ inch per foot. In practical application this slope varies from ⅛ to ½ inch per foot. Of course, the more slope, the faster the water flows. If you increase the slope of a fixture drainpipe, be careful not to make the outlet from an unvented length of pipe lower than the bottom of the fixture trap it serves. If it is lower, it is likely to siphon the water from the trap.

The Vent System

Building codes require a vent system that is arranged and sized to provide the best possible pressure and suction relief for each fixture in the system. Systems that don't follow the code may have back-pressure

problems: sinks that drain too slowly, toilets that need several flushes to get rid of all their contents, and first-floor fixture traps that allow sewer gas to enter the house when an upstairs toilet is flushed.

A poor vent system can also allow too much negative pressure (suction), which siphons the water from traps, or positive pressure, which forces bubbles of sewer gas through the liquid in the traps (blowback). Either way, the smell is undesirable.

Vent-Pipe Sizes

Vent pipes cannot be smaller than the sizes required by the code. The sizes are based on the kind of fixture, the diameter of the drain being vented, and the length of the vent pipe. For each dwelling unit, most codes require a 3-inch or 4-inch main stack extending through and above the roof, or equivalent smaller vents. If you have a usable attic, you probably want to combine vents so that just one or two larger vents stick through the space. The diameter of an individual vent can never be less than 1¼ inches or less than one half the diameter of the drain it serves, whichever is larger.

Traps

Building codes everywhere require that each fixture connected to the household drain system have a water-seal trap. Some fixtures—toilets and bidets, for example—have built-in traps as an integral part of the fixture. The trap most commonly used in the home is the

Cleanouts

Stack

Cleanout

House drain

Stack

Cleanout

House drain

P-trap. It's called a P-trap because to some people it looks like the letter *P*. It is used on sinks, wash trays, and all other fixtures that do not have their own built-in traps.

Building codes contain many restrictions about traps because they are so important in protecting health. The following restrictions appear in almost every code.

• Traps must be self-cleaning—that is, smooth inside so hair, lint, and other material cannot be caught and retained.

• No trap can depend on moving parts for its seal.

• No trap outlet can be larger than the fixture drain it serves.

• Each trap must have a water seal not less than 2 inches and not more than 4 inches in depth.

• To prevent siphoning, all traps must be installed level in relation to their water seals.

• Almost always, each plumbing fixture must have its own trap. A notable exception is a double sink, in which case adjacent units can be connected to a single trap.

• No fixture can be double-trapped. A toilet with an integral trap, for instance, cannot be connected to another trap.

Consult with a plumbing supplier, licensed plumber, or local building department for advice on the requirements for traps in your area.

Cleanouts

In recognition of the importance of accessible cleanouts, all building codes now require cleanouts in all new construction. The requirements regarding location, size, and minimum distance between cleanouts are all spelled out very specifically in the local code. The list that follows presents specifications from representative codes.

• A cleanout is required where the house sewer crosses the property line or connects to the public sewer. This cleanout allows the cleaning of stoppages that may occur in the public sewer. It also provides a place where tests can be performed on the entire house system.

• Some codes require and others allow a cleanout within 5 feet of the outside of the house.

• Accessible cleanouts are required on all horizontal drain lines and where a change of more than 45 degrees occurs in the direction of the drain.

• A cleanout is required at the base of all stacks.

• All cleanouts must have at least 18 inches of clearance

around them to allow the access of cleaning rods, snakes, and other tools.

Codes often define the roof vent of a one-story house to be the cleanout for the stack it serves. Certain requirements involving pipe sizes and changes in direction must be met for this to be the case, however. Before using a roof vent in this way, be sure to check the local code for pertinent details and discuss the matter with the building department.

Drainage From Below Sewer Level

Homeowners occasionally want to install wash trays; a washing machine; or even a whole bathroom, including a sink and toilet, in a basement area. In these cases sometimes it is necessary to dispose of waste water that accumulates below the main sewer line.

In some situations the problem can be solved by lowering the house sewer line, providing it can be joined to the public sewer at a point farther downstream. This usually requires obtaining an easement from neighbors to run the house sewer line across their property.

An easier solution is to install a sewage ejector or

up-flushing toilet to remove waste water from basement fixtures.

In some areas building codes allow single-unit up-flushing toilets. These toilets usually depend on high water pressure, 40 pounds per square inch or more, to break up the solids into small pieces and siphon them upward to an overhead drain line. Up-flushing toilets are fairly easy to install yourself. They come with complete, illustrated instructions that must be followed exactly.

A sewage ejector is a special tank with a pump inside. Material from a regular toilet is flushed into the tank and then pumped up, as much as 10 feet or so, to the sewer line. You may find that it is more convenient to walk upstairs to the bathroom than to pay for this installation, however. The cost of a toilet, the ejector, and all the pipe and fittings can be five or six times that of a medium-priced toilet alone—even if you do all the installation yourself. And having a plumber install it, would cost even more.

Typical Pipe Sizes

This table cites the pipe sizes usually found in most bathrooms.

Fixture	Fixture Units	Drain-pipe (In.)	Vent Pipe (In.)	Supply Pipe (In.)
Bathtub	2	1½	1¼	½
Washbasin	1	1¼	1¼	⅜
Shower	2	2	1¼	½
Toilet	4	3	2	⅜

ROUGHING-IN THE PLUMBING

Now that you know all the components your plumbing system will have and you've studied the plans to see where they all go, you can actually get started installing them. Installing plumbing is done in two stages: rough plumbing and finish plumbing.

Providing Plumbing Access

At this point in the building process you will rough-in the plumbing. This stage involves installing all the plumbing systems under and within the walls of the house. The second stage consists of installing finish plumbing, which involves installing fixtures and fittings. It may seem patronizing to tell you that the installation is fundamentally simple, but the fact remains: It is simple! One person can do the rough plumbing outlined in this section. On a difficulty scale of 10 points, consider roughing-in the plumbing a 5. The skills involved include thinking, planning, and being able to understand all codes and regulations. You must be able to measure accurately, have basic carpentry skills, and use special plumbing-installation tools.

Installing rough plumbing includes connecting the supply lines up through the stubouts, the drain lines for the toilet flanges, and the stubouts for drains. You can install some of the finish plumbing fixtures—including

☐ Round-tipped shovel
☐ Square-tipped shovel
☐ Pickax or maddock
☐ Tool belt
☐ Framing hammer
☐ Handsaw
☐ Power circular saw
☐ Reciprocating saw
☐ Power drill and bits
☐ Brace and bits
☐ Steel tape measure
☐ 24-inch level
☐ Combination square
☐ Framing square
☐ Carpenter's pencil
☐ 10- or 12-inch crescent wrenches
☐ Screwdrivers

For Threaded Pipe
☐ 2 or 3 pipe wrenches
☐ Pipe vise
☐ Pipe cutter, pipe reamer, and pipe threader
☐ Joint compound or tape with Teflon nonstick coating

For Copper Pipe
☐ Tubing cutter
☐ Tubing bender
☐ Propane torch
☐ Solder and flux
☐ Emery cloth
☐ Steel wool
☐ Wire brush for tubing

For Plastic Pipe
☐ Hacksaw and miter box
☐ Tubing cutter
☐ Utility knife
☐ Solvent cement
☐ Sandpaper

Sewer Line Under Foundation Forms

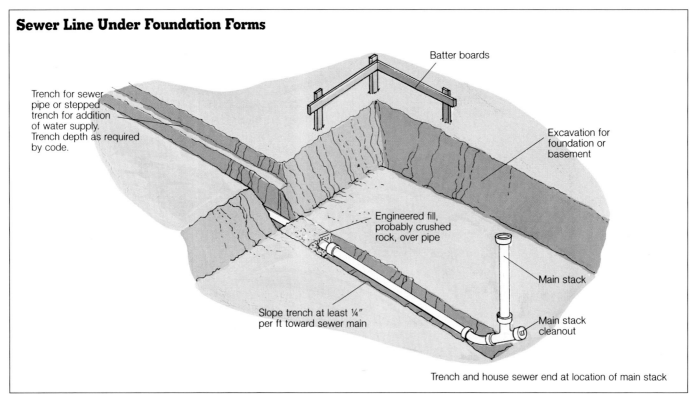

Batter boards

Trench for sewer pipe or stepped trench for addition of water supply. Trench depth as required by code.

Excavation for foundation or basement

Engineered fill, probably crushed rock, over pipe

Main stack

Slope trench at least ¼" per ft toward sewer main

Main stack cleanout

Trench and house sewer end at location of main stack

bathtubs, bathtub-shower valves, shower pans, prefabricated showers, and prefabricated bathtub-shower units—at this point as well. Installing these fixtures is detailed in a later chapter. If you choose to install fixtures now, be sure to protect them from the rigors of the remainder of the construction.

The first stage of rough plumbing is dealing with access. See the illustrations for methods of pipe access through and under a perimeter foundation wall. Be sure you make arrangements for this access when you plan, form, and pour the foundation.

The water supply pipe is connected to the meter. It runs under the foundation and into the basement or crawl space. Under the foundation you should have dug a trench for the pipe and provided a protected access hole for it.

Installing pipes in new construction is a matter of doing the various jobs in the right order and making sure that the framing accommodates the piping and fixtures. If you carefully plan your work, you should be able to proceed through the whole thing in an easy step-by-step manner.

Choosing the Pipes

Carefully choose the kind and size of pipe you will use for each part of the installation. For the DWV system use acrylonitrite-butadine-styrene (ABS) pipe because it's so easy to work with. The size of DWV pipe is regulated according to fixture units (1 fixture unit represents a waste flow of 1 cubic foot per minute). The main drain should be 3 or 4 inches in diameter and most branch drains 1½ or 2 inches. Although the table on page 157

lists pipe sizes according to the National Plumbing Code, you should check local codes as well. Use the smallest size the code allows. The local code also sets a maximum length for the drainpipe run from fixture to stack. The length depends on pipe diameter.

The size of the vent pipe is determined by the maximum fixture unit load, length of pipe, type of fixture, and diameter of the soil or waste stack the vent pipe serves. Again, check the local codes for specifics. As a rule of thumb, the diameter of a vent cannot exceed the main drain diameter. The vent diameter cannot be less than 1¼ inches or less than half the diameter of the drain it serves, whichever is larger.

Installing Under-Floor Pipes

After the foundation is complete and the girders are in place, measure carefully to find where the soil stack and other drain and supply lines need to come up through the floor. When you install the floor joists, make sure you know where the bathrooms, laundry, and kitchen will be. Then install double joists and close parallel joists where necessary to support showers and tubs, and allow access for the soil stack and other pipes. Check the illustrations for all the special framing needed for the soil stack, toilets, bathtubs, and showers (see page 160).

If this planning isn't done when the joists are first installed, modifications can be made at the time of the rough plumbing installation. You can add extra joists and cut joists to

Framing for Bathroom Fixtures

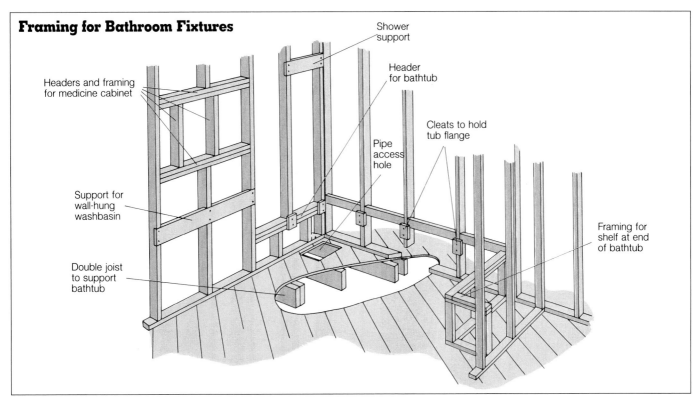

Headers and framing for medicine cabinet

Support for wall-hung washbasin

Double joist to support bathtub

Shower support

Header for bathtub

Cleats to hold tub flange

Pipe access hole

Framing for shelf at end of bathtub

put in headers, but it's better to do these jobs when you put in the joists in the first place; it's much less work then.

Run the pipes from where they enter the house, through the crawl space, and along the floor joists. Leave stubouts above the level of the floor.

If you intend to have a second-floor toilet, you need to install a soil stack for it. A soil stack is a vertical toilet drain; you don't need to install soil stacks for toilets in a one-story house. At this stage, install the first 5 to 6 feet of soil stack and a cleanout. The soil stack must be as close to the toilet as possible. Wait to extend the rest of the stack until after the wall framing is complete.

For all the toilets on the first floor, suspend the closet bend from the joists or from nailed-on braces, as shown in the illustrations. Then locate where all the drains from other fixtures will penetrate the floor and install pipes for them. From these drains work backward to the stack and install the drainpipe and the vents.

Now measure and mark where all the supply pipes for hot and cold water need to go through the floor to reach all the bathroom, kitchen, laundry, and other fixtures. If your water heater is in the basement or garage, you may want much of the parallel hot- and cold-water pipe to be under the floor. If the water heater is on the first floor, you may need to install only the main supply line to it under the floor; you can put the rest of the water supply pipes into the walls after the wall framing is done.

After the plumbing has been roughed-in under the floor—and after the furnace duct work is in, if there is any—you will have to call for an underfloor inspection before you lay the subfloor.

Installing the Remaining Rough Plumbing

You will complete the rough plumbing after the subfloor and all the wall and roof framing are done. Some plumbing fixtures require special framing. See the illustrations of the framing that must be done for toilets, bathtubs, showers, and other plumbing fixtures. The illustrations also indicate the rough plumbing dimensions and the kinds of support framing needed to support and secure the pipes as you rough them in. These illustrations give most of the positions and measurements you'll need to rough-in supply and DWV piping and install stubouts. Providing an illustration of every possible configuration is impossible, but the illustrations included should give you a general idea of what is needed. You can improvise for your individual circumstances.

Often, the wall through which the soil stack goes and any walls that are between or back up to bathrooms are made extra wide with a double row of studs set sideways making room for the stack and horizontal runs of drain between the studs. Bracing or supports can be added without cutting or notching any of the studs.

By code, horizontal drain lines must be sloped toward the sewer at a rate of at least ¼ inch per foot—⅛ inch per foot with 3-inch and larger drains. A better slope is ½ inch per foot; make all lines with this slope when possible. A horizontal drain may enter a vertical stack through a sanitary T fitting. Connecting horizontal drains to horizontal stacks and vertical drains to horizontal stacks requires a 45-degree fitting.

Doing the Rough-In Carpentry

Roughing-in a plumbing system requires a lot of work with a drill, saw, and hammer. You must plan and run pipes in your head before you do any cutting or boring. More so here than in any other part of the construction of your house, "Measure twice and cut (or drill) once."

When you do the cutting and drilling, try to make the holes as small and neat as possible. Use a compass and reciprocating saws when you need to, but whenever you can try to use a drill and the smallest bit to do the job. Make larger holes where pipes will be supported by sound-insulating devices.

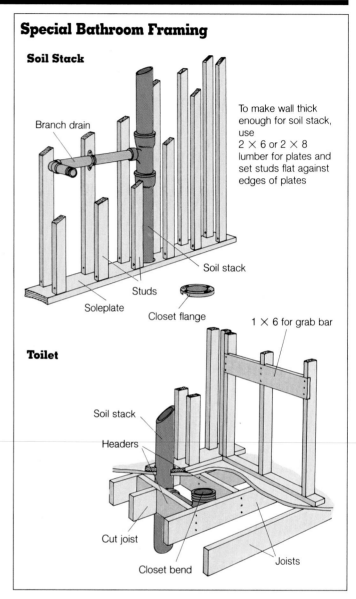

Special Bathroom Framing

Soil Stack

Branch drain

To make wall thick enough for soil stack, use 2 × 6 or 2 × 8 lumber for plates and set studs flat against edges of plates

Soil stack

Studs

Soleplate

Closet flange

Toilet

1 × 6 for grab bar

Soil stack

Headers

Cut joist

Closet bend

Joists

Rough Plumbing for a Bathroom

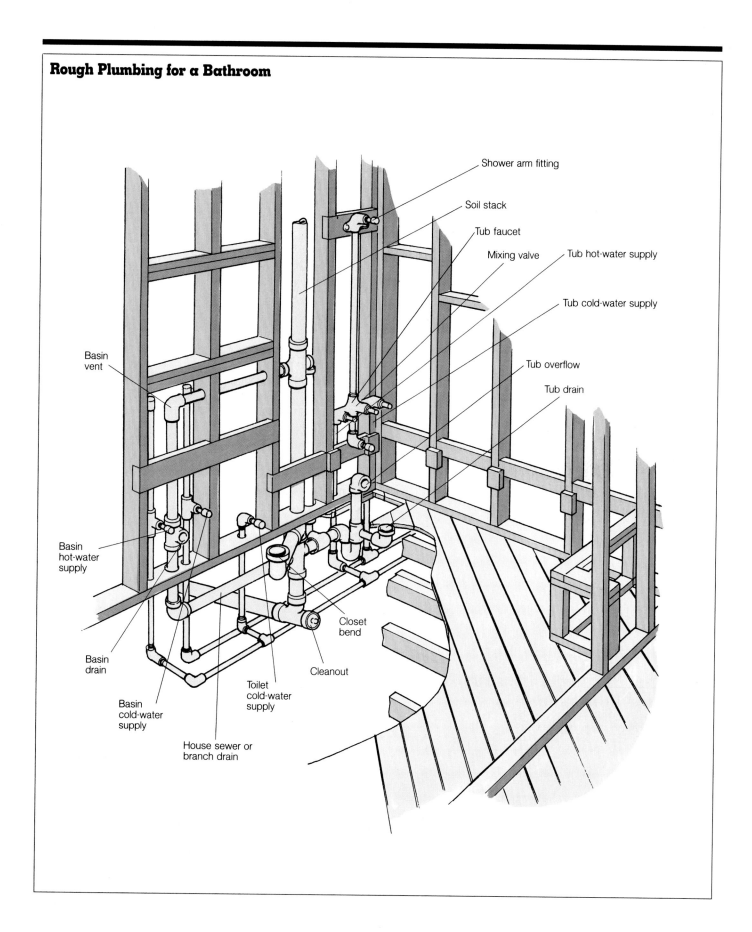

Shower arm fitting

Soil stack

Tub faucet

Mixing valve

Tub hot-water supply

Tub cold-water supply

Tub overflow

Tub drain

Basin vent

Basin hot-water supply

Basin drain

Basin cold-water supply

Toilet cold-water supply

House sewer or branch drain

Cleanout

Closet bend

Pipe Access

In Joists

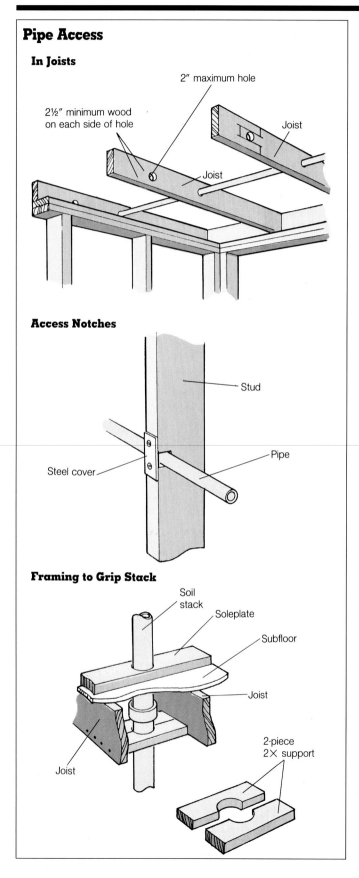

2" maximum hole

2½" minimum wood on each side of hole

Joist

Joist

Access Notches

Stud

Steel cover

Pipe

Framing to Grip Stack

Soil stack

Soleplate

Subfloor

Joist

Joist

2-piece 2× support

Using a drill will make your rough-in carpentry work neater and minimize the weakening of the framing members.

You can make holes almost anywhere along a joist if they are smaller in diameter than one quarter the width of the joist and in the center, between the top and bottom. There must be at least 2 inches of wood left between the hole and the edges of the joist.

If you have to cut notches in joists, they should be on the top, not the bottom, and they should be toward the ends rather than in the middle—in the end quarter, if possible. If the notches are in the middle half of a joist, they must be reinforced with a 4-foot 2 by 4. Notches in a joist should never go more than one quarter of the way through the joist.

Though you can bend tubing a little, you are not going to be able to get rigid pipe to go through drilled holes in studs; you'll have to use notches. Notches in studs for a horizontal pipe should be as shallow as possible. Make them deep enough to enclose the pipe, but no deeper. To protect the pipe from nails driven into the wall when the pipe is no longer visible, you must nail a steel cover plate over each notch after copper or plastic pipe is installed.

If you must put notches in the studs of a bearing wall, you have to be more careful. Codes say you can notch bearing studs in the top half only and that there must be two studs remaining whole for every one you notch. This means you can't notch all the studs in a wall to put in a horizontal pipe if the wall is a bearing wall. If you must run a pipe horizontally in a bearing wall, add studs sideways between the notched ones, as shown in the illustration at left.

Closet bends and other drainpipes are bulky and can cause problems when they don't fit easily between framing members. Whenever possible, position them between joists or studs and brace them as necessary. When you do need to notch a joist or stud, make the notch as small as possible and add bracing to compensate. If you must cut away a portion of a joist, add doubled headers and trimmers as you would in framing any floor opening. (See the illustrations here and in the section about framing floor openings.)

Soil stacks and other large drainpipes, especially those made out of cast iron, are very heavy. Even a 3- or 4-inch ABS pipe can be heavy when it's filled with water. To help take some of this weight off the pipes at the bottom of the stack, add some framing between the joists of each floor or ceiling a stack passes through. On the sides of two 2 by 4s, cut a semicircular hole the same diameter as the outside diameter of the stack. Nail them near the bottom of 2 joists to grip the stack just below a joint.

Support for Pipes

When supply pipes run along or across the bottom of joists in a crawl space, do not notch the joists. Codes require that the pipe be held or supported with clamps not more than 10 feet apart. Use copper clamps and nails with copper pipe and galvanized clamps and nails with galvanized pipe.

Plastic pipe needs to be supported at closer intervals, every 4 to 6 feet, and any kind of clamps and nails can be used. But don't make the clamps too tight. Plastic expands when it warms up, so the clamps should fit loosely.

Horizontal drain line in the crawl space or basement, where it hangs from joists, must be supported by strong pipe straps. Attach the straps to the joists with screws or lag bolts rather than nails.

Venting Drainpipes

A drainage system must be vented to operate efficiently and keep sewer gas out of the house. There are many ways to design vent systems. The best way is to make them as simple and straightforward as possible as long as they comply with the codes. Find out what is acceptable by the local code.

In areas of harsh winters, snow and ice could accumulate and block vents in the roof. In these areas the code sometimes requires that you increase the size of small, secondary vents just before they pass through the roof.

Insulating Pipes

By insulating your supply pipes, you can keep the cold-water pipes from sweating in hot weather and minimize the heat loss from hot-water pipes in cold weather. Manufactured materials are made especially for this purpose. Some are rolls of plastic foam or fiberglass that you wrap around the pipe in a spiral fashion. Others are semi-rigid tubes of foam plastic that are split so you can slide them over the pipes and secure them with tape.

Don't put the insulation on the pipes before the inspector has approved the rough plumbing though. You'll just have to remove it so the inspector can see the pipes. If you are going to insulate pipes that will be inside the walls, you will have to put on the insulation before the sheathing or wall-covering is installed.

Inspecting the Rough Plumbing

Besides inspecting all the pipe sizes and fittings, the inspector will do a gasing inspection after the rough plumbing is completed. The inspector will check supply lines for both water and sewer gas leaks. To do this, the pipes must be pressurized with water or air—just for the inspection. The inspector will also check the drainpipes for leaks. To do this, put a 10-foot riser on the drains, plug the bottoms, and fill them with water to create 10 feet of pressure on the lines. If there are no leaks, the plumbing will pass the inspection. After the inspection, remove the temporary riser.

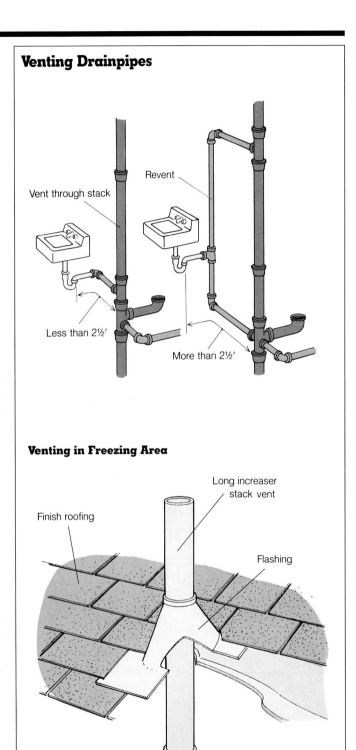

Venting Drainpipes

Vent through stack

Revent

Less than 2½'

More than 2½'

Venting in Freezing Area

Long increaser stack vent

Finish roofing

Flashing

Coupling

Vent pipe

PLANNING THE WIRING

Electricity originates in huge generators that are powered by water from hydroelectric dams or by coal-, oil-, or nuclear-fired steam plants. From the generator, electricity travels in high-voltage wires to distribution stations. From there it is directed into cities and towns and transformed into a lower voltage, 120 volts, before it enters houses.

- ☐ Your house plans
- ☐ Graph paper
- ☐ Tracing paper
- ☐ Straightedge ruler
- ☐ Architect's scale
- ☐ T square
- ☐ Triangles (45 degree and 30/60 degree or adjustable)
- ☐ Pencils
- ☐ Eraser
- ☐ Templates for fixtures and appliances
- ☐ Drawing board or drafting table

Designing Adequate Wiring

Planning your electrical needs is not difficult, but it does take some time. You must understand the basics of electricity. You must be completely versed in the latest codes for your area. You must know what you want from your system. You must be able to confidently shop for all the components needed to put it together. This section will help you determine the electrical needs for your new house.

Three wires carry electricity into most houses. Two wires are hot and carry 120 volts

each. The third wire is neutral and provides a return path for electricity back to the source or a safe ground. The presence of two incoming 120-volt hot wires makes it possible to use both for special 240-volt circuits required for major appliances, such as electric ranges or clothes dryers.

In the service panel the incoming electricity is distributed to the individual circuits in the house. The two hot wires are attached to separate bus bars in the panel. Circuit breakers are attached to these bus bars. One hundred-twenty-volt circuit breakers draw from either of the busses; 240-volt circuit breakers draw from both.

Adequate wiring means more than wiring that just meets regulations. The National Electrical Code (NEC) and local codes are concerned mainly with safety and do not consider what your particular wiring needs are or what they might be 10 years from now. So, when wiring a new home, consider your wiring needs room by room.

As time goes by, you will probably buy more appliances that draw more power. With well-planned wiring, you can run any appliance at any time without having to take others off the circuit or worry about tripping a breaker. In planning wiring that will meet your needs, you should first consider the following NEC code requirements for new wiring.

- You must have one circuit for each 600 square feet of habitable space, but it is better to have a circuit for each 500 square feet. You must have a minimum of three such circuits.
- Any wall space wider than 2 feet must have at least one outlet. Each outlet must have another outlet within 12 feet of it, measured horizontally along the wall. Any room dividers, such as bars or counters, are to be included in this distance. The code makes this requirement to minimize the need for extension cords.
- In addition to the lighting circuits, you must have at least two 20-ampere small-appliance circuits in the kitchen, dining room, and pantry, plus individual circuits for such appliances as the kitchen range, water heater, dishwasher, garbage disposer, washing machine, and clothes dryer. In addition, you must have an individual circuit for any permanent appliance rated at 1,000 watts or more, such as a built-in bathroom heater.
- If you have a two-story house, make sure you have two circuits with the outlets divided between both floors. This way, a blown fuse or tripped breaker will not darken an entire floor.

- There must be at least one receptacle in each of the following locations: behind any kitchen counter wider than 12 inches, in any room intended for laundry machines, next to each bathroom sink, in the garage, and on the house exterior.
- The receptacles in the bathroom, garage, outdoors, and some kitchen locations must be protected by a ground fault circuit interrupter (GFCI).
- There must be wall switches to control the lights at all outdoor entrances, hallways, and stairs, and in an attached garage. The switches at both ends of long hallways and stairs must be three-way switches.
- A wall switch must control lighting in every room.
- In kitchens and bathrooms, the wall switches must be wired to installed lighting fixtures. In other rooms, they may control receptacles where lamps are plugged in.

Amperage Needs

If you will have more than five circuits in your house, you should calculate the amperage demand to determine the size of the service panel you will need. Start with the general lighting circuits by calculating the square feet of the planned living space, including the garage and workshop. You must supply 3 watts for every square foot of usable space.

As an example, say you have a 1,500-square-foot house. Using the formula of 3 watts per square foot, you will need 4,500 watts (3 × 1,500) just for the general lighting circuits. In a new house, you must have two 20-ampere small-appliance circuits for the kitchen. Rate each one at 2,400 watts, for an additional 4,800 watts. The laundry circuit gets an additional 1,500 watts. By checking the faceplates on major appliances, you will come up with additional wattage.

If you have electric central heating only, add 65 percent of its rated load in watts to the total. If you have just an air conditioner, add 100 percent of its load to the total. However, if you have combined central air-conditioning and heat, add just the larger of the two (either 100 percent of the air conditioner or 65 percent of the heater) because they are not used at the same time.

Use the steps in the chart at right to calculate the wattage of electrical service for your house.

Additional Wiring Considerations

Although the NEC does not require the following steps in wiring, many local codes do. You should incorporate them as a policy of good wiring.

If there is more than one entrance to a room, plan three-way switches at each entrance so you don't have to retrace your steps to turn a light on or off. If there are more than two entrances, then go to a four-way switch. If your house is well wired, you should be able to walk from the front to the rear, turning lights on and off, without having to backtrack.

There should be an adequate number of circuits for present and anticipated needs.

Calculating the Wattage of Electrical Service

Use these figures to calculate the amperage needs of your house as follows.
1. List the wattage of each circuit, allowing the adjustments on the chart.
2. Add the individual wattages to find the total wattage (40,800).
3. Subtract 10,000 ($40,800 - 10,000 = 30,800$).
4. Find 40 percent of the remainder ($30,800 \times 0.40 = 12,320$).
5. Add back the 10,000 ($12,320 + 10,000 = 22,320$).
6. Divide by 240 volts ($22,320 \div 240 = 93$ amperes).

In this example the service should be at least 100 amperes. To be on the safe side, make it 125.

Circuit	Adjustment	Example		Typical Wattages
General purpose	3 watts/ft^2	1,500 sq ft house	=	4,500
Small appliance	1,500 watts each circuit	2 K, 1 DR, 1 Laundry	=	6,000
Kitchen range	Check faceplate			12,000
Clothes dryer	Check faceplate			5,000
Dishwasher	Check faceplate			1,500
Garbage disposer	Check faceplate			800
Water heater	Check faceplate			5,000
Central heating	65% of total rating	Rating = 9,230 $\times$ 0.65	=	6,000
Central air conditioner	Don't add if heating is electric; otherwise, 100%			
				40,800

Appliances Requiring Individual Circuits

The appliances listed in this table must have their own circuits. No other appliances, outlets, or lights can be on the same circuit. Wire sizes are for copper measured according to the American Wire Gauge (AWG).

Appliance	Typical Voltage	Wire Size	Breaker Amperage
Kitchen range	240	6	50
Built-in oven	240	8	40
Cooktop	240	8	40
Water heater	240	10	30
Clothes dryer	240	8	40
Central electric heating	240	6	50
Air conditioning	240	8	40
Food freezer	120	12	20
Dishwasher	120	12	20
Garbage disposer	120	12	20
Trash compactor	120	12	20
Fixed bathroom heater	120/240	12	20
Furnace motor	120	12	20
Well pump	120	12	20
Any permanent appliance rated at more than 1,000 watts	120	12	20

Number of Conductors Permitted in a Box

This table shows the maximum number of wires that can be connected in a single junction box. If there are more wires, add another box next to the first one.

Box Size (In.)	Maximum Number of Conductors			
	No. 14	No. 12	No. 10	No. 8
Round or Octagonal				
4 × 1¼	6	5	5	4
4 × 1½	7	6	6	5
4 × 2⅛	10	9	8	7
Square				
4 × 1¼	9	8	7	6
4 × 1½	10	9	8	7
4 × 2⅛	15	13	12	10
Switch Boxes				
3 × 2 × 1½	3	3	3	2
3 × 2 × 2	5	4	4	3
3 × 2 × 2¼	5	4	4	3
3 × 2 × 2½	6	5	5	4
3 × 2 × 2¾	7	6	5	4
3 × 2 × 3½	9	8	7	6
Junction Boxes				
4 × 2⅛ × 1½	5	4	4	3
4 × 2⅛ × 1⅞	6	5	5	4
4 × 2⅛ × 2⅛	7	6	5	4

stuffed into a box. The accompanying table tells what size you will need for particular situations.

When using this table consider the following factors.

• Each hot or neutral wire (black, white, or red) counts as one conductor.

• All ground wires together count as one conductor.

• Each receptacle or fixture counts as one conductor.

• All internal clamping devices and fixture studs count as one conductor.

Codes don't usually specify the heights of boxes from the floor, but the list that follows presents typical heights for most areas.

• Switches: 44 to 48 inches above the floor.

• Receptacles: 12 inches above the floor, 44 inches above the floor over counters.

• Boxes for baseboard heaters: Most have their own boxes built into the ends of the units.

• Ceiling light: Typically center of ceiling.

• Junction boxes: Wherever they will be accessible; they cannot be concealed inside of the walls.

The more circuits you have, the less chance any one will be overloaded. Although the codes do not limit the number of outlets you can put on any circuit, standard practice is to put no more than 8 to 12 receptacles and fixtures on one lighting circuit and 6 receptacles on one small-appliance circuit. The circuits should be divided equally around the house so that if a breaker does trip, one entire floor will not be darkened.

The wiring should have enough ampacity to handle the anticipated loads in every room. In the house lighting circuit, for instance, the NEC permits No. 14 wire, which has an ampacity rating of 15 amperes. But No. 12 wire is used a great deal—and even required by some local codes—because its 20-ampere capacity can handle larger loads.

Electrical Equipment

You need to install a box for each fixture and appliance on each circuit and a box anywhere cables are joined. There are dozens of types of boxes to choose from. The first decision is whether to use metal or plastic boxes. Plastic boxes are less expensive and do not require direct grounding. Metal boxes are easier to fit wallboard around (they provide a bigger margin for error), but they have to be grounded and are more expensive.

The shape of the box depends on what goes in it and its purpose. Switch boxes, also called utility boxes, are rectangular and are the most common type. Some metal boxes come in double, triple, and quadruple sizes to hold more than one switch, and some single boxes are made so they can

be ganged—you just remove one side from each and screw the boxes together. Plastic boxes, too, can be bought in large sizes for multiple fixtures, but they cannot be ganged.

Use octagonal and round boxes for light fixtures. Junction boxes are sometimes octagonal or round, but most often they are square. Specialty boxes are available for you to use for surface mounting where you can't cut into a joist or stud as well as for outdoor installations. Some appliances and fixtures, like wall heaters and recessed lights, have their own built-in boxes.

According to codes, you can use any shape of box that suits your purpose; the critical factor is its size. The NEC is very strict about how many wires and fittings can safely be

Electrical Fixtures

Knowing the minimum code requirements will help you place light fixtures, switches, outlets, and appliances. The specifications that follow are based on the National Electrical Code; consult with the local building department for additional restrictions. Code requirements are minimums; when going to the trouble and expense of building a house, increase the number of fixtures and outlets in anticipation of future needs.

Lights

Every room, hallway, stairway, outdoor entrance, and attached garage must have at least one permanent light fixture controlled by a wall switch at each entrance. The light can be mounted on the ceiling or any wall, and you can have as many individual fixtures as you wish. The following list includes some exceptions to these rules about lights.

• A wall receptacle controlled by a wall switch at the entrance to a room may be substituted for a permanent light fixture in any room except the kitchen or the bathroom.

• Light fixtures for utility rooms, crawl spaces, and attics without stairs can be controlled by pull chains instead of wall switches.

• Lighting for hallways, stairways, and outdoor entrances can be activated by specialized switches. These include remote, central, or automatic switches.

• Fixtures in clothes closets must be located on the ceiling or on the wall above the door. Pendant fixtures are not allowed—most codes maintain that fixtures of this type cause an overstuffed closet to become a fire hazard. Check specific codes for lighting other small, closed spaces such as pantries.

Switches

The switch for the main light fixture of a room should be at the door to the room or at each door, if there is more than one. The switch must be on the latch side of a hinged door so that the door does not interfere with the access to the plate when you enter the room. In bathrooms do not place switches where it is possible to reach them while using the shower or bathtub. Attic stairs must be illuminated by a light that is controlled by a switch at the foot of the stairs. Lights for basement stairs must have a switch at the head of the stairs as well as an additional switch at any other entrance to the basement.

Receptacles

Receptacles, also called outlets, must be in every room and no more than 12 feet apart. (The code actually states that no point along the floor line of any wall can be more than 6 feet from an outlet.) A wall with more than one door opening should have at least one outlet, unless the section of wall between the doorways is less than 2 feet wide.

For a kitchen counter place receptacles no more than 4 feet apart. Standard practice is to install at least one outlet for each foot of counter.

Laundry rooms must have at least one receptacle within 6 feet of any appliance.

Bathrooms should have at least one receptacle adjacent to the washbasin.

There must be at least one receptacle outdoors, as well as one in the garage and one in the basement.

All kitchen, bathroom, outdoor, and garage receptacles must be protected by GFCI devices.

Appliances

Any 240-volt appliance or permanent 120-volt appliance should have its own receptacle or junction box. Any built-in 120-volt appliance, such as an electric heater, must have its own circuit.

Types of Wire and Cable

Technically a wire is an individual conductor, either solid or stranded, wrapped in its own insulation. A cable is a cluster of two or more wires, each with its own insulation, wrapped together in plastic or metal sheathing. Descriptions of the most common types of wire and cable follow.

Type T Wire

Used for general indoor wiring, the thermoplastic (T) insulation protects against a wide spectrum of temperature differences.

Type TW Wire

This wire provides heavy insulation for weather resistance. It is used for outdoor wiring (but not direct burial) and for wiring in damp places such as basements.

Type THW Wire

Type THW wire is similar to Type TW, but it is more heat resistant.

Type NM Cable

This nonmetallic cable is the type of wiring that is most commonly used in residential installations. It is widely known by the trade name Romex. It consists of two or more individually insulated Type T wires and a bare copper ground wire, all wrapped in jute and paper spacers and sheathed in plastic. This cable must not be used where it will be exposed to dampness.

Type NMC Cable

This type of cable is made specifically for damp areas like basements or laundry rooms. It often has a glass wrapping on each wire. The wires are embedded in a solid plastic sheath to keep out moisture. If NMC cable is not available in your area, you can use UF cable.

Type UF Cable

This cable is so durable it is recommended for underground burial. The wires are embedded directly in tough plastic that keeps out all water. It is an excellent choice for outdoor wiring or wiring in a barn or garage where there is always a lot of moisture. SE is another type of cable that can be buried.

Armored Cable

Known by the trade name BX, this cable has heavy paper and metal spiral sheathing. The ground wire is aluminum because the metal sheathing also acts as a ground. It should not be used in damp areas. Some local codes require armored cable in places where wiring will be exposed to potential abrasion, such as in crawl spaces or along the inside of garage walls.

ROUGHING-IN THE WIRING

One person can do all the rough wiring for a typical house, although it is always easier to have a helper. To do rough wiring, you should have basic carpentry skills and be able to use some special wiring tools. You must be able to measure accurately and follow directions. On a difficulty scale of 10 points, consider roughing-in the wiring a 5.

Installing the Service Entrance

The service entrance is where the power from the supplier, whether dropped from a pole or run underground, is connected to a house. The incoming wires pass through the electric company's meter, into the service panel, to the bus bars in the panel, through the circuit breakers, and then to the branch circuits in the house. Virtually all houses are now installed with circuit breakers rather than fuses. Typically, the service entrance also contains the natural gas and water meters and main shutoff valves as well. Local codes specify the location so that emergency crews can find it quickly.

- ☐ Round-tipped shovel
- ☐ Square-tipped shovel
- ☐ Pickax or maddock
- ☐ Tool belt
- ☐ Hammer
- ☐ Handsaw
- ☐ Hacksaw
- ☐ Compass saw
- ☐ Power circular saw
- ☐ Reciprocating saw
- ☐ Power drill and bits
- ☐ Bit extension
- ☐ Brace and bits
- ☐ Steel tape measure
- ☐ 24-inch level
- ☐ Combination square
- ☐ Framing square
- ☐ Carpenter's pencil
- ☐ Slot screwdrivers
- ☐ Phillips screwdrivers
- ☐ Wood chisels
- ☐ Utility knife
- ☐ Needle-nose pliers
- ☐ Lineman's pliers
- ☐ Wire cutter
- ☐ Electrician's multipurpose tool
- ☐ Cable stripper
- ☐ Wire nuts, assorted sizes

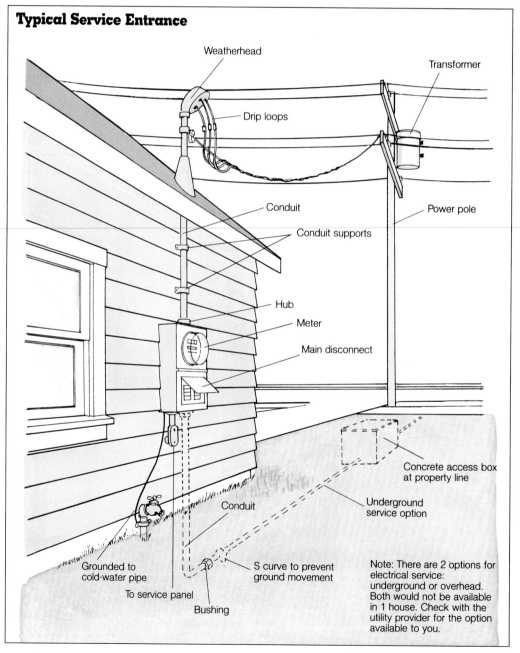

Typical Service Entrance

Weatherhead

Transformer

Drip loops

Conduit

Conduit supports

Power pole

Hub

Meter

Main disconnect

Concrete access box at property line

Underground service option

Grounded to cold-water pipe

Conduit

S curve to prevent ground movement

To service panel

Bushing

Note: There are 2 options for electrical service: underground or overhead. Both would not be available in 1 house. Check with the utility provider for the option available to you.

Service-Panel Components

Electricity originates in huge generators that are powered by water in hydroelectric dams or by coal, oil, wind, or nuclear energy. From the generator, electricity travels in high-voltage wires to distribution stations. From there, it is transformed into lower voltage and directed to community substations. Finally, the voltage is lowered again before it is directed to residential service panels. In the service panel, the electricity is distributed to the individual circuits in the house.

Mast

This galvanized steel pipe, usually 2 inches in diameter, extends up the side of the house and through the eaves to rise above the roof. The mast must be high enough so that the drip loops are at least 10 feet above ground and at least 3 feet from any door or window.

Weatherhead

Incoming wires are attached to the weatherhead, a protective cover at the top of the mast. An underground service panel does not have a mast and weatherhead; instead, a conduit comes up to the meter box.

Service Box

A metal box attached to the house designed to contain and protect the service panel.

Ground Wire

A copper ground wire is bonded (firmly attached) to the neutral bus bar and then connected, with a wire-to-pipe ground clamp, to the grounding electrode system.

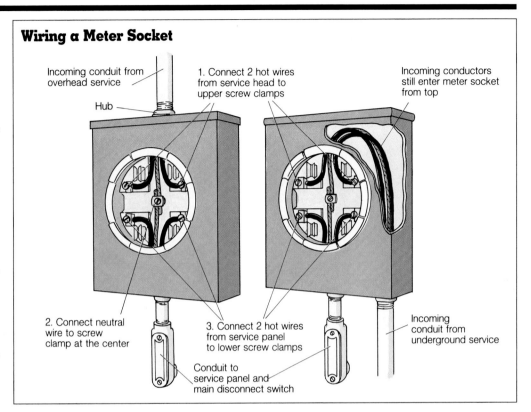

Wiring a Meter Socket

Incoming conduit from overhead service

Hub

1. Connect 2 hot wires from service head to upper screw clamps

Incoming conductors still enter meter socket from top

2. Connect neutral wire to screw clamp at the center

3. Connect 2 hot wires from service panel to lower screw clamps

Conduit to service panel and main disconnect switch

Incoming conduit from underground service

Service Panel

This box includes a hookup for the meter (supplied by the electric company); a neutral bus bar, where all the neutral and ground wires are connected; and two hot bus bars, where the incoming hot wires and breaker switches are connected. If you like, you can place the circuit-breaker panel apart from the service panel—in the house or garage, for example.

Service panels are rated in amperes, usually 100, 125, 150, and 200 amperes. What you should have will be determined by the number of circuits you are planning and the computed load for your house. To determine the size of the service panel you will need, compute the electrical load for your house (see page 165). A representative from the electric company will tell you where to place the panel.

You may install the service panel and run all the circuits, but the electric company will not connect the power until you have received a final approval from the inspector. To mount the mast, weatherhead, panel, and ground wire, take these steps.

1. Mount the service panel about eye level or a little above. Position the mounting screws in studs.

2. Directly above the service panel drill a hole, large enough for the mast, through the eaves and the roof. Drop the mast through the hole and connect it to the panel by using a hub (watertight nut). Use conduit supports to attach the mast to the side of the house.

3. Attach the flashing and an adjustable flashing seal to prevent rainwater from dripping through the hole and down the pipe.

4. Attach the insulator for the service drop wires. Make sure the mast is securely fastened to the house.

5. Drop the 1 white (neutral) wire and the 2 black wires down the mast and into the panel. There can be no splices in these wires. Leave about 3 feet sticking out the top. Make sure the wires are the correct size to accommodate the amperage of your service.

6. Run the three wires through the weatherhead and attach the weatherhead to the mast. The electric company will connect your service-entrance wires to their service-drop wires. You must leave enough wire sticking out—about 3 feet—to form a drip loop so that rainwater cannot run down the wires into the panel.

Panel Wiring

Wiring the service panel is fairly easy and straightforward.

1. First wire the meter socket. The 2 hot wires are usually large and black, but 1 may be black and 1 red. The service conductors are always attached to the top of the meter, even when they originate underground. From the meter run the cable into the service panel.

2. From the 2 screw clamps next to the lower meter sockets, connect 2 more hot wires of the same size to the main disconnect switch.

3. Connect the neutral wire coming from the meter to the neutral bus bar in the panel. Note that the neutral wire runs through the meter housing but is not electrically connected to the meter itself.

4. Connect the ground wire to the grounding electrode system of the house. The ground wire must be No. 6 or larger and should be kept as short as possible. Although not essential, encasing the ground wire in metal or plastic pipe makes your work look neater.

5. As you run each circuit through the house, connect the hot wire to the breaker switch. Connect the white neutral wire and the bare ground wire to the neutral bus bar.

The Grounding Electrode System

Until a few years ago, most residential electrical systems were grounded by connecting the service-entrance ground wire to an underground cold-water pipe. Because of the increasing use of nonmetallic pipe and insulated fittings in

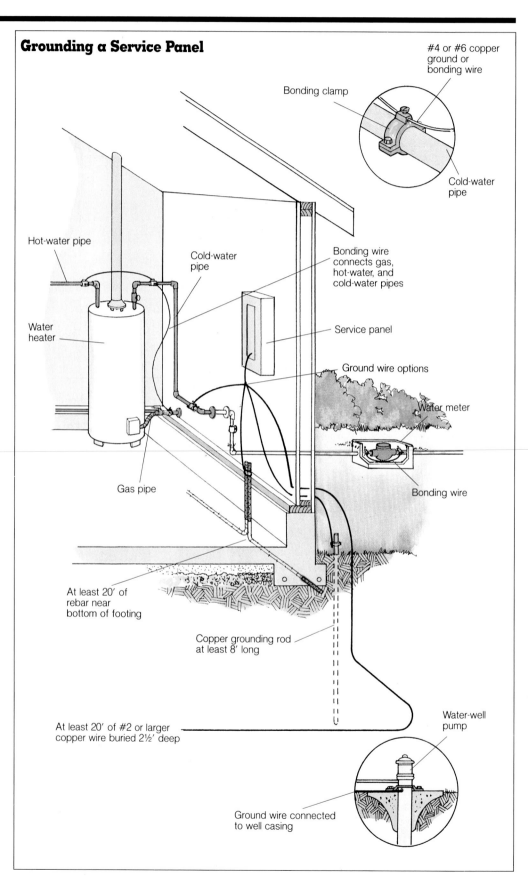

Grounding a Service Panel

#4 or #6 copper ground or bonding wire

Bonding clamp

Cold-water pipe

Hot-water pipe

Cold-water pipe

Bonding wire connects gas, hot-water, and cold-water pipes

Water heater

Service panel

Ground wire options

Water meter

Gas pipe

Bonding wire

At least 20' of rebar near bottom of footing

Copper grounding rod at least 8' long

Water-well pump

At least 20' of #2 or larger copper wire buried 2½' deep

Ground wire connected to well casing

Framing for Heater Registers

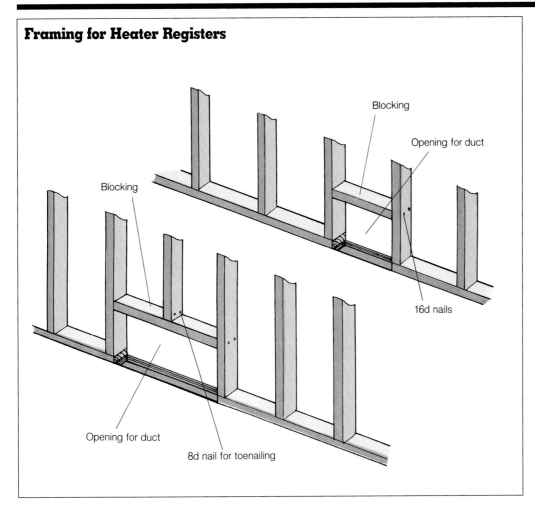

Blocking

Opening for duct

Blocking

16d nails

Opening for duct

8d nail for toenailing

Installing Vacuum Systems

Installing a central vacuum-cleaning system means that instead of lugging your vacuum around the house, you simply attach a hose to a special outlet built into the wall. The wall outlets are powered by a motor unit connected to tubing that runs to a central collection trap, which you occasionally clean out. These systems run more quietly and are more powerful than regular vacuum cleaners. Central systems make house cleaning easier and add to the resale value of the house.

Two or three national companies and many local and regional companies make central vacuum-cleaning systems. Some claim to have systems that can be custom planned and installed by the owner-builder. Others claim that these systems can't work efficiently unless they are planned and installed by professionals. They argue that only experts who have scientific knowledge about air movement and how it's affected by the lengths, diameters, and curves in the tubing can really plan and install an effective system.

The actual installation of the power unit, tubing, and outlets is not very difficult for a person with average carpentry skills. Although each manufacturer's system is similar, they are also very different in important ways. Therefore, if you are considering installing your own system, contact a couple of contractors in your area that specialize in central vacuum-cleaning systems and get the details on each installation.

If you find a system that you're confident you can install, go for it. If not, let the experts do it for you.

FINISHING THE EXTERIOR

Finishing the exterior of the house involves selecting and installing exterior doors and windows, selecting and installing the exterior siding, and putting up the outside trim. If you are building the house entirely on your own, you have completed the rough plumbing and rough electrical work. If you are having professionals help with the house, the roughing-in and the installation of doors and windows can be done simultaneously. These jobs need to be done after the roof is on but before the framing inspection and the closing-in of the walls.

Once the doors and windows are in, the house is protected from the elements. Beyond that, windows give the house a finished look that will be a big psychological boost to all the workers on the project.

Classical arches, a stucco exterior, and a tile roof are common features of a Mediterranean house. Here, fixed metal windows repeat the arch motif of the entrance; the exterior of paper and lath over sheathing awaits professional stucco application; and the roof is in the process of being tiled. Each tile is designed to lock over the strapping, which is already in place on the roof.

INSTALLING EXTERIOR DOORS

The difficulty involved in installing an exterior door depends on the style of door you choose. On a difficulty scale of 10 points, consider installing exterior doors a 6. Garage doors are trickier to install than house doors, double doors are more difficult than single doors, and site-hung doors are considerably harder than prehung doors.

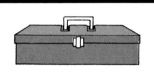

☐ Tool belt
☐ Hammer
☐ Handsaw
☐ Hacksaw
☐ Power circular saw
☐ Power drill and bits
☐ Brace and bits
☐ Hole saw
☐ Steel tape measure
☐ Combination square
☐ Framing square
☐ 24-inch level
☐ Slot screwdrivers
☐ Phillips screwdrivers
☐ Wood chisels
☐ Mortise chisel
☐ Nail sets
☐ Utility knife
☐ Awl
☐ Jack plane or power plane
☐ Belt sander
☐ Door bucks
☐ Router
☐ Hinge-mortise routing template

Choosing Door Styles

You need at least basic carpentry skills to install any kind of door, entrance set, or dead bolt. To install a single prehung door, two people need about two hours to complete the project. A single site-hung door or sliding door takes two people about four hours to install. A garage door or double door takes two people a day to install. One person can install an entrance set or dead bolt in about an hour.

The doors on the exterior of a home serve several functions. Obviously, they open to let in visitors, sunlight, and fresh air and to let out the cat; they close to keep your family and possessions safe, to keep out rain and wind and snow, and to keep in heated or cooled air. Exterior doors include the front door, one or more rear doors, and the garage door. The most common styles of exterior doors are single, double, or sliding glass doors. Most common garage doors are overhead or swing. All doors should complement the look of the home and harmonize with its architecture and decor.

In choosing a door, you must consider a number of variables in addition to style. Exterior doors are part of the weather seal of a home. You must ensure that they fit snugly and are properly weatherstripped, and you may have to install dual glass for energy savings. As protection against crime and fire, you may want a metal door. Metal doors are filled with insulating plastic and finished to resemble a quality wood door. Fiberglass doors have similar characteristics. For a front entrance, you might choose a set of double doors, which signal a broad welcome to visitors. French-paned and glass sliding doors open the house to the outside and bring in a beautiful view, but for security and privacy these are usually placed at the back of the house where they open onto the patio or garden.

Before choosing a door, you should understand how various doors are made and sold. You can buy standard exterior doors in prehung packages or build on-site the elements on which to hang the doors.

Standard Door Construction

Exterior doors are commonly 1¾ inches thick and not less than 80 inches high and 36 inches wide. Back doors are the same height—as are all doors—but sometimes narrower, down to 32 inches.

The construction of exterior doors is more complicated than it may first appear. A quality

exterior door must not only be beautiful, but it must provide security, durability, and resistance to the elements. All the exterior entrances should be hung with solid-panel or solid-core flush doors.

Panel doors have vertical stiles and horizontal rails, something like picture frames, with panels between.

Flush doors are made from two plywood veneer layers covering an interior core. Flush doors that are called hollow are actually filled with cardboard waffles. Solid doors contain a piece of particleboard. Decorative molding may be attached to the surface.

Standard doors for the exterior and interior come prehung in packages. Buying prehung doors is usually slightly more expensive than building your own jambs and mounting your own hinges, but the assembled units can save hours of painstaking work. This section will cover installation procedures for both prehung and site-assembled units, so you can choose your own level of punishment.

Hanging a door on-site can create a customized appearance. Most commonly, you would go to the trouble for an exterior door only; prehung units are usually adequate for the interior. The instructions that follow are for an exterior door. Installation for an interior door is the same except an interior door does not have a sill or threshold. An exterior door of a house usually opens to the inside, with the handle on the same side as the light switch.

Installing Doorsills

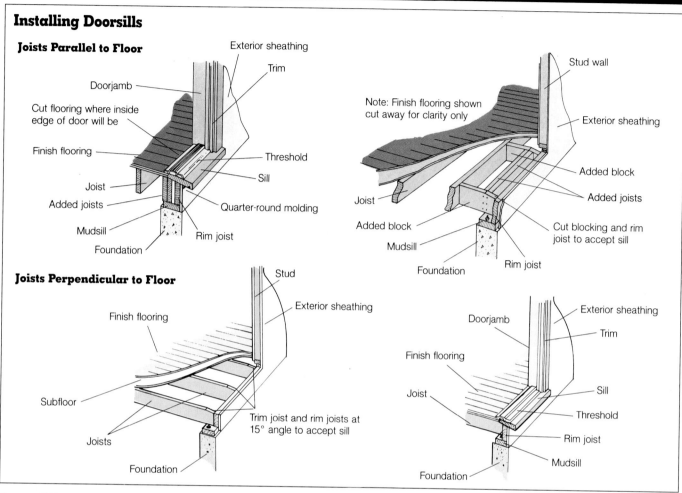

Joists Parallel to Floor

- Exterior sheathing
- Trim
- Doorjamb
- Cut flooring where inside edge of door will be
- Finish flooring
- Threshold
- Joist
- Sill
- Added joists
- Quarter-round molding
- Mudsill
- Rim joist
- Foundation

Note: Finish flooring shown cut away for clarity only

- Stud wall
- Exterior sheathing
- Added block
- Added joists
- Joist
- Cut blocking and rim joist to accept sill
- Added block
- Mudsill
- Foundation
- Rim joist

Joists Perpendicular to Floor

- Stud
- Exterior sheathing
- Finish flooring
- Subfloor
- Joists
- Foundation
- Trim joist and rim joists at 15° angle to accept sill

- Exterior sheathing
- Trim
- Doorjamb
- Finish flooring
- Sill
- Joist
- Threshold
- Rim joist
- Mudsill
- Foundation

Installing the Sill

You must install a door sill for every exterior door opening. Sills, at the base of the door, provide a finished appearance and slope downward to shed water that blows against the door. Sills are usually made of hardwood and should have a groove on the underside near the front to prevent water from running along the bottom edge toward the house. If the sill doesn't have one, use a circular saw to cut a ¼-inch-deep groove.

In most cases the floor joists must be trimmed to accept the sill so its back edge is flush with the finish floor. The threshold will cover the joint between the sill and the floor.

If the joists are running parallel to the sill, you must add a support member for the edge of the subflooring that was cut away and for the back of the sill. Do this by nailing 2 blocks, of the same dimensions as the joists, between joists on either side of the door opening. Cut 2 support joists to length and nail them through the blocks, as shown in the illustration.

Use a saw and chisel to notch the tops of the joists at the edge of the house. Make the notches 2 inches deep, then fit the sill into this trimmed area and check that it is level. Shim one end if necessary. Predrill the nail holes.

Choosing a Prehung Package

Prehung units include the side jambs, the head jamb, and a door already mounted on hinges. Sometimes, prehung exterior doors have the threshold attached to the bottom of the side jambs. Slip such a unit into the rough door opening, shim until square, then nail into place.

A prehung door is factory-assembled with the door hinged and mounted on one of the side jambs. A hole has been drilled for the entrance set. When selecting a door, order either a right-hand door or a left-hand door. The door handle of a right-hand door is

on the right when viewed from inside the room into which the door opens. Verify that the supplier knows exactly what you mean, however, because terminology does vary.

There are three basic styles of prehung doors. In one, the door is mounted inside the fully assembled jambs. In another, it is mounted on the hinge jamb only; you must nail together the head jamb and other side jamb. In the third style, called a split jamb, tongue-and-groove jambs are fitted together from opposite sides of the rough opening. The door is already hung from one of the jambs. All these styles are installed in just about the same fashion.

Anatomy of a Prehung Door

One-piece Jamb

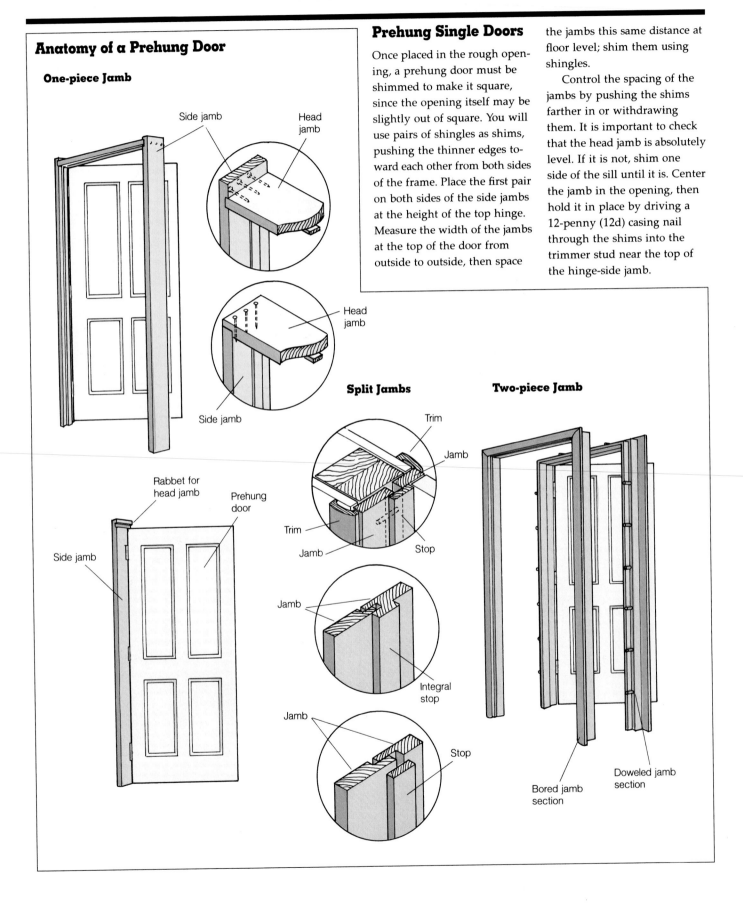

Side jamb

Head jamb

Head jamb

Side jamb

Rabbet for head jamb

Prehung door

Side jamb

Prehung Single Doors

Once placed in the rough opening, a prehung door must be shimmed to make it square, since the opening itself may be slightly out of square. You will use pairs of shingles as shims, pushing the thinner edges toward each other from both sides of the frame. Place the first pair on both sides of the side jambs at the height of the top hinge. Measure the width of the jambs at the top of the door from outside to outside, then space the jambs this same distance at floor level; shim them using shingles.

Control the spacing of the jambs by pushing the shims farther in or withdrawing them. It is important to check that the head jamb is absolutely level. If it is not, shim one side of the sill until it is. Center the jamb in the opening, then hold it in place by driving a 12-penny (12d) casing nail through the shims into the trimmer stud near the top of the hinge-side jamb.

Split Jambs

Trim

Jamb

Trim

Jamb

Stop

Jamb

Integral stop

Jamb

Stop

Two-piece Jamb

Bored jamb section

Doweled jamb section

Plumb the hinge-side jamb. Adjust the shims until it is perfectly vertical. Nail it into place through the shims, then check that it is still plumb. Set the other jambs into place. Since the head jamb keeps the top of the unit rigid, the key is to get the bottoms of the side jambs properly spaced. One trick professionals use is to drive a wallboard screw through the jambs into the trimmer stud, then tighten or back off the screw until the jambs are exactly spaced. Put the shims into place and nail them when everything is square.

With a utility knife score the shims deeply next to the jamb edge; snap them off. Install any exterior casing. Install the entrance set (see page 199). As soon as you can, finish the door with a couple of coats of sanding sealer and paint or stain and varnish. If an exterior door is left for long without being sealed, the weather can expand, shrink, or warp it out of fit.

Installing a Prehung Door

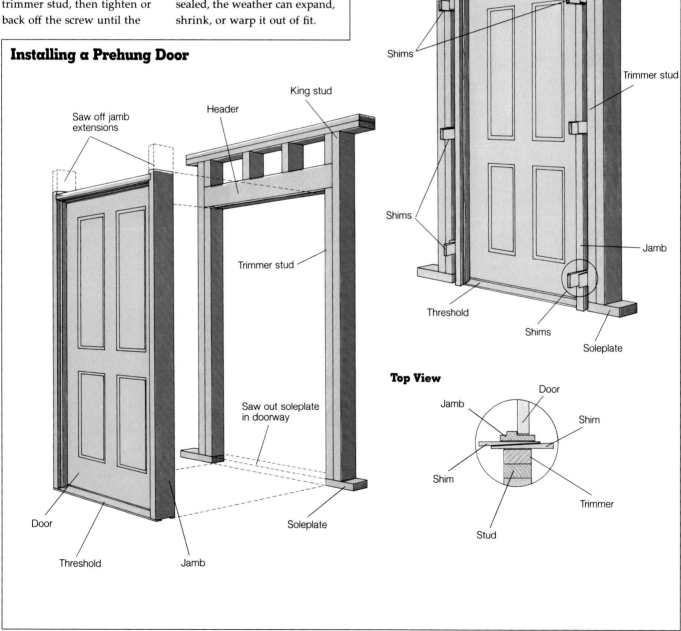

Top View

Hanging a Single Door

To hang a door on-site, you will need a door; three butt hinges; side and head jambs; sill material; a threshold; and an entrance set, which is made up of a lockset with a door handle or knob and a dead bolt. Install the sill (see page 187) and then continue here.

Jambs

It is easiest to make jambs from jamb stock, which is wood stock shaped for the purpose. Jamb stock is available in most lumber outlets. It is already routed for the head jamb and ripped to the proper width.

If you make your own jambs, use stock that is at least 1¼ inch thick and rip it to the width of the house framing material plus the thicknesses of the exterior and the interior sidings. At the top of the side jambs, rout a ½-inch-deep rabbet the thickness of the jamb material so the head jamb fits flush with the tops of the side jambs. Put the jambs together with glue and three 8d casing nails in each side.

The rough door opening should be as wide as the door, plus the thicknesses of the 2 side jambs, plus ¼ to ½ inch on each side for shimming. Install the jambs in the opening, with 2 shims behind each hinge location and 2 more spaced equally between the hinge locations. Check that the space is plumb and square, then tack the top of the hinge-side jamb into place.

Adjust the width of the jambs at the bottom to match that at the top by tightening or loosening a wallboard screw driven through the jamb into the trimmer stud. Check again that the jamb is square by placing a steel framing square in the corners. Check that the head is level; if it isn't, shim the bottom of one leg. Make sure the space between the jambs is equal from top to bottom.

Use 12d casing nails to fasten the jambs to the trimmer studs through the shims—hammer in 2 nails at the top, 2 at the bottom, and 6 more spaced evenly between the top and bottom. Trim off the shims.

Threshold

The final step of framing an exterior door is the installation of the threshold. You can either install the threshold now or wait until you've finished hanging the door. You must, however, install the threshold before the doorstops.

Measure the width between the jambs and mark the threshold so you can cut it to that width. If the threshold is metal and has predrilled screw holes, cut some metal from each end so the holes are centered between the ends.

Position the threshold as shown in the illustration on the opposite page, so that it covers the joint between the floor and the sill. If the threshold is hardwood, drill pilot holes and nail it into place. If it is a metal flatbar, put matching screws through the predrilled holes.

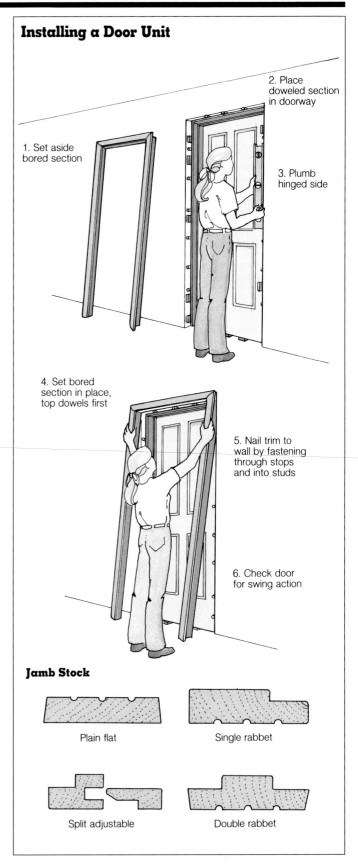

Installing a Door Unit

1. Set aside bored section

2. Place doweled section in doorway

3. Plumb hinged side

4. Set bored section in place, top dowels first

5. Nail trim to wall by fastening through stops and into studs

6. Check door for swing action

Jamb Stock

Plain flat

Single rabbet

Split adjustable

Double rabbet

Door Sizing

The door should be trimmed ⅛ to 3/16 inch smaller than the jamb width to give a 1/16- to 3/32-inch clearance on each side. In addition, trim the door to allow for weather stripping (see page 237). Do all the trimming for width on the hinge stile so you won't have to deepen the pre-bores for cylindrical locksets. Allow a ⅛-inch clearance at the top and bottom. After you hang the door, you may have to trim it some more to fit over the threshold and weather stripping.

The last step is to bevel the lock edge of the door so it will clear the jamb when the door swings. You can lay out the bevel you'll need by measuring from the center of the hinge pin (or about where it will be) to the lock edge of the door on the hinge side. Then keep the end of the scale at the axis of the hinge pin and carry this same measurement to the door-stop side of the door. Your mark should be about 1/16 inch or a little more from the edge of the door.

Frame Installation

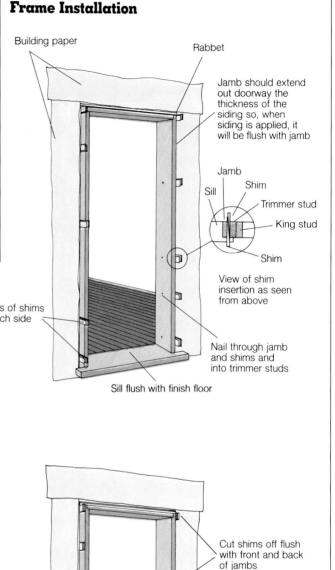

Building paper

Rabbet

Jamb should extend out doorway the thickness of the siding so, when siding is applied, it will be flush with jamb

Jamb

Shim

Sill

Trimmer stud

King stud

Shim

View of shim insertion as seen from above

5 pairs of shims on each side

Nail through jamb and shims and into trimmer studs

Sill flush with finish floor

Cut shims off flush with front and back of jambs

Wood threshold or metal bar covers joint of sill and finish floor

Building a Doorjamb

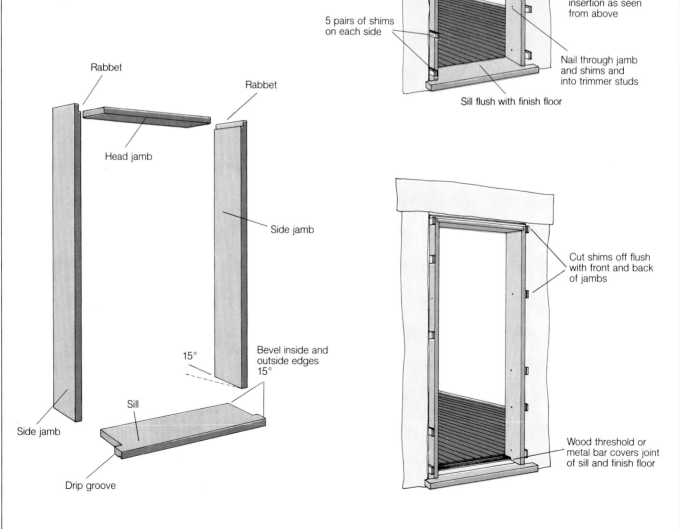

Rabbet

Head jamb

Rabbet

Side jamb

Side jamb

Sill

15°

Bevel inside and outside edges 15°

Drip groove

Suggested Door Hinge Sizes

For appearance's sake as well as utility, be sure your doors are on hinges appropriate for their width, thickness, and use.

Door Thickness (In.)	Door Width (In.)	Hinge Size (In.)
¾–1⅛ (Cabinets)	Up to 24	2½
⅞–1⅛ (Screen or storm)	Up to 36	3
1⅜ (Passage)	Up to 32	3½
	Over 32	4
1¾ (Passage or entry)	Up to 36	4½
	Over 36	5
2 (Entry)	Up to 42	5 or 6

Hinges

If you are serious about hanging doors, you should rent a butt-hinge template guide. It will allow you to rout all three mortises on the door at once and then to accurately transfer the measurements to the jamb.

On exterior doors up to 7 feet high, use three 4-inch loose-pin butt hinges (or three decorative hinges). On doors over 7 feet tall, use four hinges. To make a door fit properly, you must mortise both the door and the jamb so the hinges will be flush with the surface.

Set the door on edge. Brace it in the corner of a room or on a door buck. Hinge locations vary with taste. One common positioning is to put the top hinge 7 inches from the top of the door and the bottom one 11 inches from the bottom of the door. The middle hinge is always at the midpoint between the others.

Trace the outline of each hinge on the stile edge by using a sharp pencil, awl, or knife. Allow the leaf of the hinge to extend ¼ inch beyond the edge of the door so the knuckle won't bind against the casing when the door is fully open. Remember, the knuckle is on the side to which the door opens—inside the house on an entrance door.

When the mortises are cut, install the hinges on the door. Put the hinges in place and mark the center of each screw hole. Drill small pilot holes for the screws and be sure to drill them straight. If the screw goes in crooked, it will pull the hinge out of alignment.

Now put the door into place in the doorway and mark the position of the hinges on the

Hanging a Door

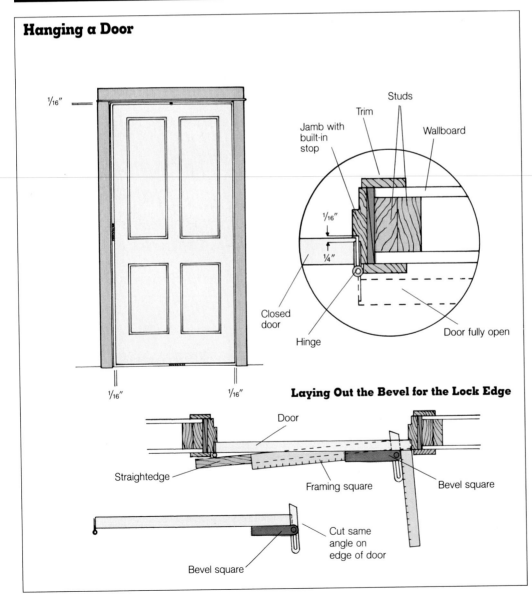

Laying Out the Bevel for the Lock Edge

jamb. Again, allow the knuckle to extend ¼ inch beyond the edge. This is easier said than done by one person, so arrange to have a helper if you can. Put small shims under the door to raise it to ¹⁄₁₆ to ⅛ inch of the top. Mark the outline of the hinges, and cut mortises in the jamb just as you did in the door.

Some pros mark and cut the mortise for the top hinge first. Then they put the door up and screw the top hinge to the jamb and use the hinge for marking the other mortises. They claim to get a consistent fit this way.

When all the mortises are cut, pull the pins from the hinges and screw the jamb leaves to the jamb. Then put the door in place, fit the hinges together, tap the pins back in, and the door is hung.

If the hinges don't line up exactly, loosen the screws on both leaves. While your helper holds the door up, tap the leaves together, insert the pins, and then tighten the screws again.

Open and close the door to check that it doesn't bind anywhere. Ideally, the door should have a ¹⁄₁₆ inch clearance on the hinge side and ¹⁄₁₆- to ³⁄₃₂-inch clearance on the lock side. If it doesn't, use a jack plane to give it the proper clearance.

If the door is sticking at the top or bottom, it could be because one of the mortises was cut too deep or not deep enough. If you discover a mortise cut too deep, put a shim of cardboard under the hinge leaf.

Cutting for Hinges

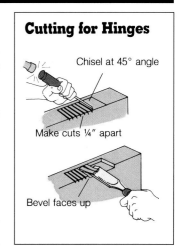

Chisel at 45° angle

Make cuts ¼" apart

Bevel faces up

Using Door Bucks

A door buck allows you to stand a door on edge while you plane it or mortise the hinges. Door bucks are easy to make and will save you a lot of time and frustration. This section describes two door bucks you can make with scrap lumber in a few minutes. Make them both and see which you find easiest to use.

To make the first buck, cut a couple of pieces of ⅜- or ¼-inch plywood 3½ inches wide and 12 inches long. Nail 2 pieces of 2 by 4, about 4 inches long, on edge near the center of each. Space them apart the thickness of a door plus ⅛ inch. Then nail square 2 by 4 legs at the ends, and you are ready to work. Just set the door on the buck and the weight will bend the strip of plywood down, clamping the door between the two 2 by 4s.

Make the second buck from lengths of 2 by 4 about 16 inches long. Cut a notch 1 inch deep and 2½ inches wide in the center of the 2 by 4s. From a scrap of 1 by 3 or 1 by 4, cut a wedge about 5 inches long (see the illustration). Set the door in the notch, and knock the wedge in to hold the door upright.

Another simple and very sturdy door buck is probably already in your arsenal of tools: a supply of pipe or bar clamps. Using clamps is a little more cumbersome and takes longer than using a real door buck, but if you have only a few doors to work on, clamps are just dandy. Just place one near each end of the door—the bars or pipes should extend in opposite directions. To protect the door, put pieces of scrap wood in the jaws of the clamp.

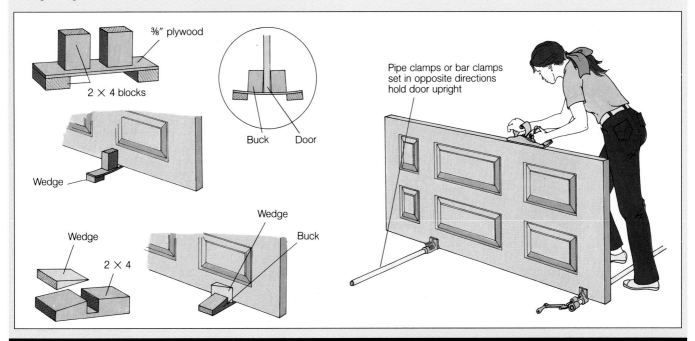

⅜" plywood

2 × 4 blocks

Buck   Door

Wedge

Wedge

Wedge   Buck

2 × 4

Pipe clamps or bar clamps set in opposite directions hold door upright

Cutting Mortises

Hinge mortises can be cut with a router and a commercially available hinge mortise template, a hinge marker, or the tried-and-true hammer and chisel. Except with the template, the outline and depth of the mortise must be marked on the wood with a sharp pencil, awl, or knife.

When using a router and template, read the instructions that come with the template carefully; be sure you understand them. You will need a straight routing bit and a guide bushing for the router. With wing nuts or knobs, clamp the template to the edge of the door. Adjust the router bit to the depth of the hinge thickness. Set the router in place and squeeze the trigger.

If the hinges have square corners, square the corners of

the mortise with a chisel. However, you can buy hinges with round corners designed to fit into router-cut mortises.

To cut mortises by hand, use a ½- or ¾-inch chisel. Score the top and bottom edges of the mortise by hammering the chisel, with the bevel inward, to the depth of the mortise. Between the scores make a series of similar cuts about ¼ inch apart. Then score the back line of the mortise as you scored the top and bottom lines.

Remove the waste wood in the mortise by driving the chisel from the edge toward the back line at the depth line; the bevel of the chisel should face up. Set the hinge in the mortise to check the fit. Make any final adjustments, and clean up the corners.

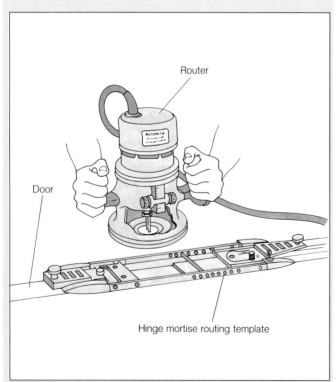

Router

Door

Hinge mortise routing template

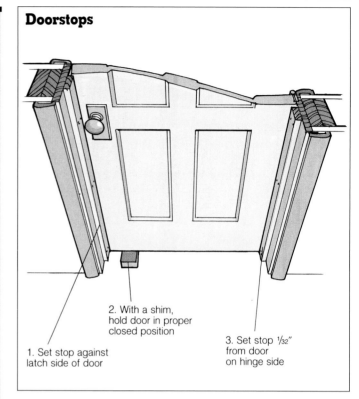

2. With a shim, hold door in proper closed position

1. Set stop against latch side of door

3. Set stop ⅟₃₂″ from door on hinge side

Doorstops

Doorstops are usually ⁷⁄₁₆ inch thick and from 1 to 2½ inches wide. You can rip the stop material yourself from 1-by stock or buy ready-made stop molding at the lumberyard. Buying the molding is much easier.

With the door closed and held in the proper position by your helper, mark the outside edge of the door with a sharp pencil. Measure and cut the stops to length. Nail the stops into place, starting with the head stop.

Weather Stripping, Locksets, and Sealing

Now you need to decide what kind of weather stripping you want around the door. Some types will require additional trimming or beveling of the door (see page 237).

Finish the installation by installing the lockset and adding the trim (see page 199). As soon as you can, apply a couple of coats of sanding sealer and paint or stain and varnish the door. Exterior doors should be sealed as soon as possible after installation, on all 6 sides, so humidity and weather changes don't damage them.

Hanging Double Doors

Double doors are generally made of solid wood. They are sometimes glazed to let light into the house. Double doors are available in many styles in both wood and metal that looks like wood. You can buy just the doors and hang them yourself or order them prehung.

Both doors in the set are hinged and both will open. The main door is the one with the

Installing a Double Door

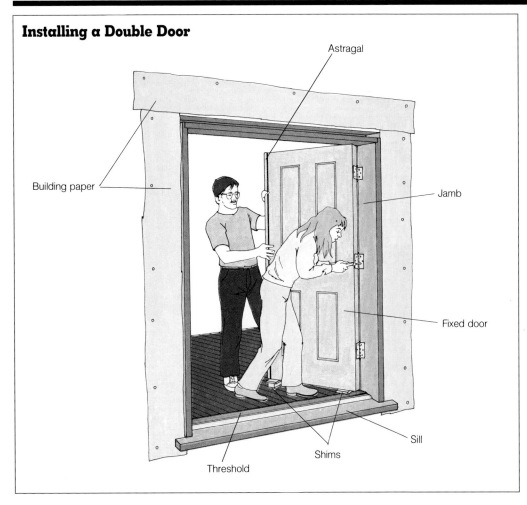

Astragal

Building paper

Jamb

Fixed door

Sill

Shims

Threshold

lockset and handle. It is the one that always opens first and is sometimes the only one that is opened for years at a time.

The other door, the one that has the astragal (that's the strip that covers the crack between the doors), is normally fixed in the closed position by sliding brass bolts. These bolts are set into the edges of the top and bottom and slide into fittings in the head jamb and threshold. If you want both doors open to admit a large party of friends or a large piece of furniture, just slide the bolts back and open the door.

Each of the double doors are installed just as a single door;

the trick is to hang them straight, true, and plumb so the crack between them is even and the tops and bottoms line up perfectly. With prehung doors, where the jambs are precision-cut and premortised, this is not difficult. Hanging your own double door requires experience and good finish carpentry skills.

The next section will describe how to install prehung double doors. To hang a double door from scratch, read Hanging a Single Door (see page 190) and do it very carefully—twice.

Jamb Installation

Construct the rough opening in the framing in the same way you would construct the framing for a standard exterior door, only wider. Install a sill (see page 187).

If the prehung doors are in the jambs when they are delivered, pull the hinge pins and remove the doors. Set the jambs in the rough opening. Plumb and level them by using shingle shims as described in the section about installing a single prehung door. So the doors hang perfectly, take extra pains to see that the top jamb is level and the jambs are absolutely plumb and square.

Door Hanging

Install the fixed door first. If the hinges are already installed, just have your helper hold the door in place while you tap in the pins. If the hinges weren't screwed to the jambs, have your helper hold the door in place as if it were half open, at about 45 degrees. Put some shims under the bottom of the door to support it. Screw the top hinge leaf to the premortised jamb first, using the long screws that should have been shipped with the doors. If possible, the screws should go through the jamb and into the trimmer stud. Then screw the other 2 hinges into the premortised positions on the jamb.

Close the door; check the gap between the door and the jamb to see that the door is hanging straight. If not, you may have to shim out a hinge, but wait to do this until the other door is up.

Now hang the main door in the same manner as the fixed door, using the long screws in the top hinge leaf. Close both doors to check the fit. Shim one or more hinges if necessary to make the doors hang straight and the joint between them even. If the doors fit too tightly, remove the hinges on the main door and plane the hinge edge as much as necessary. You will probably have to remortise the hinge locations after planing.

Score and snap off the shims. Install the entrance set and weather stripping. As soon as possible, protect the door with a couple of coats of sanding sealer and paint or stain and varnish. Be sure to protect all 6 sides.

Framing a Sliding Door

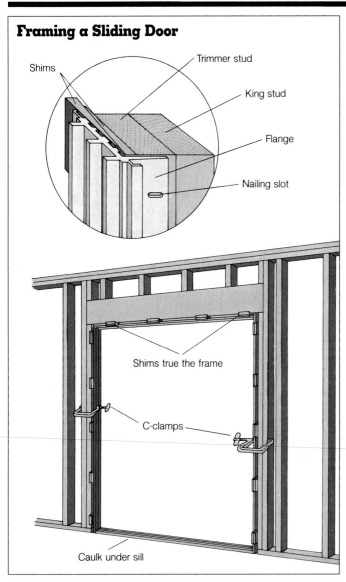

Shims

Trimmer stud

King stud

Flange

Nailing slot

Shims true the frame

C-clamps

Caulk under sill

Choosing Sliding Doors

These doors are generally sold in the standard door height of 80 inches and in widths—for two doors—from 60 inches to 16 feet. Sliding doors can be ordered in custom sizes, but they are very expensive. Sliding glass doors are easy to install, so don't hesitate to put them in yourself. You can save quite a bit in labor costs.

Shop around for a good price on sliding doors, but make sure the glass in them is of good quality. Most local codes require safety or tempered glass in sliding doors. Be sure the doors you buy have it even if it's not required by the code. The code may also require dual glass if you live in a cold-winter climate.

Security is another thing to consider. Glass is simply more vulnerable than metal or wood. You can, however, make it more difficult for a burglar to

pry the door back and snap the lock if you take a few precautions. Choose the sliding doors with the most sturdy locks, and try to find doors with track locks as well. If yours don't have track locks, cut a length of ¾-inch dowel or a 1 by 1 stick to fit closely between the movable door and the jamb on the opposite side. With the stick in the track, the door cannot be opened.

Most sliding doors are sold with screws in the head jamb that just clear the door when it slides. These screws prevent the door from being lifted up and off the track. If you get doors that don't have these screws, drill a couple of holes through the head jamb into the header and install your own.

Sliding doors usually have either a wood or an aluminum frame. If you choose aluminum, look for those with thermal-break frames. The frames have an insert of plastic that minimizes the amount of heat that the aluminum can conduct out of the house.

If you live in an area where the winters are cold, place the doors to take advantage of the low angle of winter sunlight. Then block the summer sun with a roof overhang or an outside blind. Some doors now have miniblinds between the dual panes of glass.

Sliding doors can be arranged to open either to the left or to the right. After the frame is installed, put the fixed section in place first. Put it in the outside track on the side you want it. Then put the sliding door on the inside track on the opposite side.

Hanging Sliding Doors

Try to have the doors delivered and on hand at the time you do the rough framing. If this isn't possible, be sure you get a copy of the installation instructions for your particular doors so you're sure the rough opening is the correct size. The rough opening should be whatever size the manufacturer specifies, usually ½ inch wider and ½ inch taller than the door unit.

Take special care to make sure the trimmer studs are plumb and the header is level. Minor variations can be corrected with shims, but it's a lot easier if they're perfectly true to start with.

Sliding glass doors are usually packaged and shipped with the jambs unassembled. The first step is to put them together. This is usually done by inserting screws at the 4 corners. Before putting the frame in place, lay at least 2 thick beads of caulk along the floor, where they'll be under the outside edge of the bottom track, to provide a weathertight seal.

Have your helper assist you in placing the frame in the opening by moving the frame from the outside to the inside. Align the frame so there is an equal gap on each side. Step on the sill to distribute the caulk and to make it lie flat. Check the sill with a level and, if necessary, put several shims along the low side to level it.

Screw the sill down by using countersunk brass or galvanized screws about 12 inches apart. Do not drive the screws all the way home until the rest of the frame is properly set.

Use a level to check that the frame is true in the opening—not leaning in or out. Hold it in place with a C-clamp on each side. The clamps will also draw the outside metal flanges or wood trim tight against the framing studs.

Hold a straight board against each jamb to see if it bows in or out. Correct any distortions with shims. Even if the jambs are perfectly straight, use 5 pairs of shims on each side to keep the frame solidly in place. Use at least 4 pairs of shims along the head jamb. Use the steel framing square in each corner to check that the frame is square.

For metal doors, drive screws through the predrilled holes in the side and head jambs to fasten the frames to the rough opening framing. For wood doors, hammer 12d casing nails through the shims to nail the wood frames to the trimmer studs.

Lay the head-jamb flashing, which usually comes with the unit, over the outside of the head jamb and nail it to the header so it will be covered with the siding. Do not nail it to the head jamb.

Usually, the metal sill of the bottom track overhangs the rough opening and must be supported. Cut a length of rot-resistant wood or pressure-treated lumber to the width of the sill, and rip it to a width ⅛ inch narrower than the overhang. Lay a bead of caulk along the top, push it into place against the bottom of the sill overhang, and nail it into place. Integrate the installation of the sill with that of the exterior siding.

Put the stationary section into place in the outer channel

on either side, depending on which side you want the sliding door. On many makes of aluminum doors, you will note that the top corner of the frame of the fixed section is only partially cut. The fixed section will not fit into the top channel until you complete the cut with a hacksaw and remove the extra piece of metal.

The stationary section must fit tightly into the side jamb. If you can't push it in easily by hand, place a length of 2 by 4 against the opposite edge to protect it and rap on the 2 by 4 with a hammer to force the section all the way into the jamb. On some metal frames, screws through predrilled holes secure the stationary section to the frame on the inside.

On wood doors, the rails are mortised to accept holding brackets. Put the brackets into place, drill into the head jamb and sill, and use screws to secure the brackets.

The next step is to install the sliding door. For wood doors, begin by putting the security screws into the head jamb. Then remove the head stop. Lift the door into position, and place the bottom of the door so the rollers rest on the rail in the sill. Push the top of the door into position against the weather stripping in the top track, and screw the head stop back into place.

On metal doors, begin by removing the security screws from the top track. Tip the top of the door toward the frame, and slip the top into the upper channel. Lift the door so the bottom of the door clears the bottom rail, and set the rollers on their rail. Slide the door open, and replace or install the

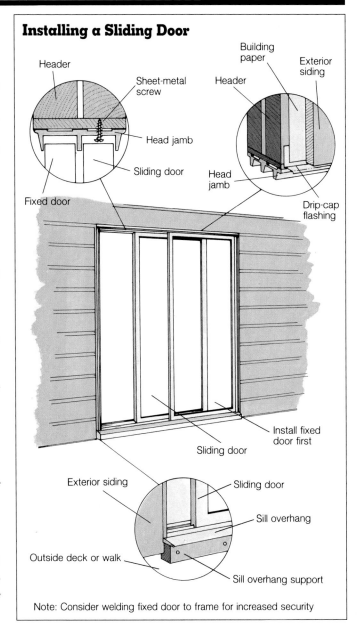

Installing a Sliding Door

Header
Sheet-metal screw
Head jamb
Sliding door
Fixed door

Building paper
Exterior siding
Header
Head jamb
Drip-cap flashing

Install fixed door first
Sliding door

Exterior siding
Sliding door
Sill overhang
Outside deck or walk
Sill overhang support

Note: Consider welding fixed door to frame for increased security

security screws in the head jamb so the door can no longer be lifted off its rail.

Slide the door back and forth a few times to check for smooth movement. Then close it and check the fit at the latch end. If one end is lower than the other, causing a poor fit or drag on the track, adjust the rollers at the bottom corners. On some brands of doors, the adjusting screw is on the edge of the door. In others, you must

unscrew and remove caps on the inside door corner, use a screwdriver to turn the recessed adjusting screws, and replace the caps.

There is also an adjusting screw by the latch. Open and close the door a few times to see if the latch fits and catches properly. Adjust it until it works just right. You are now ready to install the siding and the trim.

Garage Door Types

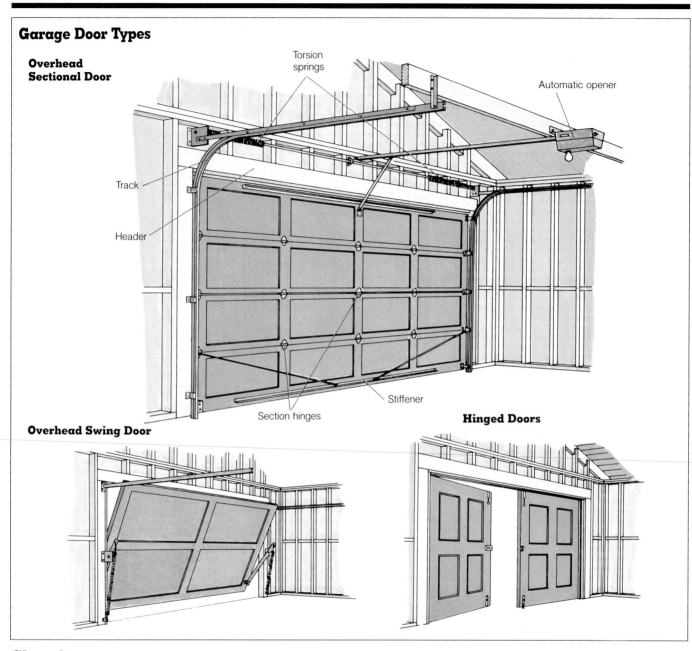

Overhead Sectional Door

Torsion springs

Automatic opener

Track

Header

Section hinges

Stiffener

Overhead Swing Door

Hinged Doors

Choosing a Garage Door

The wide variety of styles and sizes of garage doors falls into four main categories: overhead swing, overhead sectional, sectional barn, and hinged barn.

The major advantage of an overhead door is that, when it's open, the door is out of the way. The swing door is a one-piece door that operates on a pivot. It

has counterbalanced springs to help you lift it open and to hold it both open and closed. Because it is supported only at the four corners, a swing door tends to sag and warp even though it usually has a cable-and-turnbuckle truss in the middle. A swing door is cheaper than a sectional door and needs less space overhead to operate.

The overhead sectional door is the most common type of garage door. Even though it's more complex and more expensive initially, it more than makes up for it in durability and ease of operation. You need more overhead clearance for an overhead sectional door than for an overhead swing door, but you can open the former even if a car is parked right in front of it. Some city

codes require overhead sectional doors because they open straight up and cannot hit anyone passing by outside.

Sectional barn doors are similar to overhead sectional doors, but the barn doors operate horizontally. They are in sections that may or may not be hinged together. Barn doors are hung on a track that goes around one or both sides of the

198

garage. To open them, you slide them sideways. Their big advantage is size. They can be much wider than any overhead door. In fact, they can be any width you want. If you want a three-car garage with a single door or want to park your old Cessna 190 airplane in the garage, this is the door for you. Barn doors cannot be fitted with automatic openers, however.

Hinged barn doors are the least expensive kind of garage door, but their disadvantage is that they are always in the way. The two separate sections of the door are hinged to the side jambs of the frame of the garage-door opening. They, of course, must swing outward, so they block your vision as you exit the garage and block the sides of the driveway as long as they are open. Hinged barn doors are difficult to impossible to fit with automatic openers.

Hanging Garage Doors

Because of their size, complexity, and special hardware, garage doors are rarely constructed on-site. They are bought as either ready-made or custom-made kits from garage-door companies or the large catalog stores.

Installation methods and procedures will depend on the kind of doors you want and the kit you select. See the illustrations for a general idea of how the various kinds of doors are mounted and operate.

Always follow the manufacturer's directions precisely—especially when installing the large springs. On overhead swing doors, always install the spring-lift device with the door open; the spring is "loaded" when the door is closed.

Installing an Entrance Set

A visit to a hardware store or locksmith will bring you up-to-date on all the entrance sets available today. New styles, including electronic devices, are being developed continually. The most common entrance sets are cylinder locks, which are part of the door handle, and dead bolts. Dead bolts and doorknobs with or without a cylinder lock are installed in the same manner. They are installed with simple tools.

Entrance sets come in a wide variety of styles and price ranges. Choose the one that best complements your door and house style.

Cylinder locks, or key-in-knob locks, have a wide barrel that goes through the door. The lock mechanism is in the knob. It is easy to install and fairly inexpensive, but it is also the easiest kind of lock to force because of the rounded latch. If you have a damaged or malfunctioning cylinder lock, it is simpler to replace the entire unit than to repair it.

A dead bolt is intended to supplement a lockset. The bolt should extend at least 1 inch into the jamb, since prying a door will usually force the lock no more than ½ inch. The outside face of the lock is either flush with the door surface or protrudes from the door on a tapered cylinder.

When you install a lock, make sure that the door is sound. Obviously, the best lock is no good if the door is flimsy and easy to break or knock down. On a very secure door, the jambs are at least 1¼ inches thick, with the stops milled right into them.

Cylinder locks and dead bolts engage a strike plate that is set into the jamb. If the strike plate fails, the lock gives. Most strike plates are made of a flimsy metal that is held to the jamb. You can buy reinforcement plates that are made of heavy-gauge metal and include long screws that penetrate all the way through the jamb and into the stud.

Avoid double-key locks, which from the inside can only be opened with a key. They make escape very difficult in case of an emergency such as a fire or confronting a trapped intruder. Many local codes prohibit them.

Locksets should be centered 36 inches above the inside finish floor. A dead bolt is usually installed 4 to 6 inches above the lockset. In measuring for locks and marking the hole centers, always work from the "high side" of the door—the edge away from the stop.

Keep the door from moving by wedging shims under it. Install the lockset or dead bolt first, followed by the strike plate. The five steps that follow describe the installation of most cylinder locks. The installation of some locks may be different, however; be sure to read all the manufacturer's instructions before starting—especially before drilling holes in an expensive door.

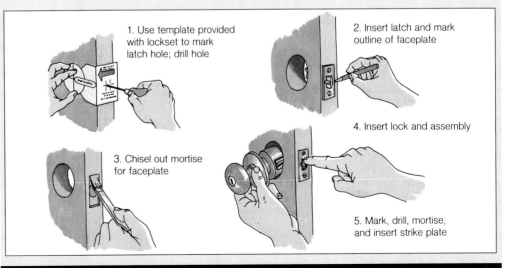

1. Use template provided with lockset to mark latch hole; drill hole

2. Insert latch and mark outline of faceplate

3. Chisel out mortise for faceplate

4. Insert lock and assembly

5. Mark, drill, mortise, and insert strike plate

INSTALLING WINDOWS

Make all window choices prior to framing the window openings to ensure that the spaces provided will fit the windows. Skylight installation will affect the roof framing and the installation of the finish roof. Your construction schedule will be greatly enhanced if the spaces you've built are the right size for the windows you ordered.

- ☐ Tool belt
- ☐ Hammer
- ☐ Framing hammer
- ☐ Handsaw
- ☐ Power circular saw
- ☐ Steel tape measure
- ☐ Combination square
- ☐ Framing square
- ☐ 24-inch level
- ☐ Slot screwdrivers
- ☐ Phillips screwdrivers
- ☐ Wood chisels
- ☐ Nail sets
- ☐ Utility knife
- ☐ Awl

Choosing Windows

The difficulty of installing windows depends on the type of window and the type of frame. On a difficulty scale of 10 points, consider installing windows a 5. Metal-framed windows are easier to install than wood-framed windows. Two people should have basic carpentry skills to install metal-framed windows and finish carpentry skills to install wood-framed windows. The two of you will need four hours to

install each wood-framed window and two hours to install each metal-framed window. Greenhouse windows take about two hours to install; skylights, about four hours each. These specialty windows may require an extra helper or two, depending on the size of the window.

Like exterior doors, windows have three purposes. One function is to admit light and present views while providing protection from heat, cold, water, and dust. The second is to provide an exit in an emergency. The third purpose is to enhance style. Windows should have a style that complements the design of the house. Consider all three purposes as you decide on the kinds of windows you want in your new house.

There are so many styles and manufacturers that make slightly different versions of the same windows that the big problem is deciding what type you want. Specialty windows—including greenhouse windows and skylights—are increasingly popular choices in new homes. Get to know the key aspects of

different kinds of windows, including both their good qualities and their limitations. Then study all the windows available from suppliers before you make your final choice.

Although there are many types of windows, your decisions fall into just a few categories. Windows are either fixed or openable. Frames are either metal, wood, or clad wood. Glass is glazed in a few different ways.

Fixed Windows

A fixed window does not open to permit ventilation or cleaning, but its sealed edges provide excellent protection against air infiltration. Fixed windows are available in almost any shape, style, or size. If you choose a large size, it should be dual glazed for energy conservation, even if dual glazing is not required by the local code. Fixed windows are often filled with colored glass or filled or covered with stained glass in interesting designs. These windows can make striking design accents.

Openable Windows

Openable windows include casement, double-hung, single-hung, sliding, awning, rotating, and jalousie styles. All can be glazed with a single pane or many panes, in designs to go with any architectural style.

Casement windows usually open outward, but they can be ordered to open inward. They provide excellent ventilation because the entire area of the window can open. Some styles have pivot hinges that allow for easier cleaning.

Double-hung and single-hung windows differ only in that both sashes of the double-hung window open; only one sash of a single-hung window does. A casual observer usually can't tell the difference by looking at them. These windows provide less ventilation than a casement window because only half the window area can be open at one time. The weight and pulley systems of old double-hung windows tended to stick, but the spring-tension devices in new styles work well for many years.

Sliding windows are generally the least expensive of all the openable windows. As with double-hung windows, only half the window area can be open at one time. The inner sash is usually designed for easy removal so you can clean both sides of both sashes from the inside.

Awning windows are hinged at the top and open out. Hopper windows are hinged at the bottom and open in. Their design allows airflow and easy cleaning from the inside, even though the whole window doesn't open.

The rotating window can pivot on its central axis to open partially. It can turn 90 degrees for maximum ventilation or swivel 180 degrees to aid in cleaning the outside.

Jalousie windows, with their many small, pivoting panes, provide good ventilation when open. Unfortunately, they don't seal well when closed and they are prohibited by many energy codes. They are easy to reach for cleaning, but the cleaning is tedious. Jalousie windows are suitable only for porches in warm-weather areas.

Many window styles are available in a double-glazed version with a miniblind between the panes to control light and heat.

Frames

Aluminum windows come with or without thermal breaks, which minimize the transmission of heat or cold. Thermal breaks encase the exterior of the frame. You'll never need to paint them, but color selection is limited.

Metal frames without thermal breaks transmit cold and heat, which may result in condensation problems. They are durable if painted regularly to prevent rust.

Traditional wood frames have excellent insulating qualities and seal tighter than metal frames. However, a skilled carpenter must install them and they must be painted regularly.

Clad-wood frames are factory-covered with protective vinyl on the exterior so no painting is required. In extreme cold, however, vinyl is brittle and may crack. A wide variety of colors is available. To contribute to a traditional look, clad-wood frames are often unpainted on the interior.

Glazes

Glazing refers to how glass is installed within a window. Different glazes are appropriate for different uses. The type of glazing affects the thermal qualities of the glass, and these thermal qualities affect the energy efficiency of the house. If you live in a moderate climate, you may be able to use single-pane windows throughout. This would be fortunate because single-pane windows are quite economical and easy to handle. But in most areas, especially those with cold-winter climates, the building codes demand windows with better thermal qualities. This is fortunate also, because in cold climates thermal windows will prove cost-effective in the long run and contribute to the comfort of the house.

Single-pane glazing is the least expensive glazing. A single-pane window has poor thermal qualities and is commonly used in small-pane windows.

A double-pane window contains a factory-sealed air space between panes to provide a markedly improved thermal barrier.

Tempered glass provides strength. It is required for glass doors, including sliding doors and shower doors and for windows that are installed close to the floor. Tempered glass also provides the strength needed for large picture windows. Tempered glass is available in various glazes for different thermal qualities.

Acrylic glazing provides a virtually unbreakable window. Unfortunately, though the plastic is clear initially, it scratches easily and dulls with age.

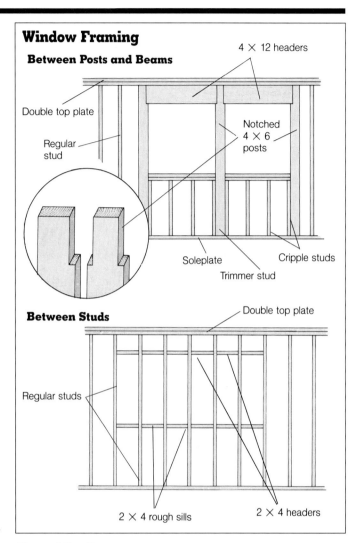

Window Framing
Between Posts and Beams

4 × 12 headers

Double top plate

Regular stud

Notched 4 × 6 posts

Soleplate

Trimmer stud

Cripple studs

Between Studs

Double top plate

Regular studs

2 × 4 rough sills

2 × 4 headers

Considering Fixed Windows

Custom window shops sell fixed windows in any size or shape, all made up and ready to install. They can be bought already set into wood jambs that fit into the rough opening or in metal frames with nailing flanges. Buying windows in frames makes them easier to install but adds to the cost.

As an alternative, this section will take you through all the fundamentals of installing your own fixed window, including how to make and set a sill, how to build the jambs, and how to set the window.

The job is somewhat complex but still within the reach of the amateur owner-builder.

Careful work is needed. Take a few practice runs by installing fixed windows in the garage, workshop, or utility room before attempting the big one in your living room.

Framing

There are several ways to frame the rough openings for fixed windows. The most common way is to frame a standard opening, as described on page 82. A standard opening consists of the king studs, trimmer studs, header, and rough sill.

Installing the Windowsill

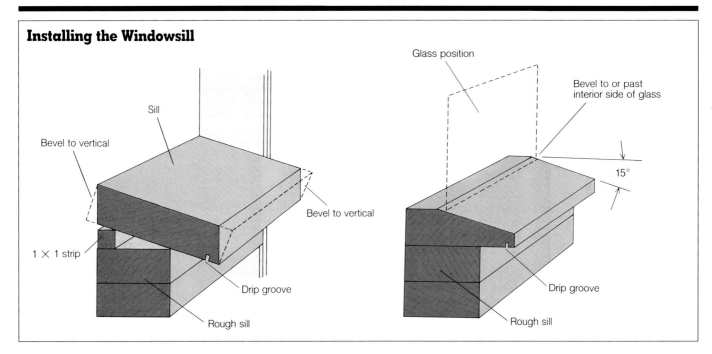

An alternative opening is often used to frame a wall for a bank of high fixed windows. This consists of a series of 4 by 6 support posts spaced 4 feet on center. As the illustration shows, the top ends are notched on each side to accept lengths of 4 by 12s as headers. In rooms of standard height, 4 by 12s are commonly used as headers in door or window openings—they fit right under the top plate and no cripple studs are needed above them. The rough sill is set conventionally, on cripple studs, since it will be covered by the interior wall material.

An unconventional way to frame an opening is to set the windows directly between studs. In this case, no header is needed as long as you maintain standard stud spacing, which is 16 inches on center for 2 by 4s and 24 inches on center for 2 by 6s. It may sound like this window spacing would chop up the view, but in fact the series of narrow windows breaks the view into attractive individually framed pictures that many people prefer. In addition, a series of narrow windows suits many more architectural styles than does one huge pane of glass.

If you choose to experiment with alternative methods, your primary consideration is to maintain proper structural support of the wall. Essentially, that involves using headers of the correct size for the opening. If you are in any doubt, consult a licensed contractor or the building inspector.

Windowsill

The sill must be angled to shed water. Setting a fixed window on a level sill would surely cause water that is blown against the window to leak inside. This would not only stain the interior wall, but could cause wood rot.

Sill material can be purchased at a hardware or lumber store, or you can make your own quite easily. To make your own, choose 2-by stock that is at least 2 inches wider than the distance from interior to exterior wall. Before installing it, set the blade on the circular saw to make a cut ¼ inch deep. Make this cut along the bottom of the exterior side of the sill, about ½ inch from the edge. This will prevent water from creeping up the underside of the sill to the house.

The sill can be prepared in two different ways. In the first, the sill is raised on the interior side by resting it on a length of 1 by 1. Begin by beveling the edges of the sill with a circular saw so that they are vertical when the sill is in place. Do this by setting the sill on the 1 by 1, then using a level to mark a vertical line along one end. Set the blade on a circular saw to that angle and cut the sill. Flip the sill over and cut along the edge.

The other way eliminates setting the sill on a 1 by 1. Clamp the sill in a vise and then rip a bevel cut along the top exterior side. The angle need be only about 15 degrees, but it should extend to the interior side of the glass. A bevel deep enough to reach the exterior side of the glass could allow water to creep underneath the pane. Once in place, the sill is covered on the interior by the stool and the apron.

Jambs, or Not

Fixed windows can be installed either with or without jambs. The better way is to construct jambs that frame the glass and are then set in the rough opening. The jambs can be shimmed to be square if the opening is not. In addition, the jambs are independent of the house structure and thus, if it shifts, the windows will remain in place. If the glass is set between framing members only and the house settles an inch or so, a gap may open up along the edges of the window.

On the other hand, it is much easier simply to place the windows between framing members than to construct jambs. Not all houses settle significantly, and the window can be recaulked if necessary.

Without a Jamb

Install windows without a jamb by either using stops or using rabbets. The choice is yours and should be based on which you think is easier for you.

In an installation using stops, windows are set between verticals spaced 4 feet on center and the glass is held in place between the verticals by ¾-inch stops on each side of the glass. A standard header and rough sill must be installed.

First put the sill into place on the rough sill. Position the inside stops by measuring in 1½ inches from the outside edge (the thickness of two ¾ inch stops), plus the thickness of the glass (usually ⅝ inch for double panes), plus ¼ inch. The additional ¼ inch allows an ⅛-inch clearance on both sides of the glass for a strip of butyl glazing tape all around the window. The butyl tape, available at custom window shops, acts as a seal and remains pliant to allow the wood to expand or contract without disturbing the windowpane.

Once the measurements are made and marked, nail 1 by 1 stock (actually ¾ by ¾ inch) around the window opening to form the inside stops. Note that you'll need to bevel the bottom stop at an angle to match the sill. Lay a narrow strip of butyl

Installing a Window Without Jambs

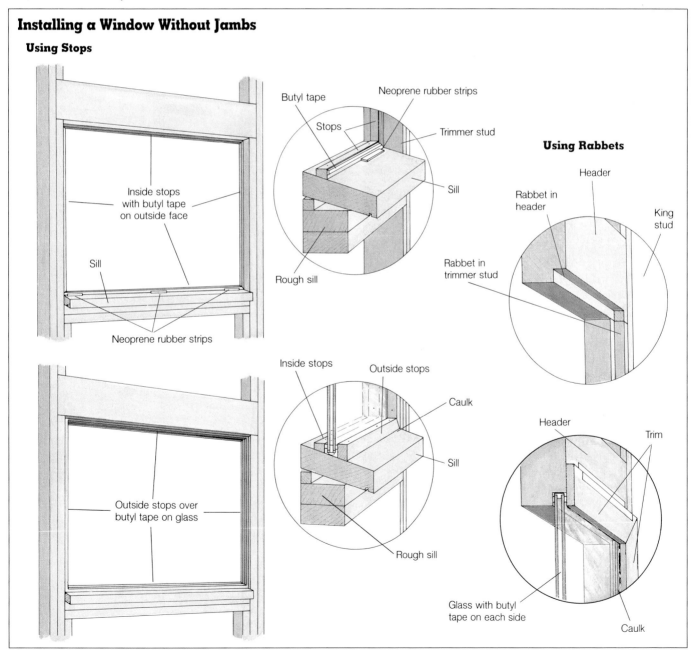

Using Stops

Inside stops with butyl tape on outside face

Sill

Neoprene rubber strips

Butyl tape

Neoprene rubber strips

Stops

Trimmer stud

Sill

Rough sill

Outside stops over butyl tape on glass

Inside stops

Outside stops

Caulk

Sill

Rough sill

Using Rabbets

Header

Rabbet in header

King stud

Rabbet in trimmer stud

Header

Trim

Glass with butyl tape on each side

Caulk

tape around the stop, where the glass will fit against it.

Cut 3 strips of neoprene rubber, called setting blocks, the same thickness as the glass, 4 inches long. Place these strips, which will cushion the glass, on the sill next to the bottom stop, one strip at each side and one in the center.

With a helper put the glass into place against the stops so it rests on the setting blocks. While your helper holds the glass, apply the butyl tape around the outside edges of the window.

Place the outside stops so they are snug against the butyl tape but not crushing it. Nail the stops into place. For this particular style, no exterior trim is necessary.

The second method is a modification of the first. A more finished appearance is obtained by using dado blades on a table saw or a router to cut a rabbet around the edges of the support posts and the header. Make the rabbet ½ inch wide and as deep as the glass is thick plus ¼ inch for the butyl tape. Apply the rabbet where the pane will fit, and put the setting blocks into place on the sill.

With the help of a second person, put the glass into place and put the butyl tape around the outside edge of the glass.

Nail the exterior trim into place so that it overlaps the window by ½ inch, the same amount as the rabbet. Apply caulk to seal the gap between the trim and the glass.

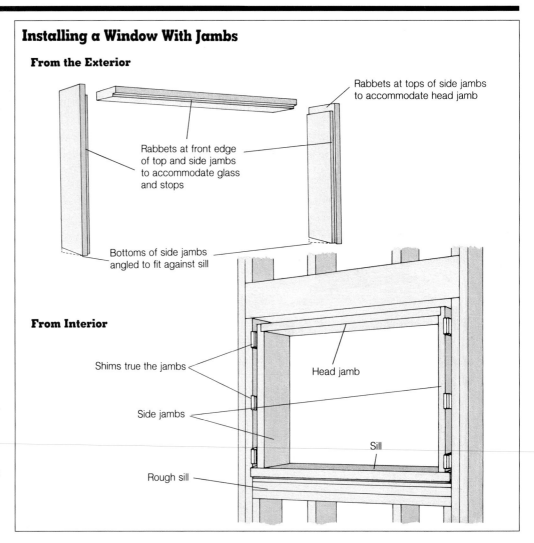

Installing a Window With Jambs

From the Exterior

Rabbets at tops of side jambs to accommodate head jamb

Rabbets at front edge of top and side jambs to accommodate glass and stops

Bottoms of side jambs angled to fit against sill

From Interior

Shims true the jambs

Head jamb

Side jambs

Sill

Rough sill

With a Jamb

A jamb allows you to set a window in an opening that is not square. Make the jamb from kiln-dried wood, if available, so that it will not warp and shrink as it dries. Use 2-by stock wide enough to cover the opening from the interior or to the exterior siding. You will probably have to use lumber that is wider and rip it to size.

With a table saw and dado blade or a router, rabbet the exterior edges of the jamb stock. Cut the rabbet to a depth equal to half the size of the outside stops. The rabbet width of should be ¾ inch for the outside stop, plus the thickness

of the glass, plus ¼ inch for the butyl tape on both sides.

Construct the jamb for the size of the glass, with the side jambs rabbeted on the tops so the head jamb is flush with the tops. Construct the jamb so there will be ½ inch clearance from the rough opening on the 2 sides and the top. No jamb material is needed on the bottom, but the sill must be perfectly level. If it isn't, shim it on one side to level it.

As described in the section about installing doorjambs, place the jamb in the rough opening and place shingle shims from inside and outside

to secure the jamb. Use a steel square and a level to ensure that the jamb is plumb. Fasten it into place by nailing through the shims.

Put the setting blocks on the sill, put the butyl tape in the rabbet where the glass will press against it, then put the glass in place.

While a helper holds the glass, tape the exterior edges of the glass and then nail on the stops. Caulk along the edges between the stops and the glass, then install the trim around the window.

Later, after the wallboard is installed, install the stool, apron, and interior trim.

Installing a Wood-Frame Openable Window

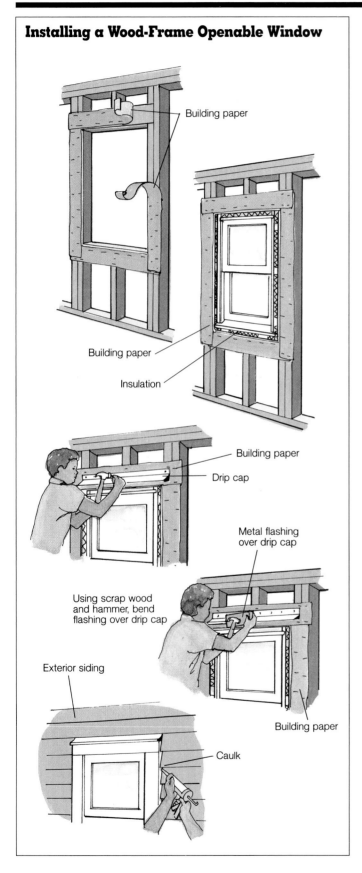

Building paper

Building paper

Insulation

Building paper

Drip cap

Using scrap wood and hammer, bend flashing over drip cap

Metal flashing over drip cap

Exterior siding

Building paper

Caulk

Considering Wood-Framed Openable Windows

Most wood-framed openable windows, of whatever style, are installed in the same fashion. If your window is a standard size, you can find one ready-made that will fit. Custom-fit windows can be made up in window shops but are considerably more expensive. Whether your new window is ready-made or custom-fit, you must make sure that the rough opening is the correct size. Different manufacturers specify different gaps between the window jamb and rough opening to allow for shimming. This gap is usually ¼ to ½ inch.

The depth of the wood-frame material must match the depth of the overall wall thickness, which is from exterior to interior covering. The interior of the window jamb must be flush with the inside wallcovering. When you order windows, specify the jamb width based on the wall thickness. Jambs should be about ¹⁄₁₆ inch wider than the wall thickness.

Premade flashing is available for most window sizes; check for it where you buy other window components.

Wood-Framed Windows

Before each window is installed, it should be squared. Lay it facedown on a flat surface, then place a steel framing square inside the corners. Both sides of the square should rest flush against the window jambs. If they don't, push at

diagonal corners until the window is square. Then tack 2 thin pieces of wood across 2 corners to hold it square. Trim off any overhang so that the frame can be inserted into the rough opening.

With building paper or special paper flashing, cover the sheathing and the studs forming the rough opening. Bend the paper around the trimmer studs, rough sill, and header. Place the bottom piece first, then the sides, then the top piece; each should overlap the one put on before. Staple the paper into place.

Install the premade flashing under the siding at the top of the opening. The flashing that protrudes should be long enough to overlap the top edge of the window frame by ½ inch. When the window is in place, bend this down over the top trim.

Now put the window into place. While a helper holds it there, check that the frame is flush with the interior wall. If it extends into the room, push it back flush with the wall.

With everything ready, have the helper hold the window in place while you center it in the opening from inside. Use shims to raise the windowsill from the rough sill until the gap equals that between the head jamb and rough header. Place a level on the jamb to check it, and shim both sides to wedge the window into place. With 8d casing nails, nail the sill to the rough sill, through the shims. Fasten the jambs to the trimmer studs with 12d casing nails through the exterior stops. With a nail set, sink the nails so the heads are below the wood surface. When the

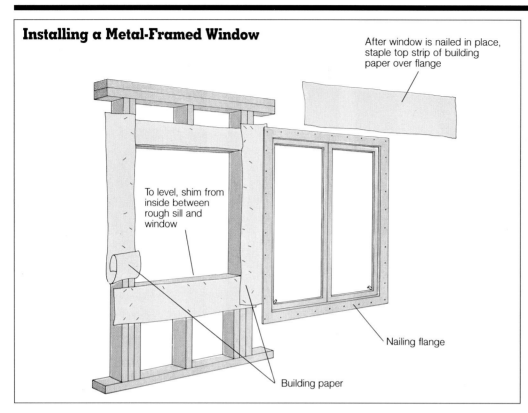

Installing a Metal-Framed Window

After window is nailed in place, staple top strip of building paper over flange

To level, shim from inside between rough sill and window

Building paper

Nailing flange

window is finally stained or painted, fill the holes with wood putty.

Later, bend the flashing over the head casing and install building paper and the exterior siding over the flashing.

Considering Metal-Framed Windows

The metal window frame with a nail-on fin or flange is used for virtually every type of window, openable or fixed.

Metal-Framed Windows

If openable, metal window frames are shipped with the sashes in place. Keep the windows closed and locked during installation.

Manufacturers make windows fractionally smaller than the size specified. This will give

you all the clearance you need. Thus, for a window 3 feet wide you need a rough opening 3 feet wide, with no additional clearance. However, it is always prudent to discuss the exact dimensions with the window supplier.

The first installation step is to cover the edges of the rough opening with building paper or special paper flashing. Note in the illustration how it is stapled into place: The bottom strip is put on first, and the 2 side strips overlap the bottom strip and extend 6 inches above window height. The top strip goes on after the window is installed and overlaps the nail-on flashing.

Once the paper is up, the actual installation is simple. Run a bead of caulk around the inside of the fin. Have a helper

put the window into place, with the nail-on fins tight against the rough opening. From inside, use shingle shims to raise the window until the gaps at top and bottom are equal. Center the window in the space.

Place a level on the bottom edge of the frame. Adjust the frame until it is perfectly level. Open the sash to see that the window slides smoothly and closes evenly.

Hold the window firmly in place, and drive 8d nails through the flanges into the rough opening frame. Space nails every 12 inches. Staple flashing paper across the top.

Later, when installing the exterior siding, the siding should be fitted over the flange and snug against the window frame. Run a bead of caulk between siding and frame. Then trim around the window, as desired.

Considering Clad Windows

A clad window is a combination of a standard wood window and a metal window. The outside of a clad window usually has a nailing fin made of aluminum or vinyl, which you nail into place in the same manner you would nail any metal window. The inside is installed and trimmed in the same manner as a standard wood window.

Considering Greenhouse Windows

A greenhouse window is an attractive and practical addition to any house, but it is particularly nice in the kitchen. A variety of herbs and flowers can be kept growing in it the year around to provide culinary treats and color. Even though the greenhouse window extends only 16 inches at most, its open design enlarges the room visually. Proper shading of greenhouse windows is important. Overheating is one of their biggest problems, and it kills many plants.

Aluminum-framed greenhouse windows are commonly sold through glass and window outlets and building-supply stores. The windows come in standard sizes or can be made to fit your particular need. They are either single- or double-glazed.

Also consider the venting system. To protect the plants, venting is essential during hot weather. The most efficient

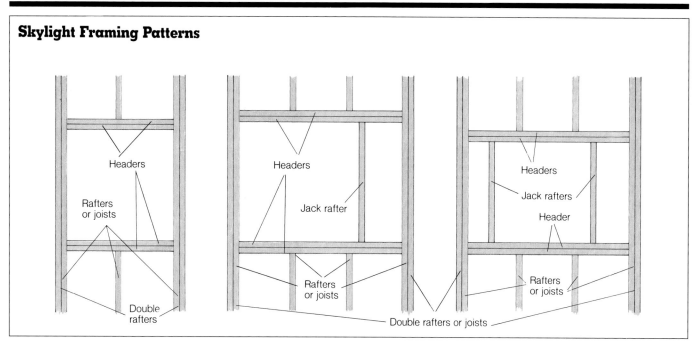

Greenhouse-Window Installation

vents are side casement or sliding windows that provide cross-ventilation. A single vent at the top, to release hot air, is just as effective. Less effective is a ventilation system with small windows opening only at the sides. The hot air at the top of the window cannot escape to the outside; instead, it's pushed back into the house.

To order a greenhouse window, you must have the rough opening measurements. Virtually all greenhouse windows are metal, with nail-on fins.

Greenhouse-Window Installation

The standard greenhouse window is installed in the same manner as other metal-framed windows (see previous page). Even though the greenhouse window protrudes from the side of the house, it is lightweight and no additional supports are needed.

Considering Skylights

In choosing a skylight location, consider the kind of light you'll be letting in. On a roof slope facing south or west, the skylight will admit a lot of direct summer sun. That can increase room temperature and fade rugs and furniture. Placing it on an east or north slope will give you nearly as much light but less direct sun. If you must place a skylight where it will receive a lot of direct sunlight, choose one that is tinted.

Skylights usually range in width from 16 inches to 4 feet and in length from 2 feet to 6 feet, but you can have them custom-made to fit nearly any opening. Smaller skylights, which are less expensive, generally admit ample light. In addition, skylights that are only 2 feet wide will fit between most rafters. This simplifies the installation.

In addition to size, consider the kind of skylight you want.

Some have a tinted bubble to reduce light, some have a frosted bubble to diffuse light, and others have clear plastic or glass. Bubbles can be single- or double-paned. The latter is usually required by code in cold climates.

Some skylights open to provide summer ventilation. The most elaborate of these are operated electrically through thermostats set at a temperature of your choice or by sensors that close the window at the first sign of moisture.

Some skylights are self-flashing, which means they are quite simple to install, but some roofing professionals consider these slightly prone to leaks. The other style is mounted over a wood frame called a curb, which must be flashed. Whichever you decide on, do some comparative shopping because prices vary considerably. This book will show you how to install both kinds.

Curb-Mounted Skylights

The curb is made from 2 by 4s or 2 by 6s. Measure and cut carefully so that it is ½ inch smaller all around than the interior dimension of the skylight. This allows the skylight to fit over both the curb and its flashing.

When the curb is nailed together, square it with a framing square. Then tack 2 light pieces of wood across the diagonal corners to hold it in position.

The illustrations show the different patterns of framing an opening. The simplest way is to use regular rafters rather than building one or more jack rafters.

When you sheath the roof, leave the opening for the skylight flush with the inside edge of the framed opening.

Set the curb over the hole in the sheathing when you are ready to install the roofing. Double-check the curb to ensure that it is centered square and on an even plane, then toenail it to the rafters by nailing through the decking.

Some skylights are sold with a flashing kit as an optional extra. Curb flashing is often called saddle flashing, a term that refers to the way the head and base flashing fit around the top and bottom of the curb. If you give the outside measurements of the curb to a sheet-metal shop, they will make the flashing for you.

Install the flashing with the roofing. To install the flashing, first fit the base flashing into a bed of roofing cement around the bottom edge of the curb. Nail the flashing along the top of the curb. Note that the apron rests on top of the shingle course along the bottom edge of the curb.

Fit the first piece of step flashing so it overlaps the base flashing. Slide it beneath the shingles of the next course, embedding in roofing cement the edge next to the curb. Nail it to the curb along the top edge. Continue up both sides in this fashion until you reach the top. Fit the head flashing around the top of the curb, embed it in cement, then nail it. Spread

roofing cement around the top and side edges of the apron that extends onto the roof deck, then nail the next shingle courses down over it. Set each shingle edge in roofing cement for added protection.

Apply a bead of caulk or some cushioned weather stripping to the top of the curb. Then drop the skylight over the curb and flashing. Use

Flashing Skylights

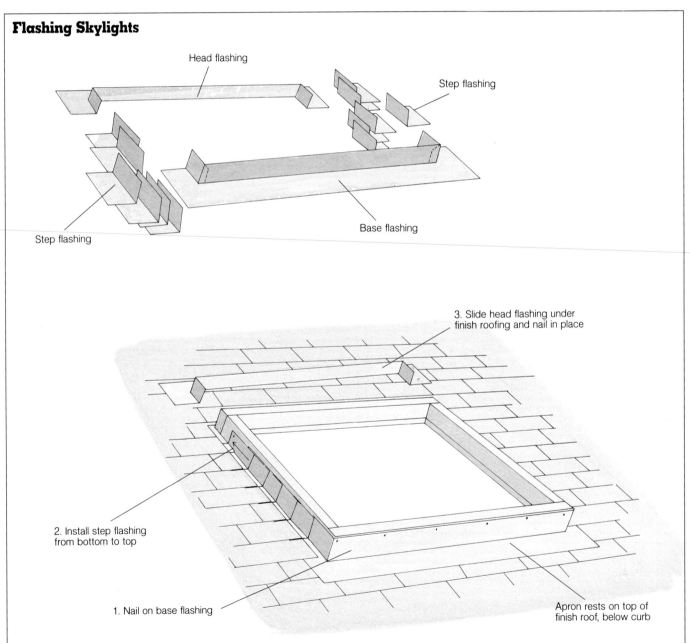

Head flashing

Step flashing

Step flashing

Base flashing

3. Slide head flashing under finish roofing and nail in place

2. Install step flashing from bottom to top

1. Nail on base flashing

Apron rests on top of finish roof, below curb

galvanized screws or special aluminum screwnails with neoprene washers to attach the skylight to the curb by placing the fasteners along the upper edge or through the factory-drilled holes. Screw the skylight in temporarily, until you finish the interior. Later, screw it firmly into place and cover each screw head with a dab of roofing cement.

Self-Flashing Skylights

Construct the opening for a self-flashing skylight in the same manner as a curb-mounted skylight. Frame an opening the same size as the inside dimensions of the skylight in the rafters; in the sheathing leave a hole that is flush with the inside edges of the framing opening.

When you have shingled to the lower edge of the skylight opening, set the skylight on the sheathing. The lower part of the flange should lie on top of the shingles. With roofing cement, coat the deck and the top edge of the shingles. Then lay the skylight on the cement and press the flange into it. Check that the skylight is centered and square, then use roofing nails spaced 6 inches apart to nail down the top and sides of the flange—not the bottom. Coat the edges and the top of the flashing flange with roofing cement. Then shingle around the skylight. As a final touch, lay a bead of caulk or roofing cement along the edges of the shingles where they fit next to the skylight.

Installing Skylights

Skylight With Curb

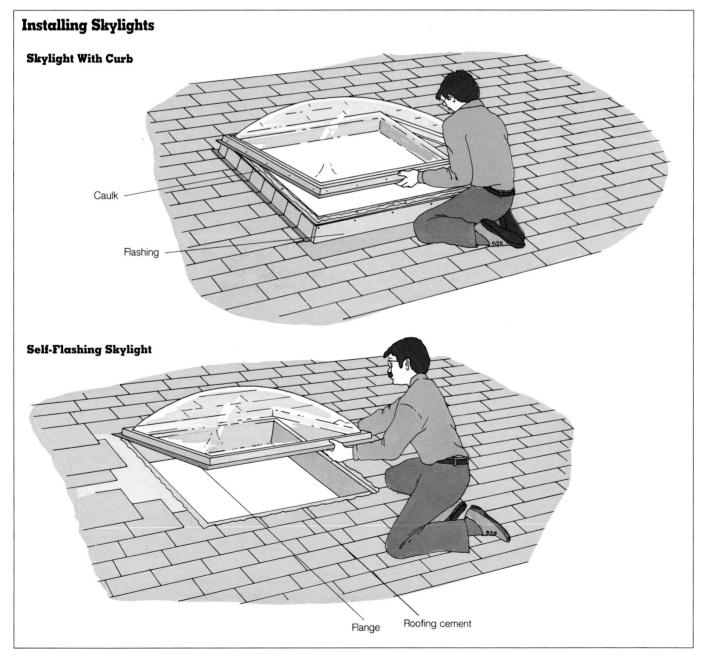

Caulk

Flashing

Self-Flashing Skylight

Flange   Roofing cement

The exterior siding is a major design feature of any building. Siding affects the appearance and value of a house for many years. Exterior maintenance varies greatly with the different sidings as well, so choose carefully. You'll be glad you did when you see your sparkling new home on the day you move in.

☐ Tool belt
☐ Hammer
☐ Framing square
☐ Combination square
☐ Bevel square
☐ Steel tape measure
☐ Story pole
☐ Handsaw
☐ Power circular saw
☐ 24-inch level
☐ Chalk line
☐ Nail sets

For Shingle Siding
☐ Tool belt
☐ Roofing hatchet
☐ Utility knife

Choosing a Siding

You can save a great deal of money by installing the exterior siding yourself, but the work is fairly complicated. On a difficulty scale of 10 points, consider installing exterior siding a 6. It takes three people with basic carpentry skills three days to install wood panels, six days to install board siding, and nine days to install shingles on an average house.

This section contains a guide to selecting the exterior siding

that is best for your house style, instructions for bracing and flashing the exterior walls, and methods for installing several popular siding materials. Though not all styles of exterior siding can be installed by the owner-builder, many can. Styles you can install yourself are board siding, wood panels, and wood shingles.

Choose the siding with all the care and consideration you will give to the interior of your house. Among the aspects to consider are your personal preferences, the house style, the prevailing styles in the neighborhood, the durability of each style, the initial cost, the cost of maintenance, and the complexity of the installation.

Your choice of siding material dictates the order of the next steps in the construction process. If you choose wood panels, install the door and window casings after the siding. If you choose board siding or shingles, put the window and door casings on the sheathing prior to the siding so the siding can butt up to it.

The style of your house will narrow the choices in siding material and color. The finish roofing may suggest a particular siding. Your choice should complement the prevailing

styles and color combinations in the neighborhood—you don't want your house to stand out in an unneighborly way. Some neighborhood associations have restrictions on siding materials and colors.

The region you are building in also plays a part in siding choices. Some sidings are particularly suitable for certain weather patterns, and making the appropriate siding choice will mean low maintenance. Not all natural materials are native to all parts of the country. If you choose a material that must be shipped a great distance, expect to pay the cost of shipping.

Shop around to compare siding prices; they can vary widely. Since you are going to cover an entire house, yours is not just a little do-it-yourself project. Ask the supplier for a contractor's discount or at least a quantity reduction.

Wood Boards

Solid-wood siding, installed either horizontally or vertically, is the most widely used residential siding in the country. It is available in a confusingly broad variety of choices. Of the various types of siding patterns available, the interlocking styles are somewhat more expensive than those that simply overlap, but they go up faster and form a tighter seal.

Installed horizontally, wood boards work particularly well on saltboxes, Cape Cod cottages, Victorians, and Ranch-style houses. The long clean lines will enhance the appearance of virtually any house.

Vertically-installed wood boards give height to multi-storied houses such as Greek

and Gothic Revivals. The boards are usually ¾ inch thick and range in widths from 3½ inches to 11¼ inches. Some styles, such as channel siding, have rabbeted edges for a weather-tight fit. Shiplap and tongue-and-groove boards are also used for vertical installations.

In another common style called board and batten, standard boards are nailed up vertically and the joint between each one is covered with a narrow board called a batten. Battens are generally made from 1 by 2, 1 by 3, or 1 by 4 stock. The wider battens are used with the wider boards. The pattern is reversed in the style called batten and board.

Wood-board siding does not go up as fast as wood-panel siding, but the individual boards are much easier to handle. Redwood and cedar boards are often left to weather naturally. Pine or fir must be protected by regular painting or staining.

Wood Panels

Wood-panel sidings are made of plywood or hardboard, which is constructed of heat-processed wood pulp pressed into sheets. Panels are normally 4 by 8, 4 by 9, or 4 by 10 feet.

Wood panels are available in many different finishes, which allow them to be used on just about any style of house. Plywood siding styles include smooth and rough finishes and grooved panels that imitate board siding. Hardboard siding comes in an even wider variety of styles, which may be embossed to imitate stucco or shingles.

Installing Vertical Board-and-Batten Siding

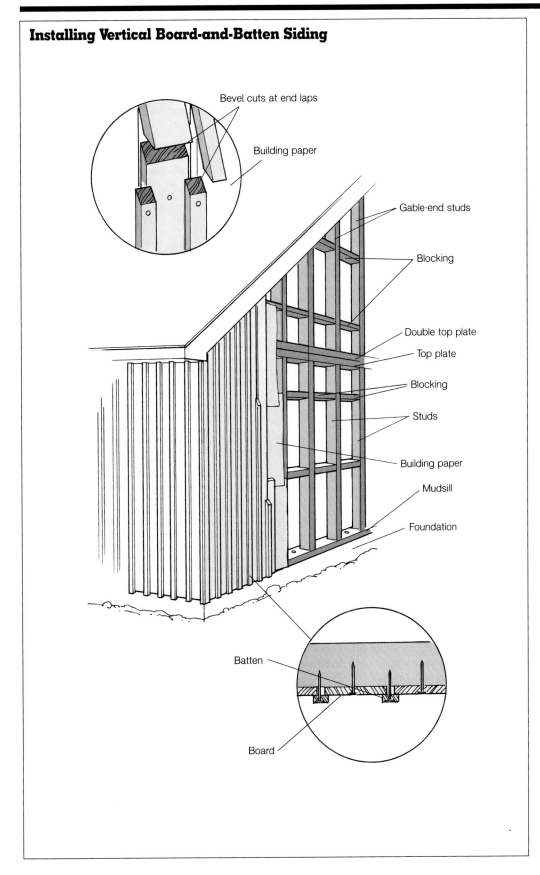

Bevel cuts at end laps

Building paper

Gable-end studs

Blocking

Double top plate

Top plate

Blocking

Studs

Building paper

Mudsill

Foundation

Batten

Board

For board-and-batten siding, leave a ¼-inch gap between the boards. If you butt them, they may swell when damp and then buckle. Nail the boards into position first; then add the battens. Where vertical boards must be end-lapped, bevel-cut the ends to prevent water infiltration.

Gable-Ends Finishing With Vertical Boards

Find the slope of the roof by placing a sliding bevel square along the side of the house and adjusting the bevel to the angle of the rafter. Transfer this slope to siding that must be cut to fit the gable ends. Gable ends with vertical siding can be installed in several different ways. You can install the siding all the way to the roofline, in a continuous sweep. This is commonly done with narrow redwood or cedar boards. Or, depending on the material you are using and the style you want to set, you can put horizontal siding over the gable ends or shingle them.

Corner Treatments

The standard corner treatment for vertical siding consists of overlapping 1 by 4s or a 1 by 4 overlapping a 1 by 3. Caulk the building corners before nailing on the corner pieces. If you splice two boards end-to-end, cut each board on a bevel where they join together so the joint repels water.

Installing Shingle Siding

Shingles are sold in lengths of 16 inches, 18 inches, and 24 inches. The maximum exposure should be ½ inch less than half the overall length, which works out to 7½ inches, 8½ inches, and 11½ inches respectively. These exposures can be reduced for better appearance.

Wood shingles are sold in bundles made up according to the length and number of shingles. To order enough for your house, all you need to know is the square footage of the walls. From this figure, a supplier can quickly estimate your needs. Allow 10 to 15 percent extra for waste. You can return any unused bundles, but you might keep one on hand for later repairs.

Apply shingles over solid sheathing. Cover the corners with building paper to protect against possible water infiltration. Wrap the solid sheathing with red resin paper. It is similar to 15-pound building paper, but it is not asphalt impregnated. Resin paper allows the shingles to breathe while still blocking wind.

Install metal flashing above wood-framed windows and door openings (see page 213). The flashing should extend 2 to 3 inches up the wall. Paint all window sashes and casings before the shingles go on—it's almost impossible to paint the casing neatly around the edges of rough shingles.

After the wall is prepared, use the story pole to lay out shingle exposures (see page 217). The goal is to have the shingle butts in line with the bottom of the windowsill and the top of the drip cap, if

possible. This arrangement minimizes the need to cut shingles to fit. In addition, the house will look better without short shingle exposures above or below openings or at the top of the run.

Double the first shingle course across the bottom. To keep this course level, put a shingle at each corner of the building; the butt of the shingle should be 1 inch below the sheathing. Tack a small nail to the bottom of each shingle, and stretch a string between the two. Align all intervening shingles on the string line. As you go along, be careful not to depress the string with the shingles or you will have a curved row of shingles.

For all successive courses, tack a straight 1 by 4 across the shingles and in line with the story-pole marks. Then lay the shingle butts on the 1 by 4 as you nail them.

If the guide board won't fit between windows, snap chalk lines between the story-pole marks. Or, if you have a few spaces between windows that are similar in width, make a short guide board.

Fasten shingles by using 2d or 3d aluminum nails or galvanized box nails. Use ring-shank nails to keep the shingles from working loose in windy areas. This is particularly important when nailing shingles to ⅜-inch plywood sheathing, which doesn't hold nails as well as thicker sheathing does.

Use 2 nails to fasten each shingle, regardless of its width. Place the nails 1 inch above the butt line for the next course and ¾ inch in from the edges.

Shingles can be spaced about ⅛ inch or more to allow for expansion. However, many shingles are being sold green, or freshly cut. If you get some of these, they will tend to

shrink as they dry. Ask the shingle dealer if the shingles are green, and act accordingly.

No gap between shingles should be closer than 1½ inches to a gap in the adjacent course. No gaps should be in line with others less than 3 courses away. When putting a course above a door or window, don't let a gap line up with the window or door edge.

Where shingles must be cut to fit around obstructions, measure and then make the cut with a handsaw or power jigsaw. For curves, use a coping saw or power jigsaw. For fine trimming when fitting along casing or trim boards, use a block plane on the shingle edge. If shingles must be shortened to fit above a window or door opening, trim the shingles from the butt end; trimming along the top would mean thicker shingles under the row above, causing a bulge.

Beginning Shingle-Siding Installation

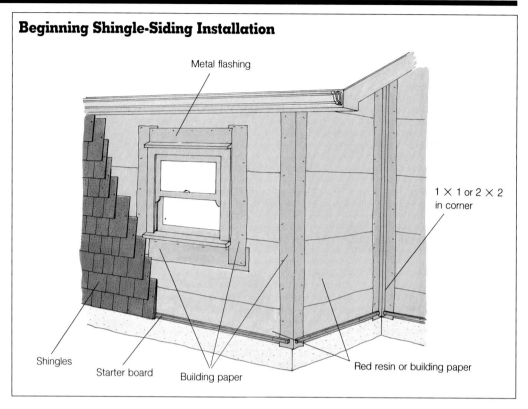

Metal flashing

1 × 1 or 2 × 2 in corner

Shingles

Starter board

Building paper

Red resin or building paper

Installing Shingle Siding

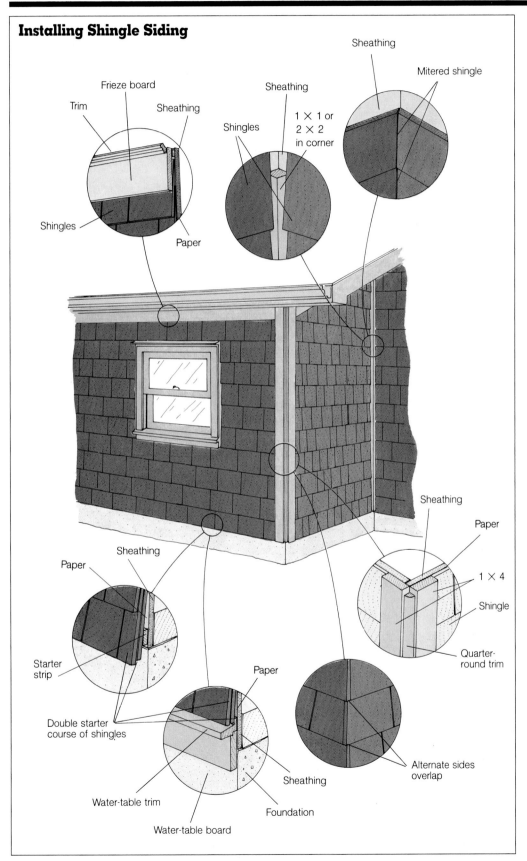

Frieze board
Trim
Sheathing
Shingles
Paper

Sheathing
Shingles
1 × 1 or 2 × 2 in corner
Paper

Sheathing
Mitered shingle

Sheathing
Paper

Sheathing
1 × 4
Shingle
Quarter-round trim

Sheathing
Paper
Starter strip
Double starter course of shingles

Paper
Sheathing
Foundation
Water-table trim
Water-table board

Alternate sides overlap

Corner Treatments

Where shingles meet at corners, they can be woven or butted against trim boards. Woven corners provide better weather protection and are more commonly used, but they must be individually fitted and then cut.

To weave corners, nail the bottom layer of the doubled starter course around the bottom of the house. Now start the next layer of shingles. Consult the illustration to see how the top shingle on side A should extend beyond the corner. Put the side-B shingle against the extended shingle, and trace its outline along the back of the side-A shingle. Cut along that line with a saw, and nail the shingles into place. On the next row up, repeat the process, this time extending the end shingle on side B beyond the corner and, on its back, marking the outline of the shingle on side A. Continue up the wall in this manner, with courses overlapping in alternate rows.

The most effective weather protection and the fastest way to shingle corners is to use trim boards. These should be 2 by 6 redwood or cedar so they will weather naturally with the shingles. With the edges overlapping to form a tight seal, place the boards on the corners; then butt each course of shingles to the board edges. For a smooth fit against the board, use a plane to trim shingle edges where necessary.

Inside corners can also be woven, or the shingle edges can be butted against a 1 by 1 or 2 by 2 board nailed in the corner (see page 219). Put a bead of caulk between the shingles and corner boards.

INSTALLING EXTERIOR TRIM

The exterior of any building must function as a weatherproof skin that enables you to maintain a controlled temperature inside.

- ☐ Tool belt
- ☐ Hammer
- ☐ Framing square
- ☐ Combination square
- ☐ Bevel square
- ☐ Steel tape measure
- ☐ Handsaw
- ☐ Compass saw
- ☐ Coping saw
- ☐ Power circular saw
- ☐ Power drill and bits
- ☐ 24-inch level
- ☐ Chalk line
- ☐ Nail sets

Choosing Trim

Trim is necessary to cover gaps or cracks where materials meet or where different elements of the house come together to prevent the flow of air.

You need basic carpentry skills to install exterior trim. On a difficulty scale of 10 points, consider installing exterior trim a 5. Although you won't need a helper for most of the jobs, an assistant will be welcome when working with long and awkward parts of trim. You don't need any special tools or equipment. It should take you about five days to install all the exterior trim on an average house.

This skin must also shed water so none enters the house or gets in, under, or between the parts or construction members

to cause deterioration of the wood. Since gravity controls the flow of water, every part of the house—from the peak of the roof to the ground—must overlap in such a way as to carry the water easily from one part to the next, without letting it stop or seep between members into places it can do damage.

On most modern houses, exterior trim consists of casings and moldings around doors and windows, moldings and cornices where the roof meets the side walls, and various treatments to gables.

If the architectural style—Gothic or Victorian, for example—calls for complex kinds of trim, look in books about period architecture for examples. You can usually find a good selection of moldings and decorative shingles in at least one or two of the better building-materials outlets in most cities. In areas such as Seattle, New York, New Orleans, Baltimore, and San Francisco, where the restoration of old buildings is popular, specialists are again manufacturing gingerbread architectural decorations.

If you installed wood-panel siding, you need to install door and window casings now (see page 205). Door and window casings should be done before other types of siding. Install cornices and gables after the

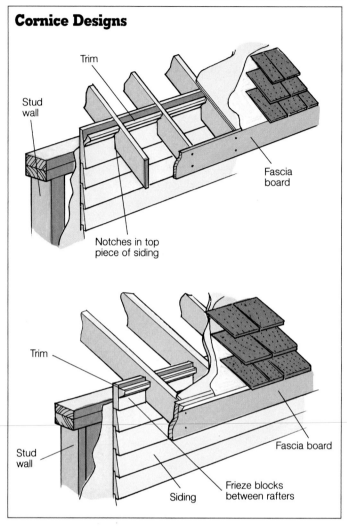

Cornice Designs

Trim

Stud wall

Fascia board

Notches in top piece of siding

Trim

Stud wall

Fascia board

Siding

Frieze blocks between rafters

siding is all installed. Some attic vents should be attached to the framing before the siding is put on.

Installing Cornices

A cornice is the trim that covers the joint where the roof and side walls of a house meet. Since the end and sometimes the underside of the rafter is part of the cornice, how it is cut determines how the cornice is made. Therefore, determine the kind of cornice you want before you frame the roof.

At the gable ends, where the intersection of the roof and

wall is at an angle, you will need a raked cornice. It can be constructed in the same way as the horizontal cornice under the eaves, but the raked cornice angle must match the angle of the roof slope.

If, after the roof is all framed, you decide that the eaves and gable overhang aren't wide enough for the kind of cornice you want, you can add to both. Extend the rafters by attaching tail rafters. These are just pieces of rafter material that are nailed to the

Installing Open Cornices

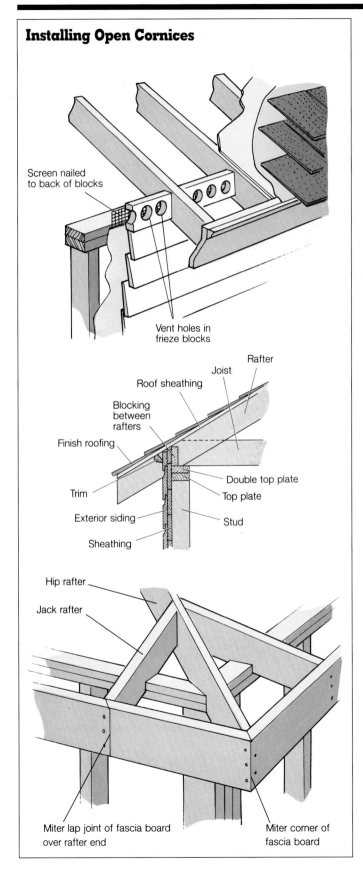

Screen nailed to back of blocks

Vent holes in frieze blocks

Rafter

Joist

Roof sheathing

Blocking between rafters

Finish roofing

Trim

Double top plate

Top plate

Exterior siding

Stud

Sheathing

Hip rafter

Jack rafter

Miter lap joint of fascia board over rafter end

Miter corner of fascia board

side of the existing rafters. To extend the gable overhang, add lookout rafters on outriggers. These changes must be made prior to installing the roofing.

Although there are many styles of cornices, they are all classified as either open or closed. In an open cornice the space between the rafter ends or tail rafters is left open so you can see the roof sheathing by looking up from the ground. A closed cornice includes a panel called a soffit that covers the underside of the rafters. The soffit can be attached directly to the bottom of the rafters or mounted on lookouts.

Open Cornices

The open cornice is the easiest and least expensive to make. It is made up of the frieze, which covers the area above the wall top plates and between the rafters, and the fascia, which is nailed to the ends of the rafters and covers them and the spaces between the rafter ends. If you like the look of exposed rafter ends, you can omit the fascia. You might even want to decorate the ends of the rafters with fancy cuts, such as an S curve or a simple animal design.

The Frieze

There are several ways to cover the frieze area. One is to notch the sheathing or siding for each rafter and run the siding right up to the roof decking. Then you can add a strip of cove, crown, or bed molding or square-edged trim to cover the intersection of the siding and the decking.

Another way is to stop the siding at the wall top plates and fill the frieze area with frieze blocks. Cut lengths of 2-by lumber to fit exactly between the rafters. Nail them into place either against the face of the siding or on top of the siding and against the bottom of the roof decking.

You can drive the nails through a rafter into one end of each block. Then you will have to toenail the other side because the last block you put in is in the way.

If you want vents in any of the blocks, put them in before you nail in the blocks. To make vents, drill holes as needed and tack wire mesh on the back.

You can add decorative cove, crown, or bed molding at the top of the blocks if you want to add a little ornamentation. All the joints in an open cornice should be cut carefully and made to fit precisely. All the work on the trim should be done exactly because it is easily seen from the ground.

The Fascia

To trim the ends of the rafters, rip a 1 by 6 or 1 by 8 so that it is just wide enough to cover the ends of the rafters. Any splices in the fascia board must occur at the center of the end of a rafter so that each side of the break can be nailed securely to the rafter. To minimize splits, drill small pilot holes for the nails. When the fascia turns a corner, miter the joint carefully so the ends fit tightly.

Installing Closed Cornices

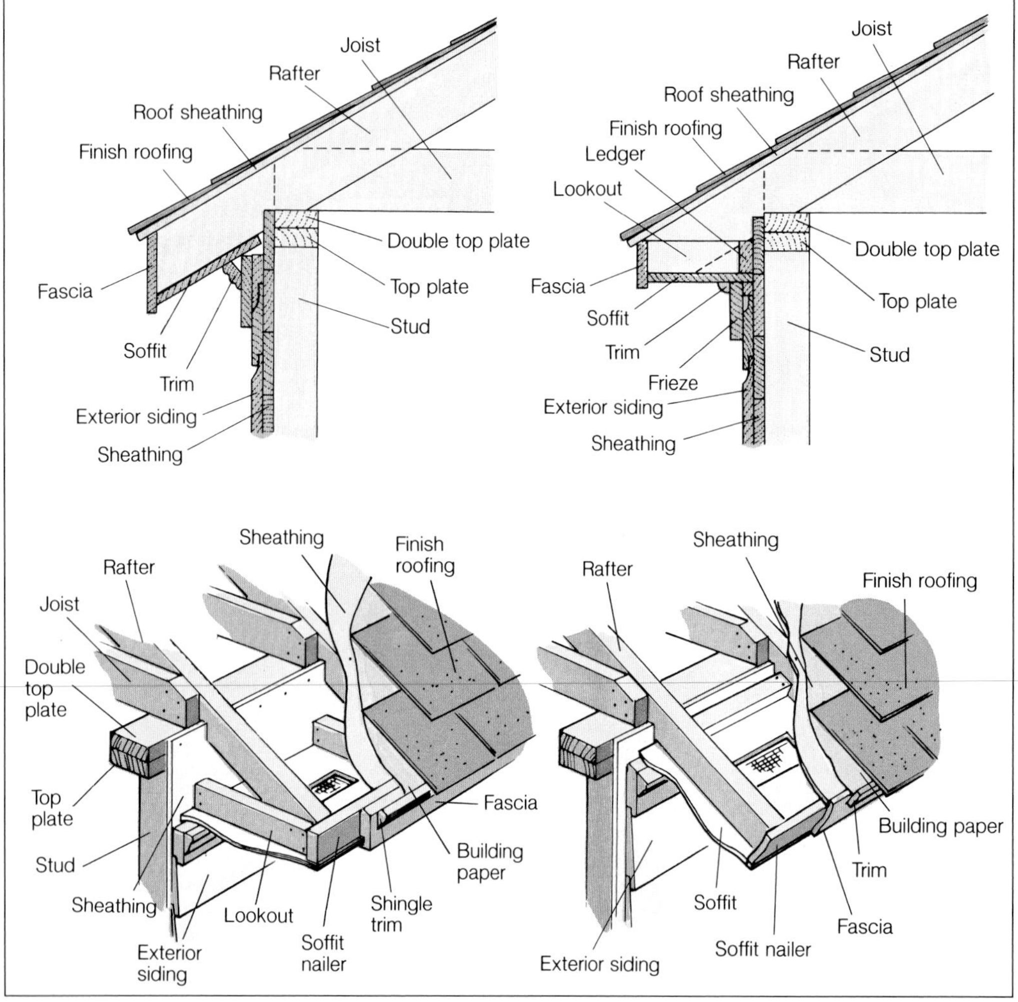
Joist
Rafter
Roof sheathing
Finish roofing
Double top plate
Top plate
Stud
Fascia
Soffit
Trim
Exterior siding
Sheathing
Joist
Rafter
Roof sheathing
Finish roofing
Ledger
Lookout
Double top plate
Fascia
Top plate
Soffit
Trim
Stud
Frieze
Exterior siding
Sheathing
Sheathing
Finish roofing
Rafter
Joist
Double top plate
Top plate
Fascia
Stud
Building paper
Sheathing
Lookout
Shingle trim
Exterior siding
Soffit nailer
Sheathing
Rafter
Finish roofing
Building paper
Trim
Soffit
Fascia
Soffit nailer
Exterior siding

Closed Cornices

The entire rafter area in a closed, or box, cornice is closed off by the roof on top, the fascia on the ends, and the soffit underneath. Except for the soffit and its supports, if any, the elements of an open and closed cornice are the same.

For a neater appearance and so they last for a long time, soffits are commonly supported in front by a groove in the fascia. This groove is about ⅜ inch up from the bottom edge of the fascia. In addition to supporting the soffit, the groove allows the ⅜-inch edge of wood to hang below the soffit and act like a drip edge.

The simplest of closed cornices is the one with a sloping soffit. The soffit is nailed directly onto the bottom of the rafters, so it slopes just as the rafters slope. For this kind of cornice, the ends of the rafters can be plumb, like tail cuts, or they can be cut square.

The sloped soffit is a little easier to install if the ends of the rafters and, therefore, the fascia are perpendicular to the soffit. This allows the groove for the soffit to be perpendicular to the surface of the fascia. If the tail ends of the rafters are plumb, the groove must be cut at an angle.

The Lookouts

Lookouts are usually 2 by 4s that go horizontally from the ends of the rafters to the wall. If you want the fascia to be as wide as the rafter ends, the lookouts can be attached to the rafters as is. If you would like the fascia to be narrower, for a lighter appearance, trim off the bottom of the rafter tail by marking a horizontal line with a level and cutting along with a circular power saw.

Toenail the lookouts to the wall and facenail them to the ends of the rafters. Lookouts for the rake cornice should be spaced every 16 inches from the eaves to the ridge. Toenail the lookouts to the gable wall and end-nail them through the barge rafter.

The Soffit

Soffits can be made from any of several materials. The popularity of wide overhangs makes materials that come in large sheets suitable for this purpose. Exterior grades of plywood, wallboard, and hardboard are all used. Aluminum soffit material comes in rolls and is available in several widths. The aluminum is perforated so separate vents are not required.

If your rafters are 16 inches on center, ⅜-inch plywood is sufficient for the soffit. Measure and cut the plywood or other soffit material into long strips. On the strips measure and mark the locations of all the rafters and lookouts, then cut 4- by 8-inch vent holes in the soffit so they fall between the lookouts. Tack or staple screen to the back of the holes. Position the soffit so the front edge overhangs the rafters so it will fit into the fascia groove. Nail the soffit to the bottoms of the lookouts.

Metal and ⅛-inch hardboard soffit material can be secured with aluminum channel material made for the purpose. See the manufacturer's instruction sheets for details of installation.

To install the rake soffit between the barge rafter and the gable wall, you'll have to put nailers—pieces of 2 by 4—on the wall between the lookouts.

The Frieze

For a closed soffit, the frieze is one or more boards or strips of molding that cover the joint of the soffit and the siding decoratively. For a deep shadow line, you can use 2 by 4 or 2 by 6 material. For a lighter look, use 1 by 2, 1 by 3, or 1 by 4 stock. You can add moldings at the top, at the bottom, or both.

The frieze on the rake should be exactly the same as the one on the eaves. The rake frieze, however, must stop when it reaches the return of the eave cornice, and small pieces of frieze or at least the moldings must be cut to make the connection.

The Fascia

Rip the fascia to the width of the rafter end, plus the thickness of the soffit material, plus the ⅜-inch drip edge between the groove and the bottom. The fascia for the rake cornice must be the width of the barge rafter, plus the thickness of the soffit material, plus ⅜ inch.

Nail the fascia board to the ends of the rafters and the side of the barge rafter so the protruding edge of the soffit fits in the groove. Be sure any joints are over the ends of rafters and nailed securely. Miter all the corners carefully and make sure all the joints fit tightly.

Installing Attic Ventilation

Codes vary, but figure 1 square foot of free vent area for every 150 square feet of attic. A 2¼-square-foot gable vent, with louvers and screening, should have 1 square foot of free vent area. You can reduce the required vent area by half if half the vents are soffit vents in the eaves and the other half are at least 3 feet off the attic floor.

Roof and gable vents are easy to install. Just measure and cut out a piece of the roof or wall, and then insert the vent into the hole. Frame any hole cut into the roof or wall with a system of 2 by 4s, and use caulk or flashing to seal the hole after the vent is installed.

If the rafters are insulated, such as in an occupied attic or a vaulted ceiling, an effective vapor barrier must be on the heated side to prevent moisture from inside the house from getting into the rafter cavity.

☐ Windows installed
☐ Exterior doors installed
☐ Exterior siding installed
☐ Exterior trim installed
☐ Exterior work approved

Venting

Summer

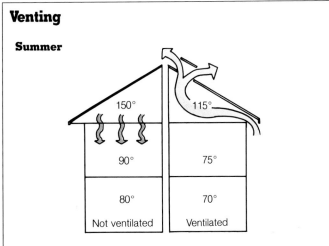

In hot weather, proper ventilation prevents attic from becoming a hot box

Winter

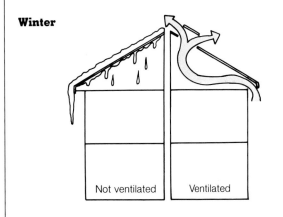

In cold weather, proper ventilation helps prevent moisture from condensing on insulation, structural timbers, shingles, or roof

STEPS, STAIRS, PORCHES & DECKS

Every house requires some kind of step, stairway, porch, or deck for exterior access to the front and rear doors. Multistory houses need interior stairways for travel between levels. Beyond meeting these basic needs, steps, stairways, porches, and decks are architectural features that play a big part in actualizing the design style of the house. They also expand the living space of the house, from stairway nooks used for quiet reading to massive decks used for entertaining.

Steps, stairways, porches, and decks must be designed to fit the architectural style of the house and built to take years of wear and tear. Both these aspects require thorough planning, numerous mathematical calculations, and careful concrete and carpentry work.

While considering the style of stairway or deck that is right for your house, look again at the gallery of house styles beginning on page 16. In planning outside access, look at the surrounding houses to make sure that your design is in keeping with the styles of the neighborhood.

A rural site is the perfect setting for this traditionally styled house. Although the all-American look makes you want to sit on a porch swing, this almost-completed house is most modern. The roof is covered with aluminum shingles; the horizontal siding is vinyl; and the openable windows are vinyl-clad metal.

INTERIOR STEPS AND STAIRWAYS

Most owner-builders with some carpentry experience are able to build a few steps for access. However, building stairways that connect two entire levels is probably one of the most difficult parts of building a house.

- ☐ Tool belt
- ☐ Hammer
- ☐ Framing hammer
- ☐ Framing square
- ☐ Combination square
- ☐ Bevel square
- ☐ Steel tape measure
- ☐ Handsaw
- ☐ Power circular saw
- ☐ Table saw or radial arm saw
- ☐ Power drill and bits
- ☐ Router and bits
- ☐ 24-inch level
- ☐ Chalk line
- ☐ Nail sets
- ☐ Screwdrivers

For Steel Stairways
- ☐ Wrenches
- ☐ Nut drivers

Stairway Styles

Stairways are difficult partly because of the repeated precision necessary, but mostly because of the mathematics. A lot of figuring is needed to make a stairway fit in the place you want it and be uniform in increments throughout its length. On a difficulty scale of 10 points, consider building steps and stairways an 8. The difficulty increases with the length and type of stairway. You could

certainly use at least one helper to assist in the placing of the stringers and the repetitious installation of risers and treads. You don't need any special tools, but your skill as a finish carpenter will be tested.

In designing stairways remember that they will be used for the passage of people and furniture. Above all they should be safe and have adequate headroom and width. They should also be attractive and add to the beauty of the house. The basic parts of all stairways are the same, and all stairways are planned in the same way.

Whether only a couple of steps or several flights, all stairways are one of four general types: principal, utility, spiral, and disappearing. The principal stairs are the main or only stairs in the house and are designed for ease of use and beauty. They can be straight or curved. A principal stairway is often a featured design element of the house.

Utility stairs are for service but not necessarily great looks. They usually go to the attic or basement or are an extra stairway from upstairs rooms to the kitchen. Compared to principal stairs, utility stairs are often slightly steeper, less easy to use, and made of less expensive materials.

Anatomy of a Stairway

Grand multiple-level stairways and a couple of steps between the back door and the yard look different but all steps and stairways are made up of the same components.

Stringer, String, Carriage, or Horse	One of the inclined pieces that supports the treads and risers. Plain, or open, stringers are cut to follow the lines of the treads and risers. Closed stringers have parallel sides and support the risers and treads by means of cleats attached to them or grooves cut into them. A finish stringer is any similar member applied to decorate the stairway.
Riser	The vertical face of a step.
Tread	The horizontal surface on which you step.
Nosing	The projection of the tread beyond the riser.
Unit Rise	The vertical measurement from the surface of one tread to the surface of the next.
Total Rise	The vertical measurement between the surfaces of the floors from the bottom of the stairway to the top.
Unit Run	The horizontal measurement from the face of one riser to the face of the next.
Total Run	The horizontal length of the stairway.
Stair Width	The distance between the sides of the stairway. Stair width can be measured between walls, from wall to side of tread, or between sides of tread.
Headroom	The clearance from an imaginary line connecting the noses to any overhead ceiling or obstruction.
Landing	A floor where the stairway begins or ends.
Platform	The intermediate area, wider than the treads, between two parts of a stairway.
Winders	Wedge-shaped radiating treads where a stairway turns.
Railing	Any barricade on the open side of a stairway to prevent falling.
Handrail	The top of the railing on the open side of the stairway or a special member attached with brackets to the wall on the closed side of a stairway. A handrail is usually a finished piece of wood or metal to grip while going up or down a stairway.
Balusters	Any vertical members supporting the handrail on the open side of the stairway. For safety, balusters should be spaced no wider than 6 inches.
Gooseneck	In some decorative railing systems, a specially curved piece of handrail that attaches to the lower side of a landing newel.
Newel or Newel Post	The main post of the railing at the start of a stairway and any post where a handrail turns.

Anatomy of a Stairway

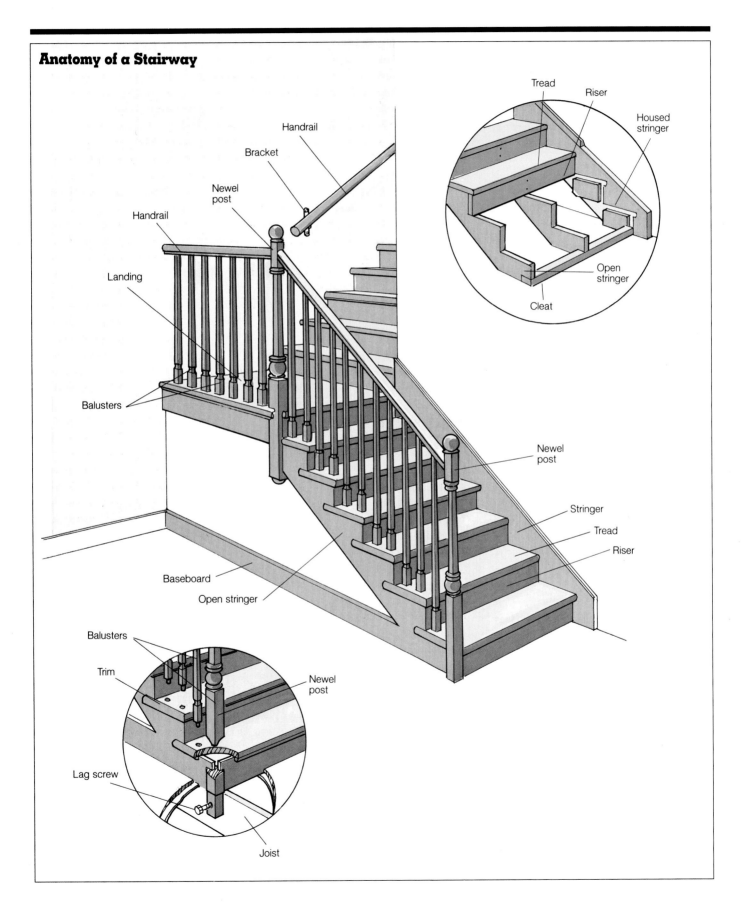

Handrail

Bracket

Newel post

Handrail

Landing

Balusters

Baseboard

Open stringer

Balusters

Trim

Newel post

Lag screw

Joist

Tread

Riser

Housed stringer

Open stringer

Cleat

Newel post

Stringer

Tread

Riser

Stairway Types

Stringer and Cleat

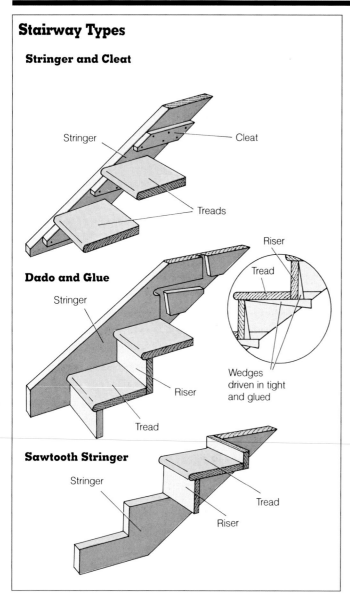

Stringer

Cleat

Treads

Dado and Glue

Stringer

Riser

Tread

Riser

Tread

Wedges
driven in tight
and glued

Sawtooth Stringer

Stringer

Tread

Riser

Spiral stairways take less overall space than straight stairs and are an interesting design element. Keep in mind, however, that children and others with less than full mobility will find them difficult to maneuver and that it is nearly impossible to move furniture up or down a spiral stairway. In some areas small-radius spiral stairways may not meet code requirements for multilevel access and can be installed only in addition to a principal stairway.

Disappearing stairs are usually used for attic or loft access. They are spring-loaded, folding stairs that hide in a trapdoor. They are seen only when they unfold for use.

Prefabricated stairways are available at most building-supply outlets. You can choose from metal units—straight and spiral—that are set in place and a selection of precut wood stairway parts that you put together yourself by following an accompanying instruction sheet. Some suppliers have catalogs of precut stairways or style sheets of stairways available to be cut and assembled on the site.

One widely available stairway is called housed construction. You buy it in a kit consisting of routed stringers; dadoed and rabbeted risers and treads; and sometimes an elaborate railing with decorative newel posts, balusters, and handrail. The kit is manufactured in a mill; customized for your rise, run, and number of steps; and assembled on the job with glue and wedges. When installed properly such a kit results in a handsome, strong, and squeakless stairway that will give excellent service for many years.

How you plan to finish a stairway affects its construction. Stairways that will be carpeted can be built of rough treads and risers finished on the sides with trim boards and skirts. When the carpentry is finished, the steps are far from elegant. But, after you install the carpet, voilà—a beautiful stairway.

Building elaborate stairways, curved ones in particular, requires the same skills as fine furniture making. Building intricate stairways may be best left to a qualified, specialized contractor. In addition to providing the necessary skills and special equipment, such a specialist is familiar with the local codes that regulate stairway design and construction.

Placing a Stairway

Convenience should be the primary consideration when placing a stairway. The stairs should be easily accessible from as many rooms as possible. Make sure that there will be enough headroom; if the stairway is too close to the eaves, you will have no room to stand up when you reach the top. Also consider noise, which travels freely up and down stairs. For instance, a room for formal entertaining or quiet retreat should be away from a stairway that would pipeline noise from other rooms.

Regard the principal stairs as a major design element rather than a utilitarian afterthought. Going up and down stairs can be a dramatic transition. Try to arrange for an appealing view at the top—a window or attractive alcove rather than a stark hall or blank wall. Also consider the view as you descend. Place a window or an inviting room where the steps terminate.

The most logical site for a stairway is directly above another stairway. Place attic stairs above the principal stairs or basement stairs, for example. If this isn't practical, try to position the flight so the steps run parallel to the joists. If the steps must run perpendicular to the joists, position the stairway along a bearing wall or add a wall or posts to support the trimmer joists.

Optional Configurations

Stairways take up a lot more space than most people realize. A typical straight-run stairway must be 3 feet wide by 9 to 13 feet long, not to mention an additional 9 square feet of floor space for a landing at the bottom. The well opening eliminates another 36 feet of floor space upstairs. Such a stairway occupies approximately 85 square feet of valuable floor space. Other configurations, such as L-shaped stairways or stairways that turn 180 degrees, require an even larger area.

Space-saving configurations include steeper stairs, circular stairs, spiral stairs, and the use of winders. Making stairs steeper to save room is safe only to a point. The preferred angle of incline is from 30 to 35 degrees. A circular configuration saves some space, but circular stairs are much more difficult to build and are best left to professionals.

Prefabricated spiral stairs come with diameters ranging from 4 to 6 feet. Most codes specify that a spiral stairway serve only as a secondary flight if the upper story contains more than 400 square feet.

Winders save space by eliminating the level platform where the stairs change direction. Codes have strict requirements regulating the size of winders, however. In some areas the local code does not permit them at all.

Code Requirements

Considering that 50 percent of all household injuries occur as a result of falls, many of them on stairs, the fact that codes are strict about stairs comes as no surprise. Most codes require that the width of principal stairways be at least 36 inches between finished walls. Handrails may project into the width no more than 3½ inches from each side; finish stringers or trim no more than 1½ inches from each side. Allow a minimum headroom of 80 inches. If you have room, increase

Stairway Inclines

The usual range of stairway inclines is illustrated below. Building codes generally require an incline between 20 and 50 degrees. The most comfortable and preferred incline is between 30 and 35 degrees. The 20-degree stairway shown is the flattest within the preferred range. The 50-degree stairway is very steep and suitable only for a basement or utility stairway.

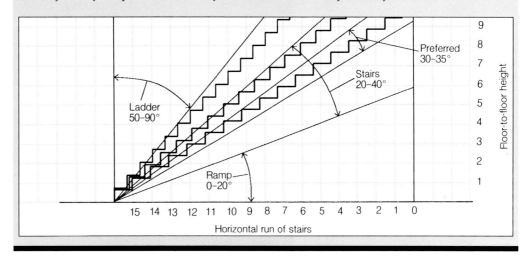

the width and headroom to enhance comfort and convenience.

Most codes require a handrail on at least one side of the stairway. You will probably need one on any open side. The rail should be a consistent height of 30 to 34 inches as measured from the nosing of each tread and 1½ to 2 inches wide for gripping. The handrail should terminate at both ends in such a way that it will not catch cuffs and loose clothing. Allow at least 1½ inches of clearance between the handrail and the wall.

Doors at the top of stairways should open away from the stairs. If the door must open toward the stairs, then there must be a landing at least as large as the door swing. Landings must be the same width as the stairs and at least 3 feet deep. No stairway should rise more than 12 feet without a landing.

Rise and Run

Local codes specify the acceptable height (the rise) and depth (the run) of each step. To a significant degree, the rise and run determine the safety of a stairway. Most codes specify a rise between 7 and 8 inches and a tread width between 9 and 11 inches. Added together, the tread and riser should total between 17 and 18 inches. This relationship must be constant. A higher riser requires a narrower tread—an 8-inch riser with a 10-inch tread; a gentler slope calls for wider treads—a 6-inch riser with an 11-inch tread, for example.

Codes also specify that an individual riser may not deviate by more than ⅜ inch in height from the others in the run. If you build an enclosed stairway, you must cover the walls with wallboard at least ½ inch thick and put fire blocks at the line of the stringer between all the studs in the walls.

Headroom

Headroom is measured from an imaginary line connecting all the nosings to the lowest point of the ceiling, soffit, or obstruction directly overhead.

Basement stairs under the principal stairway do not usually present much of a headroom problem, but a principal stairway under stairs to an attic can. Although the minimum headroom required by code is normally 80 inches, this is not enough. The minimum headroom often looks cramped and dark, and the ceiling is too low when you must carry large items of furniture up the stairs. A headroom between 88 and 92 inches is the most pleasing and practical for a principal stairway. This height allows most furniture to be carried up without problem, and the average person can swing an arm in a complete circle overhead without hitting any obstruction.

Riser to Tread Relationship

The local code tells you the acceptable height and depth of steps. The correct relationship between these two is absolutely essential for proper stairway construction. If the ratio is incorrect, the stairs will be either too steep or too gradual. This will make them uncomfortable and unsafe.

For principal stairways, most codes specify risers between 7 and 8 inches and a tread between 9 and 11 inches. For utility stairs, the maximum allowable riser is 8 inches and the minimum tread width is 9 inches. Added together the unit rise and unit run should total between 17 and 18 inches.

To determine the proper rise and run accurately, measure the distance from finish floor to finish floor. This measurement includes the floor-to-ceiling height plus the depth of the joists, subfloor, and finish floor. If the finish floor is not installed when you are doing the planning, find out what its depth will be and include it in your calculations.

Convert the measurement of the distance from finish floor to finish floor to inches and divide by 7. Say the floor-to-floor height is 108¾ inches. Dividing by 7 yields a little over 15½. Because you must have a whole number for risers, drop the fraction. Now divide 108¾ by 15 risers and get the exact riser height: 7¼ inches.

To be comfortable and safe the sum of the unit rise and unit run should be between 17 and 18 inches. So to determine the tread width, subtract 7¼ from 17½ and get 10¼.

Table of Risers and Treads

This table shows combinations of unit rises and unit runs that fit typical floor-to-floor heights and total runs. All fall in or near the preferred incline range.

Floor-to-Floor Height	Unit Rise	Unit Run	Number of Risers	Number of Treads	Total Run
9'	7¼"	10¾"	15	14	12'6"
9'	6¾"	10¾"	16	15	13'
9'	6"	11"	18	17	15'8"
8'6"	7¼"	10½"	14	13	11'4"
8'6"	7¼"	11½"	14	13	12'6"
8'6"	6⅜"	10⅜"	16	15	13'
8'6"	6⅜"	11"	16	15	13'9"
8'	7⅜"	10"	13	12	10'
8'	7⅜"	11"	13	12	11'
8'	6"	10⅜"	16	15	13'
8'	6"	12"	16	15	15'

Ideal Riser-to-Tread Relationship

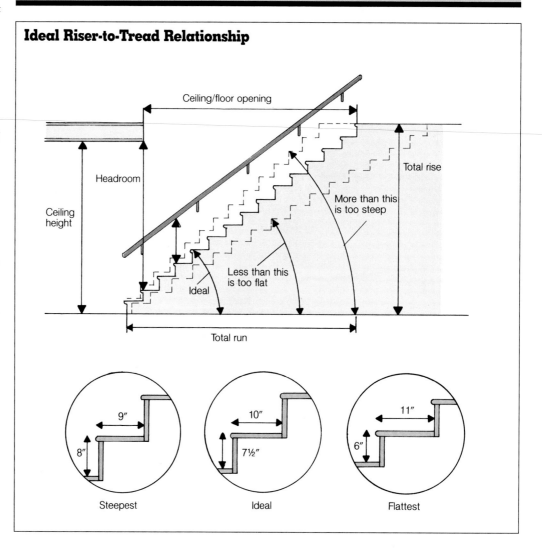

252

Laying Out a Stairway

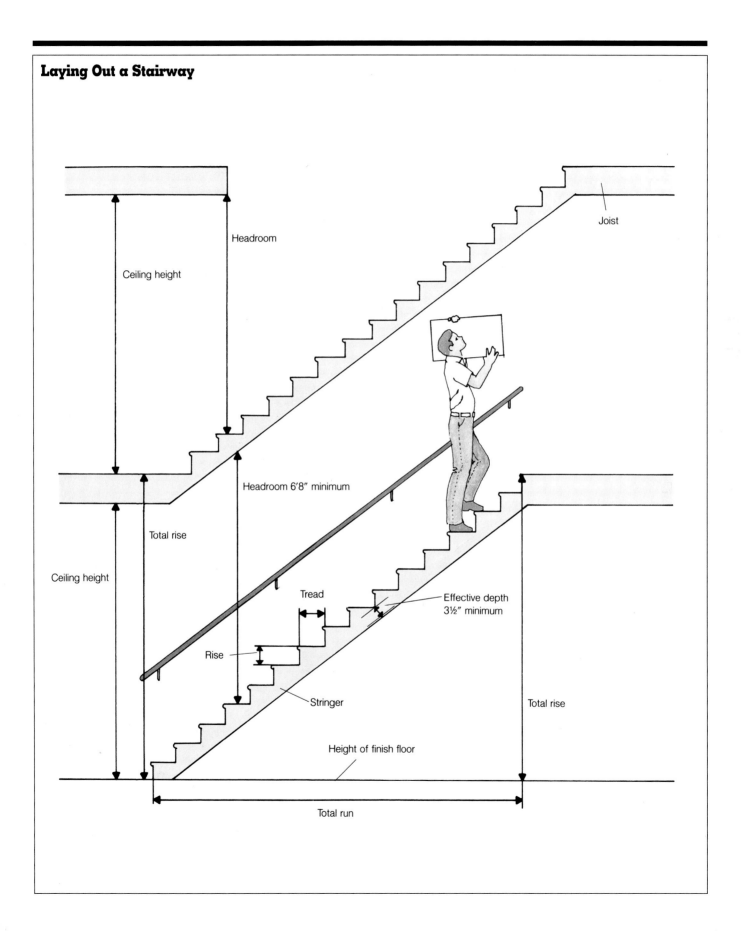

Headroom

Ceiling height

Joist

Headroom 6'8" minimum

Total rise

Ceiling height

Tread

Effective depth 3½" minimum

Rise

Stringer

Total rise

Height of finish floor

Total run

Because the last riser leads to the finish floor and not another tread, there is one more riser than the number of treads. In our example, you will have 14 treads. To find the total run of the stairway, simply multiply the number of treads by the unit run—that is, 14 × 10¼ inches. The total run or horizontal length of the stairway will be 143½ inches.

Building a Principal Stairway

Stairway planning should take place prior to the framing phase of construction.

Before you launch ahead and take on the building of a complete stairway yourself, see if a local manufacturer will prefabricate and deliver the stairway as a unit that you can install. Take the stair dimensions to a building supplier or a stair specialty company and order precut parts that you will assemble on-site. A supplier can probably produce difficult finish details—hardwood balusters, posts, and railings—more efficiently than you can.

If you plan thoroughly and work carefully, you can build a simple flight of stairs.

The Rough Opening

Carefully study the illustrations that show the proper framing for the rough opening of a stairway.

When you calculate the width of the rough opening, take into account the width of any handrails or railings required by the code. Also include the thickness of any finish material to be applied later, such as wallboard, paneling, or wainscoting.

Framing a Stairway

Parallel to Joists

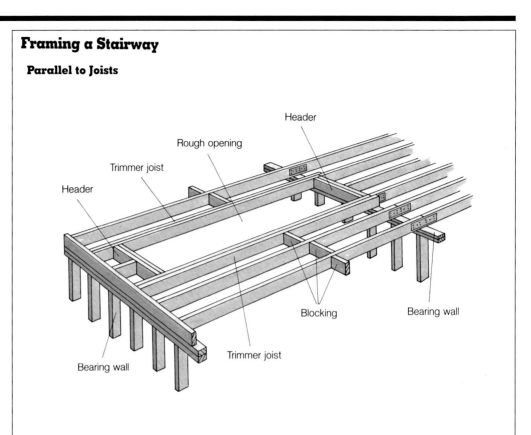

Perpendicular to Joists

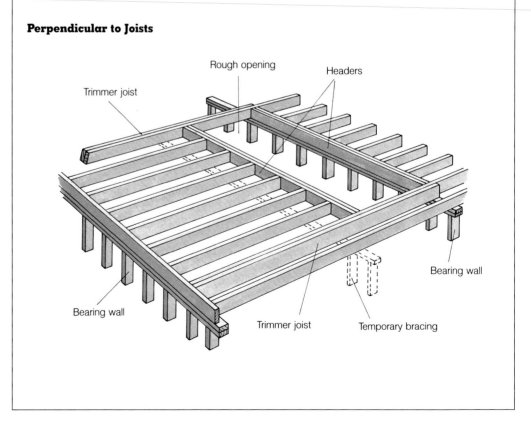

If possible, make the opening as long as the stairway. If you need to limit the opening, calculate it according to the minimum headroom required. To continue the previous example, assume a ceiling height of 99 inches. If the desired headroom is 7 feet (84 inches), you have 15 inches with which to work. With a riser height of 7¼ inches, the minimum height is reached over the second step: 7¼ × 2 = 14½ inches. The rough opening will extend from the top of the stairs to the nosing edge of the second step. If a shorter opening is desired, lower the minimum headroom you will settle for and recalculate.

Stringers

For the kind of stairway under discussion, stringers are generally cut from 2 by 12s. This creates a strong, closed stairway. The simplest stairway has two stringers cut into a sawtooth pattern. The cutouts in the stringers support the risers and treads, which are nailed or screwed to the stringers. To allow for trimming, order the stringers at least 24 inches longer than the finished length you'll need. Ordering stringers at least 4 feet longer than the stairway run should give you enough extra length. If you are building a basement stairway, make sure that any wood that will touch the concrete floor is pressure-treated or coated with preservative.

Treads are usually precut a full inch to 1¼ inch thick and made from hardwood or Douglas fir. The nosing will extend over the riser an inch or so. Risers are usually made of ¾-inch stock that matches the

Cutting a Stringer

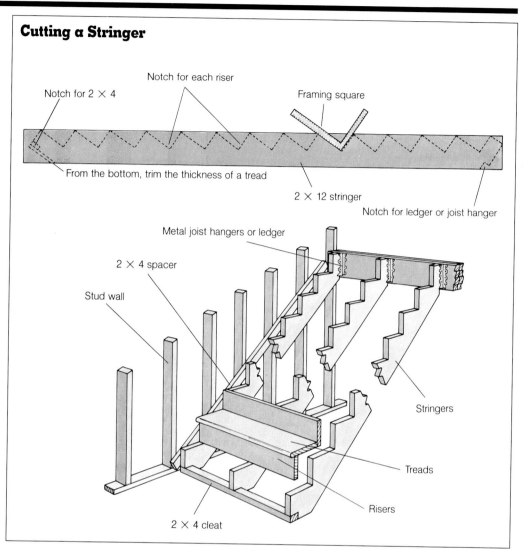

tread stock. If the stairs are to be carpeted, however, the treads can be 2 by 12s cut to fit and the risers can be ¾-inch plywood or 2-by lumber ripped as needed.

Use a framing square to mark the cuts for the first stringer. Measure the unit run dimension along the blade and the unit rise on the tongue. Special screw-on clips that you buy at the hardware store can help you to mark these measurements, or mark them with a crayon or colored tape.

Start about a foot from the end of the stringer that will be the top of the stairway. With the 2 marks directly on the edge of the stringer, mark the outline with a sharp pencil. Continue the process, as shown in the illustration, until all the risers and treads are laid out on the stringer. Take great care in your measuring. The finished stairs must meet a code requirement that demands no more than a ⅜-inch variance from one riser and tread to the next; a smaller variance is better. The codes were written to prevent stairway accidents caused by

inconsistent riser and tread ratios. Building inspectors do measure.

Double-check all markings, then use a portable power circular saw to make the cut to the pencil line. Use a handsaw to finish the cut where the curve of the blade didn't reach. Be sure all the cuts are square and the corners sharp.

To make the first stair the same height as the others, you will have to trim the bottom of the stringers by the thickness of the tread material.

If the stringer is not attached to walls, you need to anchor the stringer to the floor with a 2 by 4 kicker. If a kicker is needed, mark the bottom corner of the stringers for a 1½- by 3½-inch notch.

Place the stringer in the rough opening to be sure it fits just right. When you are sure it does, use it as a pattern and mark and cut the second stringer.

For a stairway over 36 inches wide, a third stringer is required to provide additional support in the middle. Adding the third stringer is advisable even for a narrower stairway; it will make the stairway feel sturdier and last longer without squeaks. The third stringer can be made by nailing the cutout blocks from one of the first stringers to a 2 by 6 or 2 by 8.

Assembly of Stringers, Risers, and Treads

Now install the stringers. At the top use 16-penny (16d) or larger nails to fasten a 2 by 4 ledger to the header; fit the notched stringers over it. Or butt the stringers directly up against the header and secure them with metal joist hangers.

Place a 2 by 4 flat between one or both stringers and the side wall framing to act as a spacer. Drive 16d or larger nails through the stringer and into the studs.

If you're installing a kicker, nail it to the floor and toenail it to the bottom of the stringers.

For concrete floors, drill holes for expansion shields and attach the kicker to the floor with lag screws.

Once the stringers are secured, install the treads and risers. This 2 by 4 spacer creates

Assembling a Stringer Stairway

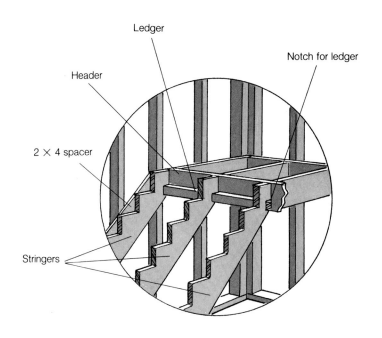

Ledger

Notch for ledger

Header

2 × 4 spacer

Stringers

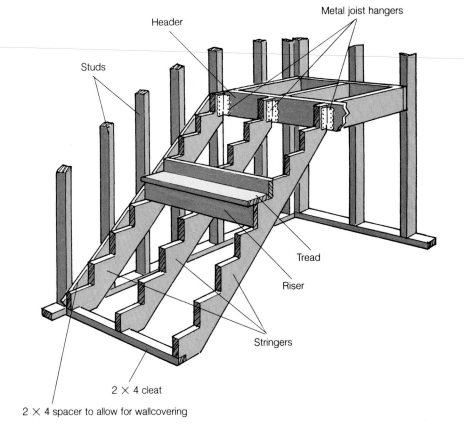

Metal joist hangers

Header

Studs

Tread

Riser

Stringers

2 × 4 cleat

2 × 4 spacer to allow for wallcovering

a gap for sliding wallboard or other finish materials between the wall framing and stringers. Starting at the bottom, use 8d finishing nails or wallboard screws to fasten 2 or 3 risers to the stringers. Apply construction adhesive to each joint before nailing to prevent squeaks later on. After nailing the risers to the stringers, nail the corresponding treads to the stringers, on top of the risers. From the back, with nails spaced about every 8 inches, fasten each riser to its tread. If the treads and risers are hardwood, drill pilot holes for each of the nails; this will prevent splitting.

For enclosed stairways install a line of fire-stops between the wall studs and where the stair stringers are attached. Check the local code for other requirements, such as fire-stops between stringers and the use of Type-X wallboard for finishing the walls.

Note: If the stairs are to be finished wood, consider installing temporary rough-wood treads now and replacing them with better-quality wood when construction is completed. If you install the good wood now, be sure to protect it.

If the stairs are to be carpeted, rough-wood treads are adequate.

Railing Installation

All stairways should have at least one handrail extending from one floor to the next. To attach a handrail on the closed side of a stairway, use metal brackets made for the purpose to fasten the rail to the wall. Preshaped handrails for principal stairways are available from building-supply outlets. A 1½- to 1¾-inch dowel is satisfactory

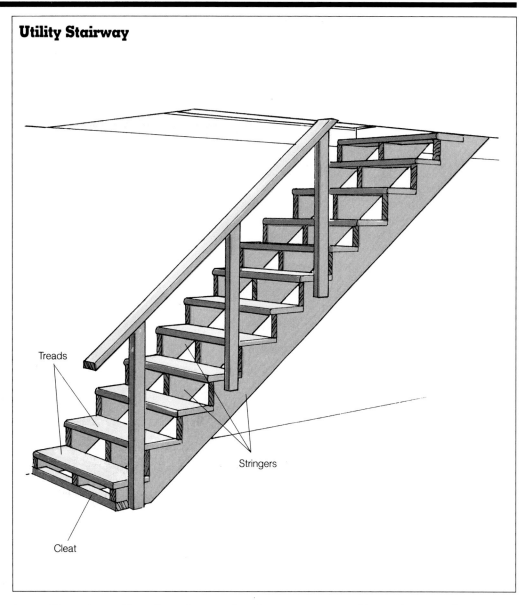

Utility Stairway

Treads

Stringers

Cleat

for a utility stairway. The rail ought to be placed between 30 and 34 inches above the nose of the treads and 38 inches above the floor of any landing.

Building Utility Stairs

You can build utility stairways with less expensive, lower-grade materials than principal stairways. Utility stairs can be made either with or without risers, but many homeowners prefer them with risers,

because risers improve appearance and facilitate cleaning. Utility stairs are usually made with cutout stringers, which were described in the section about principal stairways (page 255). The bottom end of basement stairs is usually anchored to a kicker that is bolted to the concrete floor.

If you want a utility stairway with risers, build it just as you would build a principal stairway. To save some money and much of the work, however, there are a few alternatives.

You can leave out the risers. And if you leave out the risers, you can use 2 by 10s or 2 by 12s for the treads to give the stairway a more substantial appearance.

If you really do decide you want to go without risers, you may want to consider a stairway construction technique that is even easier than using cutout stringers. This technique makes use of cleats, and the result is a serviceable utility stairway attractive enough for its setting.

Cleat Stairways

As with other stairways, the first job in building a cleat stairway is to determine the total rise and run. Make a diagram to determine the length of the stringer, the angle at the bottom, and the configuration of the cuts at the top.

If you would rather do the figuring on the site, drop a plumb line from the edge of the top level to the bottom level. Measure the run from this point and make a mark. Lay a straight 2 by 4 or other board from the top level to this mark, and set this angle on a bevel square.

To build cleat stairs with solid stringers, use wood or metal cleats to suspend the treads, which should not be wider than 3 feet, between 2 solid stringers. For spans less than 10 feet, the stringers can be 2 by 8s; for spans longer than 10 feet use 2 by 10s. All else being equal, rough lumber provides more strength because it is larger than the same nominal size of surfaced lumber.

Mark risers and treads on the stringers as if you were going to cut them. Each tread should overhang the one below it by 1 inch.

Like the principal stairway, the utility stairway will be secured to the bottom floor with a kicker. Since a cleat stairway has no risers, however, you will place the kicker in the middle bottom rather than in front. Use a 2 by 4 for the kicker, pressure treated if the floor is concrete, and mark its end shape on the stringer. Cut the notches in the stringers. Use nails or screws to secure the kicker to a wood floor; use

expansion shields and lag screws on a concrete floor.

When you have the first stringer laid out, transfer all the marks to the second stringer. Cut the top and bottom of the second stringer. Now you are ready to add the cleats.

The cleats can be metal stair brackets or you can cut them from 2 by 4s. Make them long

enough to just meet the edges of the stringers when they are in position on the lines you drew. Attach the cleats with construction adhesive and screws or nails long enough to clinch after they penetrate the stringer, then fasten the cleats to the stringers so the top edge of each cleat is on one of the lines.

Place the stringers into position. Be sure they are the same

distance apart at the top and at the bottom. Nail them to the joists at the top, to the kicker at the bottom, and to studs in the wall if one or both stringers are against a wall.

Cut the treads to length. Nail them into position on the cleats. Start at the bottom and you can sit on the nailed ones while you attach the rest.

Figuring Stringers and Cleats

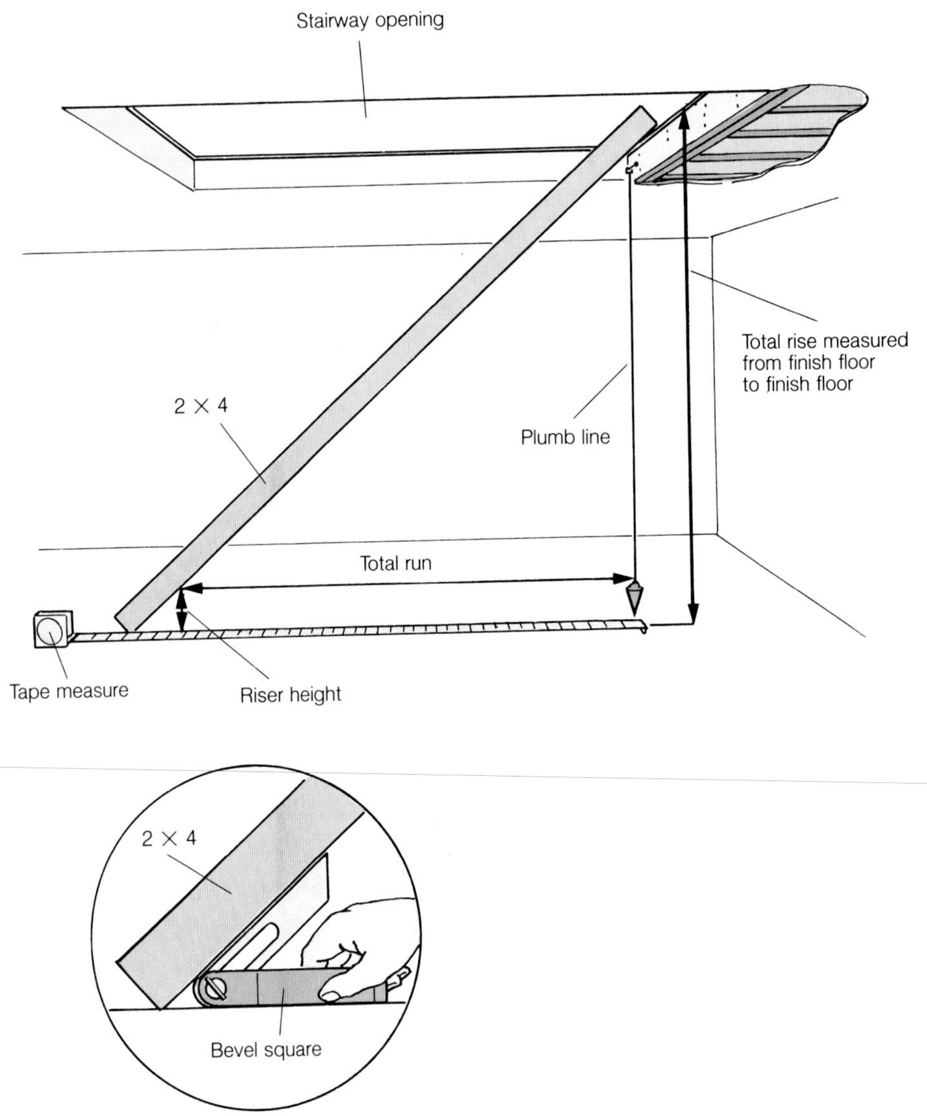

Stairway opening

2 × 4

Plumb line

Total rise measured from finish floor to finish floor

Total run

Tape measure

Riser height

2 × 4

Bevel square

this manner, frequently measuring the distance from a couple of places along each course to the peak. Make the adjustments necessary to ensure that the strips will be parallel to the ridge board. Place the insulation as you go if you didn't staple it in earlier. A ridge board that protrudes below the strips can be edged with moldings, or it can serve as a nailer for a piece of bevel-ripped 1-by board that is nailed over it.

Tiled Ceilings

Ceiling tiles are usually acoustic tiles made of fiberboard. They are available in many colors and patterns. The tiles are factory-finished and require no painting or other finishing. These tiles can be installed over any flat surface, such as wallboard that you put on first, or furring strips.

To avoid cutting more tiles than necessary, start by marking the exact center of the room. Measure from there out to the walls to determine how many rows of tiles will fit on each side. If there is a half row or less at the outer edge, adjust the center point so there is a half tile or more all around.

You will use either wallboard or furring strips to anchor the tiles. To install wallboard, follow the instructions beginning on page 274 but skip the mudding and taping. For furring strips, use 1 by 2 pine or fir boards nailed across the joists. Fasten the strips the same distance on center as the width of the tiles you select.

To install the ceiling tiles, start by attaching 4 tiles at the adjusted center point you determined earlier. If you are

placing the tiles on wallboard, secure them with glue. Attach tiles to furring strips by using small nails or a staple gun or as the manufacturer's instructions direct.

Suspended Ceilings

A suspended ceiling can be attached either before or after the finished surface of the walls. It is the easiest and fastest ceiling covering you can install. A suspended ceiling is great if you are putting a ceiling in a basement or attic room with overhead irregularities, such as beams or pipes, that you want to hide. To keep from having to cut small pieces around the edges, determine the position of the ceiling seams by using the method described for positioning rows of ceiling tiles.

Suspended ceilings have standard parts regardless of the manufacturer. These parts are wall angles, main Ts, and cross Ts. Attach the wall angle all around the room at the height you want the ceiling. Check continually with a level to make sure the wall angle is true. Position the main Ts so they are perpendicular to the joists, spacing them according to the size of the panels and the calculations you made to position the seams.

Suspend each main T by attaching wires to the joists every 4 feet. If splices are necessary, install a wire on each side of the splice. To allow twisting, let the wires hang at least 2 inches lower than the level of the ceiling will be. Feed the wires through the holes in

the main T, then twist them. When all the main Ts are up and level, fit the cross Ts into place between the main Ts. The ends of the main and cross Ts rest on the wall angle for support.

Set the panels into place. You can do any cutting with a utility knife and a straightedge. Panels with a decorative pattern are marked with an arrow on the back and should be placed with all the arrows pointing in the same direction.

Choosing Wall and Ceiling Finishes

There are really only two styles of standard walls and ceilings: wall and ceiling framing covered with stained or painted wood boards and framing covered with wallboard finished with paint, wallcoverings, sheet panels, or ceramic tiles. Wallboard, despite its name, covers both ceilings and walls. Its installation is described beginning on page 274. Typical finish materials are described in the sections that follow.

Wood Boards

Real wood boards add warmth and character to any room. Wood evokes the rich woodwork of fine old homes and, as a result, often plays an important part in imitating older home styles. As long as it preserves the character of the design, wood boards work equally well with contemporary architecture.

Board installation requires few tools and skills. The individual boards, usually tongue-and-groove, are attached directly to studs or foundation walls as the finish wallcovering.

There are several good reasons for using boards rather than other finish wall materials. Wood is extremely durable and almost maintenance free—facts that make it a very popular choice, particularly for a family room. It provides richness and warmth and, once installed, needs little, if any, finishing.

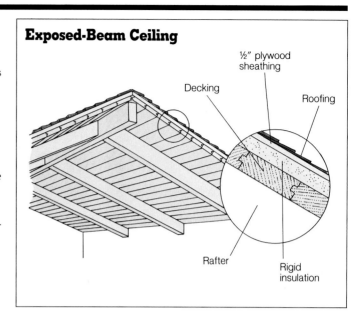

Exposed-Beam Ceiling

Decking

½" plywood sheathing

Roofing

Rafter

Rigid insulation

Wood must be used with discretion. Wood can be overpowering; if finished with a dark stain, it can cause a room to feel gloomy.

As long as the surface is waterproof and all the joints are carefully caulked, wood boards can be used on the walls even in wet areas.

Sheet Paneling

Today the most common form of paneling consists of sheets of plywood or hardboard covered with wood veneer or printed or embossed to mimic wood grains. The range of textures, colors, patterns, grains, and wood species is wide enough to suit just about any kind of design and pocketbook.

The greatest variety of paneling is available in sheets. Paneling sheets are usually 4 feet wide by 8, 9, or 10 feet long. One type of paneling has plywood backing. Plywood thicknesses vary from 3/16 inch to 5/8 inch. The other type of paneling uses hardboard backing, which consists of wood fibers pressed under heat. Most hardboard is 1/4 inch thick.

Sheet surface options are almost endless. In some cases real wood strips, called veneers, are glued to the plywood backing to produce a surface identical to individual boards but much less expensive. Some hardwood veneers are thick enough to have V grooves, and the sheets come completely finished.

To prepare a surface for paneling, on the floor and ceiling mark the position of all the wall studs so you know where to drive nails when you can no longer see the studs. With a long straightedge, check for high spots and low spots along the studs. If all areas are within 1/4 inch of a flat plane, that's good enough. If the stud wall is irregular, straighten the studs or plane them so the surface is within 1/4 inch of being flat.

You can install wood paneling at this point, on the bare studs. However, the walls will be firmer, better insulated, and more soundproof if you apply wallboard over the studs before you install the paneling.

Exterior Siding

Siding—ranging from old barn boards to new pine, redwood, or cedar siding—can be used indoors. It can be installed vertically, horizontally, or diagonally, and it comes in various patterns, such as shiplap, V groove, and channel rustic. Install it on the studs or over wallboard. It can be painted, stained, or finished with sealer.

Using exterior siding on an interior surface can be very effective when installed as a wainscoting—that is, just on the bottom half of walls in rooms that you want to have an outdoors or old-fashioned feel, such as a family room, library, or an informal living room.

Ceramic Tiles

Both ceramic and dimensioned stone tiles can be installed in wet and dry locations. Tiles can be installed from floor to ceiling, as a wainscoting, or as a decorative accent around doors and windows. Ceramic tiles are most popular in kitchens and bathrooms. But, because tiles are durable and easy to keep clean, they can be quite effective as a wall finish in family rooms, laundry rooms, halls, and children's bedrooms. Tiles can be installed by a handy owner-builder.

Ceramic tiles specified for walls are thinner than those specified for floors. In areas that are dry or that have a limited amount of moisture, install tile directly over wallboard that has been sealed and primed with material that is compatible with the tile adhesive to be used. Wet locations, such as tub and shower surrounds, require a waterproof backing. The best installation method for these areas is to install tile-backing units, which are specially made glass-mesh mortarboards, in lieu of standard wallboard. Tape the joints with fiberglass mesh tape, and fill the joints with tile adhesive. Using the thin-set method, install the tile with adhesive recommended for wet locations.

Wallcoverings

Wallcovering is a general term for paper, vinyl, and fabric products designed to cover walls. Wallcoverings add richness to any room. Manufacturers stipulate those that are appropriate for wet areas.

Commonly available wallcoverings are machine-printed in widths ranging from 18 to 27 inches. Those easiest to hang are pretrimmed and prepasted.

Hang wallcoverings over wallboard that is as smooth as possible; texture or roughness may show through. Seal the wallboard so that it neither draws too much moisture from the paste nor permits alkalis or corrosive elements to leach from the surface and discolor the wallcovering. Remember to paint the ceiling and trim before hanging the wallcovering.

Paint

The color of a room affects its size and mood. Paint is the easiest way to color a room. Generally, light colors seem to enlarge a room and dark colors seem to shrink it.

Choosing colors is perhaps the most difficult task of painting. The amount of natural light should affect the choice. A sunny room with windows facing west will tend to get hot, so use cool blue and gray tones to keep it feeling comfortable. Rooms with north-facing windows feel cold and benefit from warm red, orange, and brown tones. When choosing paint colors, the use of the room should also be considered as should the colors of other finished surfaces, such as the floor covering, and fairly permanent items, such as plumbing fixtures, countertops, and cabinets.

Paint over wallboard that has been properly taped and sealed or primed. Purchase the highest-quality paint you can afford and buy the type of paint appropriate to the location. Purchase enough paint for the entire area, checking batch numbers to maintain color consistency throughout the job.

Sound Insulation

Radios; televisions; powerful stereo systems; dishwashers; washing machines and clothes dryers; and video games with their electronic beeps, pings, and burps have made providing sound-insulated areas in a home very important. Sound isolation of bedrooms and bathrooms is also very important to many people.

One way to prevent interior sound pollution is to isolate "active" rooms from "quiet" rooms in establishing the floor plan. However, this is not always practical. The other prevention technique is effective sound insulation.

How Sound Gets Around
Sound is the molecules of a substance, usually gaseous or solid objects, bumping into each other and forming waves, very much like the ripples on a pond when you toss in a stone. Sound radiates outward from the sound source, through the air. When it strikes a solid object—such as a wall, floor, or ceiling—it causes it to vibrate. If the solid object can vibrate freely all the way through, it will cause the air on the other side to vibrate and pass the sound, almost unaltered, into the next room.

To keep the sound from going into the next room, you must find a way to stop the vibrations on one side of a wall from going through to the other. In the building business, the resistance of a wall to the transmission of sound has been given a rating. This rating is called the Sound Transmission Class (STC). The higher the rating, or class, the more effective the sound barrier.

At an STC rating of 25, normal speech can be heard through a wall. At a rating of 45, loud speech is only heard as a quiet murmur. At a rating of 60 or higher, loud speech is not audible at all and even loud music is only heard if it has a very loud beat. Of course you need a solid stone wall over 12 inches thick or a 6- to 8-inch wall filled with sand to make a barrier this effective.

Most sound engineers agree that a rating of 50 or more is quite adequate for a multi-occupancy building, whereas they consider a rating of 40 or less poor.

Insulating Against Sound
In a conventionally framed house, the studs and joists are the sound conductors. They transmit the vibrations from the wall and ceiling on one side to the other. Floor receptacles and light switches placed back-to-back are especially good conductors of sound. Doors, especially thin-walled hollow-core doors that don't fit well, can also cause sound leaks. Of course, a thin door can cause some loss of sound, but not enough to make much difference if the sound is loud.

Walls, floors, and ceilings of very dense material stop sound almost completely. A solid masonry wall or ceiling, or thick walls filled with sand, as in sound studios, have a very high STC rating. In the conventional wood-frame house you are building, however, the structural needs and increased costs of including these kinds of heavy walls or ceilings are prohibitive.

Deadening Walls
There are several ways to provide acceptable sound-resistant walls at an affordable cost. One is to nail a layer of ½-inch sound-deadening board to both sides of the studs and then glue a layer of ½-inch wallboard—or better yet, ⅝-inch wallboard—to that. This will provide an STC rating of around 45, at which you must really concentrate to hear loud speech through the wall.

The second system uses resilient metal between the wallboard and the studs to deaden the sound vibrations. You can nail light and flexible extruded aluminum channel across the studs horizontally and then screw the wallboard to the metal between the studs. Or you can nail small resilient metal clips to the studs and screw the ½-inch wallboard to them. In either case the sound vibration of the walls is deadened by the springiness of the metal. With either of these systems, you should get an STC rating of between 45 and 50, depending on the materials.

Another way to deaden sound between 2 rooms is to install a double stud wall. Of course you have to plan on this before you frame the house—changing the framing costs a lot of extra money and work. To install a double stud wall, you need 2 by 6 or 2 by 8 plates instead of the usual 2 by 4s. Stagger the studs so each one falls between a stud on the other side of the wall. You will have to install twice as many studs because the distance between studs must still be 16 inches on center.

Between the layers of studs, weave a layer of 1½- or 2-inch fibrous insulation. Use nails to attach ½-inch wallboard to the double wall of studs. Or leave out the insulation and apply the double layer of board we described above: a ½-inch sound-deadening board to the studs and glue ½-inch or ⅝-inch wallboard on top. Each of these insulation methods produces a wall with an STC rating of about 50, whereby loud speech cannot be audible at all through the wall.

Deadening Ceilings and Floors
The sounds coming through a ceiling are not only the air-borne sounds described earlier; in addition, you have the sounds of impact as things strike or roll along the floor—footsteps, pacing, or the tea cart being moved. Appliances that vibrate can also send considerable sound through the floor.

Ceilings and floors benefit from some sort of vibration-suppression material to keep the ceiling covering isolated from the joists.

Installing conventional carpet as a finish floor on upper levels of the house may be the best way to keep sound from traveling to the levels below.

INSTALLING WALLBOARD

Wallboard is a versatile and inexpensive building material used—despite its name—to cover both walls and ceiling. It is also called drywall, gypsum board, gypboard, and Sheetrock (a brand name). Wallboard is easy to install, although it takes some practice to finish it properly.

- ☐ Tool belt
- ☐ Wallboard hammer
- ☐ Wallboard saw
- ☐ Utility knife
- ☐ Steel tape measure
- ☐ Steel straightedge
- ☐ Panel T square
- ☐ Carpenter's pencil
- ☐ Chalk line
- ☐ Wallboard screw shooter
- ☐ Foot lever
- ☐ Caulk gun
- ☐ Compound tray
- ☐ 3- or 4-inch filling knife
- ☐ 6-inch filling knife
- ☐ 10- or 12-inch filling knife
- ☐ Inside-corner filling knife
- ☐ Outside-corner filling knife
- ☐ Sanding block
- ☐ Pole sander
- ☐ Sandpaper
- ☐ T braces

Planning a Wallboard Project

Installing wallboard on ceilings is a little more difficult than installing it on walls, but both jobs are similar and you should be able to do them yourself with one helper. On a difficulty scale of 10 points, consider installing wallboard a 6. Besides standard wallboard tools, consider renting a ceiling jack to raise the wallboard to the ceiling and hold it there while you nail it.

Wallboard is dimensionally stable, it can be moisture- and fireproofed, it cuts easily, and it creates an excellent surface for painting, wallcoverings, sheet panels, or ceramic tile. It can be doubled up to provide thermal mass. It can even go on the outside of buildings as a fire-resistant sheathing. When damaged, wallboard is easy to repair or replace.

Wallboard does have disadvantages, however. It can be monotonous as a finish wall if used without relief. It is sometimes heavy to handle, though not prohibitively so. And it takes skill to tape and finish the joints to an absolutely smooth surface. In spite of these limitations, wallboard is still the universally recommended wallcovering for interior walls.

One of the first planning decisions to make is how much of the work you are going to do yourself. Most people find it fairly easy to install wallboard themselves, as long as help is available for handling the heavy panels. However, if the final appearance is important or if there is a large area to cover, it is best to have the taping and texturing done professionally. If you choose to tape and texture yourself, start with out-of-the-way areas so that you can develop your proficiency before tackling the most visible walls.

Another early planning step is to calculate the placement of panels so you can order the types and sizes you need. For a large project, calculate the total square footage, allow a small percentage for waste, and order an equivalent square footage in the largest panels you will be using. It is a good idea to order extra, especially since wallboard is so inexpensive.

You may also need to buy, borrow, or improvise a few specialized tools. With some practice you can use a regular hammer to install wallboard, but for large projects you should get a wallboard hammer. The rounded head prevents breaking through the paper, and the angle of the handle keeps knuckles clear of the wall. You will also need extra blades for the utility knife, a wallboard saw, and a wood or metal straightedge. A foot lever helps snug panels up against the ceiling.

Types of Wallboard

Wallboard is a manufactured panel, made of gypsum or similar material, that is sandwiched between two layers of heavy paper. One side is smoother than the other, and the two long edges are beveled slightly to create a recessed cavity when two panels butt together. This cavity makes it possible to cover the joint with a special paper tape and layers of taping compound. When done properly, the final result is a smooth, flush wall with no visible joints.

The three types of wallboard are regular, Type X fire-resistant, and moisture-resistant panels. Building codes specify where extra fire-resistant and moisture-resistant panels must go. Typically, Type X fire-resistant panels must be used in residences for common walls between the garage and living space, for enclosed closets under stairs, and in closets containing gas water heaters. Moisture-resistant panels must be used behind bathtubs, sinks, and similar moisture-producing fixtures; they provide a good backing for tile in these locations. Moisture-resistant panels benefit from the use of a special joint compound and a sealant for coating all cut edges.

Wallboard is sold in ¼-, ⅜-, ½-, and ⅝-inch thicknesses. Install ⅝-inch-thick panels to give the house a feeling of solidity. Use thinner panels, ¼-inch or ⅜-inch thick, for special applications such as round corners. Panels are typically 4 feet wide and 8 feet long, but they are available in 10-, 12-, and 14-foot lengths. To provide effective sound insulation, hang ⅜-inch-thick sheets in a double layer to make ¾-inch-thick walls.

FINISH FLOOR OPTIONS

A floor is actually a series of layers. The part of the floor seen most is the finish floor. This is essentially a membrane over the real floor— the structural floor that holds everything up and keeps out moisture and drafts.

Learning About Finishes

Not all floors have all the layers, but it is important for you to understand how the layers relate to each other so you know what to put in and what you can leave out as you construct a floor.

Choose the finish floor for every space in the house before you install the subfloor. Different finish floors require different subfloor materials. Subfloors are installed during framing (see page 79).

Because the floor is such an important part of the way a room looks, select flooring coverings carefully. Remember that the finish flooring will last for many years, so choose one that is flexible in terms of design and use. It is much less expensive to change the color of your walls or to introduce new furnishings than it is to install a new floor.

As a general rule, good design is simple design, although simplicity is not always easy to achieve. Simple design requires a high level of restraint, thoughtfulness in planning, and care in execution.

If you want a dramatic and exciting floor, then be bold. Let it be the keynote for the rest of the decor. More often, however, the floor will play a background role. It will be the visual foundation that pulls the other elements of the decor

together. This section will describe the most common types of floor covering and their subfloor requirements.

Wood Floors

The warmth, beauty, and durability of wood make it one of the most popular flooring materials. Wood adds a feeling of quality and permanence to any room, and a wood floor will last the lifetime of a house if properly installed and maintained. If well protected and cared for, wood will never even have to be refinished; it will just look better as it takes on the patina of age. Wood also has insulating properties and is resilient to walk on.

However, wood is subject to moisture damage, from either spills or humidity. Take precautions when installing it around plumbing fixtures, over an enclosed crawl space, or below grade. Although modern floor finishes are tough, a wood floor is still vulnerable to scratches and surface abrasion. This might be a drawback in high-traffic areas or in beach areas where sand is common.

Wood flooring is milled in three basic formats: strip, plank, and block. Strip flooring is narrow, 2 to 2¼ inches wide and ⁵⁄₁₆ or ¾ inch thick, with tongue-and-groove edges.

Plank flooring is wider, consisting of random widths of up

to 9 inches. It is also ⁵⁄₁₆ or ¾ inch thick with tongue-and-groove edges. Wood blocks— often called parquet tiles—are available in various-sized squares with tongue-and-groove edges.

Most styles are available prefinished, although this option adds to the flooring cost. Most are hardwood—red oak, white oak, teak, walnut, maple, pecan, or hickory. Softwoods— such as pine, Douglas fir, and redwood—can also be used as flooring materials, but they will scratch and pit more easily than the hardwoods.

Before installing wood floors on a framed floor, install a ¾-inch tongue-and-groove CDX plywood subfloor over the exposed joists. Lay building paper over the subfloor. If you plan to finish a concrete slab by laying a wood floor, install a wood sleeper floor and building paper over the slab.

Some wood blocks can be glued directly to a concrete subfloor.

Resilient Flooring

Resilient flooring is available in sheets and tiles. Both come in a wide range of colors and patterns that make them appropriate for any room in the house.

Resilient flooring is both practical and elegant. It is durable, comfortable, and easy to maintain. The patterns and textures range from glossy to matte, from lightly mottled to highly textured, from monochromatic to marbleized, and all are available in almost any color imaginable.

Most resilient flooring is made of vinyl or a vinyl composition. Rubber sheet, cork tiles, and wood tiles finished with

polyurethane are also available. Solid vinyl and vinyl-covered cork are the most expensive and have the most resiliency and best sound-insulating qualities. Vinyl-composition flooring is generally less expensive. The resiliency varies with the thickness of the material.

Though your own color preferences and design needs will guide you in selecting a pattern, keep in mind a few general guidelines. Do not use patterns that simulate natural materials in places where the real material would never be used. For instance, do not curve a Spanish floor-paver pattern up a wall. Avoid patterns that will overwhelm a room. The bigger and more intricate the pattern, the larger the room should be. If you like an intricate pattern for a small room, but fear that it may appear too busy, check to see if it is also available in neutral, monochromatic tones. If sheet materials need to be seamed in prominent places, conceal the seams by choosing a pattern with straight lines, such as simulated tile with grouted joints.

Most tiles measure 12 inches square and are sold by the piece. Resilient sheet is sold by the square yard. It usually comes in 6- or 12-foot-wide rolls, although 9- and 15-foot widths are sometimes available. Plan to install sheet flooring so that seams fall in the narrowest part of the room or away from highly visible, heavily trafficked areas.

Resilient materials are thin and therefore reveal any dents, bumps, cracks, or depressions in the subsurface, including recessed nail heads. Resilient materials must be installed over a surface that is entirely free of potential moisture. To prepare an exposed joist floor for a resilient flooring finish, install a ¾-inch tongue-and-groove CDX plywood subfloor, then install a ¼- or ½-inch particleboard underlayment. Fill all joints and underlayment nail depressions, and sand the particleboard until smooth.

Concrete slabs must be perfectly smooth before you cover them with resilient flooring.

Ceramic Tile

Ceramic materials have been installed on floors for centuries. Tile materials for finish floors include ceramic tiles, dimensioned stone tiles, tile mosaics, paver units, and brick veneers.

The wide range of colors, textures, sizes, and shapes makes tile suitable for installations that vary from simple and angular to warm and textural. Tiles can cover a large area, or they can be used as an accent to other materials to provide contrast and interest.

Install a ceramic tile floor over a double subfloor. First install ⅝-inch tongue-and-groove CDX plywood directly over the joists. Then install exterior-grade plywood or special tile-backing units over the subfloor. Make sure a concrete slab is smooth and dry before you install tile on it.

Carpeting

Wall-to-wall carpeting is soft, warm, and comfortable. Carpeting comes in a very wide choice of colors, patterns, and textures. Carpet is suitable for open expanses or intimate spaces. It can be used in any room. It needs to be maintained and is not as permanent as most of the other flooring materials, however.

With the wide range of colors, fibers, and textures to choose from, carpet is one of the most luxurious choices of flooring. The softness and resilience of carpet invite you to sit down or stretch out on it, and the broad expanse of color provides an excellent background for any decor.

Carpet is made from natural wool and man-made products such as nylon, polyester, acrylic, and polypropylene olefin. Conventional carpet requires a pad. Cushion-backed carpet has a built-in pad.

The typical subfloor under conventional carpet is ¾-inch tongue-and-groove plywood. The pad covers any roughness in the subfloor. If you are installing cushion-backed carpet, install a ¾-inch tongue-and-groove CDX/PTS plywood subfloor, fill all joints, and sand the subfloor smooth.

When installing carpet on top of concrete, make sure the floor is dry and that there are no moisture problems. Floors with radiant-heat pipes deserve special consideration if you are installing conventional, not cushion-backed, carpet. Because the tackless strip has to be nailed into the concrete, you risk puncturing the pipes. To locate the pipes, moisten the concrete around the perimeter of the room wherever you intend to install pieces of tackless strip. Turn up the heat. Mark the areas that dry first. Avoid these spots when nailing.

Anatomy of a Slab Floor

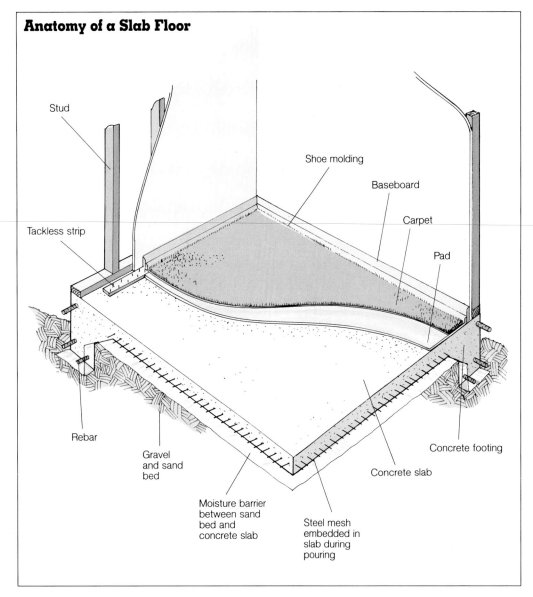

Stud

Shoe molding

Baseboard

Carpet

Tackless strip

Pad

Rebar

Concrete footing

Gravel and sand bed

Concrete slab

Moisture barrier between sand bed and concrete slab

Steel mesh embedded in slab during pouring

Anatomy of a Wood-Frame Floor

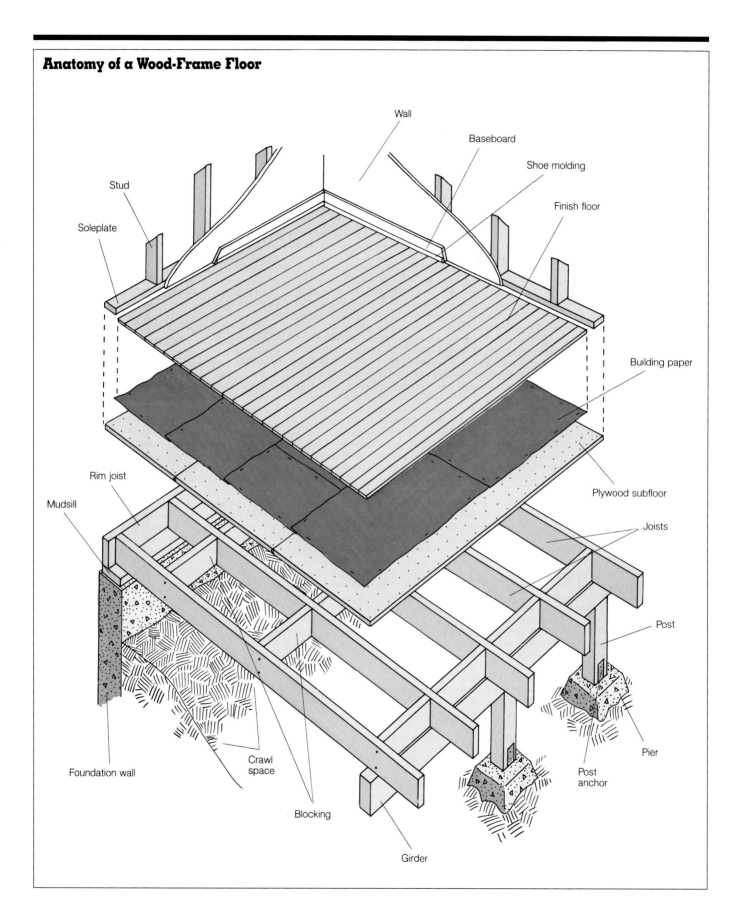

Wall

Baseboard

Shoe molding

Stud

Finish floor

Soleplate

Building paper

Rim joist

Plywood subfloor

Mudsill

Joists

Post

Foundation wall

Crawl space

Pier

Blocking

Post anchor

Girder

INSTALLING INTERIOR DOORS

Interior doors are similar to exterior doors except they need not be quite as heavy or weatherproof. Another difference is that interior doors seldom have a threshold. Unless there is a change of floor height between rooms, the floor from one room flows through the doorway and into the next, without interruption.

- ☐ Tool belt
- ☐ Curved-claw hammer
- ☐ Handsaw
- ☐ Hacksaw
- ☐ Power circular saw
- ☐ Power drill and bits
- ☐ Hole saw
- ☐ Steel tape measure
- ☐ Combination square
- ☐ Framing square
- ☐ 24-inch level
- ☐ Slot screwdrivers
- ☐ Phillips screwdrivers
- ☐ Wood chisels
- ☐ Mortise chisel
- ☐ Nail sets
- ☐ Utility knife
- ☐ Awl
- ☐ Jack plane or power plane
- ☐ Belt sander
- ☐ Door bucks
- ☐ Router
- ☐ Hinge-mortise routing template

Choosing Interior Doors

On a difficulty scale of 10 points, consider installing interior doors a 5. You must carefully measure and level components. Depending on the style of door you install, some finish carpentry is involved. Because of all the holding, measuring, and leveling involved, a helper is desirable for this job.

Many interior doors are flush hollow-core. They are made of two unadorned sheets of plywood or hardboard, with a light framework inside. The interior of the door is actually hollow or filled with cardboard to reduce noise transmission.

Solid-core interior doors are used for bedroom and bathroom doors where soundproofing is desired. The outside of these doors is, again, two sheets of plywood or hardboard. The core is usually a solid piece of particleboard.

Solid-wood doors are more expensive than core doors. Solid doors are often paneled, designed in architectural styles popular prior to the 1930s. Solid-wood doors block sound and have a solid look—they are worth the investment. These doors are made of either hardwoods or softwoods.

All door styles are available in paint grade. This means they have plugged knots or seams in the wood that would be unattractive if the door were stained or left natural. Paint will cover the imperfections.

Hollow-core, solid-core, and solid-wood doors are available in a variety of wood species suitable for finishes that show off the grain and beauty of the wood. These are, of course, more expensive than doors that are going to be painted.

Hanging Hinged Doors

A regular hinged door, such as most of those in any house, is installed exactly like an exterior door (see page 190). Interior doors are available prehung or you can hang them yourself, just as exterior doors.

The big difference between an interior and exterior installation, however, is that an interior door does not have a threshold. This will affect your measurements. Another difference is that an interior door does not need flashing or building paper around it.

Doorknobs and Locks

Interior knobs and locks are installed in the same manner as the exterior entrance sets (see page 199). You can purchase interior doors with the holes for the knob or lock cylinder and the latch bolt already drilled. Most interior latches are cylinder-lock type and are installed in these holes. If the knob you chose is something other than standard, buy doors that do not have bores; drill them yourself.

Installing Pocket Doors

Pocket doors are available as ready-made units, complete with the door, or as hardware units to which you add the door of your choice.

Ready-made units are available in widths from 24 to 36 inches for a standard 80-inch door frame. All you do is rough-frame a doorway according to the instructions, insert the unit, add wallcovering and trim, and it's done.

Kits that supply just the hardware include adjustable overhead tracks and wheels that attach to the top of the door and fit the track.

The Opening

Make the opening width equal to 2 times the door width plus 2½ inches for jambs and shims. Make the rough opening height 83 or 84 inches (check the tracks and doors before framing the opening). Install trimmer studs and a header across the entire opening.

Ready-made Units

Set the pocket frame into the side of the opening where the door will be recessed. Make sure it is plumb and level. Nail it to the framing.

Install the side jamb and head jamb. Again, make sure they are plumb and level before nailing them.

Screw the overhead track to the center of the head jamb. Mount the wheels on the top of the door, and lift it into place so that the wheels hook onto the track. Adjust the wheels until the door hangs straight. Finish the walls and trim the opening, as needed.

Hardware Units

These units are kits that include everything you need to install a pocket door but the door. The first thing you have to do, then, is select the door you want and frame the opening to fit it. Read the kit manufacturer's instructions to find the size of the rough opening you'll need to accommodate the door you have chosen.

The first step in hanging the door is to place the overhead track in the opening so that both ends butt against the trimmer studs. Check that it is centered on the header, and make sure it is level. Use shims to level it, if necessary, and nail it to the studs.

Snap chalk lines on the floor between the outside edges of the trimmer studs. Then place the split jamb at the midpoint of the opening, where the edge of the open door will be, and screw the top of the jamb to the track. Screw the bottom flange to the floor, using the chalk lines as guides and a level to check plumb.

Repeat this step with the second part, the split stud. Place it between the split jamb and the trimmer as required by the manufacturer's instructions. Again use the chalk lines to position the bottom, and be sure it is plumb.

Mount the wheels on the door and hang it on the track. Adjust the wheel mechanisms to make the door the proper height. Install door guides at the base of the split jamb, and adjust them to allow ⅛-inch clearance from the door.

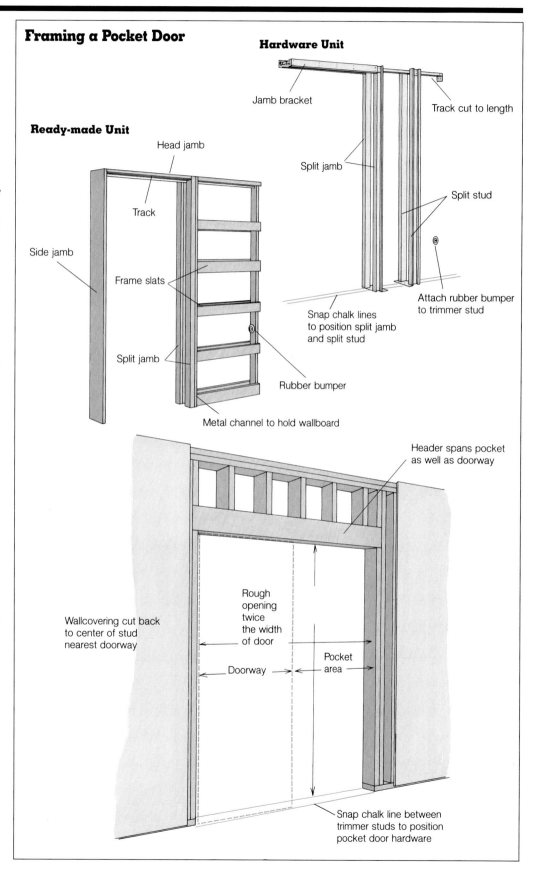

Framing a Pocket Door

Hardware Unit

Jamb bracket

Track cut to length

Split jamb

Split stud

Attach rubber bumper to trimmer stud

Snap chalk lines to position split jamb and split stud

Ready-made Unit

Head jamb

Track

Side jamb

Frame slats

Split jamb

Rubber bumper

Metal channel to hold wallboard

Header spans pocket as well as doorway

Wallcovering cut back to center of stud nearest doorway

Rough opening twice the width of door

Pocket area

Doorway

Snap chalk line between trimmer studs to position pocket door hardware

Install the bumper where the midpoint of the door will hit it. Adjust the bumper with shims or washers so that the door will extend ⅜ inch beyond the split jamb when it is open.

Cover the exposed trimmer stud with jamb stock and the framing with wallboard or whatever wallcovering you are using in the room. Use 1⅛-inch doorstop material to conceal the track and split jambs. Leave a ⅛-inch clearance on both sides, then trim the opening with casing material.

Installing Bypass Doors

Also called sliding doors, bypass doors are commonly used for closets because they take up less space than swinging doors. Sliding doors are also useful as room dividers. They are typically used to block off an area used for a home office. Sliding doors are easy to install. Virtually any type of door can be used as a sliding door; typical sliding doors are hollow-core doors and many are mirrored.

Mirrored doors are often installed in metal frames like sliding glass doors.

The basic hardware for sliding doors consists of an overhead track, a pair of wheels that attach to the top of each door, and door guides that are fastened to the floor. You can buy this hardware separately and use inexpensive hollow-core doors or buy the doors and hardware in a kit.

The doors should be 1½ inches shorter than the opening to allow 1¼ inches for the track and ¼-inch clearance above the floor or carpet. Each door should be ½ inch wider than half the width of the opening, so that the doors overlap by ½ inch when closed. If you cannot find doors of the proper width, either make them narrower by trimming the edges of the door with a power saw or add trim to the inside of the doorway.

The Track

To install a top track, frame the door opening with side and head jambs. If the overhead track is not adjustable, cut it to length with a hacksaw. Then place the track against the overhead jamb and mark on the jamb locations of the predrilled screw holes. Remove the track and drill pilot holes for the screws. Install the track with the open channels facing into the opening. Conceal the track with an extrawide top casing or a separate strip of wood nailed to the jamb.

The Doors

Mount a pair of wheels on the top edge of each door, about 2 inches in from each end. With the overhead track installed and the wheels mounted, hang the inside door on the inside channel first, then hang the outside door. Push the doors back against the side jambs, and check how straight they hang by visually comparing them to the jambs.

If a door hangs unevenly, loosen the adjusting screws on the wheel mounts and raise or lower one corner of the door until it is hanging straight.

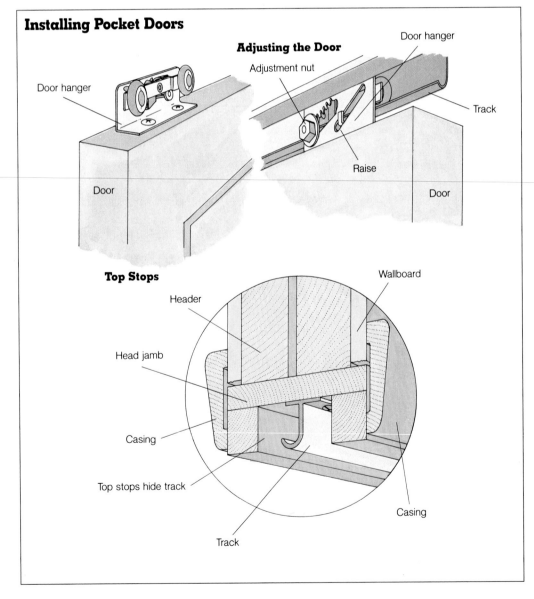

Installing Pocket Doors

Door hanger

Adjusting the Door

Door hanger

Adjustment nut

Track

Raise

Door

Door

Top Stops

Wallboard

Header

Head jamb

Casing

Top stops hide track

Track

Casing

The Floor Guides

The guides are small plastic or metal pieces screwed into place over the finish flooring. Screw the guide to the floor between the doors in the center of the opening, where they meet. If the guide is adjustable, move the side pieces until there is a ⅛-inch clearance from the doors. If the guide is too low, place a shim under it to raise it.

The Trim

Finish the installation by installing trim around the doors. Fasten casings around the opening and a strip of molding across the head jamb to hide the overhead track.

Note: Both bypass and bifold doors can be installed without wood jambs and casings. In this style, after the tracks and doors are installed, the rough-frame opening is covered in wallboard. This is a less expensive way to finish these openings, and the result is a very modern look.

However, the absence of the protective wood jambs and casings causes the wallboard around the opening to get dents and dings when people and furniture bump through the door. The wallboard also tends to show fingerprints more than does wood. To case or not to case is really a matter of interior-decorating style.

Installing Bypass Doors

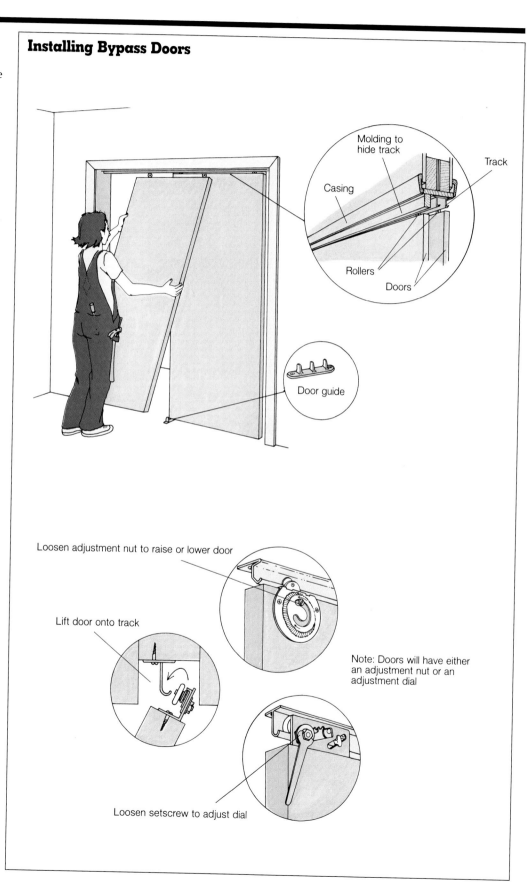

Molding to hide track

Casing

Track

Rollers

Doors

Door guide

Loosen adjustment nut to raise or lower door

Lift door onto track

Note: Doors will have either an adjustment nut or an adjustment dial

Loosen setscrew to adjust dial

Installing Bifold Doors

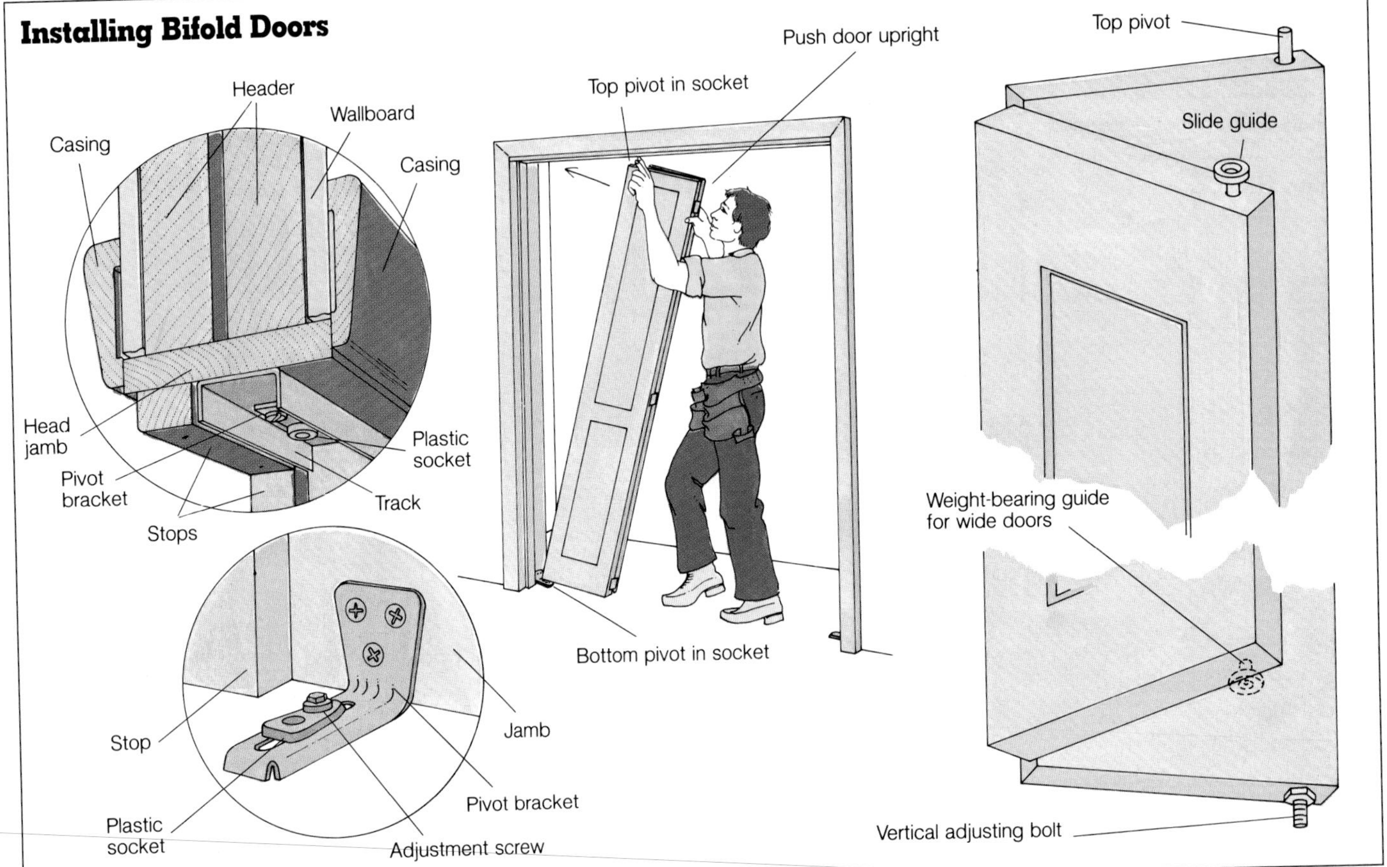
Header
Wallboard
Casing
Casing
Head jamb
Pivot bracket
Stops
Plastic socket
Track
Stop
Plastic socket
Adjustment screw
Pivot bracket
Jamb
Top pivot in socket
Push door upright
Bottom pivot in socket
Top pivot
Slide guide
Weight-bearing guide for wide doors
Vertical adjusting bolt

Installing Bifold Doors

Bifold doors come to the rescue where a conventional door would be in the way when open. When they are closed bifold doors provide a warm and interesting break in the wall. Bifold doors come in pairs (two doors equal one pair; four doors equal two pairs for a double bifold). Bifold doors can be flush, paneled, or louvered.

You can install bifold doors easily in any regular door frame. They come in a variety of widths so, by using one or two pairs, you can arrive at the right width for almost any standard opening. Even then, if the doors do not fit the opening exactly, you can narrow all the doors by trimming them at the edges or building up the sides of the jambs to make the opening slightly smaller.

The hardware includes an overhead track, a bottom pivot for each pair of doors, a slide guide, and an adjustable bolt that goes in the bottom corner of each pivot door. The hardware is available separately or as part of a complete package, which includes the doors.

The Track

Cut the overhead track to fit inside the opening. Insert the bumper into the track, placing it where the slide guides attached to the top of the doors will hit it. Slip the pivot guides into each end of the track, and screw the track into the center of the head jamb.

The Brackets

Wait to install the brackets until the finish floor is complete. Position the bottom brackets on the floor by dropping a plumb bob from each pivot guide in the top track. Screw the bottom brackets to the side jambs, leaving all adjusting screws loose for later adjustment.

The Doors

Measure the opening carefully and trim the doors equally to allow a total clearance of ¼ to ½ inch, depending on the number of hinges and doors. Install the hinges that join each pair of doors. Then install the top and bottom pivots and the slide guide necessary for each pair.

Now you will set each pair of doors into place. Set the bottom pivot into the bottom bracket first. Tilt the door toward the center of the opening, and slide the top pivot guide to the center of the track so that you can insert the top pivot of the door into it. Tilt the door back to a vertical position, inserting the slide guide into the track as you push on the door.

Guide Adjustment

When the door is in a plumb position, tighten the top and bottom adjusting screws. Open the door to test it for clearance. If it binds on the top track or is too low, adjust the height by turning the adjusting nut on the bottom pivot of the door. If you are installing double bifold doors, repeat the process for the second pair.

INSTALLING INTERIOR TRIM

The various pieces used to finish a room are called trim. Some trim parts—casings, baseboards, window stools, and aprons—are made from standard square stock. Trim that is shaped is referred to as molding. Trim covers gaps and provides decorative relief for flat wall surfaces.

☐ Tool belt
☐ Curved-claw hammer
☐ Handsaw
☐ Coping saw
☐ Miter box and backsaw
☐ Steel tape measure
☐ Combination square
☐ Sliding bevel gauge
☐ Framing square
☐ Wood chisels
☐ Nail sets
☐ Utility knife
☐ Awl

Types of Trim

In general, molding is used sparingly in contemporary architecture. However, in homes designed in the older architectural styles, it is widely used and often quite elaborate.

The difficulty of installing trim and the time needed to do it depends on the intricacy of the interior. Simple trim is simple to install. On a difficulty scale of 10 points, consider installing trim a 3. Two people with basic carpentry skills can install basic trim for an average room in a few hours.

Traditionally, moldings have been made of wood. Today, many moldings are made from pressed foam. These foam moldings mimic intricately cut wood moldings for Victorian and other period architectural styles. Because moldings serve no structural purpose, the foam versions work perfectly. They are cut and put into place in the same manner as wood moldings. Foam molding is generally less expensive than the comparable wood version, and foam is lighter and therefore easier to install.

Wood moldings are usually standard dimension lumber, such as a 1 by 4 milled to a decorative or purposeful shape. Each shape is produced by running dimension lumber through a shaper, or molding machine. Although some manufacturers have their own classification system, most use standard profiles established in 1957 by the Western Wood Molding and Millwork Producers. Ask a lumber supplier for a profile chart for the WM or WP series to see what is available. No lumberyard stocks all available shapes, but a supplier can order many of them for you.

Most wood trim is made of ponderosa pine. Manufacturers also use sugar pine, Douglas fir, larch, white fir, cedar, and hemlock. Hardwood trim is also available, chiefly oak and mahogany. The best trim is made from a single piece of wood. Choose one-piece trim if you plan to stain it.

Short lengths of wood finger-jointed together form less expensive paint-grade trim. The glue in the joints is not waterproof, so use this type in dry areas only.

The most common types of interior trim are casings around doors and windows; baseboards at the bottom of walls; crown moldings at the top of walls; picture molding, usually about 1 foot below the top of the wall; and chair rail, which covers the seam between wainscoting and finish wall. Most building- and home-center stores carry fairly simple, basic styles only, but you can combine two or three different shapes to match the more ornate versions that are found in historic house styles.

Always try to match trim to the architectural style of the house. If you need a type that is out-of-date, start by trying to duplicate the pattern with two or more pieces of stock lumber. If that won't do, look for a salvage yard that stocks old materials, or see if a local lumberyard can mill a special piece.

Special moldings make a plain house look pleasingly fancy if they harmonize with the character of the home. Avoid highly ornate moldings, unless they obviously fit in with the rest of the design.

If you want to dress up door and window casings of simple dimension lumber, such as 1 by 4, merely add a piece of decorative molding across the tops of the head casings. Add short pieces of the same molding at each end, and simply miter the corners.

Another simple touch that dresses up a plain room is to run a strip of chair rail around the wall from 3 to 3½ feet above the floor or at the same height as the windowsills. Finish the wall below the rail differently from the rest of the room by using paneling or a darker paint.

Trim breaks up large expanses of wall and adds visual interest to a room. It can make rooms and hallways seem larger through visual deception—a valuable trick in smaller homes. If you want a room to appear higher, place horizontal trim near the ceiling at a height slightly lower than the tallest pieces of furniture. The added horizontal line creates a feeling of space above the furniture. The deception works better if you install trim around the top of the walls. To complete the artificial enlargement, add horizontal trim around the bottom of the wall, about 18 inches above the floor. Bottom trim enhances the definition of the walls, taking visual impact away from furniture and windows.

If a small room has a vaulted ceiling, take advantage of the expansive effect by installing trim around the walls at the same level as the top of the doors and windows. The

Trim Types

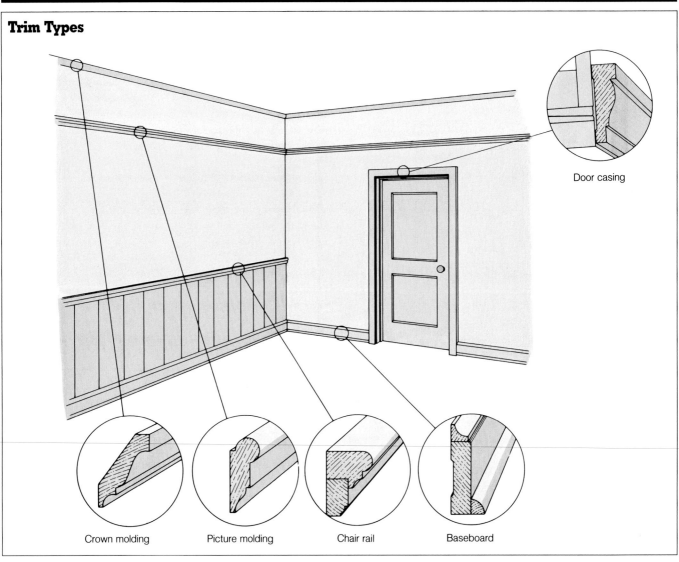

Door casing

Crown molding

Picture molding

Chair rail

Baseboard

trim accentuates the beginning of the ceiling and emphasizes the height. A similar trim around the bottom of the walls, about 18 inches above the floor, makes the room seem even larger. Use trim to outline the fireplace or other architectural feature.

There are many unconventional uses for molding, such as trimming a flush door to make it resemble a panel door or trimming posts and other structural members. Trim is most effective when it enhances existing architectural lines, not when it creates new shapes.

Working With Trim

Store trim where rough construction will not damage it. Do not install trim until all the walls are completely dry—shrinkage could open the joints. Priming the back of trim before installation minimizes shrinkage. If you choose to stain the trim, do so before installation if possible.

Try to use full-length pieces wherever trim will be prominent. If you have to join two pieces end to end, cut both

pieces on a 45-degree bevel so one overlaps the other. Do not use a butt joint.

Neat trim requires precision measuring and cutting. Make all your marks with a knife blade, sharp scribe, or sharp pencil. Cut with the sharpest saw blade available. If you saw by hand, use a backsaw or a miter box. The most accurate power saws are the power miter saw and the radial arm saw. Use one of these saws if you can. Run the blade slowly through the wood for a smooth cut. Some professionals use a

tool called a miter trimmer, which slices instead of saws. You may be able to rent one.

Nail trim with 4-penny (4d), 6d, or 8d finishing nails. Always countersink the nail heads, and fill in the holes with wood putty or filler. If it is necessary for the trim to bend and flex for it to hug an irregular wall, use thin trim or trim with recessed backs. If you have a lot of trim to install, rent a finishing-nail gun and compressor, which will speed the work considerably.

enter the house and every room within it. Track lights running the length of a hall can be spotted to highlight doors and artwork. Low-voltage fixtures installed along the molding around doors, picture molding, and chair rails provide interesting illumination along halls and stairways.

Types of Fixtures

Although there are numerous lighting effects, there are just a few basic types of fixtures and a few different kinds of bulbs to put in them. The fixture types are pendant, surface-mounted, translucent panels, recessed, and track. There are three kinds of bulbs available for home use. Each has special features and uses.

Incandescent Lights

Compared to daylight, light from incandescent bulbs seems yellowish or reddish. Incandescent light flatters skin tones and highlights warm colors. The light is easy to direct. However, incandescent bulbs cost more to operate, expend more energy in heat than light, and do not last as long as fluorescent styles.

Fluorescent Lights

Available as tubes and bulbs, fluorescent lights spread light wider and are about four times more economical to operate than incandescent bulbs. In addition, fluorescent lights do not produce as much heat as incandescent lights, and fluorescent lights last longer. They are available in many colors from cool blues to full-spectrum whites to warm tones similar to those cast by incandescents.

Quartz Halogen Lights

These produce a brilliant white light. One powerful bulb can produce enough light to illuminate an entire room, cast interesting shadows, and bathe a space in "sunshine." Because these bulbs put out so much heat, they must be used in special fixtures only.

Installing Fixtures

Besides the normal precautions you should always take with all electrical wiring, here are some safety considerations unique to lighting.

Recessed fixtures generate heat that will build up if it is trapped. Do not cover such fixtures with insulation in the attic. All around the fixture allow at least 3 inches of clearance between the fixture and insulation.

Take care to observe the limit the manufacturer sets for maximum wattage. Never use a bulb that's larger than recommended.

Lights in a bathroom should have moisture-proof housings. Switches should not be beside the tub or shower.

The lights in a child's bedroom should be at a safe height so they will not be broken during normal play. Avoid placing lamps in the room of an infant or toddler.

Be sure you observe all code requirements for placing, switching, wiring, and grounding all light fixtures. These requirements were written for your protection.

Each individual fixture mounts a bit differently. Be sure to check the manufacturer's instructions. The installation of almost all fixtures

Anatomy of a Ceiling Fixture

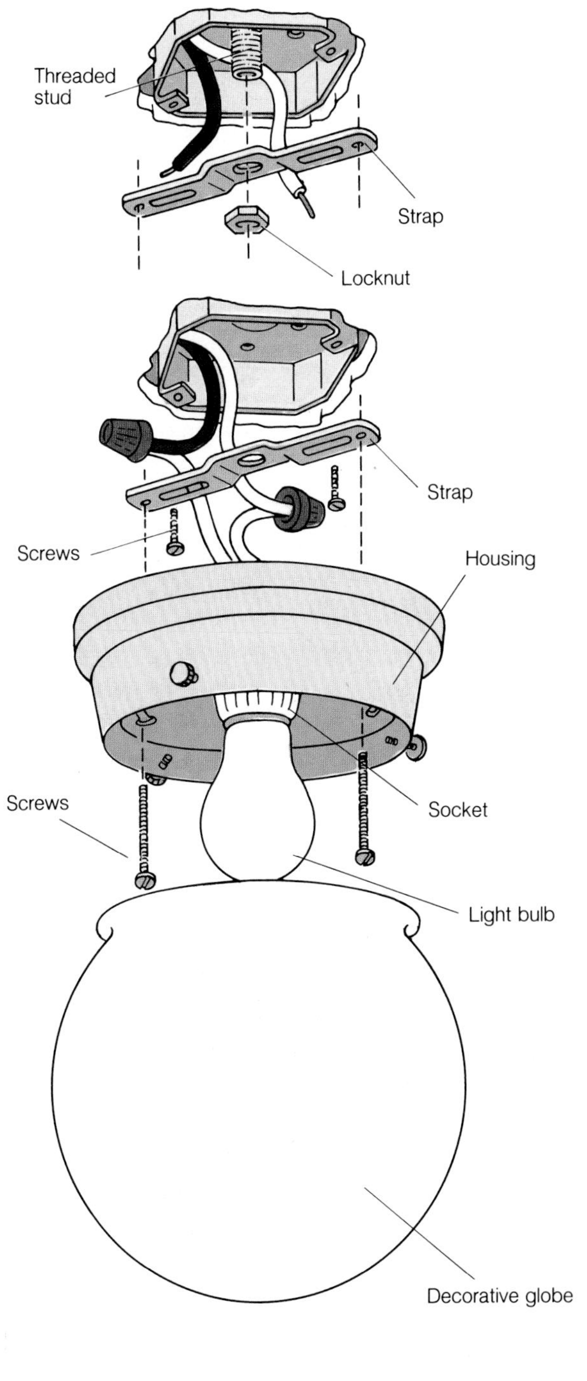

Threaded stud

Strap

Locknut

Strap

Screws

Housing

Socket

Screws

Light bulb

Decorative globe

Note: Ceiling fixtures are attached with either a threaded stud and locknut or screws

consists of three steps. The first is exposing the wires by stripping the protective coverings off the cable that sticks out of the boxes. Then you connect the wires in the cable to the wires or screws on the fixture. And, finally, you secure the fixture to the wall or ceiling and affix any protective plates or escutcheons.

The following instructions include turning on the power to check lighting angles and to see that you have connected each fixture correctly. Since you won't have power until after the final inspection, you'll have to wait until then to do these last steps.

Wire Stripping

To expose wires, first remove the sheathing, which is usually plastic on Type NM, or nonmetallic, cable but which may be rubber or armored cable. The sections that follow tell how to remove different types of sheathing.

Type NM Cable

The best way to strip the plastic sheathing from Type NM, or nonmetallic, cable is with a tool made especially for the purpose. It's called a cable stripper and is available at any hardware or electrical-supply store. You just slip the stripper over the cable to where you want the sheathing removed, usually about 6 inches from the end, squeeze it so the little blade penetrates the sheathing, and pull it off the end.

If you don't have a stripper, lay the wire flat on a smooth surface. Six inches back from the end, insert the tip of a sharp knife in the sheathing and make a shallow cut down

the center to the end. This cut provides a guide for successive passes with the knife. Be careful to cut deep enough to penetrate the sheathing without cutting the insulation around the interior wires.

Once the sheathing is split, peel it back and cut it off with a knife or a pair of wire cutters to expose the wires.

Armored Cable

Stripping metal requires a hacksaw. Make the cut about 8 inches from the end so you will have plenty of wire for the connections. Hold the saw at a right angle to the spiral strip of the armor rather than at a right angle to the cable itself. Cut through the armor only; do not cut the aluminum grounding strip or the wires inside. This is not easy and may take some practice. Once you have made a cut through the top of the armor, give the cable a sharp bend at the cut point and twist it back and forth to break the rest of the armor. Insert a plastic anti-short bushing into the cut end to protect the wires from the sharp armor.

Insulation

To strip insulation, use a wire stripper or an electrician's multipurpose tool—they will make the work much faster and easier. Place each wire in the correct hole in the stripper or multipurpose tool (the holes are numbered by wire size), squeeze the handles, and rotate the tool to cut the insulation. Then slide the tool to the end of the wire to pull the insulation off.

Stripping wire with a knife is not recommended, because you may partially cut the wire and weaken it. If you have nothing but a knife, don't cut at a right angle to the wire—you are more likely to damage the wire that way. Hold the knife blade at about a 60-degree angle, then twirl the wire back and forth until you have cut through the insulation all around the wire. Pull the insulation off with your fingers.

Splices

When wires are spliced or joined together, the connection must be very tight. A poor connection leads to a drop in voltage, overheating of the wires, and the possibility of a fire from a spark as the electricity tries to jump between loose wires. Wires that are stripped and then spliced together must be fully insulated again. For a tight, safe connection, the best way to splice wires No. 8 and smaller is with a solderless connector, more commonly called a wire nut.

This connector is a hard plastic shell with a threaded, tapered copper interior. Wire nuts come in different sizes, corresponding to wire sizes. Check the chart on the package to see which size to use.

To make the splice, first remove the insulation from the end of the wire. Remove only enough so that, when wires are joined inside the nut, no exposed wire will be visible. Insert them in the nut, then screw the nut down as tightly as you can with your fingers. If some bare wire is still showing, untwist the nut, clip off a little wire at the end, and screw the nut on again.

Splicing Wires

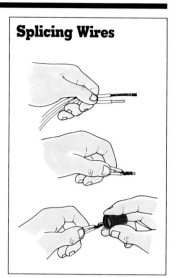

Pendant and Surface-Mounted Fixtures

Fixtures to be mounted to the ceiling surface or suspended on rods or chains all have a housing that is attached to the electrical box with screws or a central threaded stud. Generally, fixtures weighing over 30 pounds must be supported by a threaded stud mounted inside the box.

Prepare the electrical box by attaching whatever stud or bracket is required. For screw-mounted fixtures make sure the holes in the fixture canopy line up with the threaded holes at the edge of the electrical box, or use a mounting strap.

Use wire nuts to attach the fixture wires to the house wires. If the fixture is heavy, have a helper hold it.

Secure the fixture canopy to the ceiling with the 2 finish screws provided or with a decorative nut for the threaded stud. Install the light bulb, turn on the power, and verify that the light is functioning before you add the finish pieces.

Installing Pendant Fixtures

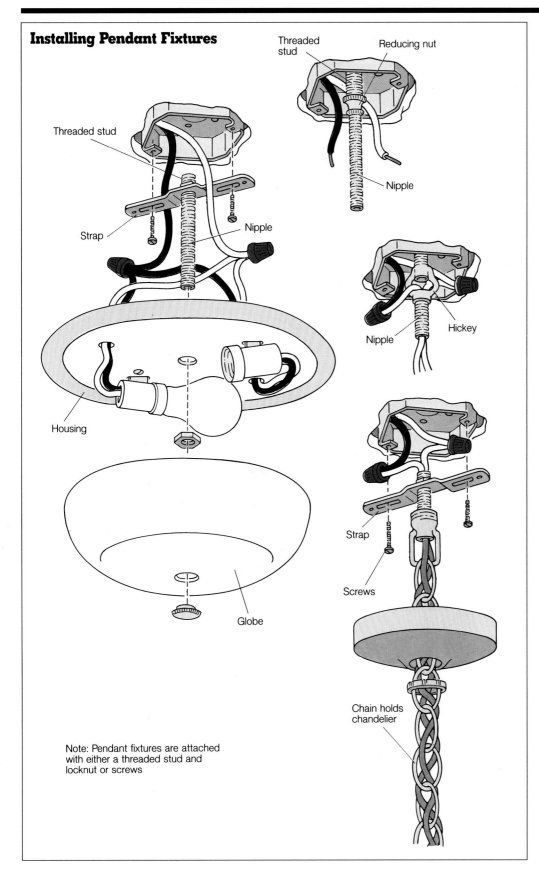

Threaded stud

Strap

Nipple

Housing

Globe

Note: Pendant fixtures are attached with either a threaded stud and locknut or screws

Threaded stud

Reducing nut

Nipple

Nipple

Hickey

Strap

Screws

Chain holds chandelier

Track Lights

In general, tracks are mounted to a canopy plate that fits over a standard electrical box. The box can be wired so the switch or switches operate all the track lights at once or so each of two separate switching circuits operates only certain lights. A plate can be at the end of the track, in the middle, or at the intersection of a T. There is an appropriate attachment for each location.

Mount the canopy bracket supplied with the track on the ceiling electrical box. It is grooved or slotted to accept the track and wire connector. If the holes in the bracket don't match up with the holes in the electrical box, use an adapter ring that offers several adjustable combinations of holes. Use wire nuts to connect the wires of the track connector to the house wires, and screw the canopy bracket to the electrical box or the adapter ring.

The track will be held to the ceiling or wall with mounting clips aligned with holes in the track. Use the edge of the track or a straightedge to mark on the ceiling the points where the mounting clips should be. Predrill the holes, then use screws or toggle bolts to attach the mounting clips. Snap the track into the wire connector and the mounting clips.

Snap the light fixtures into the track, and secure them with the locking levers or similar devices provided by the manufacturer. Turn on the power and adjust the lights to achieve the best effect. Slide them closer together or farther apart as necessary, and then relock the levers.

Translucent-Panel Fixtures

Use translucent panels individually or across the room to create a luminous ceiling.

Fluorescent fixtures with one or two translucent panels come in self-contained units that are either mounted on the surface or recessed into the ceiling. Install surface-mounted units directly beneath an electrical box, threading the house wires through a knockout in the top of the fixture. Attach the fixture to the ceiling using wood screws driven into ceiling joists or toggle bolts inserted through holes in the ceiling surface. Use a clamp to secure the house wires, and connect them to the fixture wires with wire nuts. Install the fluorescent tubes, test the light, and set the translucent panels in place.

A recessed fixture requires a large cutout in the ceiling. Joists or blocking should frame the opening above the surface material. Some fixtures are small enough to fit between the ceiling joists; others are too wide. For wide fixtures you must cut out a section of a joist. Support the cut ends with headers nailed between adjacent joists. Run Type NM cable or similar approved wiring to the general area of the opening. Thread it through a knockout in the fixture box as you lift the fixture housing into place. Use screws or nails to secure the housing to the framing. Make the wiring connections inside the housing. Install the fluorescent tubes, turn on the power, test the light, and set the translucent panels into place.

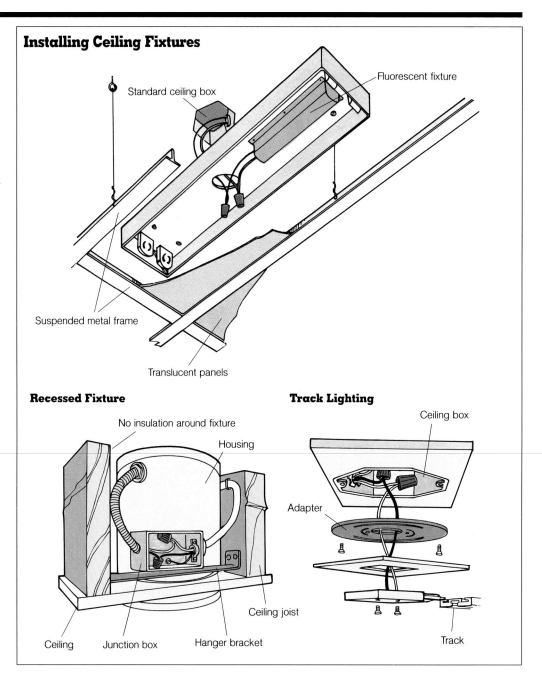

Installing Ceiling Fixtures

Standard ceiling box

Fluorescent fixture

Suspended metal frame

Translucent panels

Recessed Fixture

No insulation around fixture

Housing

Ceiling   Junction box   Hanger bracket   Ceiling joist

Track Lighting

Ceiling box

Adapter

Track

Recessed Fixtures

The metal housing for most recessed fixtures is installed before the wallboard goes on the ceiling. Once the wallboard is in place, install the trim ring and the light bulb. Be sure that the housing is installed according to the manufacturer's instructions, and follow any specified precautions concerning insulation and clearances.

Because the finish trim and the hardware are installed so much later than the housing, they can easily be misplaced or damaged in the interim. Mark the cartons well and store them in a safe place. There are various methods of installing trim rings. On each side most models have a spring device that hooks onto tabs inside the metal housing. Needle-nose pliers make installation easier.

INSTALLING SWITCHES AND RECEPTACLES

Now is the time to wire the switches and receptacles for lights, power, and any special systems you've chosen to include in the house. Install the plates over all the switches and receptacles after you've finished the walls with paint, wallcoverings, or tile, as desired.

Types of Switches And Receptacles

On a difficulty scale of 10 points, consider installing switches and receptacles a 5. You must pay attention to detail in regard to the type of material and tool to use and to which wire connects to which.

The three most common switches and receptacles are the side-wired, back-wired, and combination types. They all work equally well, the difference being primarily in the design. With the side-wired unit, the cable wires must be wrapped around the screw terminals on the side. The back-wired switches and receptacles are somewhat easier to use and a little more expensive. The

wires are stripped on the end and pushed into the appropriate slots. With the combination units, you can use either the terminal screws or the push-in terminals. In addition, front-wired and end-wired switches are available, but they are not commonly found.

Wires are connected to switches or receptacles in two basic ways—under a binding screw terminal or in a push-in terminal. Aluminum wire can be used under a screw terminal only if the device is marked "CO/ALR." Aluminum wire cannot be used at all in push-in terminals. Also, it must be spliced with special connectors, not twist or wire nuts, and it cannot be mixed with copper wire.

Binding Screw Terminals

Connecting wire to a binding screw terminal is a relatively simple procedure, but it must be done correctly. Loosen the screw so the stripped end of the wire will fit easily under it. Strip away only enough insulation so that the wire will wrap two thirds to three quarters of the way around the screw. Use needle-nose pliers to bend the wire in a small loop and hook it around the screw clockwise. The wire must be looped in a clockwise direction so that, as the screw is tightened, the loop

will be pulled tightly about it. Make sure that the tip of the wire is not bent up or down. Do not bring the wire so far around that it overlaps—this would cause a poor connection. Professionals strip off about 1½ inches of wire, wrap it around the screw, snug down the screw, wiggle the wire back and forth at the three-quarters point in the turn to break it there, and then snug down the screw again.

Finally, make sure the screw is thoroughly tightened. A loose connection can cause a gap in the wire, which causes a drop in voltage. Worse, as the electricity tries to jump the gap, it could result in sparks that might cause a fire.

Terminal screws on switches and receptacles are mounted in different ways, and you may find one type easier to work with than another. Despite this,

keep in mind that switches, receptacles, and their mounting straps are all standardized so they will fit into any kind of box; any type of faceplate will fit over them.

Push-In Terminals

To connect a push-in terminal, simply strip off about ¾ inch of wire—the amount shown on the strip gauge on the reverse side of the switch or receptacle—and push the wire into the opening. A spring holds the wire in place and makes contact. If you must remove the wire, release the spring by pushing a screwdriver tip into the slot just above the hole.

Remember, do not use push-in terminals with aluminum wire. They are generally acceptable for copper-clad aluminum wire, but check local codes before using these terminals.

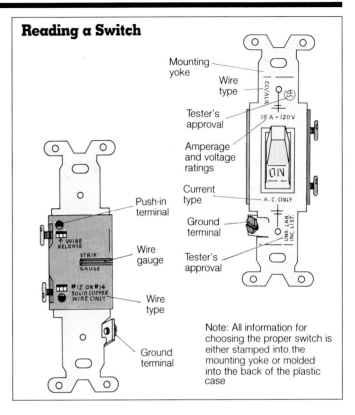

Reading a Switch

Mounting yoke
Wire type
Tester's approval
Amperage and voltage ratings
Current type
Ground terminal
Tester's approval

Push-in terminal
Wire gauge
Wire type
Ground terminal

Note: All information for choosing the proper switch is either stamped into the mounting yoke or molded into the back of the plastic case

One Screw, Two Wires

Sometimes you have two wires and only one screw terminal to put them on. A common example involves connecting the ground wire to the switch or receptacle. The incoming and outgoing ground wires cannot both be put under the same ground screw—you can't get a proper connection this way and it is against the code. The solution is to use a wire nut and a pigtail, a 6-inch-long piece of wire the same size as the other wires and stripped at both ends. Twist the 2 wires and the pigtail together with a wire nut. Make a loop in the other end of the pigtail, place it under the ground screw, and tighten the screw.

Choosing Switches

Four basic types of switches are used in houses. Although the house plans may not call for all four, they probably do call for two or three of them. You need to know how all four work in case the plans specify them or you decide to install them. These switches cannot be used interchangeably, so be sure you use the proper switch for the wiring that was done.

Single-Pole Switches

Single-pole, or two-way, switches are the most common switch in any house. They are used primarily to turn on a light or receptacle that is operated by only one switch. The handle, or toggle, is marked with "ON" and "OFF" labels. The switch has two brass-colored screws or two holes to insert copper wire. Traditionally, pushing the toggle up turns the circuit on.

Three-Way Switches

Contrary to what the name implies, the three-way switch is used to control a light or receptacle from two different points, not three. But you can always tell the three-way switch by its three terminal screws and its toggle, which has no "ON" or "OFF" labels. Two of the screws are brass-colored, and the third is black or copper-colored. Three-way switches are commonly used at the top and bottom of stairs or at different ends of a hallway or multiple-entrance room. They are always used in pairs. Connecting them also requires special three-wire cable.

Four-Way Switches

The four-way switch is used in conjunction with two three-way switches to control lights from three or more locations, such as in workshops or large living rooms. You can easily recognize the switch by its four terminal screws, all brass-colored. The toggle has no "ON" or "OFF" labels.

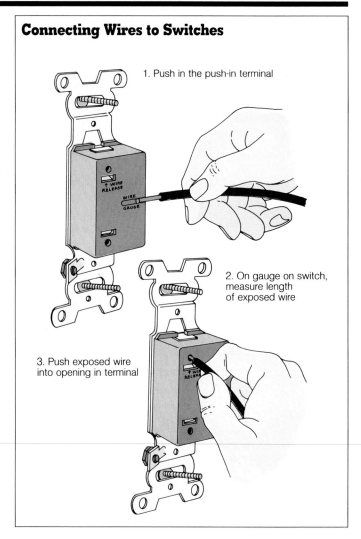

Connecting Wires to Switches

1. Push in the push-in terminal

2. On gauge on switch, measure length of exposed wire

3. Push exposed wire into opening in terminal

Double-Pole Switches

A double-pole switch looks similar to a four-way switch in that it has four brass-colored screws. The key difference is that the toggle has "ON" and "OFF" labels. It is called a double-pole switch because it handles two hot wires at the same time, rather than one hot wire, as in the single-pole switch. It is commonly used for 240-volt appliances or motors.

Specialty Switches

Following are some specialty switches that you may wish to use in lieu of standard toggle switches. Most of them are available as either single-pole or three-way switches.

Quiet Switches

Most standard switches now sold are quiet switches. They are less expensive than mercury switches but despite their name, are not quite as quiet.

Dimmer Switches

Also called rheostats, these switches are used to change the intensity of light. A dimmer reduces the flow of current to the light. Not only does such a switch allow you to create different lighting effects, but it will eventually pay for itself if the light is kept no brighter than necessary. Dimmers are available as two-way switches, three-way switches, and for either incandescent or fluorescent lights.

Mercury Switches

Mercury conducts electricity. When a mercury switch is turned on, mercury in the switch slides down to make contact with the hot wire. When turned off, the switch slides the mercury away from the contact point. It is absolutely silent and, because it has few moving parts, is commonly guaranteed for 50 years.

Mercury switches must be put into place right side up. The end that must be on top is conveniently marked "TOP." For smooth operation, make sure the switch is vertical.

Lighted-Handle Switches

If you have a room where you might be constantly groping for the switch in the dark, you need a lighted-handle switch. A miniature neon bulb keeps the toggle glowing in the dark. The bulb uses virtually no electricity.

Another type of lighted switch is used when the light fixture and the switch are not within sight of each other.

Many basement or garage lights are controlled by a switch inside the house, for example. The handle of the switch or a light on the switch glows when the outside light is on, giving you a gentle reminder to turn the outside light off if it's not in use.

Timer Switches

A time-delay switch goes off about 45 seconds after you flip it to "DELAY," giving you time to get inside.

A manual-timer switch has a spring-wound timer that can be set for a few minutes or up to 12 hours. If you have an appliance that you want to be turned off or on while you are out, you can set this timer to the desired time, plug it in, and it will do its thing.

A time-clock switch turns whatever is connected to it on and off at preset times. If you are away from home in the evenings, it can turn on lamps and a television to make it appear that you are home. Similar items turn on watering systems for landscaping.

A clock switch is both a conversation piece and a handy item for kitchen, bathroom, or dressing room. A digital clock built into the switch reminds you not to be late.

Locking Switches

With a locking switch you can keep small children from turning on power tools in your shop. Rather than a handle, it has a key you insert in the switch to turn it on or off. Wire this switch into a circuit that has outlets and, when you lock it off, the outlets don't have power. Locking mechanisms

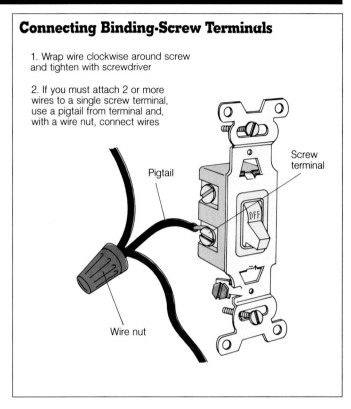

Connecting Binding-Screw Terminals

1. Wrap wire clockwise around screw and tighten with screwdriver

2. If you must attach 2 or more wires to a single screw terminal, use a pigtail from terminal and, with a wire nut, connect wires

Screw terminal

Pigtail

Wire nut

are handy for outlets powering dangerous tools you don't want children to accidentally turn on or televisions you'd rather they not watch when they should be doing homework.

Reading a Switch

The type of switch you install depends not only on what you want it to do but also on how it is rated. This important information is stamped on the metal mounting strap or yoke.

First, look for the marking indicating Underwriters Laboratory's testing and approval for safety standards. A switch without the "UL" marking may be cheaper but may also be of lesser quality.

Be sure to check the amperage rating. Switches should not be used for an amperage higher than that stamped on them.

Most lighting circuits use No. 14 wire, which has a maximum ampacity of 15 amperes. If that is the case in your house, then use a switch marked "15A-120V." Suppose you are putting in a new switch where No. 12 wire is used. No. 12 wire has an ampacity of 20 amps, so you should confirm that the local codes permit using a 15-amp switch on the circuit. Most do.

New switches are stamped with "AC ONLY," which means they can be used only with alternating current, the only type now available in residences.

Note: If you are using aluminum wiring in your house, make sure the yoke is stamped with the letters "CO/ALR." This means the switch can be used with aluminum wire. If it is marked "CU/AL," it can be used only with copper wire or copper-clad aluminum wire.

Wiring a Single-Pole Switch

Source Through Switch

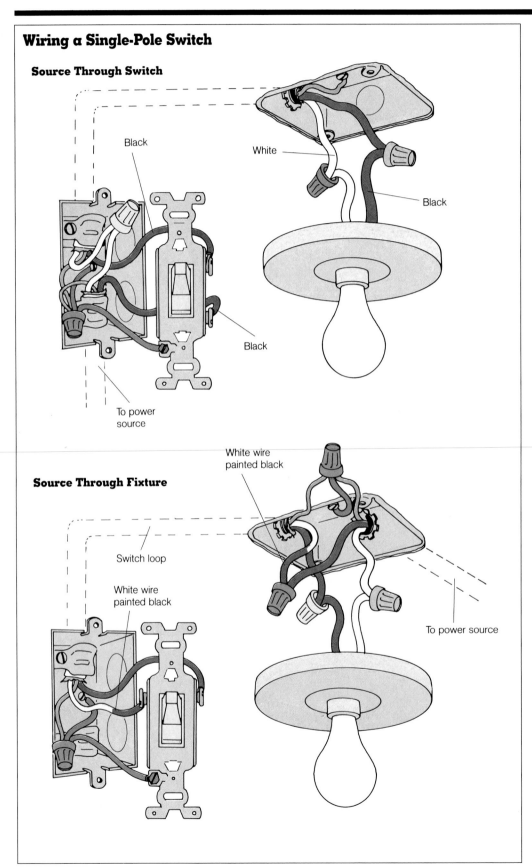

Black

White

Black

Black

To power
source

Source Through Fixture

White wire
painted black

Switch loop

White wire
painted black

To power source

Installing a Switch

When only one switch will control a ceiling light or an outlet with a lamp plugged into it, use a single-pole switch. How you wire the switch depends on whether the power goes to the light or outlet and a switch loop comes to the switch or whether the power comes to the switch and the switch loop goes to the light or outlet.

In the first case, in which the power goes to the light or outlet, only one cable comes into the switch box. The cable is called a switch loop. In this situation both wires in the cable are part of a loop in the hot wire to the light; the switch is just a break in that loop. It doesn't matter which wire of the cable, the white or black, goes to which screw on the switch. When you complete the connection, permanently cover the first inch or so of the white wire with black tape to show anyone who opens the switch in the future that both the wires are hot.

In the second case, two cables come into the box. One is the power from the service panel and the other is the switch loop that goes to the light or outlet. Again, the switch should "break" only the hot wire to the light, so the two neutral (white) wires are connected together with a wire nut and the two hot (black) wires are connected to the screws on the switch.

In both cases, connect the bare ground wire to the green hexagonal screw on the switch. If there is only 1 cable, just attach the ground wire directly to the screw. If there are 2 cables, use a pigtail. Cut a single piece of wire, preferably green, about 4 inches long. Secure one end to the ground (green) screw on the switch; connect the 2 bare wires from the cables and the other end of the pigtail all together with a wire nut. You can buy green pigtails and pigtails in other colors, which help you keep the various wires organized.

When you install any new switch, make sure that it is vertical. The box may be crooked, but the mounting-screw slots are wide enough so you can adjust the switch if necessary. Note that each end of the yoke has a pair of "ears." If the box is recessed, these ears keep the switch flush with the wall. If the box is already flush with the wall and the ears are in the way, snap them off with a pair of pliers.

Note: Connect only the hot wire to the switch, never the neutral wire. The light will work perfectly well with the neutral wires connected to the switch, but there will be power at the fixture even when the toggle is off. This is very dangerous.

Three-Way Switches

The *three* in the name of this switch refers to the number of terminals on the switch, not to how it works.

The toggle on a three-way switch does not have "ON" and "OFF" labels. Either the up or down position can turn the light on or off, depending on the position of the other switch.

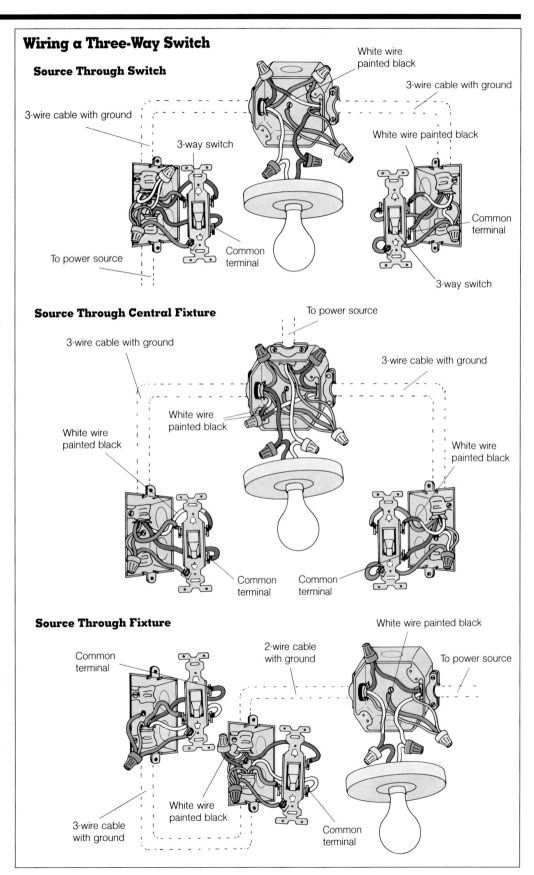

Wiring a Three-Way Switch

Source Through Switch

White wire painted black

3-wire cable with ground

3-wire cable with ground

3-way switch

White wire painted black

Common terminal

To power source

Common terminal

3-way switch

Source Through Central Fixture

To power source

3-wire cable with ground

3-wire cable with ground

White wire painted black

White wire painted black

White wire painted black

Common terminal

Common terminal

Source Through Fixture

White wire painted black

Common terminal

2-wire cable with ground

To power source

3-wire cable with ground

White wire painted black

Common terminal

One of the terminals on a three-way switch is a common, or pivot, terminal. You must identify the common terminal and the common wire to connect the switch correctly. On most switches the common terminal is a darker color than the other two. Sometimes it is copper and the others are brass. On some switches the word "common" is stamped in the switch, and the common terminal is often alone or on the opposite side of the switch from the others. The configuration varies with the manufacturer, but it is usually indicated on the packaging if it is not obvious by looking at the switch itself.

Several combinations of lights and switches are possible in three-way switch wiring. As with a single-pole switch, the connections vary depending on where the power source enters the circuit and where the light fixtures are in relation to the switches. This section will describe how to wire a three-way switch in general and show you illustrations of all the various combinations of switch-light relationships.

Making three-way connections involves five basic steps.

1. Connect the white neutral wire from the power source to the silver-colored terminal on the light fixture. Sometimes the power source is at the fixture and you connect it directly. Other times the power goes into a switch box. Then you connect the white wires directly to each other in a line from switch box to switch box until the neutral wire from the power source connects to the fixture without connecting to any switches.

Wiring Switches and Receptacles

Source Through Switch

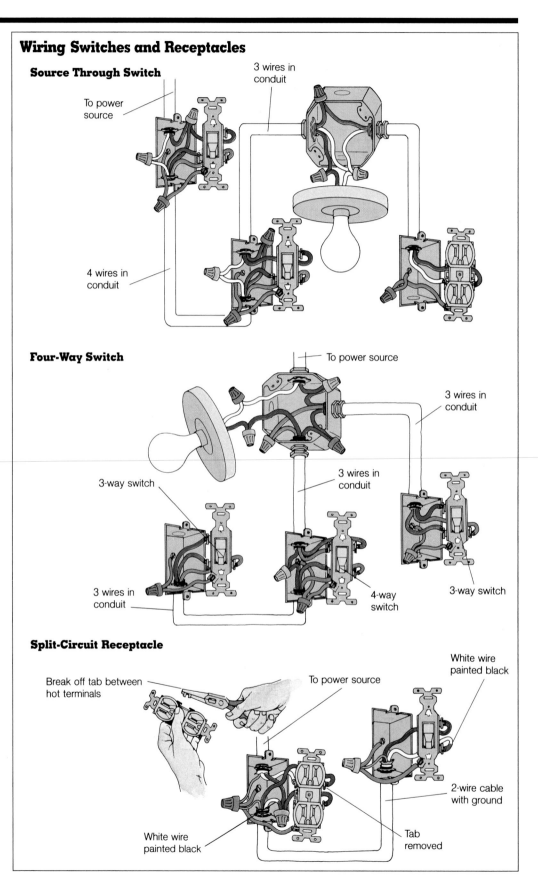

To power source

3 wires in conduit

4 wires in conduit

Four-Way Switch

To power source

3 wires in conduit

3-way switch

3 wires in conduit

3 wires in conduit

4-way switch

3-way switch

Split-Circuit Receptacle

Break off tab between hot terminals

To power source

White wire painted black

2-wire cable with ground

White wire painted black

Tab removed

2. Connect the black wire, the hot wire, from the power source to the common terminal of switch 1 (the first switch you bring power to).

3. Connect a black wire from the brass terminal on the light fixture to the common terminal of switch 2 (the second switch you bring power to).

4. Run three-wire cable, with a ground, between the 2 switches. To complete the wiring, connect the 2 wires that are not the ground. These 2 wires are the traveler, or switching, wires. Connect white and red wires that go between the 2 switches to the lighter-colored terminals on the 2 switches. Color the ends of the white wire black. These 2 wires must not connect to anything else.

In some cases, the white wire has already been used to connect the neutral wire from the power source to the fixture. Then you have to use the remaining black wire to make this connection.

5. Connect the ground wires at each box.

Four-Way Switches

You can use one or more four-way switches between two three-way switches to provide additional points from which lights can be turned on and off. By adding four-way switches between the two three-way switches, you can have as many control locations as you want. These locations are called four-way switches because they have four terminals.

1. A four-way switch goes between 2 three-way switches. Install the three-way switches as the preceding section directed. In between these connect the four-way box so that

the switch "breaks" the 2 traveler wires but not the hot wire.

2. At the box for the four-way switch, switch 2, connect the 2 black wires to each other with a wire nut. The resulting black wire does not connect to switch 2. Connect the traveler wires, red and white, from both cables to the light-colored terminals on the switch. Connect the wires from each cable to screw terminals directly opposite each other.

3. At the box for switch 3, connect the black wire to the common terminal screw. Connect the red and white wires to the 2 light-colored terminals.

4. Connect the ground wires at each box.

Dimmer Switches

Also called rheostats, dimmer switches come with a dial to turn the lights up or down, or they appear to be a standard wall switch (the amount of light is controlled by the relative movement of the switch). Some models have a sliding toggle to preset the light level and a separate on-off button. Dimmers can handle only a certain amount of wattage—the amount is stamped on the switch. Dimmers with knobs and some slide-type toggles usually can handle up to 600 watts; those with toggle switches usually have a 300-watt capacity. Do not exceed the wattage limit.

Dimmers are normally used to control overhead incandescent lights. Special dimmers are also available for fluorescent fixtures. In addition, simple

dimmers are attached in the middle of a lamp cord to control floor or table lamps. Both types of dimmers are available in most hardware or electrical-supply stores. Wall-mounted dimmers are available in single-pole and three-way switches. When used in a three-way switch, however, only one of the two switches dims the light. Both continue to turn the lights on or off.

A single-pole dimmer is hooked up just like a standard single-pole switch. Some dimmers come with switch leads (wires) already attached to the mechanism. These are joined to the existing wires (black to black, white to white) with wire nuts.

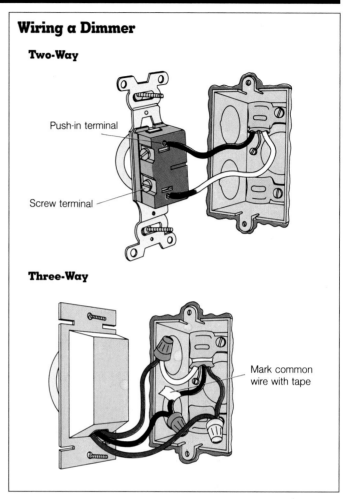

Wiring a Dimmer

Two-Way

Push-in terminal

Screw terminal

Three-Way

Mark common wire with tape

Timers

Switches that turn lights on and off at preset times must be installed in middle-of-the-run wiring. Determine which black wire is the incoming hot wire. To the box attach the special mounting plate that comes with the timer switch.

Using wire nuts, join the incoming hot black wire to the black wire on the timer switch. Join the red wire on the switch to the outgoing black wire. Finally, join the 2 white wires in the box to the white jumper wire from the switch. Put the switch into place, turn the power on, and test the switch according to the manufacturer's instructions.

Reading a Receptacle

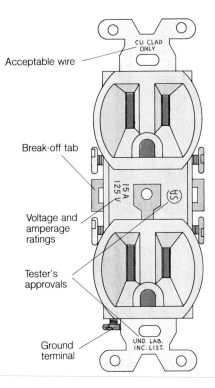

Acceptable wire

CU CLAD ONLY

Break-off tab

Voltage and amperage ratings

15 A
125 V

Tester's approvals

Ground terminal

UND. LAB.
INC. LIST.

Side Wired

Back Wired

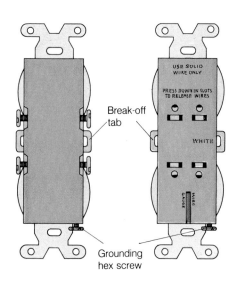

USE SOLID WIRE ONLY

PRESS DOWN IN SLOTS TO RELEASE WIRES

WHITE

Break-off tab

WIRE GAUGE

Grounding hex screw

Types of Receptacles

Three-hole grounding-type outlets are now required in all new house construction and are advised for any rewiring work in old houses. You must attach a ground wire to the outlet and to the box if it is metal. If the box is plastic, it will not conduct electricity and need not be grounded.

All receptacles in bathrooms, garages, and outside must be protected by a ground fault circuit interrupter (GFCI). Many codes require GFCI receptacles in kitchens and other areas as well. To provide GFCI protection, use a GFCI circuit breaker in the panel or a GFCI receptacle. Regular outlets can be GFCI-protected if they are wired through the GFCI receptacle.

There are two basic types of receptacles: side wired and back wired. The side-wired receptacle has four terminal screws, two brass-colored and two silver-colored. The hot wires, black or red, go on the brass-colored screws. The white neutral wires go on the silver-colored screws. The green screw at the bottom is for the ground wire.

The back-wired or push-in receptacle has holes in which to insert the wires. A strip gauge on the back of the outlet shows you how much insulation to strip off the end of the wire. The word *white* is stamped on one side of the receptacle, indicating that the white neutral wires go in there. The hot red or black wires go in the other side. To release the wires, push a screwdriver into the slot above or below the holes. Some receptacles have both push-in holes and terminal screws.

Most receptacles are duplex receptacles—that is, they have two units. Both units are hot at the same time because they are joined by a brass tab on one side that passes the current from one side to the other. On the other side is a chrome tab that keeps current flowing in the white neutral wire. If the brass tab is broken off by twisting it with a pair of pliers, only that outlet that is actually wired will be hot. The current will not pass to the other. This is done for split-receptacle wiring with three-wire cable, a complex process not covered in this book. The next section describes a simple way to install a three-wire appliance circuit.

Reading Receptacles

A receptacle should be stamped with "UL," which indicates that the outlet has met the rigid safety standards of Underwriters' Laboratory. The receptacle should also have a stamp indicating the maximum amperes it can handle and the number of volts. Typically, it reads "15A-125V." Stamped on the outlet or the mounting yoke is a series of letters indicating what type of wire may be used with this receptacle. If the stamp reads "CU" or "CU CLAD," use only copper or copper-clad aluminum wire. If your house has aluminum wiring, you must use a receptacle stamped "CO/ALR."

Types of Plugs and Receptacle Slots

Receptacles are made with several different slot combinations. Each type is designed so plugs for one cannot fit into another. This prevents an appliance designed for one kind of electricity load from being plugged into another and doing damage to the circuits or the appliance.

The Ungrounded Two-Prong Type

This 120-volt plug is commonly used on lamps, toasters, irons, and other small appliances with insulated frames although the receptacle is no longer allowed in most areas. In many instances one prong is slightly larger than the other. The small prong is hot and the large one is neutral. The plug can be inserted into an outlet only one way. If the receptacle is wired properly, the incoming hot black wire is connected to the side of the outlet with the short, narrower slot. The white neutral wire is connected to the long, wide slot.

The Grounded Three-Prong Type

A three-prong 120-volt plug indicates that the cord contains a ground wire. When this plug is in a properly wired three-slot outlet, any short circuit that might occur in the tool or appliance will be directed through the ground wire in the cord to the ground wire in the receptacle, rather than through you. Three-prong plugs are usually for 15 amperes. The 20-ampere grounded plug has one prong angled differently from the others and will fit a 20-ampere three-slot outlet only, as shown in the illustration.

The Grounded Clothes-Dryer Type

This type of 120/240-volt, 30-ampere plug and receptacle is designed specifically for clothes dryers. Note that the L-shaped ground prong will fit only into a similarly shaped slot in the outlet. This outlet is wired with both 120 and 240 volts. The 240 volts are for the heating coils of the dryer, and the 120 volts are for the inside light and the timing mechanism.

The Grounded Range Type

A 120/240-volt, 50-ampere plug and outlet are used primarily for electric ranges. The prongs are all angled a specific way and will fit in a matching outlet only. The 120 volts are used to power the clock, lights, and burners when on low settings. The 240 volts power the oven and the burners when on high settings.

The Grounded Conditioner Type

This 240-volt, 30-ampere plug, again with a set of prongs that will fit a matching outlet only, is commonly used for air conditioners and water heaters, if these are not hard wired.

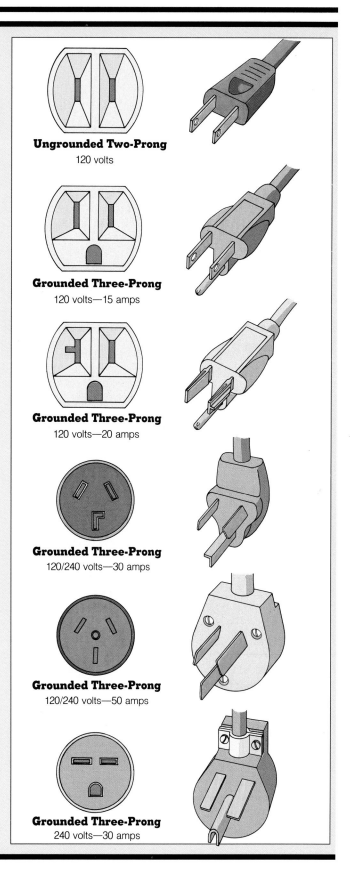

Ungrounded Two-Prong
120 volts

Grounded Three-Prong
120 volts—15 amps

Grounded Three-Prong
120 volts—20 amps

Grounded Three-Prong
120/240 volts—30 amps

Grounded Three-Prong
120/240 volts—50 amps

Grounded Three-Prong
240 volts—30 amps

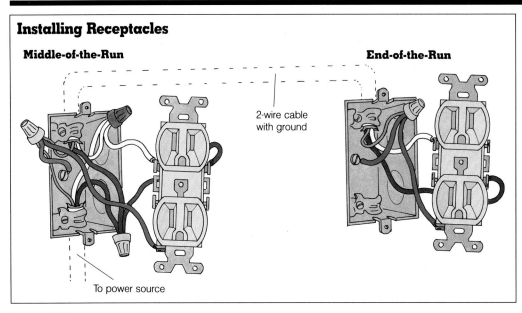

Installing Receptacles

Middle-of-the-Run

End-of-the-Run

2-wire cable
with ground

To power source

Installing Receptacles

All outlets currently sold are designed to handle three-prong plugs. The U-shaped hole is for the ground connection. All new installations must have three-prong receptacles.

Middle-of-the-Run Receptacles

A middle-of-the-run receptacle has four wires in the box: a hot black and a white neutral wire coming in from the source and the same going out to the next receptacle. In addition, there are incoming and outgoing ground wires.

To wire this receptacle, attach a black pigtail to the two black wires, a white pigtail to the two white wires, and a green pigtail to the two ground wires; if the box is metal, attach another pigtail to the box. Then attach the pigtails to their respective screw terminals or slots in the receptacle: black pigtail to brass screw, white pigtail to silver screw, green pigtail to green screw.

Armored-Cable Wiring

If the wiring is done with armored cable, the device box must be metal and have special clamps for armored cable. Be sure an anti-short bushing is inserted into the end of the armored cable before it is clamped into the box.

Receptacles and switches are wired to armored cable the same as nonmetallic cable, except that a grounding pigtail must always be attached to the metal box.

End-of-the-Run Receptacles

If a receptacle is the last receptacle on the circuit, only 2 wires come into the box. Attach the hot black wire to one brass-colored screw and the white neutral wire to one silver-colored screw. Attach the ground wire from the cable to both the green terminal screw on the receptacle and, with pigtails and a wire nut, to a metal box.

If you are using armored cable, there is no bare ground

wire. In this case, ground the receptacle by running a pigtail from the green ground screw on the receptacle to a machine screw in the back of the box.

Combination Receptacles

Suppose you want a receptacle where there is also a switch. To install this combination, you must use middle-of-the-run wiring because an outlet must always be hooked to a white neutral wire to complete the circuit. The appropriate receptacle has one silver-colored, one copper-colored, and two brass-colored screws. To start, use a wire nut to attach a white pigtail to both neutral wires and to the silver-colored screw.

To have the outlet and the light controlled by the switch, attach the black hot wire to the copper screw and the black switch wire to either brass-colored screw.

If you want the outlet hot all the time, attach the black hot wire to either brass-colored screw and the black switch wire to the copper-colored screw.

Connect a green pigtail ground wire to the back of the metal switch box and another to the green hexagonal screw on the switch receptacle. Tie the 2 pigtails into the bare ground wires with a wire nut.

A light-receptacle combination is not a common thing in a new house, but you might use one if you wanted a light over the stove or sink or some other work area to be controlled by a switch that can also have a receptacle. This kind of light is sold with the fixture wires already installed, and the receptacle can be installed in end-of-the-run wiring. In addition to following the installation instructions in the next two paragraphs, be sure to install a GFCI receptacle if required.

At an end-of-the-run connection, the outlet will be hot only when the light is on. The light and the receptacle need both hot and neutral wires. Using a wire nut, attach the 2 black wires from the fixture to the incoming hot black wire. Attach the 2 white neutral wires from the fixture to the incoming white neutral wire with a wire nut. Connect a green ground jumper wire to the back of the metal switch box and then, with a wire nut, link that to the incoming bare ground wire and the green ground wire from the fixture.

At a middle-of-the-run connection, the outlet will be hot all the time. Using a wire nut, connect the black wire from the receptacle part of the fixture to the 2 black wires. Connect the white wire marked black (the hot wire) to the black wire from the light. Attach the

2 neutral wires from the fixture to the incoming white wire. Connect a green ground pigtail to the back of the switch box and join it with a wire nut to the incoming bare ground wire and the green fixture wire.

Note: If you are installing a combination light and receptacle in a location that requires GFCI protection, install a GFCI breaker in the panel for the circuit or a GFCI combination receptacle.

Three-Wire Appliance Circuits

Small-appliance circuits in the kitchen are usually wired with two separate 120-volt lines. You can wire two separate circuits, each with its own cable, but it's easier to run one three-wire cable and operate both circuits from the one cable. Every other outlet is then on a circuit separate from the one next to it. This allows two powerful small appliances to be used side by side without overloading a single circuit.

A three-wire circuit contains a black hot wire, a red hot wire, a white neutral wire, and a bare ground wire. The red and black wires are connected to separate circuit breakers at the breaker panel. Their handles must be connected, however.

Connect the receptacles just as you would a standard two-wire circuit except for one small difference: Wire alternating outlets with the black wire and red wire. In other words, connect the first with black and white wire, the second with red and white wire, the third with black and white wire, the fourth with red and white, and so on.

Make sure the white neutral wire connects to all receptacles and the black and the red never connect to the same one. One neutral wire can serve a maximum of two circuits.

Installing Doorbells

All the wiring and the transformer for your chimes or bell should be in place before you install the wallboard. There should be one set of wires protruding from the siding at the position of each push button and a set of wires protruding from the wall at the location of the chimes.

Check the manufacturer's instructions to see how to connect the wires to the buttons and the chimes (see page 182).

Installing Specialty Systems

Now is the time to install the boxes and mount the fixtures for all prewired systems—smoke alarms, security systems, intercoms, stereo speakers, and vacuum cleaners (see page 178). Wait to install the faceplates until after you've completed the wall finish.

Since systems vary greatly according to the manufacturers, this book can't give you specific installation instructions. Refer to the instructions supplied with each system and follow them exactly.

☐ Ceiling wallboard installed
☐ Wall wallboard installed
☐ Garage door installed
☐ Exterior painted
☐ Finish floorings, except carpet, installed
☐ Interior doors installed
☐ Interior trim installed
☐ Switches installed
☐ Receptacles installed
☐ Light fixtures installed

Wiring a Three-Wire Appliance Receptacle

Electric box

240-volt receptacle

Metal conduit

Neutral conductor

PREPARING FOR OCCUPANCY

To obtain an occupancy permit, your house must undergo a final building inspection. The exact requirements vary from location to location, but typically the house must have a working kitchen and at least one operating bathroom to pass. This chapter provides the information you need to install cabinets, countertops, plumbing fixtures, and bathroom accessories. Because of the variety of appliances and brands, however, this chapter does not describe the installation methods for the appliances within the kitchen. Likewise, it does not discuss how to install finish floor materials and final wall and ceiling finishes. Check the Reading List on page 345 for books to guide you through appliance installation and room finishing.

Plenty of auto space was high on this homeowner's wish list. However, simple accoutrements—such as the octagonal vents under the repetitive gables, the wide trim, and soon the doors—will dress up the multiple garages. The siding on this Ranch-style house, most of which has been primed but not yet painted, is made of plywood panels applied vertically.

INSTALLING CABINETS AND SHELVES

Cabinets are the showpieces of most kitchens and bathrooms. They can be custom-built or purchased in modular units to be installed. Custom cabinets are expensive. If you have extraordinary finish carpentry skills, you can build your own. If you contract someone to build custom cabinets, you probably want the carpenter to install them.

- ☐ Tool belt
- ☐ Steel tape measure
- ☐ 24-inch level
- ☐ 48-inch level
- ☐ Combination square
- ☐ Framing square
- ☐ Chalk line
- ☐ Curved-claw hammer
- ☐ Flat pry bar
- ☐ Nail sets
- ☐ Handsaw
- ☐ Compass saw
- ☐ Coping saw
- ☐ Slot screwdrivers
- ☐ Utility knife
- ☐ ¾- and 1-inch chisels
- ☐ Power drill and bits
- ☐ Jack plane or power plane
- ☐ 6-, 8-, and 10-inch crescent wrenches
- ☐ Adjustable or C-clamps
- ☐ 6- or 8-foot stepladder

Planning an Installation

Installing cabinets is a meticulous and demanding task. It's easy to underestimate the time required to do it right. For an average-sized kitchen, figure about a week of work for cabinet installation. For each bathroom, allow one or two days. On a difficulty scale of 10 points, consider installing prefabricated cabinets and shelves a 7. You'll need help for holding cabinets in place and finish carpentry tools.

Cabinets are installed relatively late in the construction process. All the walls, ceilings, and soffits (if any) should be finished. The painting should be completed, wallcoverings may be up, and rough wiring for under-the-counter lighting should be installed. If the finish floor is in place, protect it with plywood or cardboard while the cabinets are being installed.

In a successful cabinet installation, the units are level, plumb, and square. All joints are tight and flush. All the doors and drawers are aligned.

Choosing Kitchen Cabinets

Modular cabinets are available in many styles, configurations, and finishes. Besides standard cabinets, you can get desks, tabletops, microwave-oven containers, and pantry units all fabricated to match.

When selecting cabinets you'll need to make decisions about whether you want cabinets with or without face frames, the materials and colors you prefer, and the sizes, types, and storage options for your needs.

Face-frame cabinets have frames around the doors and drawers. They can be fitted with flush doors and drawers, but they are usually fitted with doors and drawers that have a lip that overlaps the face frame and covers the crack between the door or drawer front and the frame.

Frameless cabinets, also known as Euro-style, have no face frames, only the thickness of the top, side, and bottom material between the edges of the doors and drawers and the sides and bottoms of the cabinets. The doors and drawers either overlay the top, sides, bottom, and front of the cabinet (so there is just a narrow crack around the doors and drawer fronts) or are inset between the top, sides, bottom, and front (so there is no lip on the doors or drawers to overlap the cabinet).

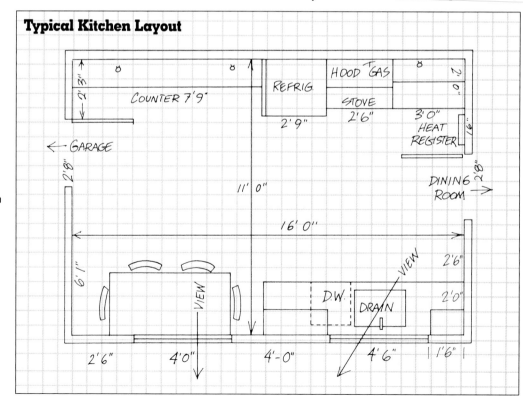

Typical Kitchen Layout

Kitchen Cabinet Sizes

This table shows typical sizes of various kitchen fixtures and appliances and the sizes of cabinets or openings needed to install them.

Appliance		Size of Cabinet (or Opening)
Sinks	24″ × 21″ single	30″
	30″ × 21″ single	33″
	32″ × 21″ double	36″
	42″ × 21″ triple	45″
Cooktops	30″	33″
	36″	36″–39″
	42″–45″	45″–48″
Range	Drop in or slide in	30″
Oven	Built-in	27″–30″
Range hoods	30″, 36″, 42″, 48″	Same size as hood
Dishwasher	24″	Add ½″
Compactors	12″, 15″, 18″	Add ½″
Refrigerator	Varies	33″–36″

Cabinet Types

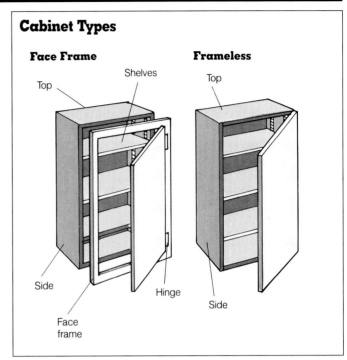

Face-frame cabinets provide a traditional look and a substantial feel, and they are easier to install than frameless cabinets. Frameless cabinets provide more efficient storage because the width of the door opening is the width of the inside of the cabinet. With face-frame cabinets, the inside of the cabinet is an inch or so wider than the door opening.

Frameless cabinets can cause some problems in tight corners where doors cannot open fully and drawers cannot clear obstructions on the sides. Filler pieces are available to solve these problems.

Preparation

Besides the tools listed on page 312, you will need a countersink bit for the drill, a 6-foot straightedge or a long level, shims, masking tape, and a bar of soap.

An extra electric drill with a Phillips-screwdriver bit is handy to have. You will also need a supply of 1½-, 2½-, and 3-inch quick-drive wood screws, 3-, 4-, and 6-penny finishing nails, 1-inch brads, and whatever special connecting screws are provided with frameless cabinets.

Inspect all the cabinets for defects and verify the sizes. Make sure that the doors fit, that none of the boxes is warped, and that all the drawers slide perfectly. Remove all the doors, mark on each door which cabinet it belongs with, and put the cabinets back into the cartons. Store them until you need them.

Start the layout for the cabinets by locating the highest point of the floor in the area where the base cabinets will be installed. Use a long level or a straightedge with a level on it. If the highest point is not against the wall, use a level and a pencil to transfer the height

of that point to the wall. Having marked the wall at the appropriate height, measure up from the mark and make a second mark at the height of the base cabinets (usually 34½ inches). Add an allowance for the thickness of the finish floor if it is not yet down and make a third mark. Using the straightedge and a level, draw a line on the wall at this third mark. This line represents the tops of all the base cabinets. (The line will be covered by the counter or the back splash. Make heavy marks on the wall only where they will be covered by cabinets; elsewhere use a faint pencil.)

Now draw another level line for the tops of the wall cabinets. Most wall cabinets are 30 inches tall and 18 inches above the countertop. For most installations, then, this line will be exactly 84 inches (36 + 18 + 30) above the highest point of the floor.

If the wall cabinets extend up to a soffit or up to the ceiling, check it for level. Find the lowest point of the ceiling or soffit in the area over the cabinets and draw a level line on the wall at that height for the cabinet tops. You can now see how much of a gap there will be between the ceiling or soffit and the cabinets. Plan to cover this gap with a strip of molding.

If the installation includes a full-height cabinet, measure it now to make sure that it will fit beneath the ceiling or soffit. You may have to trim the top or the base, according to the manufacturer's instructions.

Using the lines on the wall for horizontal guides and a level for plumb, lay out the cabinet dimensions on the wall. Make sure that they line up properly with each other and with the various corners, windows, sinks, appliances, and so forth. Make any adjustments necessary.

Next, mark the location of each stud just above the line for the base cabinets, in the area where the upper cabinets will be hung. To find a stud, tap on the wall lightly and listen for a solid sound. Probe the area with a hammer and nail until you locate both edges of the stud. Mark the exact center on the wall. Hold a level vertically against the mark and draw a line for the stud. Repeat for each stud behind the upper cabinets. If there is blocking between the studs, mark another level line at the center of the blocking where the cabinets will be hung.

It is usually easier to install the wall cabinets before the base cabinets. However, if the back splash will be full-height laminate that extends up to the wall cabinets, the base cabinets and the countertop must be installed first. It is also better to install the base cabinets first if there is a full-height cabinet in the middle of a run.

Installing Wall Cabinets

Start a run of wall cabinets with a full-height cabinet or a corner cabinet if you have one. Otherwise start at whichever end will not require a filler piece. The first cabinet is the most critical—it must be perfectly level, plumb, and square, or the entire run will be out of alignment.

Measure where the studs line up behind the first cabinet and transfer these measurements to the inside of the cabinet at the top and bottom hanger rails. Countersink and drill holes through the back of the cabinet at these marks;

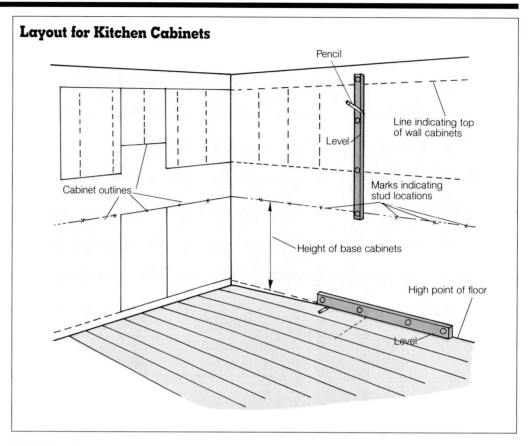

Layout for Kitchen Cabinets

Pencil

Line indicating top of wall cabinets

Level

Cabinet outlines

Marks indicating stud locations

Height of base cabinets

High point of floor

Level

make the holes just large enough for the 3-inch screws.

If the cabinets are frameless, they may require a metal support rail, provided by the manufacturer. Install this rail next. It must be attached to the wall behind the cabinets, which will be hung from it. Cut it to length and screw it securely to each stud at the height recommended by the manufacturer.

There are several methods for holding the cabinets in place while you attach them to the wall. One is to build a T brace slightly longer than the distance between the floor and the bottom of the cabinet. Another method, used when the base cabinets are installed first, is to build a simple rectangular frame out of 2 by 4s; this frame should be just high enough to support the wall cabinets when

it sits on a makeshift countertop. A third method can be used if the walls have not yet been finished. Simply screw a 1-by cleat to the wall to support the bottom of the cabinets. Specialty jacks are useful here, if you know a professional who might lend you one.

To begin, lift the first cabinet into place and slide the brace up under it. You will need a helper to stabilize the cabinet while you do this. Screw it to the studs with 3-inch screws, tightening only one of the top screws and leaving the others slightly loose. Place a shim behind the cabinet, next to a screw, at any point where the wall bows inward. Use a level to check that the cabinet is plumb and horizontal in all directions.

Now transfer the stud dimensions to the inside of the second cabinet and countersink and drill the screw holes. Drill 2 more screw holes through the vertical stile on the side that will be attached to the first cabinet. Drill where the hinges will cover up the screw heads.

For frameless cabinets the side holes are already partially drilled, about 3 inches back and 2 or 3 inches up from the bottom or down from the top. Simply complete the drilling. Special fasteners go into these holes; they screw into each other, leaving a smooth head on each side that is covered with a plastic cap.

Lift the second cabinet into place and support it, but do not screw it into the back wall. Instead, clamp the 2 cabinets together so that the joint between them is tight and flush.

Installing Wall Cabinets

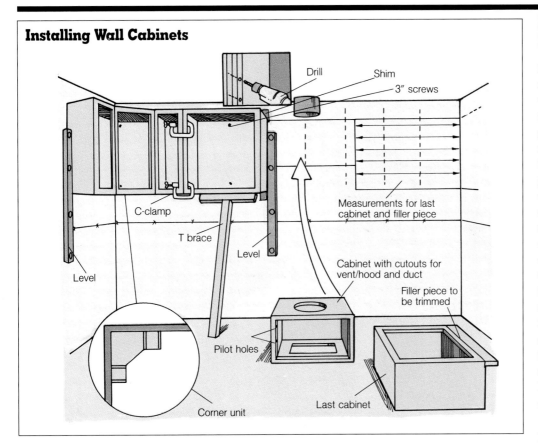

Drill   Shim
3" screws

Measurements for last
cabinet and filler piece

C-clamp

T brace

Level

Level

Cabinet with cutouts for
vent/hood and duct

Filler piece to
be trimmed

Pilot holes

Corner unit

Last cabinet

Use wood scraps to protect the cabinet finish from the clamps. Choose a drill bit slightly smaller than the shank of a 1½-inch screw and center it in the first side hole of the second cabinet. Drill about two thirds of the way into the adjoining stile of the first cabinet. Do the same for the second side hole. Now lubricate two 1½-inch screws with bar soap and drive them firmly into the holes that you have just drilled. If the cabinets are tall or if the face frames do not align perfectly, predrill more holes and add more screws. Then screw the cabinet to the back wall, the same way as you did the first cabinet.

Repeat this process for all the wall cabinets in the same run. If a vent/hood will be mounted to a wall cabinet, cut holes in the cabinet for the duct before you install it.

If the final cabinet will end next to a sidewall, there may be a gap that needs a filler piece. These come in 3-inch and 6-inch widths and must be cut to fit snugly. Before you install that cabinet, attach the filler piece to the stile in the same way as you would attach 2 cabinets together. Then take a series of measurements between the wall and the last cabinet installed. Transfer these measurements to the face of the final cabinet, marking them on the filler piece. Now connect the marks with a line. Cut along the line with a fine-toothed keyhole saw, angling the back of the cut toward the

cabinet. The cut will follow any deviations in the wall so that the filler piece will fit perfectly. Filler pieces for corners are installed in the same way but need not be scribed and cut. Some manufacturers provide cabinets with wide stiles, called ears, already attached. Ears function as filler pieces and are trimmed in the same way.

When the full run of wall cabinets is in place, check for level, plumb, and squareness (measure diagonals). Use shims to make any necessary adjustments, loosening the back screws to slip them into place. After all the screws are tightened, make a final check. Be especially careful with frameless cabinets. The slightest warp will make the doors hang crooked.

Frame and frameless base cabinets are installed in the same way, except that with the frameless style there is no margin for error. Start with a corner cabinet, unless a cabinet in the middle of a run must be perfectly aligned with some other feature, such as a window or the sink plumbing. Set the cabinet in place and shim under the base until the top is even with the layout line. Countersink and drill through the top rail at each stud and attach the rail to the stud with 3-inch screws. If the wall is not straight, place shims behind the cabinet. Use a level to check the top, sides, and front. Hold it against the frame and not against a door or drawer.

Set the second cabinet in place and attach it to the first cabinet, using the same method used for the wall cabinets. Screw it to the back wall.

Complete the run of base cabinets. Some cabinets, such as lazy-susan corner units and sink fronts, have no box to attach to the wall. They are held in place only at the face frames. (With frameless styles, the sink fronts have sides that extend back just far enough to attach them to the adjacent cabinets.) Because these cabinets have no backs, you will have to provide support for the countertop along the back. Screw cleats of 1-by lumber to the wall just below the layout line.

You will also need to fabricate a floor for some sink fronts. Cut it out of a piece of ¹/₂- to ³/₄-inch plywood and support it on cleats screwed to the wall and the adjacent cabinets. Seal it or paint it before you install it.

If there will be an appliance—a dishwasher, trash compactor, or slide-in range—in the middle of a run, you must allow for it when you install the base cabinets. Check the appliance specifications to determine the exact width of the space. To keep the cabinets on both sides of the gap aligned, bridge the space with a long straightedge at the front and back. Install filler pieces at the end of the run and at the corners, the same way as you did for the wall cabinets.

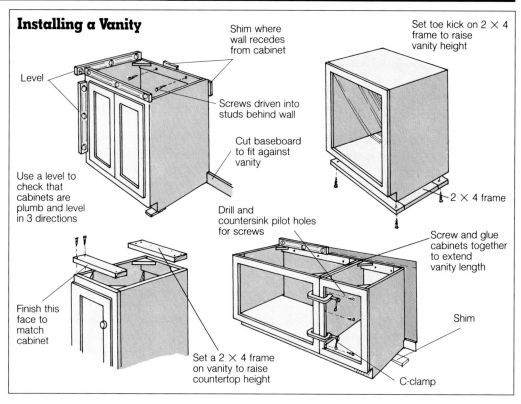

Installing a Vanity

Shim where wall recedes from cabinet

Set toe kick on 2 × 4 frame to raise vanity height

Level

Screws driven into studs behind wall

Cut baseboard to fit against vanity

Use a level to check that cabinets are plumb and level in 3 directions

Drill and countersink pilot holes for screws

2 × 4 frame

Screw and glue cabinets together to extend vanity length

Finish this face to match cabinet

Shim

Set a 2 × 4 frame on vanity to raise countertop height

C-clamp

Finishing Touches

Finish panels, doors, trim, and handles are the most noticeable features of your cabinet installation. Take care to attach them correctly. Try to set aside one day just to do this part of the job; don't try to do it at the end of a long day's work.

In some cabinet lines, finish panels must be installed on all the exposed faces of every cabinet. These panels come either precut or as a full sheet of plywood paneling from which you cut out each piece to fit. If the panels have grain patterns, match each one carefully with the patterns on the adjacent cabinets.

Measure and cut each panel to size. Spread contact cement on the back of each panel and on the side of the cabinet where it goes. Wait for the cement to set, according to the

instructions. Press the panel in place, clamp it, and leave it overnight to dry. If necessary, use 3d nails to help hold it in place. The nail heads can be countersunk and the holes filled with putty after the cement dries.

When you put the doors back on the cabinets, some of them may not line up perfectly. Most hinges have a mechanism for making slight adjustments to correct this problem.

Before you install trim pieces, be sure that the cabinets are aligned and securely fastened. Stain or paint the trim; use a miter box to cut it to length, and stain or paint the ends before you attach the trim. Predrill it and fasten it with 3d, 4d, or 6d finishing nails. Sink the heads with a nail set and fill with putty.

For frameless cabinets, attach the trim pieces from inside the cabinet, with screws. Predrill holes through the cabinet large enough to take the screws; use a smaller bit to drill pilot holes in the trim itself. Most manufacturers provide plastic caps to cover the screw heads.

To finish the toe kick, cut baseboard or similar molding to length and paint or stain it a dark color. Attach it to the cabinet kicks with finishing nails.

Installing Shelving

Most cabinet lines include open shelf units to match the cabinets. You can also construct custom-made shelving from hardwood, plywood, or particleboard covered with laminate. You can make a single shelf from an extra filler piece.

Larger units should have adjustable shelves. The simplest and least obtrusive way to

build them is to drill a series of holes in the side of the shelf unit into which small brackets can be inserted. These brackets will support the shelves.

There are several ways to harmonize the shelving with the cabinets. You can use the same kind of wood as was used for the cabinets and stain it or paint it to match. Use touch-up stain provided by the cabinet manufacturer. You may want to experiment first with scraps of the same wood. You can also harmonize the shelving with the cabinets by using the same moldings and trim. Finally, you can make the shelf unit the same height as the cabinets and set the shelves at the same heights as the countertop, vent/hood, and other prominent features of the cabinets.

Vanity Cabinets

It is relatively easy to install a bathroom vanity. It is also easy to individualize one to meet your special needs. If you want a large vanity, you can combine two or more modular units, or you can have a cabinet custom-made. The standard height for a vanity, including the counter-top, is 30 to 32 inches, but you can make it higher, as explained below.

Vanity cabinets are generally open in back to accommodate the plumbing. If yours is not, you can cut out a section of the back to make an opening for the water supply stubs and the drain stubs. You can install the shutoff valves after the vanity is in place, just before you install the countertop, but it is easier to install them beforehand.

Be sure that the floor is level. If it is not, put shims under the cabinet or trim down the base to level it. The walls surrounding the cabinet should be flat, without any bumps, bulges, or depressions.

If you wish to make the vanity or the countertop higher, there are four ways to do it. You can use a modular kitchen base cabinet, which is 34½ inches high and 24 inches deep. You can build a base out of 2 by 4s and set the vanity on top of it. You can raise the toe kick by turning the cabinet upside down and screwing wood cleats to the bottom. Finally, you can elevate the countertop by screwing wood cleats to the top of the vanity and attaching the countertop to them. You can finish the faces of the cleats to match the vanity.

Measure the height of the cabinet. Using a level, draw a line on the wall at that height. If the vanity is in a corner, draw lines on both walls. Drill pilot holes into the hanging cleat on the cabinet. Make sure that each hole is centered over a stud. Attach the hanging cleat to the wall with 2½-inch screws. Be sure that the weight of the cabinet rests on the floor, not on the screws. Shim behind the screws if there is a gap between the floor and the front of the cabinet.

If you are combining two or more units, fasten them together with C-clamps. Drill pilot holes into the side of the stile of one cabinet and drive screws through these holes into the stile of the adjacent unit. Make sure that the cabinets are level and that the face frames are tight and flush. Tightening the screws will often pull a unit out of line. If this happens, add shims or remove them.

Medicine Cabinets

Most medicine cabinets are designed to be recessed into the wall so that only the thickness of the mirrored door protrudes. You can use surface-mounted cabinets where framing, insulation, ducts, or other obstacles make it impossible to install a recessed cabinet. Surface-mounted units extend 4 to 6 inches from the wall and have finished sides. Typical sizes for a single-door cabinet are net 14 inches wide (to fit easily between studs placed 16 inches on center) and 26 to 36 inches high. Sizes for double- or

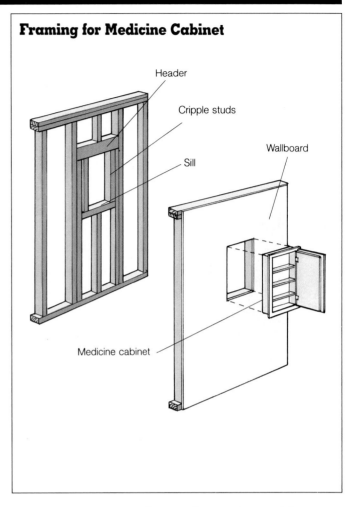

Framing for Medicine Cabinet

Header

Cripple studs

Sill

Wallboard

Medicine cabinet

triple-door units are typically 30, 36, or 48 inches wide by 26 to 36 inches high. Larger units, some from 52 to 80 inches wide and 36 to 40 inches high, are available.

You have many options when it comes to mirrors, doors, and shelves. Doors can be hinged or sliding. Most single doors can be reversed to open from the left or right. Some units are designed for corner installation. Others are designed to be installed in pairs with a wall mirror between them to create an adjustable three-way mirror. Most units have adjustable shelves. Instead of a mirror, you may prefer a door that matches the other

cabinets, a louvered door, or, one that is concealed by a favorite painting.

In choosing a medicine cabinet, consider its dimensions and proportions in relation to other features of the room. For example, if you are installing a medicine cabinet above a vanity and mounting a light bar across the top, all three items should align evenly and be in proportion to each other. If the medicine cabinet is too small, it will be overwhelmed by the vanity. If it is too large, it will draw the eye away from the vanity and diminish the impact of the beautiful design.

INSTALLING COUNTERTOPS

Installing countertops is exacting but very rewarding work. It involves handling large and fragile pieces of expensive material, taking exact measurements, making precise cuts, producing flawless joints, and attending to minute details. But when it is finished, the large expanse of countertop has a dramatic impact on the kitchen or bathroom.

- ☐ Tool belt
- ☐ Steel tape measure
- ☐ 24-inch level
- ☐ 48-inch level
- ☐ Framing square
- ☐ Power circular saw
- ☐ Saber saw
- ☐ Fine-toothed handsaw
- ☐ Compass saw
- ☐ 16-oz hammer
- ☐ Router and bits
- ☐ Power drill and bits
- ☐ Utility knife
- ☐ Chalk line
- ☐ Screwdrivers
- ☐ Small open-end wrench
- ☐ Sandpaper
- ☐ File
- ☐ Jack plane or power plane
- ☐ Mixing bucket
- ☐ Tile cutter

Planning The Installation

Some countertop installations consist simply of laying a slab of material on top of the cabinets and attaching it. Others require joining two or more slabs together or fitting the countertop into an awkward space. The most complicated installations involve exotic materials, which must be joined and cut with precision equipment. These installations should be done by professionals. The following techniques cover the installation of plastic laminate countertops, butcher block, marble and granite slabs, solid-surface materials, and ceramic tile countertops. In some cases you can do the entire installation yourself; in others, you should hire a professional to fabricate the countertop, which you can then install.

For a simple bathroom vanity or short kitchen counter, figure half a day to install a slab countertop (not including sink installation). For a complete kitchen with multiple counters, figure a day. On a difficulty scale of 10 points, consider a slab or prefabricated countertop installation a 4. If you fabricate your own laminate top, figure a 7. For a tile installation, figure a 5.

Preparation

The key to a successful installation is careful scheduling, planning, and measuring. Plan ahead. Some materials must be ordered months in advance, and it may take weeks to schedule a professional fabrication or installation. Be sure that the sink, cooktop, and other built-in appliances are on the site at the time the installation is done, or get the manufacturers' specifications for rough-in dimensions. That way you or the installers can make accurate cutouts.

Make as many decisions as possible in advance. Of course, you have already chosen the type of material you will use for the countertops. You must, however, make other decisions about edge details, corners, type and height of back splash, and where to put seams. Try to keep seams away from the sink area in order to prevent water from seeping under the countertop surface.

If you are having countertops fabricated at a shop, do not take final measurements until the walls are finished and the base cabinets are installed. If possible, have the shop take field measurements. If you take your own measurements, make an accurate sketch of the counter area with the dimensions. Keep it handy and make sure to attach a copy to your order so that you and the fabricator can coordinate last-minute changes over the telephone.

When measuring, figure a 1-inch overhang in front of the cabinets and at the open ends. Figure a ⅛-inch overhang where the countertop terminates for an appliance, such as a refrigerator or slide-in range. Where an end butts into a wall that is not square to the back wall, measure the countertop from the longest point. If you are measuring for stock materials that you will cut yourself, such as a butcher block or a postformed laminate top, allow for the thickness of any backsplash and side-splash material that will be attached to the end of the countertop where it abuts a wall. This dimension (which is usually ¾ inch) should be subtracted from the total length of the countertop piece. Make all measurements at least twice.

Finish painting or staining the cabinets before installing countertops. Make sure the cabinets have cleats in the corners or along the top edges to which the countertops can be attached. Check the cabinets for level in all directions and build up any low spots by nailing shims to the top edges. If the countertop has a lip it may block the upper drawers, the cutting board, or the dishwasher door. Should this happen, raise the countertop. Nail strips of ½- to ¾-inch plywood to the top edges of the cabinet, over the leveling shims, or have the fabricator install padding strips where the countertop will rest on the cabinet.

Installing Laminate Countertops

High-pressure laminate is a thin membrane about 1/16 inch thick that is bonded to a stable substrate of particleboard or plywood.

You have three options. You can buy the laminate and fabricate your own top; buy sections of ready-made postformed countertop and cut them to size; or order a custom countertop, with or without installation. Postformed countertop is the least expensive and most convenient option—local home centers stock it—but the color selection is limited, the back splash and edge details are fixed, and the sections come in only one width. If you order a custom top, most local shops can obtain nearly any laminate and fabricate a top in any shape. You can save money by installing it yourself, using the techniques described below for postformed tops. You can save more money and customize the work even more by doing the whole job yourself, as long as there are no mitered joints, for which it is virtually impossible to make the proper cuts without specialized equipment.

Installing a Postformed Laminate Countertop

Measure the length of countertop needed, allowing for overhangs and the thickness of any back-splash pieces on the ends. Buy separate end-splash pieces and end caps as needed, as well as drawbolt

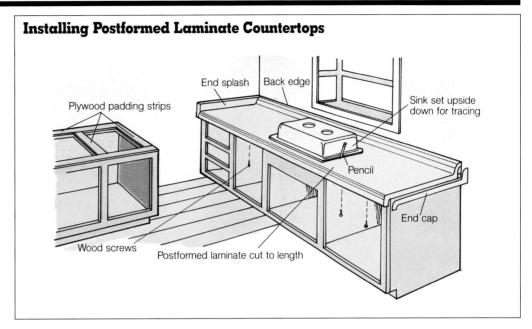

Installing Postformed Laminate Countertops

Plywood padding strips • End splash • Back edge • Sink set upside down for tracing • Pencil • End cap • Wood screws • Postformed laminate cut to length

connectors for any joints. If the countertop is L shaped, requiring two sections with mitered ends, be sure that each section has the cut at the proper end.

Use a framing square to mark the cut line along the top of the counter and up the back splash. If the corner of the wall is out of square, adjust the cut line to compensate. Place masking tape over the line and draw a fresh line on the masking tape. This protects the edge of the laminate from chipping when it is cut. Make the cut with a sharp crosscut saw that has 10 or 12 teeth to the inch, a saber saw, or a circular saw with a sharp blade. Cut from the back side with a saber or circular saw. Smooth cut edges with a file or plane.

Now attach the end splash, if there is one. This piece is usually a simple rectangle with laminate applied to one side, one long edge, and both short edges. Fit it so that the top edge is flush with the top of the back splash and the front edge is flush with the front of the countertop. Attach it to the end of the countertop with water-resistant glue and screws. Pre-drill pilot holes through the back of the end splash for the screws.

If there is no side splash, cover the exposed end of the countertop with a special end cap. To support the bottom and back edges of the end cap, glue or screw 1/2-inch by 1/2-inch wood strips to the bottom and back of the countertop, flush with the end. Then sand the wood surfaces smooth and glue the end cap in place with contact cement. Seal the bottom of the countertop with primer.

Set the countertop in place, snug against the back wall and the sidewall. If gaps appear due to irregularities in the wall, you need to do a little custom fitting. By sliding a pencil along the wall, scribe a line along the top edge of the back splash that is parallel to the back wall. Then pull the countertop out from the wall and trim away any excess on the backside of the line with a file, block plane, or belt sander. For L- or U-shaped countertops, set both sections in place and fit them snugly together before scribing them. Scribe and cut one side and fit the countertop back into place before scribing the second side.

Next, lay out the openings for the sink, the cooktop, and the drop-in range. A sink cutout should start 1¾ inches back from the front edge. Mark a line at this point. This will be the front line. Now find the centerline of the sink by measuring from the sidewall to the center of the sink cabinet. Transfer this line to the countertop. Allow for any overhangs. If the sink has its own rim, set it upside down on the countertop. Center it over the centerline and pull the front edge of the sink about ½ inch forward of the front line. Trace around it. Then remove the sink and draw the cut line about ½ inch inside the tracing. This ½-inch allowance should be adequate to support the rim and still clear the bowl. Check your measurements again. Make sure that the bowl of the sink will clear the cabinets, too. Some sink manufacturers include a paper template for tracing. Rimless sinks require a separate rim, usually of stainless steel. Set this rim on the countertop and trace around it in the same way as you would for a rimmed sink.

You can cut out the opening now or after the countertop is installed. Support the cutout from below while you cut, to prevent it from falling through the opening too soon and cracking the laminate. If you cannot support it from below, cut a 1 by 2 or similar scrap of wood long enough to span across the cutout and beyond it at least 1 inch at each end. Lay it across the top of the section to be cut out and drive one screw through it, into the center of the cutout. The stick will keep the cutout from falling through the opening.

Drill a ¾-inch hole inside the cut line at each corner to start the saber saw. When you reach the back splash, there may not be enough room for you to use a saber saw. Cut from the bottom of the countertop or use a keyhole saw. Avoid making square corners on cutouts; they tend to start cracks. Drill holes at each corner or round the corners with a saber saw.

For L- and U-shaped countertops, assemble the sections before you attach them to the cabinets. After checking the fit, slide the pieces slightly forward so there is room to separate them and move them around. Make sure that you have access to the bottom of the joint. If necessary, set the pieces upside down, in position, on padded sawhorses or a makeshift workbench.

Apply waterproof glue or silicone sealant to the edges to be joined and slide the pieces together. Align them carefully. Install the drawbolts in the recessed cavities and tighten them with an open-end wrench. Feel along the top of the joint as you tighten them to be sure that the 2 surfaces are absolutely flush.

Fasten the countertop to the cabinets from below with screws that are long enough to penetrate the countertop ½ inch. Apply a thin bead of caulk between the countertop and the wall.

Fabricating a Laminate Countertop On-site

Use ¾-inch high-density particleboard (minimum 45-pound grade) or dense plywood for the substrate. Cut all countertop and back-splash pieces to exact size. Glue and screw ¾- by ¾-inch strips beneath the front and side edges of the countertop for the overhang. The base should be clean, smooth, and dry, and joints in the base should not coincide with joints in the laminate.

Cut the laminate to size, allowing an extra ¼ inch along any edges that can be trimmed. Mark the cutting lines with a knife blade. Cut with a specialty tool called a laminate cutter or use a saw with a fine-toothed blade. Cut the laminate facedown if you use a saber saw or circular saw, and faceup if you use a handsaw or a table saw. If you use a table saw for cutting narrow strips, clamp a piece of wood onto the fence just high enough above the table to keep the laminate from chattering as it passes through the blade.

If 2 pieces will be joined, overlap the ends and cut both pieces at the same time with a router. Guide the router with straightedges clamped along both sides. Use a straight carbide cutting bit.

Attach the edge strips first. Apply contact cement to both surfaces. When the cement is dry to the touch, bond the laminate to the substrate, being careful to position it perfectly before the surfaces make contact. Go over the laminate with a roller or with a hammer and padded wood block to ensure a good bond. For rounded edges, soften the laminate with a flameless heater, such as a hair dryer, and then bend it. Use a router with a straight carbide flush bit to trim the edges. File the top edge so that it is flush with the substrate.

To attach the top piece, spread contact cement on both surfaces with a paint roller (unlike most adhesives, contact cement only sticks to itself). While it is drying, lay clean sticks on the substrate to keep the laminate from making contact as you position it. Lay the laminate on the sticks and align it. Then, working from the center, slide the sticks out from under the laminate and press it down into place. Trim the edges with a router, using a carbide bevel cutter with a ball bearing tip, to produce a beveled edge.

Install the countertop the same way as you would a post-formed unit. If you use wood trim for the edges instead of laminate, attach the top first and trim it as you would an edge strip. The wood edging should be stained and sealed, or painted, ahead of time. Seal the exposed edge of the substrate as well. Attach the wood strip with glue and finishing nails.

Installing Butcher-Block Countertops

Made from hardwoods, such as sugar maple, red oak, and white ash, butcher-block countertops are available in 25-inch widths and in various lengths. Most blocks are 1½ inches thick. They can form an entire countertop or a section of one.

Measure for butcher block the same way as you would for any countertop and cut the block to exact length. Cut from the top with a handsaw or from the bottom with a circular power saw, using a straightedge. Paint the cut end immediately with a urethane or lacquer sealer to prevent splitting.

If the back edge will not be covered by back-splash material, set the block in place, check for irregularities in the back wall or sidewalls, and trim the block to fit. Seal the raw wood.

Before the final installation, drill holes through the cabinet cleats to take the mounting screws. Changes in humidity cause the wood block to expand and contract in width (although not in length). To allow for these fluctuations, use a bit at least ⅜-inch larger than the diameter of the screws. This will permit the mounting screws to move with the block. Set the countertop in place and secure it with screws or lag screws long enough to penetrate 1 inch into the block. Predrill to avoid splitting, using a bit smaller than the diameter of the threads. Use a washer to hold the screw against the cabinet cleat and tighten the screw only enough to make contact. Set a screw in each corner of the block.

You can detail the edges and the corners of a butcher-block countertop in various ways: Trim the corners by sawing off the tips; round the edges with a router; put a bevel or an ogee on the edges with a router; or round the corners with a saber saw. After cutting, sand the raw surfaces smooth and seal them with one or two coats of a satin urethane finish.

Installing Natural-Stone Slab Countertops

Natural marble has been used on counters and tabletops for centuries, and other natural stones, such as slate and granite, are becoming popular. A slab is heavy and difficult to cut; have a simple slab cut to size and edged by the supplier. You can then install it yourself. Leave large or complicated installations to professionals. Be sure to tell the dealer not to leave sharp corners on countertops for islands and peninsulas. They are dangerous, especially if the household includes toddlers.

Measure carefully for the top and the back splash. If the marble section will be lower than the adjacent countertops (if you are installing a marble confectioner's slab, for example), allow for side pieces where the counter returns to the standard height. These side pieces can be made of matching stone or any other appropriate material. Take the measurements to a marble dealer and have the pieces cut and edged.

Position the counter, back, and the end pieces to make sure that they are even with the other counter surfaces and back splashes. If they are too low, nail plywood shims to the top of the cabinet frame to bring them up.

Apply an adhesive recommended by the supplier to the top of the cabinet frame and set the counter slab in place. Use the same adhesive to attach the back splash to the stone top and to the back wall. Follow this procedure for the end pieces as well.

Run a bead of silicone sealant along all the seams and points of contact with the back wall and the adjacent counters. Shape and smooth the bead with a damp rag wrapped around your finger.

Finish the countertop with sealer, using whichever product the supplier recommends. Apply it according to the instructions on the label.

Installing Solid-Surface–Material Countertops

Solid-surface–material countertops, known by brand names such as Avonite, Corian, Fountainhead, and 2000X, can be fairly easy to install if it is a simple slab. Large countertops or complicated installations with laminated edges, joints, and inlays should be left to professionals.

Sheets in ½- and ¾-inch thicknesses are used for countertops. Countertops can have sinks molded into them. Special 5-inch-wide strips are available for back splashes.

Start by measuring the length and width of the countertop area. Allow about 1 inch for each overhang. Install a ¾-inch plywood base over the cabinets to mount the countertop on. Shim, if necessary, to make it level. For a recessed sink, cut out the opening and then rout a groove around the edge so that the sink rim rests flush with the top of the plywood. Provide extra support for the sink by attaching cleats under the edges of the opening.

Cut the countertop and the back splashes to size. Use a circular power saw with a carbide-tipped blade and cut from the backside of the slab, or according to manufacturers' instructions. Wear goggles. Clamp a straightedge to the countertop to guide the saw. (Protect the finished surface with masking tape.) For sink openings, cut the straight lines with a circular saw and the corners with a saber saw. Set the top in place to check for fit.

To create a thicker edge, turn the top over and attach pieces of trim along the edge, using an adhesive recommended by the manufacturer. Clamp the joints and let them dry overnight. You can do the same for the back splash, or you can attach it after the top is in place.

Fasten the countertop to the plywood base or to the cabinet tops, using a mastic recommended by the manufacturer. Attach the back splash and seal all joints with silicone. Wipe away the excess and smooth the sealant with a damp rag.

Installing Ceramic Tile Countertops

Tile is an excellent do-it-yourself material for countertops and back splashes. It is especially suitable for tops that have many corners, angles, and complicated shapes. Tile installation is relatively inexpensive, although special trim pieces and epoxy adhesives can drive the cost up quickly.

Unglazed tiles are not appropriate for countertops. They stain easily and they absorb moisture. Always use glazed ceramic tiles for countertops—especially around sinks and as food preparation surfaces.

Purchase tiles that are rated for use on horizontal surfaces. These tiles are thicker than the ones that are manufactured for use on walls. If they are made of ceramic, they will usually be ½ inch thick. Polished dimensioned stone tiles ⅜ inch thick can be used for countertops as well.

Choose the trim and accent pieces early and buy them with the tile. Trim tiles are not always available to match every tile pattern, so you may have to choose a different pattern if you need to buy trim.

Installing tile countertops always involves these same basic steps: Prepare the backing, perform a dry tile layout, draw the working lines, apply the adhesive, set the full tiles, set the cut tiles, grout, caulk, and seal. All but the first two of these steps are the same as those for installing ceramic tile on floors. Both jobs also require the same tools.

Installing Ceramic Tile Countertops

Mortar-Bed Underlayment

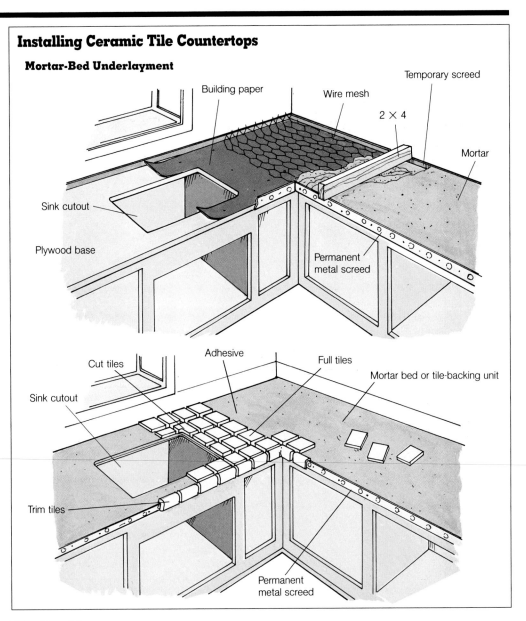

Tile Backings

Start by installing a ⅝- or ¾-inch plywood substrate over the base cabinets. The best installations are done on a bed of mortar ¾ inch to 1 inch thick, but an acceptable installation for kitchen counters would be ½-inch tile backing boards nailed to a ¾-inch plywood base. Tile backing units are cement and fiberglass boards designed as a backing for tile installations; they are especially suited for use in wet areas. They can also be used as a backing for the back splash.

Cut tile backing units by scoring and snapping, using a utility knife or a saw. Work on the coated side of the unit. Precut each unit and make any necessary cutouts prior to installation. Position the backing board over the plywood with the coated side up. Secure each unit with 1½-inch galvanized or rust-resistant nails or 1¼-inch galvanized coarse-thread sharp-point screws. Drive the fasteners flush with the coated surface but do not countersink them.

To prevent any leakage through the tile backing unit, apply 2-inch glass mesh tape over all joints and around all cutouts. Cover the tape with the setting adhesive. For best results allow these joints to dry overnight before you begin to install the tiles.

Tile can also be attached directly to a plywood backing, but this method requires sealing the plywood carefully, using epoxy-based mastic, and adding latex or epoxy modifiers to the grout mix.

If you are not adding a mortar float or tile backing unit to the top, raise the plywood by attaching 1 by 3 strips to the bottom along the edges. This provides a backing for the tiles along the front edge and keeps them from interfering with the drawers. Screw the top in from below to make future removal easier. Use shims if necessary to make it level.

Cut out openings for the sink and the surface appliances. If you are installing a recessed sink, set it in place now. Surface-mounted sinks are installed after tiling.

To install a mortar float, nail a special metal screed strip around the outer edges of the countertop with the top edge extending 1 inch above the plywood substrate. Measure and cut a piece of building paper to cover the plywood. Cut reinforcing wire mesh to size, lay it over the paper, and staple it to the plywood. Mix mortar to a consistency dry enough that it will stick in a ball and not ooze water. Lay a strip of wood lath 1 inch high against the back wall. Spread the mortar over the countertop and screed it level by dragging a straightedge along the tops of the screed strips. Remove the back screed and fill the void with mortar. Then let the mortar set up for an hour or two before setting tile.

Dry Tile Layout

Dry tile layout is the act of completely designing the tile installation before a single tile is stuck in place. It allows you to position tiles in their exact location so that you use as many full tiles and as few cut tiles as possible. A dry tile layout is practical only for small installations, such as countertops.

First, tape any trim tiles along the edge; then start taping the field tiles. If the counter is L shaped, start the layout at the inside corner and work outward. The inside corner piece should be a full tile. For straight counters, start with full tiles at the front and work toward the back. On islands and peninsulas without sinks or other inserts, begin setting full tiles at the measured center point of the field and work out toward the trim in all directions. Use tile spacers to maintain uniform grout lines. All the trim pieces should be laid out so that the grout lines match up with the grout lines of the field tiles.

Because they tend to be less stable, avoid setting very small cut tiles at the counter back and around the sink and other inserts. If the sink is surface mounted, mark tiles for cutting by laying them in place and scribing them from beneath. Cut them with a tile cutter or nippers. The sink rim will cover the raw edges. If the sink is recessed, fit the trim pieces around it and cut the field tiles where they abut the trim

pieces, allowing for the grout line. These cuts must be smooth and accurate because they will not be covered by a sink rim, so it is best to make them as you are setting the tile.

Once you are satisfied with the design, mark working lines on the setting bed so that you can reproduce it when you install the tiles. For a countertop with a sink or range insert, mark working lines around the cutout to position the trim tiles around the fixture. Extend the countertop working lines up the back wall to keep the backsplash tiles aligned.

Installing Tiles

Spread the adhesive and set the tiles exactly as if you were installing floor tiles. When you have finished the last row of countertop tiles, work up the back-splash wall. Use bullnose tiles along the top edge. When you have finished, remove the excess adhesive from the tiles as quickly as possible. Then let the work dry for one or two days. You may need to tape the back splash and trim tiles in place while the adhesive dries.

After about 24 hours, grout the joints. Then cover the countertop with plastic sheeting for two or three days to let the grout cure properly.

Special Situations

Most countertops are installed directly over base cabinets at a standard 36-inch height, but there are exceptions. Sometimes, for example, you may want to change the height of the countertop. If a tall cook prefers a higher countertop, raise the cabinets by building a simple platform of 1-by or 2-by

lumber to set them on. Many cooks, on the other hand, prefer a lower countertop for baking, or wheelchair access, or to match the height of a standard 30-inch table. Base cabinets are almost always 34½ inches high, but you can use 24-, 27-, or 30-inch wall cabinets and install them on a platform set back slightly to provide a toe kick. Typically, wall cabinets are only 12 inches deep, while base cabinets are 24 inches deep, so either set them 12 inches out from the wall or install a narrow countertop.

Countertops that are not adequately supported by cabinets require other structural support. Examples are a sideboard mounted on a wall, or a peninsula countertop that extends beyond the cabinets so that stools or chairs can be pulled up beneath it. For a countertop, such as a sideboard, that is wholly unsupported by cabinets, set the back or the ends on wall cleats and use diagonal braces. For a countertop that extends beyond the cabinets, you can support a wide overhang by using 1-inch or 1¼-inch plywood as the base. This distance is limited for fragile countertop materials like tile. This works best with plastic laminates, which have some flex and can be used this way for very wide extensions.

Some kitchen countertops are not intended for food preparation or eating. Examples are desktops and laundry counters. Use appropriate materials for these countertops and the same installation techniques described above.

INSTALLING PLUMBING FIXTURES AND FITTINGS

Preparation for installing plumbing fixtures and fittings begins way back in the planning stage. Obviously, all the work to install these fixtures isn't done at once. Instead, you perform phases of the jobs as you build the house.

- ☐ Tool belt
- ☐ Steel tape measure
- ☐ 24-inch level
- ☐ Combination square
- ☐ Framing square
- ☐ Curved-claw hammer
- ☐ Slot screwdrivers
- ☐ Phillips screwdrivers
- ☐ Utility knife
- ☐ 10- and 12-inch crescent wrenches
- ☐ 12- and 14-inch pipe wrenches
- ☐ Basin wrench
- ☐ Pliers
- ☐ Flashlight
- ☐ Power drill and bits
- ☐ Masonry bits
- ☐ Caulk gun

Planning Fixtures

You need a general idea of the type, size, and placement of all bathroom and kitchen fixtures—sinks, washbasins, bathtubs, showers, and toilets—to put the pipes in the correct spot while you're pouring the foundation, to frame the space properly to hold the fixtures, and to run the pipes and electrical wires to the right spots.

Since each fixture is quite different and the phases extend throughout building, it's impossible to say how long it will take to install a given fixture. On a difficulty scale of 10 points, consider installing plumbing fixtures and fittings a 5. No special equipment or tools are needed, just regular carpentry tools and some plumbing wrenches. Many plumbing fixtures are quite heavy. You will need help to lift fixtures into place and to hold them there while connecting fittings.

Installing Basins and Sinks

Kitchen sinks and wall-mounted, pedestal, and counter-top washbasins for bathrooms are installed in basically the same way but at different points in the sequence of construction.

Basins and sinks that are recessed below the countertop must be installed before the finish material is applied. This material will either cover the rim or butt up to it to form a flush surface.

Basins and sinks mounted on top of a countertop are installed after the finish material. Some of these are self-rimming models; others have a separate metal rim that creates a low profile.

A pedestal basin is installed after the walls are finished and the floor coverings are in place.

Fittings

Crawling around under a basin or sink is unpleasant and uncomfortable, especially when it is installed in a vanity or base cabinet. Make your task easier by attaching as many fittings as possible to the basin before you set it into place.

To attach the drain fitting to the basin or sink, first unscrew the flange piece from the top end of the drainpipe. Then screw the tightening nut down to the bottom of the threads, and slip the washer and gasket over the threads all the way down to the tightening nut. Apply a ring of plumber's putty around the top edge of the drain hole. Insert the drain fitting up through the hole from below. Screw the flange down onto it from above. Then tighten the nut under the sink to draw the flange piece snugly down onto the putty. Some

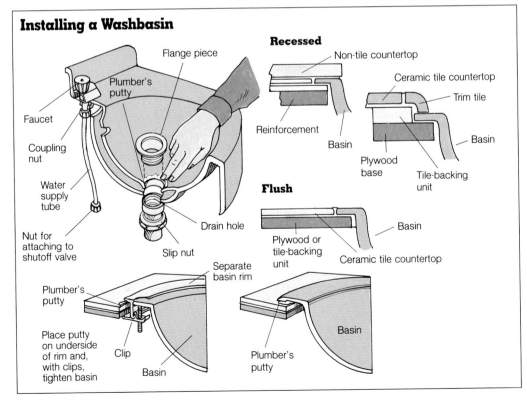

Installing a Washbasin

- Flange piece
- Plumber's putty
- Faucet
- Coupling nut
- Water supply tube
- Nut for attaching to shutoff valve
- Slip nut
- Drain hole

Recessed
- Non-tile countertop
- Ceramic tile countertop
- Trim tile
- Basin
- Reinforcement
- Basin
- Plywood base
- Tile-backing unit

Flush
- Plywood or tile-backing unit
- Basin
- Ceramic tile countertop

- Separate basin rim
- Plumber's putty
- Place putty on underside of rim and, with clips, tighten basin
- Clip
- Basin
- Plumber's putty
- Basin

kitchen sink drains with strainers use a retainer with wing nuts. Read the manufacturer's instructions to learn the proper configuration.

Attach the faucets according to the manufacturer's instructions. A one-piece center-set faucet is the easiest to install. It has 2 bolts or threaded stubs. Insert these down through the holes in the sink or basin and attach nuts to them from below. When the sink or basin is in place, connect the water supply lines to the threaded stubs. In single-control units, 2 copper supply lines should attach to the faucet; connect these to the shutoff valves.

Installing wide-set faucets for bathroom basins is more complicated than installing a one-piece faucet. Each basin has a spout and 2 handle units. All are inserted through holes in the basin or holes drilled into the countertop. Working from underneath, use flexible hosing (if allowed) or copper tubing provided by the manufacturer to connect each handle unit to the spout. You may have to cut or extend the length of the copper tubing. To extend the length, use compression fittings and ⅜-inch soft copper tubing.

Attach the hot and cold supply lines to their respective handle units. Install the linkage for the pop-up drain assembly for washbasins after the basin is in place.

Countertop Models

The most typical washbasins and sinks are countertop models. Washbasins installed into a bathroom vanity and sinks

installed into the kitchen countertop are available in recessed and rimmed models, which are often called self-rimming.

A recessed basin or sink is installed in the plywood countertop before the finish material is applied. Determine whether you want the rim of the basin to be set flush with the finish material, set under it, or trimmed. If the sink is to be set flush, mount it on the surface of the plywood. The rim of the basin is usually the same thickness as the tile. If the rim is to be recessed, putty the groove and set the sink into it so the rim sits flush with the surface of the plywood. You can also use mounting clips to suspend a recessed basin under the plywood top. Recessed models may be trimmed with a ring if the sink or basin edge will be covered with tile and grouted. If the unit has a separate metal rim, slip the rim onto the basin then set the basin into place. Working from underneath, slip mounting clips into the rim and tighten them with a screwdriver to hold the basin in place.

Install a self-rimming sink or basin after the finish material is applied. Apply a bead of caulk or plumber's putty around the edge of the countertop hole and set the basin into it.

For either version, connect the water supply lines to the shutoff valves. Then hook up the drain. Before you turn the water on, remove the aerator attachment from the end of the faucet spout and leave it off for a few days. Normal use will clear out any debris left in the pipes when the plumbing was roughed-in.

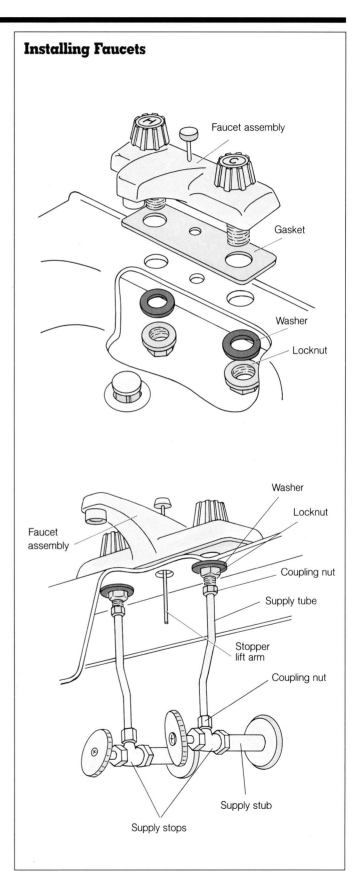

Installing Faucets

Faucet assembly

Gasket

Washer

Locknut

Washer

Locknut

Faucet assembly

Coupling nut

Supply tube

Stopper lift arm

Coupling nut

Supply stub

Supply stops

Installing a Wall-Mounted Sink

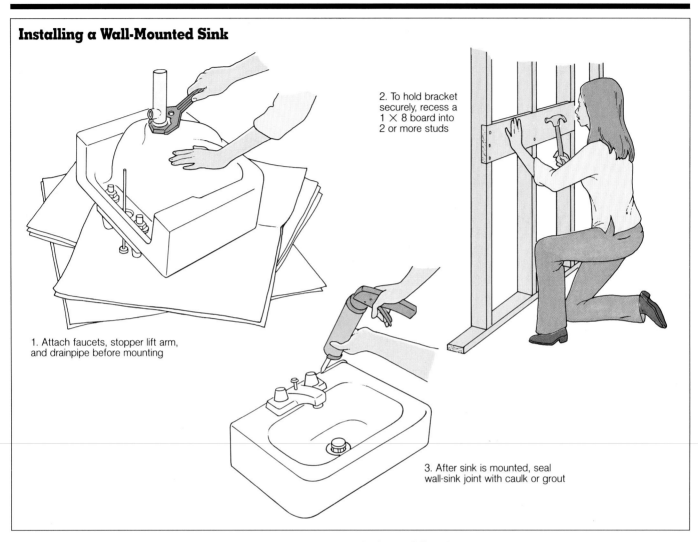

1. Attach faucets, stopper lift arm, and drainpipe before mounting

2. To hold bracket securely, recess a 1 × 8 board into 2 or more studs

3. After sink is mounted, seal wall-sink joint with caulk or grout

Wall-Mounted Models

Wall-mounted washbasins leave the space below the washbasin virtually empty, which makes them an excellent choice for a bathroom used by people who must use the basin while in a wheelchair. Because these basins can be mounted at any desired height, they are also an appropriate style for a bathroom used by children. As the children grow, the basin can be moved up. Wall-mounted sinks are often installed in laundry or utility rooms to be used for hand laundry, pet grooming, and plant potting.

A wall-mounted washbasin hangs on a bracket provided with it. Install the bracket according to the manufacturer's instructions. Using ¼- by 2½-inch lag screws or other heavy screws, anchor it into the wall studs or into blocking installed between the studs. Then lower the basin onto the bracket, making sure that it catches securely. Use a level to straighten the basin. Connect the drain and the water supply lines.

Pedestal Basins

Pedestal washbasins are an excellent choice for small bathrooms because they take up so little floor space.

The basin and the pedestal are two separate pieces. In some installations, the basin is hung on the wall first and the pedestal is installed under it. In others, the pedestal is installed first and the basin is set on top of it. If the basin is secured to the wall, make sure that there is blocking between the studs. Instead of a bracket, many models are supported on heavy lag screws inserted through holes in the back of the basin.

The pedestal is bolted to the floor. If you have to drill through tile to secure the bolts, use a special tile bit or a carbide-tipped masonry bit.

The plumbing connections for pedestal basins are the same as those for other basins except that you will usually have more space to work in and the fittings should be attractive. If the water supply lines show, use the smooth type rather than the flexible type to give a better appearance. Use a tubing bender to shape them into a graceful arc or an S curve, being careful to avoid kinks. You can cut the lines to the correct length with a tubing cutter.

Installing a Prefabricated Bathtub or Shower

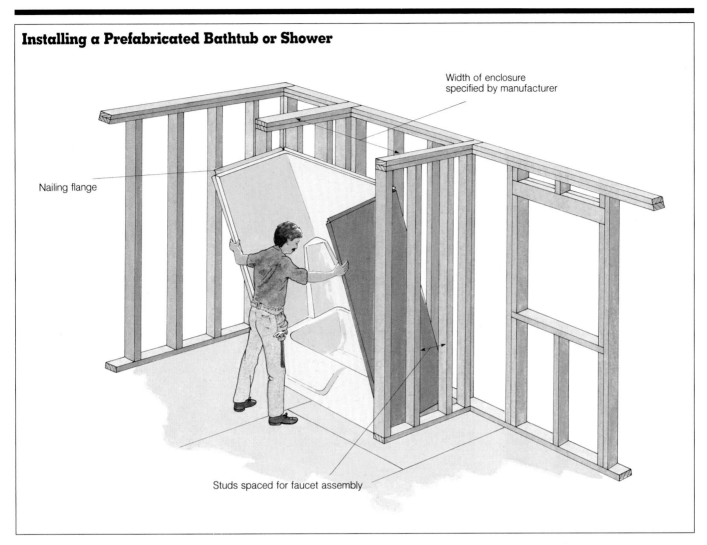

Width of enclosure specified by manufacturer

Nailing flange

Studs spaced for faucet assembly

Installing Shower Stalls

Options for shower stalls include using prefabricated one-piece units, custom-built stalls with a prefabricated shower pan, or custom-built stalls with a custom-built shower pan. A prefabricated unit is the easiest to install. You can build a shower stall with a prefabricated base if you have basic carpentry, plumbing, and ceramic tile–setting skills.

Put in prefabricated shower units, bathtubs, and shower pans during the rough plumbing phase.

Prefabricated Units

Plastic or fiberglass shower stall and combination bathtub-shower units include everything except the plumbing. These showers can be installed by one person in less than a day. The most difficult part may be getting the unit into the bathroom—most are too large to pass through a standard doorway. You may want to put the shower into the space before you frame the walls completely. Some units have a ceiling and others utilize the bathroom ceiling.

The list that follows presents the steps for installing a prefabricated shower unit.

1. Build conventional framed walls to support the unit. Space the studs evenly, but adjust the spacing where the plumbing will go so the studs will not interfere with the faucet. The width of the enclosure must be exact, so check the manufacturer's specifications or measure the unit at the base.

Note: Some codes require you to install fireproof wallboard in the opening before you install the shower. This

provision applies particularly to buildings with multiple dwelling units.

2. Rough-in a 2-inch P-trap under the floor, and stub up the 2-inch drainpipe out of the floor where the drain hole will go. Cut the drainpipe at the height specified by the manufacturer. Rough-in the faucet and the showerhead, and cut holes in the walls of the stall to fit the showerhead stub and the faucet stems.

3. Install the drain fitting in the floor of the shower unit, using plumber's putty around the flange. Remove the gasket and the retaining ring.

4. Lift the shower unit into place, centering the drain fitting down over the drain stub. Some manufacturers recommend setting the unit on a ½-inch bed of mortar or quick-setting plaster compound to provide maximum support. With galvanized roofing nails attach the top and side flanges to the studs. Secure the drain fitting by slipping the gasket down around the 2-inch drainpipe and screwing the retaining ring down on it to compress it.

5. Stub out the faucets and showerhead.

6. During the room finishing, apply wallboard or tile-backing units to the framing, bringing it over the wall flanges of the shower unit. With paint, tile, or other materials, finish the walls to match the surrounding areas.

7. Apply caulk around the cutouts and attach the fittings and escutcheons to the rough plumbing. Test the plumbing.

Custom-built Stalls

You will need to have the dimensions of the shower pan or the pan itself on hand before you frame the walls. Before you begin construction, decide what special features you want. For instance, shower faucet handles are normally set 42 to 48 inches above the floor, and showerheads are set 66 to 78 inches above the floor. However, you may want to set the handles at another height or include several individually activated showerheads at different heights to accommodate different users. You can also plan to have grab bars, a seat, or recessed shelves or alcoves.

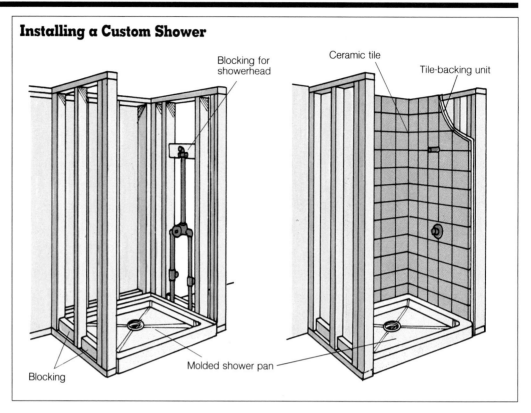

Installing a Custom Shower

Blocking for showerhead

Ceramic tile

Tile-backing unit

Molded shower pan

Blocking

The list that follows presents the steps for installing a custom-built shower stall.

1. Construct the side wall, which will take the plumbing, at a right angle to the back wall. Space the studs so they will not interfere with the plumbing. Where the top edge of the shower pan will go, nail blocking between the studs.

2. Rough-in a 2-inch P-trap under the floor, and provide a vertical drain stub that comes up through the floor where the drain hole will go. Rough-in the water supply pipes, the shower valve, and the special drop-ear elbow for the showerhead. If possible, provide shutoff valves that can be reached from a door on the back of the plumbing wall.

3. Install the drain fitting in the shower pan, and remove the retaining ring and gasket from the fitting. Spread a ½-inch layer of quick-setting plaster on the floor. Set the pan in place and level it. Slip the gasket down around the 2-inch drainpipe, and screw the retaining ring down to compress it. Test the plumbing for leaks.

4. Finish the framing around the shower pan. At the top of the pan, insert blocking between the studs. With galvanized roofing nails, secure the nailing flanges to the studs and blocking.

5. Line the inside of the stall with tile-backing units up to the point where the tile will end. Use galvanized roofing nails to attach them to the studs, lapping the backing over the flange of the shower pan.

Leave a ¼-inch gap around the bottom of the panels. Seal the joints with fiberglass mesh tape and waterproof joint compound or thin-set tile adhesive, as recommended by the manufacturer. Cover the upper portion of the stall and the outside of the walls with wallboard.

6. Finish the inside of the stall with ceramic tile or other appropriate surface material. Finish the outside to match the surrounding walls. Install the finish plumbing and a shower door according to the manufacturer's instructions. If you have to drill holes into the tile to secure the door frame, use a carbide-tipped bit. If possible, align the holes with the grout lines to make drilling easier.

Water Supply Pipes for Bathtub and Showers

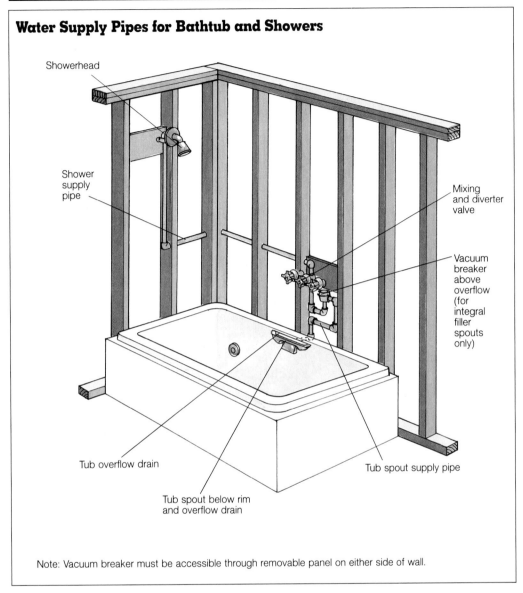

Showerhead

Shower supply pipe

Mixing and diverter valve

Vacuum breaker above overflow (for integral filler spouts only)

Tub overflow drain

Tub spout below rim and overflow drain

Tub spout supply pipe

Note: Vacuum breaker must be accessible through removable panel on either side of wall.

Installing Bathtubs

Install bathtubs as part of the rough plumbing, before the walls are closed in and before the floor is finished. The tub is the hardest of all bathroom fixtures to install. It is big, cumbersome, and heavy, and the plumbing connections are usually made inside a tight space. To install even a lightweight fiberglass tub, you will need at least one helper. If the bathtub is made of cast iron, you will probably need several.

For purposes of installation, there are two types of bathtubs. Tubs with one finished side are designed to be installed in an alcove. Tubs with no finished sides are designed to be completely surrounded by a built-in platform. Differences in size, material, and configuration can pose special problems, however, so be sure to get installation instructions from the dealer or the manufacturer.

Alcove Tubs

The following guidelines explain how to install a standard enameled steel recessed tub 30 inches wide by 60 inches long. They should give you a general sense of how to install any bathtub into an alcove.

1. Frame the walls so that the opening is just large enough to enable you to slide the tub into place against the studs. Check that the studs will not interfere with the installation of the faucet.

2. Slide the tub into place, level it with shims, and mark where the bottom of the rim touches the studs. Pull the tub out again and, just under the marks, nail 2 by 4 ledgers to the studs. These ledgers will support the rim of the tub. (Ledgers are not needed if you are installing a cast-iron tub.) Mark, measure, and nail carefully; the ledger boards must be just the right height off the floor to enable the rim to make full contact. Slide the tub in again and double-check all your measurements. If the P-trap has not yet been roughed-in, mark on the floor the exact center of the drain hole. Slide the tub back out.

3. If the P-trap and the drainpipe have not been roughed-in, cut an access hole in the floor. The hole should be 4 to 6 inches wide and extend 12 inches out from the center of the end wall. Rough-in a 1½-inch P-trap below floor level, centering the slip nut directly under the tub's overflow pipe.

4. You can rough-in the water supply pipes, the mixing valve, and the stubs for the spout and showerhead now or after the tub is installed, depending on how easy it will be to get behind the tub later. The spout is usually installed 4 inches above the tub rim. Place the faucets 4 to 6 inches above the spout if this is a tub-only unit. If there is a showerhead, install the faucets 18 inches above the spout and the showerhead 66 to 78 inches above the floor. Adjust these heights to suit your needs. You can even place the faucets on one wall and the showerhead or the spout on another, if you wish. Install shutoff valves for both hot and cold water.

5. Apply a ring of plumber's putty under the flange of the drain elbow, and connect the elbow to the tub. Tighten it by holding the drain fitting steady with the handle of a pair of pliers or with a similar forked tool while you tighten the nut underneath the fitting. You can attach the overflow pipe and the tailpiece now or when the tub is in place. Cut the tailpiece so it will fit 1 to 1½ inches down into the P-trap.

6. If the tub is not insulated, fit pieces of fiberglass blanket insulation around it. If there is room, put some under the tub as well. Do not compress the insulation.

7. Slide the tub into place. Use shims where necessary to make it stable and level. Drive 7-penny (7d) or 8d galvanized box nails above the steel flange and into the studs so that the nail heads hold the flange to the walls. If the tub is made of fiberglass, drill pilot holes into the flange before you nail through it. A cast-iron tub need not be secured to the walls.

8. For the rough plumbing inspection, cap the drain and fill the drain-vent lines to the highest vent with water.

9. After the inspection, connect the drain. The tailpiece below the drain tee should slide into the P-trap below the floor. Tighten the slip joints on the P-trap and the drain tee securely. Install the stopper mechanism according to the manufacturer's instructions. Fill the tub with water and let it sit for a few hours to test for leaks. Then open the stopper and let the water run down the drain.

10. Apply tile-backing units or moisture-resistant wallboard to the framing around the tub. Lap it over the tub flange, but

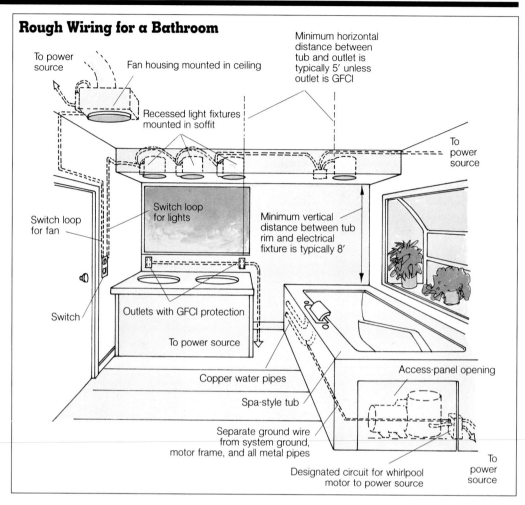

Rough Wiring for a Bathroom

To power source

Fan housing mounted in ceiling

Minimum horizontal distance between tub and outlet is typically 5' unless outlet is GFCI

Recessed light fixtures mounted in soffit

To power source

Switch loop for lights

Switch loop for fan

Minimum vertical distance between tub rim and electrical fixture is typically 8'

Switch

Outlets with GFCI protection

To power source

Access-panel opening

Copper water pipes

Spa-style tub

Separate ground wire from system ground, motor frame, and all metal pipes

Designated circuit for whirlpool motor to power source

To power source

leave a ¼-inch gap around the top of the rim. This gap should be caulked when the tile or other finish material is installed. Seal the joints with fiberglass mesh tape and moisture-resistant joint compound or tile adhesive.

11. If you install tile, use a level to mark guidelines for the first (bottom) row. Not all tub rims are level, so don't use the tub rim as a guide.

Platform Tubs

Most luxury tubs, whether they are whirlpool units or conventional models, are designed for platform installation. Some come with an optional matching skirt to finish the

side, but most units are finished with custom materials applied over a frame that is built on-site. The guidelines presented here are applicable to most installations, but you may need to modify them to accommodate a particular type of tub, choice of finish, or detail in the plumbing.

For instance, if the tub is light enough to allow two or three people to lift it into place, you can build the platform first and then lower the tub into it. You may have to exercise ingenuity in doing some of the finish work before the rough plumbing so that the rim of the tub will rest on a finished surface. If you want the rim to be covered or to be flush with the

surrounding surface, you can finish the top of the platform deck at the same time you finish the sides. In some cases there may not be enough room to install a platform all the way around the tub, so the finish walls will come down to the rim on one or more sides as they do with an alcove tub. This eliminates the need to set some of the rim on a finished surface, but it requires a waterproof joint to prevent water spilled onto the rim from leaking behind the wall.

Tubs made of acrylic and other plastic materials can expand and contract with changes in temperature. They must have strong support around the rim.

Installing a Platform Tub

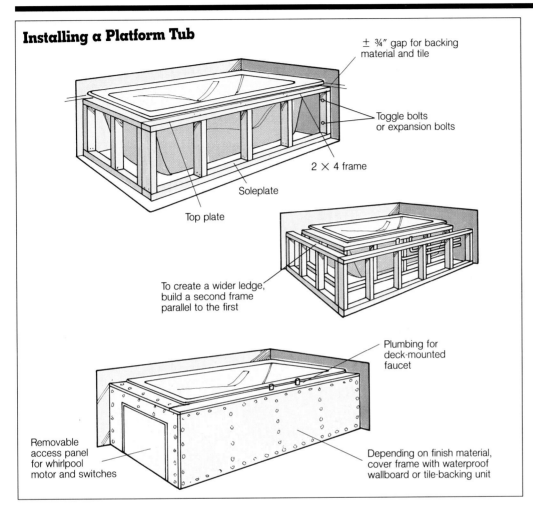

± ¾″ gap for backing material and tile

Toggle bolts or expansion bolts

2 × 4 frame

Soleplate

Top plate

To create a wider ledge, build a second frame parallel to the first

Plumbing for deck-mounted faucet

Removable access panel for whirlpool motor and switches

Depending on finish material, cover frame with waterproof wallboard or tile-backing unit

The list that follows presents guidelines for installing platform tubs.

1. It is usually easiest to install the tub first and then build the supporting framework in place so that it fits properly and so that you can leave just the right amount of clearance under the rim of the tub to install the finish material. This is the only option if the tub is made of cast iron. Be sure that the drain line and the P-trap are roughed-in below the floor and that there is an access hole through the floor for connecting the tub drain to the P-trap.

2. Build the back and side frames out of 2 by 4s, spacing the studs 16 inches apart. If you want a wider ledge, use 2 by 6 lumber or build another 2 by 4 frame outside the first one. Build a third frame if you want the platform to be more than 16 inches wide. You can rough-in the water supply pipes now or in step 5.

3. Raise the tub about 1 inch, using pry bars, and support it temporarily on blocks. Install plywood and then tile-backing units to the top of the framing, and seal the joints with mesh tape. Install the tile or other finish material along the top of the ledge, where it will be covered by the rim of the tub. Plan the layout carefully to allow for an overhang or nosing around the outside edge. If you plan to install a deck-mounted faucet or spout, remember to allow for the holes. After the adhesives have set up thoroughly, apply a bead of caulk around the bottom of the rim then lower the tub into place. If the tub is acrylic or similar plastic material, spread a ½-inch layer of mortar or quick-setting plaster on the floor below the tub before lowering it.

4. Hook up the drain in the same way you would for an alcove tub. Some drains are along the side of the tub and others are at one end.

5. Rough-in the water supply pipes and install the mixing valve and the spout. If there is an integral filler spout below the rim of the tub, you must install a vacuum breaker between the spout and the mixing valve. Because the vacuum breaker must be mounted at least 6 inches above the rim of the tub, you will have to run the water line from the mixing valve back to the nearest wall, up the wall to the vacuum breaker, and back to the spout. The vacuum breaker must be accessible for servicing, so install a removable panel or door on one side of the wall.

6. If the tub has a whirlpool unit, it will probably come with the motor and the circulating pipes already installed. The feed wires for the motor should be connected to a separate 120-volt or 240-volt circuit, the voltage depending on the motor. Most local codes require that all metal pipes be bonded to the motor with a separate No. 12 copper ground wire. Some codes also require that the ground wire between the motor and the house grounding system be continuous and that it be separate from the electrical conduit or cable. The switch that activates the motor must have GFCI protection. Some units have a push-button air switch on the rim of the tub that activates an electrical switch mounted on the motor. Electrical switches must be placed so that they cannot be reached by someone in the tub.

7. Test the plumbing for leaks by filling the tub.

8. After the plumbing has been inspected, insulate the tub and cover the framing with a backing appropriate to the finish material. If the tub has a whirlpool, install a removable panel to provide access to the motor.

Installing Shower Doors

You can install doors for most standard tub installations or simple shower stalls yourself. Doors that are integrated into glass wall units should be installed by professionals. Install tub enclosures and stall doors after the finish work is completed.

Tub Enclosures

Most bathtub enclosures consist of two side rails that are attached to the walls, a top rail that rests on them and holds up the doors, and a bottom rail that provides a water barrier along the top of the bathtub rim. The doors rest in open bottom tracks and channel bottom tracks. Open tracks are preferable because channel tracks tend to fill with gunk.

Install the bottom rail first. Begin by measuring the exact distance from wall to wall along the top of the bathtub rim. Then cut the bottom rail to this length, using a hacksaw and miter box or a power miter saw with a carbide-tipped blade. Install the vinyl gasket or bead on the bottom of the rail and set it into place. Then hold each side rail in place, making sure it interlocks over the bottom rail and is plumb. Mark the locations for the screws on the walls and remove the rails.

Drill a pilot hole for each screw. To drill through the tile, use a tile bit or a bit with a carbide tip. The hole through the tile should be slightly larger than the diameter of the screw shank.

After drilling through the tile and backing, use a wood bit of smaller diameter to complete the drilling of the pilot holes into the wood framing. Apply a small bead of silicon caulk around each hole before attaching the side rails.

Then use screws to fasten the side rails to the walls. Cut the top rail to length, and set it down onto the side rails. Hang the doors on it, as described in the manufacturer's instructions. Finally, run a bead of silicone caulk along the inside of each side rail where it meets the wall. Do not apply caulk along the inside edge of the bottom rail, or water will not be able to flow under it and back into the bathtub.

Stall Doors

The door for a shower stall is installed like a bathtub enclosure. When installing the bottom rail, however, apply a bead of caulk inside the exterior edge to augment the vinyl gasket. Most models have a special sleeve on the side rail where the door is hinged so it can be adjusted to fit the exact width of the door opening.

Installing Toilets

Even toilets are available in a variety of styles. There are one- and two-piece models, low-profile styles, and styles that use minimum amounts of water per flush. There are also many colors of toilets to choose from. Besides the colors, the differences do affect the installation. Be sure to choose this important fixture during the planning stages to ensure that your foundation, framing, and rough plumbing will work.

Toilets are usually installed at the very end of finishing a bathroom, after the walls have been painted and the flooring

Ventilating Bathrooms

A bathroom must have adequate ventilation to prevent the buildup of excessive moisture, mildew, and unpleasant odors. A window that can be opened and shut fulfills most code requirements for bathroom ventilation, but an exhaust fan that is ducted to the outside, not just to the attic, is practically a necessity. It can be installed in the ceiling, and it should have a switch that is separate from the light switch. Some fans are incorporated into a light fixture and have separate switches for the fan and the light. Try to place the fan at the highest point in the ceiling if it is pitched or in a skylight well if there is one. Otherwise, place it near the shower or tub to intercept vapors as close to the source as possible. Fans are rated by the volume of air they move in one minute, measured as cubic feet per minute (cfm). The minimum fan capacity for most bathrooms is 50 cfm, but larger units are available. Consult the manufacturer's recommendations to determine the appropriate capacity for your room. Fans are also rated for sound, and the ratings are expressed in units called sones. A sound level of 4 sones or less is desirable. Roof-mounted fans tend to be quieter than ceiling-mounted fans.

Although a window provides ventilation and lets in fresh air, it may not exhaust steam and vapor efficiently if it faces into the prevailing breezes. The best method for removing steam and vapor without a fan is to install a working skylight. Motorized units open and close automatically. Manual units are cranked open by means of a long handle.

In cold climates, where an open window is usually undesirable, the only way to bring fresh air into the bathroom may be with an air-to-air heat exchanger. This device draws stale air out of the house, draws in fresh air, and uses heat from the former to warm the latter. Fit the exhaust fan with a damper to prevent the back flow of cold air when the fan is not in use.

(except carpet) has been installed. Putting in a toilet is quite simple. The technique varies with the model, so follow the manufacturer's instructions. Be sure that the rough-in

Installing a Toilet

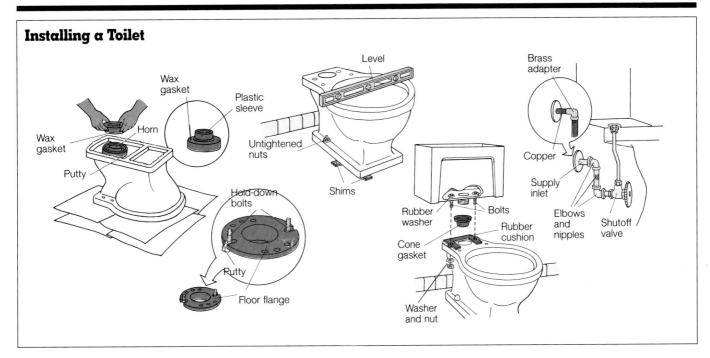

dimensions for the drain and the shutoff valve are correct for the toilet.

The steps that follow explain how to install a toilet. Before you start, remove the temporary cover from the floor flange. The flange should be screwed securely to the floor.

1. Turn the new toilet bowl (or the whole toilet if it is a one-piece model) upside down and rest it on a bed of old towels or padding to protect it. The vitreous china will scratch, so treat it gently. Place a new wax ring around the horn of the outlet opening, pressing it firmly into place. If the closet flange is recessed below the level of the finish floor, use a wax ring with a plastic extension sleeve. The sleeve should face up when the bowl is in the upside-down position. Apply a bead of plumber's putty or

caulk around the bottom edge of the base of the toilet.

2. Slip closet bolts into the slots on each side of the floor flange. If necessary, press plumber's putty around the heads of the bolts to hold them in an upright position.

3. Turn the toilet bowl right side up and set it in place on the flange, making sure the 2 closet bolts slide up through the holes in the base of the toilet. Twist the bowl back and forth and rock it slightly as you press it down.

4. Make sure the bowl is level in both directions. If necessary, slip shims of water-resistant material, such as scraps of vinyl flooring, under the base to level it; apply caulk around the shims. Place the

washers and nuts on the closet bolts and tighten the nuts snugly. Don't overtighten them or you will crack the base. Cover the nuts with the ceramic or plastic caps provided with the toilet. You may have to trim the closet bolts with a hacksaw so that the caps will fit over them.

5. Install the tank according to the manufacturer's directions. Most tanks come with rubber washers and gaskets that must be put on in the proper sequence to prevent leaks. The tank will be connected to the bowl with 2 or 3 bolts. Tighten them carefully and just enough to hold the tank in place, but not so tight as to crack either piece or put a strain on the porcelain of the tank.

6. Hook up the water supply line between the shutoff

valve and the inlet stub of the flush valve. Open the shutoff valve and let the tank fill. Stop any leaks around the fittings by tightening the nuts where the leaks occur. Flush the toilet and watch for leaks around the base. If possible, have someone watch from under the floor, where a leak may otherwise go undetected for a long time.

If there is a leak under the toilet, it means that the wax ring has slipped out of place. The only solution is to pull up the toilet and start all over again, using a new wax ring.

7. Install the toilet seat by fitting the seat bolts into the holes at the back of the bowl and securing them with washers and nuts.

PLANNING ACCESSORIES

Adding accessories to the kitchen and bathrooms is a normal part of making a house a home. Since you're building a house from scratch, you can plan for accessories before the framing and wallboard installation, thereby making accessories more stable, functional, and attractive.

Choosing Accessories

Kitchen and bathroom accessories include towel and grab bars, towel warmers, and mirrors. None of these accessories is difficult to install, except for extra framing and wallboard procedures. On a difficulty scale of 10 points, consider installing accessories a 2.

If you have a chance, take a photograph of the open walls with a wide-angle lens to create a record of where all the studs, blocking, plumbing, and electric lines are. After the framing is covered with wallboard, these photographs will be a helpful guide to installing accessories.

Providing Towel Bars

In the kitchen, plan to install bars for both cloth and paper towels wherever they will be most convenient. You may want to conceal towels behind doors or under cabinets to avoid a cluttered look, or you might prefer the splashes of color provided by a display of decorative towels. Place bars at heights so that the hanging towels will not interfere with burners, sinks, or drain boards. Choose towel bars to add a

touch of opulence; an accent of bright color; or an emphasis on clean, crisp lines.

In the bathroom, provide large towel bars to hold bath towels as they dry between uses and install smaller bars to hold guest towels or washcloths. Place the bars with plenty of room below them so the hanging towels will not interfere with switches, fixtures, heaters, and cabinets.

Figure where you'll want towel bars while your walls are still open. Install horizontal blocking between the studs at the towel bar contact points.

After the wall finish is installed, drill holes through the wallboard and into the wall studs. With screws, fasten the bars to the walls.

Installation techniques for towel bars vary. Some towel bars have concealed brackets that are attached to the wall first. The bar is then slipped onto them and secured with a hidden set screw. Others have wood or metal flanges at the ends of the bar that are held to the wall with face screws that are either exposed or concealed with small plugs.

Providing Towel Warmers

There are two styles of bathroom towel warmers: those that use electricity and those that use hot water. Electric warmers are attached to the wall and plugged into an electric outlet. If you will install this type, plan ahead and place an electric box where you will install the warmer. Other warmers are plumbed directly to the hot-water lines. These store hot water for the shower or tub and heat the towels while you bathe. Towel warmers are a wonderful luxury item. If you opt to have one, plan the rough electrical and rough plumbing accordingly. Add horizontal blocking between studs for attaching the warmer. Follow manufacturer's instructions for specific installation.

Providing Mirrors

Mirrors serve as an aid to grooming, amplify the light in a room, and make a strong design statement. They profoundly affect the perception of the space. In the case of multiple mirrors, they create interesting illusions that can work for or against the design.

Large expanses of mirror must be planned carefully in terms of design and structural support.

When planning bathroom mirrors consider your family's grooming needs first. The vanity or washbasin should have a mirror that is well lighted and at a convenient height for everybody who will be using it. Also consider the effects gained by a mirrored wall, shower surround, or ceiling.

Full-length mirrors are helpful in any dressing area. If your house includes a special exercise area, there should be full-length mirrors there, too.

Consider the use of mirrors in kitchens as well. Installing a mirrored back splash can greatly expand the illusion of space in a small kitchen and amplify light in a dark corner.

Use mirrors to expand the apparent space in any small or long and narrow room. If one whole wall is covered with mirror, it makes the room appear twice as large. However, it also causes you to see things in double, which is distracting to some people.

Mirrors that come together at the corner create a fascinating effect. In addition to doubling the apparent size of the room, they also let you see yourself as others do, not as a mirror image—in other words, the part in your hair is on the correct side instead of on the opposite side as it is when looking into a single mirror.

Mirrors on opposite walls create the familiar barber shop or beauty salon tunnel-to-infinity effect. This can be fun for your guests, but some people might find it uncomfortably disconcerting on a daily basis.

If you want to use mirrors to expand the space without overdoing it, the safest approach is to use one or two fairly large mirrors, maybe 5 feet wide and 3 to 4 feet tall, rather than floor-to-ceiling or wall-to-wall mirrors. If you use only one large mirror, place it on a wall at a right angle to the entry.

Install mirrors over wallboard. Be sure to secure large mirrors to studs.

Gravel stop   A metal edging for a built-up roof; keeps the gravel or crushed rock from falling off the edge.

Groove   A rectangular channel cut with the grain of a piece of lumber.

Ground   A connection between an electrical circuit and the earth or something taking the place of the earth.

Grounded   Connected to the earth or something serving as the earth, such as a cold-water pipe. The ground wire in an electrical circuit is usually bare or has green insulation.

Grout   Thin mortar that can flow into the cavities and joints of any masonry work, especially the filling between tiles and concrete blocks.

Gusset   A flat piece of metal, wood, or plywood; used to support the connections of framing lumber. Most often seen on joints of trusses and the joist splices. Also called a truss plate.

Gutter   A wood, metal, or plastic channel attached to the eaves of a house; catches and carries rainwater to the downspouts.

Gypsum wallboard   *See* wallboard.

Hanger   Any of several types of metal devices for supporting pipes, framing members, or other items. Usually referred to by the items they are designed to support—for example, joist hanger or pipe hanger.

Hardboard   A synthetic wood panel made by chemically converting wood chips to basic fibers and then forming the panels under heat and pressure. Also called Masonite, a brand name.

Hardwood   The wood of broadleaf trees, such as maple, oak, and birch. Although hardwood is usually harder than softwood, the term has no actual reference to the hardness of the wood.

H-clip   A metal device for holding in alignment the edges of plywood or other panels. Its name describes its shape.

Header   A horizontal member over a door, window, or other opening; supports the members above it. Usually made of wood, stone, or metal. Also called a lintel. Also, in the framing of floor or ceiling openings, beam used to support the ends of joists.

Hearth   The floor and front extension of a fireplace or the fireproof floor beneath a wood-burning stove. Usually made of brick, stone, tile, or concrete.

Heartwood   In a log, the wood between the pith and the sapwood. Usually full of resins, gums, and other materials that make it dark in color and resistant to decay.

Heel   The end, or foot, of a rafter that rests on the top plate of a wall.

Heel cut   The vertical cut at the end of a rafter; helps form the bird's-mouth.

Hip   The convex angle formed by the meeting of two roof slopes. Typically set at a 90-degree angle to each other.

Hip rafter   A rafter that runs from the corner of a wall to the ridge board and forms the hip. Set at a 45-degree angle to the walls.

Hip roof   A roof or portion of roof that slopes up toward the center from all sides.

Hot wire   In an electrical circuit, any wire that carries current from the power source to an electrical device. The hot wire is usually identified with black, blue, or red insulation, but it can be any color but white or green.

Housing   A channel or groove cut at any angle with the grain and partway across a piece of lumber. Usually, cuts made in the member used in framing stair risers and treads.

I beam   A steel beam that resembles the letter *I* when seen in cross section. Often used for long spans under a house or to support ceiling joists where no bearing wall or partition is wanted.

Inlay   Any decorative piece set into the surface of another piece. In hardwood strip floors, a border of contrasting wood around the edges.

Insulation   Any material that resists the conduction of heat, sound, or electricity.

Interior finish   Any material—wallcoverings, ceiling and floor coverings, trim, and so on—used to cover the framing members of the interior of a structure.

Isolation joint   Any joint where two incompatible materials are mechanically separated to prevent a chemical or galvanic reaction between them. Also provides opportunity for shifting and settling of the earth without cracks occurring in the materials.

Jack rafter   Any rafter that spans the space between a top plate and hip rafter or a valley rafter and ridge board.

Jack stud   Any short stud that doesn't go all the way from the soleplate to the top plate. Also called a cripple stud.

Jamb   The frame surrounding a door or window; consists of two vertical pieces called side jambs and a top horizontal piece called a head jamb.

Jig   A device that serves as a guide or template for cutting or shaping several similar pieces.

Joint   The junction where two or more pieces of material meet and are held together. Examples are a dado joint, dovetail joint, lap joint, and mortise-and-tenon joint.

Joint compound   A powder mixed with water or a ready-mixed compound for application to the seams between sheets of wallboard.

Jointing   The smoothing or straightening of the edges of boards so they fit together precisely. A machine for this purpose is called a jointer.

Joist   One of a series of parallel members, usually 2-by lumber, that supports a floor or ceiling.

Junction box   A metal or plastic container for electrical connections. Sometimes just called a box.

Kerf   The cut made by a saw.

Key   A small strip of wood inserted into one or both parts of a joint; aligns the pieces and holds them together. Also called a spline.

Keyway   The slot or groove that holds the key.

Kiln drying   The drying of lumber in an oven or kiln, as opposed to air drying.

Kneewall　A short wall extending from the floor to the sloping ceiling of an attic or top-story room.

Knockout　A die-cut impression in the wall of a junction box; can be removed (knocked out) to provide access for wires or cable.

Knot　A natural, hard, dark-colored area in a piece of wood; formed where a branch grew on the tree.

Laminate　To form a panel or sheet by bonding two or more layers of material. Also, a product formed by such a process—plastic laminate used for countertops, for example.

Landing　The platform between flights of stairs or at the end of a stairway.

Lath　A building material of metal, gypsum, wood, or other material; used as a base for plaster or stucco.

Lattice　Any framework of crossed slats of wood, metal, or plastic.

Layout　Any drawing showing the arrangement of structural members or features. Also the act of transferring the arrangement to the site.

Ledger　A board or strip of wood, fastened to the side of a wall or other framing member, on which other framing members (usually joists) rest or to which they are attached. Also called ledger board or strip.

Level　The position of a line or plane perpendicular to an imaginary line from any place on the surface of the earth to the center of the earth. Also, the position parallel to the surface of a body of still water. Also, a device used to determine when surfaces are level or plumb.

Light　A builder's term for a single pane of glass or the space in a window sash for a single pane of glass.

Linear measure　Any measurement along a line.

Lintel　A horizontal member over a door, window, or other opening; supports the members above it. Usually made of wood, stone, or metal. Also called a header.

Live load　All loads on a building not created by the structure of the building itself; the furniture, people, and other things that occupy the building.

Log　A section of a tree trunk. Usually, the section suitable for sawing into lumber.

Lookout　A framing member that projects beyond the walls of a structure to support a roof overhang.

Louver　One of a series of parallel slats arranged to permit ventilation and to limit or exclude light, vision, or weather. Louvers can be stationary or movable.

Lumber　The wood product produced by sawing and planing, but with no further manufacturing.

Main drain　In plumbing, the pipe that collects the discharge from branch waste lines and carries it to the outer foundation wall, where it connects to the sewer line.

Main vent　In plumbing, the largest vent pipe to which branch vents may connect. Also called the vent stack.

Mansard　A roof that slopes very steeply around the edge of a structure, providing room for a complete story. The central area of the roof inside the mansard roof is usually flat or slightly sloped. This kind of roof was named for the architect who designed it to avoid taxes when they were levied on all stories below the eaves.

Mantel　The shelf above the opening of a fireplace. Also, any trim around the top and sides of a fireplace.

Masonite　*See* hardboard.

Masonry　Any construction made of stone, bricks, concrete blocks, poured concrete, and similar materials. Also, the technique of building this kind of construction.

Mastic　A viscous material used as an adhesive for setting tile or resilient flooring.

Meter　A device for measuring the flow of water, gas, or electricity, usually for purposes of billing.

Miter　Any cut or joint at an angle more or less than 90 degrees.

Molding　Any shaped strip of wood used for decoration or trim. Also spelled moulding.

Mortar　A mixture of sand and portland cement; used for bonding bricks, blocks, tiles, or stones.

Mortise　Any hole to hold another part and cut into or through a piece of wood by a chisel or other cutter. Mortises are cut to hold hinges and for mortise-and-tenon joints.

Mortise and tenon　A joint made by cutting a mortise, or hole, in one piece and a tenon, or projection, to fit into the mortise on the other piece.

Mudsill　The lowest member in the framing of a structure; usually 2-by lumber bolted to the foundation wall on which the floor joists rest. Also called a sill plate.

Mullion　The vertical divider between the windows in a window unit that is made up of two or more windows.

Muntin　The dividers, either vertical or horizontal, that separate the small lights in a multipaned sash.

Natural finish　A transparent finish—usually sealer, oil, or varnish—that protects the wood but allows the natural color and grain to show through.

Neutral wire　In a circuit, any wire that is kept at zero voltage. The neutral wire completes the circuit from source to fixture or appliance to ground. The covering of neutral wires is always white.

Newel　The main post at the foot of a stairway. Also, the central support of a winding or spiral flight of stairs.

Nipple　In plumbing, any short length of pipe externally threaded on both ends.

Nominal size　The size designation of a piece of lumber before it is planed or surfaced. If the actual size of a piece of surfaced lumber is 1½ by 3½ inches, it is referred to by its nominal size: 2 by 4.

Nonbearing wall　A wall that bears no load other than its own.

Nosing The part of a stair tread that projects over the riser. Also, the rounded edge on any board.

On center Referring to the spacing of joists, studs, rafters, or other structural members as measured from the center of one to the center of the next. Usually written OC.

Oriented strand board (O.S.B) A panel material of specially produced wood flakes that are compressed and bonded together with phenolic resin. Used for many of the same applications as plywood. Also known as structural flakeboard.

Outlet In a wall, ceiling, or floor, a device into which the plugs on appliance and extension cords are placed to connect them to electric power. Properly called a receptacle.

Outrigger An extension of a rafter or a small member attached to a rafter; forms a cornice or overhang on a roof.

Panel A large, thin board or sheet of construction material. Also, thin piece of wood or plywood in a frame of thicker pieces, as in a panel door or wainscoting.

Panel siding Large sheets of plywood or hardboard that may serve as both sheathing and siding on the exterior of a structure.

Parquet A type of wood flooring in which small strips of wood are laid in squares of alternating grain direction. Parquet floors are now available in ready-to-lay blocks to be put down with mastic. Also, any floor with an inlaid design of various woods.

Particleboard A form of composite board or panel made of wood chips bonded with adhesive.

Parting stop A wood strip used in the jambs of openable windows to separate the upper and lower sashes. Also called a parting strip.

Partition A wall that subdivides any room or space within a building.

Penny When referring to nails, it originally indicated the price per hundred. The term now serves as a measure of nail length and is abbreviated by the letter *d*, which was the first initial of the Roman monetary unit, the denarius.

Phillips head A kind of screw and screwdriver on which the driving mechanism is an *X* rather than a slot.

Pier A masonry support unit independent of the main foundation wall.

Pigtail A short length of electrical wire.

Pilaster A thickening or projection in a wall; supports a framing member, usually a beam or girder. Used to reinforce the wall.

Piling Long post of metal or moisture-resistant wood driven into the ground wherever it is difficult to secure a firm foundation in the usual way, usually in soft or swampy areas.

Pitch The incline of a roof.

Pitch board A template or jig used to mark the rise and run on a stairway stringer.

Plan The representation of any horizontal section of a structure, part of a structure, or the site of a structure; shows the arrangement of the parts in relation and scale to each other.

Plank A broad piece of lumber, usually more than 1 inch thick, especially one used to stand on as part of a scaffold or between ladders or sawhorses.

Plaster A mixture of lime, sand, and water plus cement for exterior cement plaster and plaster of paris for interior smooth plaster used to cover the surfaces of a structure.

Plasterboard *See* wallboard.

Plate A horizontal framing member, usually at the bottom or top of a wall or other part of a structure, on which other members rest. The mudsill, soleplate, and top plate are examples.

Plate cut In a rafter, the horizontal cut that forms the bird's-mouth. Also called a seat cut.

Platform framing A system of framing a structure where the floor joists of the first story rest on the mudsill of the foundation and those of each additional story rest on the top plates of the story below it. All bearing walls and partitions rest on the subfloor of their own story.

Plug In plywood, a piece of wood put in to replace a knot. On the cord of an appliance, the device that inserts into a receptacle.

Plumb Exactly perpendicular to level, or parallel to the imaginary line from the surface to the center of the earth; straight up vertical.

Plumb cut Any vertical cut, especially one at the top end of a rafter that fits against the ridge board.

Ply A term used to refer to a layer in a multilayered material, such as one layer of a sheet of plywood.

Plywood A wood product made up of layers of wood veneer bonded together with adhesive. It is usually made up of an odd number of plys set at a right angle to each other.

Porch A floor extending beyond the exterior walls of a structure. It may be enclosed, covered, or open.

Post A vertical support member, usually made up of only one piece of lumber or a metal pipe or I beam.

Post-and-beam A method of construction that, rather than stud walls, uses beams spanning between posts as the main support structure.

Purlin A horizontal framing member that supports common rafters in a roof. Usually the board between the slopes of a gambrel roof.

Putty A soft, pliable material used for sealing the edges of glass in a sash or to fill small holes or cracks in wood.

PVC (polyvinyl chloride) A rigid, white, plastic pipe used in plumbing for supply and DWV systems.

Quarter-round A convex molding shaped like a quarter circle when viewed in cross section.

Rabbet A rectangular channel cut in the corner of a piece of lumber.

Raceway A channel, usually made of metal, that encloses and supports wires or cable.

Radiant heating Electrically heated panels or hot-water pipes in the floor or ceiling that radiate heat to warm the room's surfaces.

Rafter One of a series of parallel framing members, usually made from 2-by lumber, that support a roof.

Rail In a balustrade, stairway, or fence, the horizontal or slanted member extending from the top of one post or support to another. Also, the bottom member of a balustrade parallel to the top rail. Also, in a door or window, the horizontal members of the frame.

Rake The inclined edge of a gable roof. The trim piece on the rake is called a rake molding.

Rake rafter The end rafter of a gable overhang, usually held in place with lookouts. Also called a fly rafter.

Receptacle In a wall, ceiling, or floor, an electric device into which the plugs on appliance and extension cords are placed to connect them to electric power. Also called an outlet.

Register In a wall, floor, or ceiling, the device through which air from the furnace or air conditioner enters a room. Also, any device for controlling the flow of heated or cooled air through an opening.

Reinforcing Steel bars or wire mesh placed in concrete to increase its strength.

Resawing Sawing lumber again, after the first sawing, to make it an unusual size or to shape it, as with bevel siding.

Ribbon A narrow board let into studs to support joists or beams, usually in balloon framing.

Ridge The horizontal line where two roof slopes meet. Usually the highest place on the roof.

Ridge board The board placed at the ridge of the roof to which the upper ends of the rafters are attached.

Ridge cut The vertical cut at the upper end of a rafter.

Rim joist A joist nailed across the ends of the floor or ceiling joists.

Ripping Sawing wood in the direction of the grain.

Rise In a stairway, the vertical measurement from one tread to the next. In a roof, the vertical measurement from the top of the doubled top plate to the top of the ridge board.

Riser Each of the vertical boards between the treads of a stairway.

Roll roofing Material made of asphalt-saturated fiber and coated with mineral granules. Comes in 36-inch rolls.

Romex A brand name for nonmetallic sheathed electric cable used for indoor wiring. Also called Type NM cable.

Roof The uppermost part of a structure that covers and protects it from weather. Also, the covering on this part of a structure.

Roofing The material put on the roof to make it impervious to the weather.

Roof sheathing Fastened to the rafters, sheet material or boards to which the roofing is applied.

Rough-in To install the basic, hidden parts of a plumbing, electrical, or other system while the structure is in the framing stage. Contrasts with installation of finish electrical work or plumbing, which consists of the visible parts of the system.

Rough lumber Lumber as it comes from the saw, before it is surfaced.

Rough plan The second stage in house design, showing rooms in proportion and including hallways, doors, windows, and other features.

Run In stairways, the front-to-back width of a single stair or the horizontal measurement from the bottom riser to the back of the top tread.

Saddle A U-shaped flashing unit, usually of metal, placed on a roof above or below a chimney, skylight, or other roof protrusion to divert water. Also a single- or double-sloped structure, usually made of wood, placed on a roof to divert water from between two surfaces that meet at an angle. Also called a cricket.

Sanding Rubbing sandpaper or similar abrasive material over a surface to smooth it or prepare it for finishing.

Sapwood The wood near the outside of a log; contains the living cells of a tree. Usually lighter in color than heartwood and more susceptible to decay and termite infestation.

Sash The frame that holds the glass panes in a window.

Sash balance A device, usually controlled by a spring, that counterbalances the sash in a double-hung window.

Saw kerf General term for the cut made by a saw.

Scaffold A temporary structure to support workers when they are working on parts of a building higher than they can reach from the ground or floor.

Scale The proportion between two sets of dimensions. On building plans, the house is drawn smaller than the actual house, but in scale so the proportions are the same. For example, when the scale is expressed as ¼" = 1'0", ¼ inch on the drawing equals 1 foot on the actual house. When the scale is expressed as ⅛" = 1'0", ⅛ inch on the drawing equals 1 foot on the house.

Screed A strip of wood used to even the surface and control the thickness of gravel beneath a foundation slab or the various layers of plaster or stucco on walls or ceilings or to strike off wet concrete.

Scribing Marking a piece of wood or paneling so it can be cut to fit precisely against an irregular surface. Also, the cutting of the scribed line.

Sealer A finishing material used to seal the surface of wood or other material before the final coats of paint or stain are applied.

Seasoning Removing moisture from green lumber either by air drying or kiln drying.

Seat cut In a rafter, the horizontal cut that forms a bird's-mouth. Also called a plate cut.

Section A drawing of part of a building as it would appear if cut through by a vertical plane.

Service entrance The place where electrical utilities enter a building.

Service panel The box or panel where the electricity is distributed to the house circuits. It contains the circuit breakers and, usually, the main disconnect switch.

Shake A thick wood shingle, usually edge-grained.

Sheathing Sheet material or boards fastened to the rafters or exterior stud walls; that to which the roofing or siding is applied.

Shed roof A roof that slopes in only one direction.

Sheet-metal work Any components of a structure in which sheet metal is used, such as ducts and flashing.

Sheetrock A commercial name for wallboard.

Shim A thin wedge of wood, often part of a shingle, used to bring parts of a structure into alignment.

Shingles A roofing material of asphalt, fiberglass, wood, or other material cut to stock lengths, widths, and thicknesses.

Shiplap siding Exterior siding, usually ¾ inch thick, shaped to patterns.

Shoe molding A strip of wood used to trim the bottom edge of a baseboard.

Shutoff valve In plumbing, a fitting to shut off the water supply to a single fixture or branch of pipe.

Shutters Flush-board, louvered, or paneled frames in the form of small doors that are mounted alongside a window. Some are made to close over the window to provide protection or privacy, others are nailed or screwed to the wall for decorative purposes only.

Siding The finish covering on the exterior walls of a building.

Sill The lowest member in the framing of a structure; usually rests on the foundation wall. Also, the member forming the lowest side of an opening, such as a doorsill or window sill.

Sill plate The lowest member in the framing of a structure; usually a 2-by board bolted to the foundation wall on which the floor joists rest. Also called a mudsill.

Site plan Drawing of all the existing conditions on the lot, usually including slope and other topography, existing utilities, and setbacks. These drawings may be provided by the municipality.

Slab A concrete foundation or floor poured directly on the ground.

Sleepers Boards embedded in or attached to a concrete floor; serve to support and provide a nailing surface for a subfloor or finish flooring.

Slope The incline or pitch of a roof.

Soffit The underside of a stairway, cornice, archway, or similar member of a structure. Usually, a small area relative to a ceiling.

Softwood The wood of conifers such as fir, pine, and redwood. Softwood is usually softer than hardwood, but the term has no actual reference to the hardness of the wood.

Soil stack In the DWV system, the main vertical pipe. Usually extends from the basement to a point above the roof.

Solderless connector A device that uses mechanical pressure rather than solder to establish a connection between two or more electrical conductors. Also called a wire nut.

Soleplate In a stud wall, the bottom member, which is nailed to the subfloor. Also called a bottom plate.

Solid bridging A single board placed between adjacent joists near the middle of a span; braces the joists and spreads the weight load.

Span The distance between structural supports, such as bearing walls or partitions, piers, columns, and beams.

Specifications The written description of all details of a building.

Splash block A small block, usually made of concrete, placed beneath the end of a downspout; prevents erosion and helps carry water away from the building.

Spline A small strip of wood inserted into one or both parts of a joint; aligns the pieces and holds them together. Also called a key.

Square A term used to describe an angle of exactly 90 degrees. Also, a device to measure such an angle. Also, a unit of measure equalling 100 square feet. Usually used in describing amounts of roofing or siding material.

Stickers Thin boards used to separate layers of lumber and allow air circulation when the lumber is being seasoned or stored for an extended period.

Stile A vertical framing member in a panel door, wainscoting, or a paneled wall.

Stool The horizontal shelf on the interior of the bottom of a window.

Story The part of a building that is between floors or the top floor and the roof.

Stringer In a stairway, the supporting member to which the treads and risers are fastened. Also called a carriage.

Strip flooring Wood flooring material consisting of narrow strips.

Stucco A plaster made to cover the exterior of buildings; made of sand, portland cement, and lime.

Stud One of a series of wood or metal vertical framing members that are the main units in walls and partitions.

Stud wall The main framing units for walls and partitions in a building. Composed of studs; top plates; bottom plates; and the framing of windows, doors, and corner posts.

Subfloor Plywood or oriented strand boards attached to the joists. The finish floor is laid over the subfloor.

Suspended ceiling A system for installing ceiling tile by hanging a metal framework from the ceiling joists.

Switch In electrical systems, a device for turning the flow of electricity on and off in a circuit or diverting the current from one circuit to another.

Tail cut At the lower end of a rafter, the vertical cut to which the fascia board is attached.

Tail joist   A relatively short joist or beam, usually used to frame an opening in a floor or ceiling; supported by a wall and a header at the other.

Taper   A uniform decrease in size from one end to the other—as of a table leg, for instance.

Template   A pattern from which parts of a structure can be made. Templates may be of paper, cardboard, plywood, and so forth.

Tenon   A projection of one piece of wood that fits precisely into a hole, the mortise, in another piece to form a mortise-and-tenon joint.

Termite shield   Galvanized steel or aluminum sheets placed between the foundation, pipes, or fences and the wood structure of a building; prevents the entry of termites.

Threshold   A shaped piece of wood or metal, usually beveled on both edges, that is placed on the finish floor between the side jamb; forms the bottom of an exterior doorway.

Tie beam   *See* collar beam.

Tile-backing units   Waterproof units made of fiberglass mesh and concrete; produced specifically as an underlayment for ceramic and dimensioned stone installed in the thin-set adhesive method.

Timber   Pieces of lumber with a cross section greater than 4 by 6 inches. Usually used as beams, girders, posts, and columns.

Toenailing   Driving a nail so it enters the first wood surface diagonally. This method is usually used to add strength or when there is no room to swing a hammer for direct nailing.

Tongue   A projecting edge on a board; fits into a groove on another board.

Tongue and groove   A way of milling lumber so it fits together tightly and forms an extremely strong floor or deck. Also, boards milled for tongue-and-groove flooring or decking that have one or more tongues on one edge and a matching groove or grooves on the other.

Top plate   In a stud wall, the top horizontal member to which the cap plate is nailed when the stud walls are connected and aligned.

Transom   A window above a doorway.

Trap   In plumbing, a U-shaped drain fitting that remains full of water to prevent the entry of air and sewer gas into the building.

Tread   In a stairway, the horizontal surface on which a person steps.

Trim   Any finish materials in a structure that are placed to provide decoration or to cover the joints between surfaces or contrasting materials. Door and window casings, baseboards, picture moldings, and cornices are examples of trim.

Trimmer   A joist or beam to which a header is nailed, usually when framing an opening in a floor or ceiling. Also, a stud next to an opening in a wall that supports a header.

Truss   An assembly of wood or metal members that serves as a relatively lightweight but strong framework to take the place of rafters and joists in the support of a roof or floor.

Truss plate   A flat piece of metal, wood, or plywood; used to support the connections of framing lumber. Most often seen on joints of wood trusses and joist splices. Also called a gusset.

Type NM cable   Nonmetallic sheathed electric cable used for indoor wiring. Also known by the brand name Romex.

Underlayment   The material placed under the finish coverings of roofs or floors to provide waterproofing as well as a smooth even surface on which to apply finish material.

Unit of rise   A division of the total vertical height of a roof slope or a stairway; used in calculating the length of rafters and the relationship of risers to treads.

Unit of run   A division of the total horizontal length of a roof slope or a stairway; used in calculating the length of rafters and the relationship of the risers to treads.

Valley   The concave angle formed by the meeting of two sloping surfaces of a roof, that come off adjacent walls to form an inside corner.

Valley flashing   A method of waterproofing the valley of a roof with metal or roofing-felt flashing.

Valley rafter   A rafter that runs from a wall plate at the corner of the house, along the roof valley, and to the ridge.

Vapor barrier   Any material used to prevent the penetration of water vapor into walls or other enclosed parts of a building. Polyethylene sheets, aluminum foil, and building paper are the materials used most.

Veneer   A thin layer of wood, usually one that has beauty or value, that is applied for economy or appearance on top of an inferior surface.

Vent   Any opening, usually covered with screen or louvers, made to allow the circulation of air, usually into an attic or crawl space. In plumbing, a pipe in the DWV system for the purpose of bringing air into the system.

Vent stack   In plumbing, the largest vent pipe to which branch vents may connect. Also called the main vent.

Wainscoting   Panel work covering only the lower portion of a wall.

Wallboard   Panels used for finishing interior walls and ceilings. Consist of a layer of gypsum plaster covered on both sides by layers of paper. Also called gypsum wallboard, drywall, and Sheetrock, á trade name.

Wall plate   A decorative covering for a switch, receptacle, or other device.

Weather stripping   Narrow strips of metal, fiber, plastic foam, or other materials placed around doors and windows; prevents the entry of air, moisture, or dust.

Wire nut   A device that uses mechanical pressure rather than solder to establish a connection between two or more electrical conductors. Also called a solderless connector.

344

READING LIST

You may want to read more about some of the specific aspects of house building covered in this book, such as home design, plumbing, wiring, and finish work. The following is a selected reading list to help you get started. It is by no means complete, but you should be able to find many of the books listed here in a local bookstore, home center, or library.

Planning to Build

Before You Build by Robert Roskind. Ten Speed Press.
Building Your Own House by Robert Roskind. Ten Speed Press.
How to Contract the Building of Your New House by James M. Shepherd. Shepherd Publishers.
House by Tracy Kidder. Houghton Mifflin.
New House Book by Terence Conran. Villard Books.
Practical Guide to Home Restoration by William F. Rooney. Van Nostrand Reinhold.

Foundations and Framing

Basic Carpentry Techniques. Ortho Books.
Basic Masonry Techniques. Ortho Books.
Carpentry and Building Construction by John L. Freirer and Gilbert R. Hutchings. Charles A. Bennett.
Housebuilding: A Do It Yourself Guide by R. J. De Christoforo. Sterling Publishing.
How to Build Additions. Ortho Books.
Roof Framing by Marshall Gross. Craftsman.
Wood-Frame House Construction. United States Department of Agriculture.

The Roof

Ortho's Home Improvement Encyclopedia. Ortho Books.
Roofer's Handbook by William E. Johnson. Craftsman.
Roofs & Sidings. Ortho Books.

Utility Systems

Basic Plumbing Illustrated by Howard C. Massey. Craftsman.
Basic Plumbing Techniques. Ortho Books.
Basic Wiring Techniques. Ortho Books.
Do-It-Yourself Plumbing by Max Alth. Sterling Publishing.

Electrical Wiring: Residential, Utility Buildings, and Service Areas by Thomas S. Colvin. American Association for Vocational Instructional Materials.
Guide to Electrical Installation & Repair. McGraw-Hill.
Guide to Plumbing. McGraw-Hill.
Home Wiring from Start to Finish by Robert W. Wood. Tab Books.
Modern Plumbing for Old and New Houses by Jay Hedden. Creative Homeowner Press.
Practical Electrical Wiring by H. P. Richter. McGraw-Hill.
Successful Plumbing by Robert Scharff. Structures Publishing.

Finishing the Exterior

Creative Home Landscaping. Ortho Books.
How to Replace & Install Doors & Windows. Ortho Books.

Heating, Cooling, and Energy Conservation

50 Simple Things You Can Do To Save The Earth. Earthworks Press.

Steps, Stairs, Porches, and Decks

Deck & Patio Upgrades. Ortho Books.
Deck Plans. Ortho Books.
Garden Construction. Ortho Books.
How to Design & Build Decks & Patios. Ortho Books.

Finishing the Interior

Finish Carpentry Basics. Ortho Books.
Floors & Floor Coverings. Ortho Books.
How to Install Ceramic Tile. Ortho Books.
Interior Lighting. Ortho Books.
Interior Views by Erica Brown. Viking Press.
Setting Ceramic Tile by Michael Byrne. Taunton Press.

Bathrooms and Kitchens

Bathroom Design by Barry Dean. Simon and Schuster.
Bathrooms by Rick Harrison. HP Books.
Designing & Remodeling Bathrooms. Ortho Books.
Designing & Remodeling Kitchens. Ortho Books.
The Kitchen Book by Sally King. Pelham Books.
Kitchens. The Knapp Press.
Kitchens by Rick Harrison. HP Books.
Kitchens & Bathrooms. Lane Publishing.
Small Kitchens by Robin Murrell. Simon and Schuster.

INDEX

U.S./Metric Measure Conversion Chart

	Symbol	Formulas for Exact Measures			Rounded Measures for Quick Reference		
		When you know:	Multiply by:	To find:			
Mass (Weight)	oz	ounces	28.35	grams	1 oz		= 30 g
	lb	pounds	0.45	kilograms	4 oz		= 115 g
	g	grams	0.035	ounces	8 oz		= 225 g
	kg	kilograms	2.2	pounds	16 oz	= 1 lb	= 450 g
					32 oz	= 2 lb	= 900 g
					36 oz	= 2¼ lb	= 1000 g (1 kg)
Volume	tsp	teaspoons	5.0	milliliters	¼ tsp	= ¹⁄₂₄ oz	= 1 ml
	tbsp	tablespoons	15.0	milliliters	½ tsp	= ¹⁄₁₂ oz	= 2 ml
	fl oz	fluid ounces	29.57	milliliters	1 tsp	= ⅙ oz	= 5 ml
	c	cups	0.24	liters	1 tbsp	= ½ oz	= 15 ml
	pt	pints	0.47	liters	1 c	= 8 oz	= 250 ml
	qt	quarts	0.95	liters	2 c (1 pt)	= 16 oz	= 500 ml
	gal	gallons	3.785	liters	4 c (1 qt)	= 32 oz	= 1 liter
	ml	milliliters	0.034	fluid ounces	4 qt (1 gal)	= 128 oz	= 3¾ liter
Length	in.	inches	2.54	centimeters	⅜ in.	= 1 cm	
	ft	feet	30.48	centimeters	1 in.	= 2.5 cm	
	yd	yards	0.9144	meters	2 in.	= 5 cm	
	mi	miles	1.609	kilometers	2½ in.	= 6.5 cm	
	km	kilometers	0.621	miles	12 in. (1 ft)	= 30 cm	
	m	meters	1.094	yards	1 yd	= 90 cm	
	cm	centimeters	0.39	inches	100 ft	= 30 m	
					1 mi	= 1.6 km	
Temperature	°F	Fahrenheit	⁵⁄₉ (after subtracting 32)	Celsius	32° F	= 0° C	
					68° F	= 20° C	
	°C	Celsius	⁹⁄₅ (then add 32)	Fahrenheit	212° F	= 100° C	
Area	in.²	square inches	6.452	square centimeters	1 in.²	= 6.5 cm²	
	ft²	square feet	929.0	square centimeters	1 ft²	= 930 cm²	
	yd²	square yards	8361.0	square centimeters	1 yd²	= 8360 cm²	
	a.	acres	0.4047	hectares	1 a.	= 4050 m²	